Climbing Up to Glory
A Short History of African Americans during the Civil War and Reconstruction

Wilbert L. Jenkins

A Scholarly Resc
Wilmingto

© 2002 by Scholarly Resources Inc.
All rights reserved
First published 2002
Printed and bound in the United States of America

Scholarly Resources Inc.
104 Greenhill Avenue
Wilmington, DE 19805-1897
www.scholarly.com

Library of Congress Cataloging-in-Publication Data

Jenkins, Wilbert L., 1953–
    Climbing up to glory : a short history of African Americans
during the Civil War and Reconstruction / Wilbert L. Jenkins.
        p. cm.
    Includes bibliographical references and index.
    ISBN 0-8420-2816-1 (alk. paper) — ISBN 0-8420-2817-X (pbk. :
alk. paper)
    1. African Americans—History—1863–1877. 2. African
Americans—History—To 1863. 3. United States—History—Civil
War, 1861–1865—African Americans. 4. Reconstruction. I. Title.

E185.2 .J46 2002
973.7'089'96073—dc21   2002017619

In memory of my father, Joe A. Jenkins Sr.,
and to my mother, Elizabeth Jenkins,
and in memory of many of my fallen relatives,
who were trailblazers in their own right

ABOUT THE AUTHOR

Wilbert L. Jenkins is an associate professor of history at Temple University in Philadelphia, Pennsylvania. He was an assistant professor of history at West Virginia University in Morgantown from 1989 to 1992. A native of Raleigh, North Carolina, he received his bachelor's degree in history from Winston-Salem State University in 1977, his M.A. degree in history from Ball State University in 1978, and his Ph.D. in history in 1989 from Michigan State University. Professor Jenkins is also the author of *Seizing the New Day: African Americans in Post-Civil War Charleston* (1998), and he has written and published numerous articles in newspapers and academic journals on the African-American experience.

CONTENTS

ACKNOWLEDGMENTS

THE FIRST OPPORTUNITY to discuss this work took place in April 1991 at West Virginia University as part of the Sojourner Truth-Nelson Mandela Colloquium series, when I presented it to both graduate and undergraduate students as well as to colleagues. Their comments and suggestions proved helpful. I was also invited by Donald West and Curtis Franks of the Avery Research Center for African-American History and Culture at the College of Charleston to present my work there in July 1993 to a large audience, and was again invited in November 1998 by W. Marvin Dulaney, the director of the Avery Research Center. Finally, I was given the opportunity to discuss my ideas at the faculty colloquium in the History Department at Temple University in February 2000. The idea to invite me originated with Kathleen Uno, a colleague of mine in the History Department. I would like to thank all of those whose suggestions contributed toward making this a better and more complete piece of scholarship.

Numerous individuals have supported this work, both directly and indirectly. Colleagues at Temple University and at other colleges and universities read and commented on several book chapters. In this regard, I would like to thank Dieu Nguyen, Peter Gran, Kenneth Kusmer, Susan Klepp, and Russell Weigley, all of Temple. In addition, thanks are extended to Joe Trotter of Carnegie-Mellon University, Peter Wood of Duke University, and Edmund Drago of the College of Charleston. I owe a debt of gratitude to Craig Stutman, one of my doctoral students, for critiquing the manuscript and making invaluable suggestions. A number of good friends who cheered me on over the years did not actually read the manuscript but might as well have done so, considering the dividends I have reaped through discussions of their work and my own. Many more people fall into this class than I can mention by name, but I wish to call attention to a few of them: Philip Evanson, Bettye Collier-Thomas, Frank Thornton, Wilbert Roget, Teshale Tibebu, and Nathaniel Norment, all of Temple University; Joseph Windham of Northern Virginia Community College; Walter Hill of the National Archives; Jo Dohoney of Samford University; and James McLaughlin and Larry Little of Winston-Salem State University. I also owe debts of gratitude to colleagues who kept an eye out for materials relevant to my research. Lenwood Davis of Winston-Salem State University provided valuable material on black colleges and universities, and Gregory Urwin of Temple University shared two of his very helpful articles on the Poison Spring massacre. In addition, Professor Urwin shared invaluable materials with me pertaining to the Fifty-fourth Massachusetts Volunteer Infantry, the most famous African-American regiment during the Civil War.

Others also assisted in beneficial ways. Stephen Massengill and Earl Ijames of the Department of North Carolina Resources and Archives went above and beyond the call of duty in locating excellent illustrations. Comments made by several of my students on a range of scholarly themes in the graduate course on the Civil War and Reconstruction which I taught in Fall 1999 benefited the final product, and I would like to extend my appreciation to Leah Alter, Jennifer Fry, Latasha Long, Bertha Adams, Anne Harney, Margaret Markmann, and Jennifer Lawrence. As they did for my first book, Rhonda Johnson, Patricia Williams, and Joanne Follmer of the History Department staff at Temple University offered much-needed moral support. Rhonda also typed earlier book chapters. Many thanks are also extended to Deborah Stuart, who with a sharp eye edited earlier book chapters. Pebbles Murrell-Farrah and Yvette Gibson typed earlier chapters, and Belinda Wilson-Hagins graciously typed the final manuscript. Their professionalism is exemplary. Harold E. Whipple of Saint Augustine's College was trusting enough to place in my possession pictures of Saint Augustine's College that were the only ones in the college's archives. Moreover, Paul Crater, Cathy Mundale, and Karen Jefferson of Atlanta University provided much-needed assistance in locating numerous photographs. Matthew Hershey, the senior acquisitions editor at Scholarly Resources, went above and beyond the call of duty in shepherding the book to publication. I would also like to acknowledge the steadfast support of my mentors at Michigan State University: Harry Reed, John Coogan, Darlene Clark Hine, Gordon Stewart, Frederick Williams, Peter Levine, and Richard Thomas, who believed in me when I had self-doubts, and for this, I will always be thankful. Thanks also go to Edward Grayson III, Alfonso Grant, Charles Brooks, Nathaniel Greene, John Watson, and Tim Howard for continuously reminding me that I had an obligation to tell the history of our ancestors. Finally, I would like to thank my ancestors for leaving a rich history for those of us engaged in scholarship to record. I sincerely hope that I have done them justice in the pages that follow.

My one regret is that my father, Joe A. Jenkins Sr., did not live long enough to see either my first book or this book published. Writing *Climbing Up to Glory* has helped me deal with his death. The numerous hours spent on research and writing proved to be good therapy and enabled me to find a fitting way to celebrate my father's life. In many ways, his experience growing up black in the South paralleled that of many of those blacks mentioned in these pages. Like many of them, my father had to endure white racism and racial discrimination on an unprecedented scale. Nevertheless, they not only persevered with a great deal of tenacity and willpower but also became the living embodiment of what can be accomplished through unflagging determination and inner strength. Since my father's life represents a continuous struggle to survive and prosper in American society, as does the black characters I write about here, I dedicate this work to him. In addition, since my mother, Elizabeth Jenkins, and my gone-but-not-forgotten relatives contributed in their own ways to creating a better society, it is appropriate to dedicate this book to them as well. Unfortunately, the list is too long for me to name them all here, but I wish to cite a few: Willie and Mary Debnam (great-grandparents), Lorenzo and Sadie Barbour and Ashe Burnette (grandparents), John D. Jenkins Sr. and Mattie Jenkins (grandparents), Jimmie Debnam, Tink, Martha, and Mary Frances Neal, Fannie Sanders, Grace Clark, Edith and Zebedee Allen, Joe Barbour, Irvin and Flora Bell Harris, Catherine Harris, James Jenkins, and Pronto Merritt. I would be remiss if I failed to dedicate this book also in memory of Alfonso Grant, a kindred spirit who taught me the beauty of life, and probably more things about life than he ever realized. In many respects, he became a role model for me and, in essence, my second father. Sleep well, my friends, for you have left your marks on the world; you will never be forgotten, and you are sorely missed. It is my hope that this book contributes in some measure to the liberation of individuals of African descent as well as to an understanding of and appreciation of their struggles to become first-class citizens in American society.

INTRODUCTION

THE CIVIL WAR AND RECONSTRUCTION mark a watershed in American and African-American history. Scholars have examined this period in depth, yet few have focused on the lives of African Americans in those years between 1861, when the first shots were fired at Fort Sumter, and 1877, when the last federal troops were withdrawn from the South. Those works that cover the experiences of African Americans represent state, regional, or community studies and generally target a scholarly audience. My book seeks to fill this void in historical scholarship. With *Climbing Up to Glory*, my aim is to appeal to both students of African-American history and laypersons. Although my book focuses mostly on the South, where the vast majority of African Americans lived and were held as slaves when the Civil War began, I also look at the lives of blacks in the North, who had been free since 1839. Like the few free blacks in the South, they were regularly subjected to white oppression and racial discrimination. A sense of powerlessness was common to all blacks, both slave and free. And thus all blacks, in the North and in the South, saw the Civil War as an opportunity to improve their condition and change their lives. Most slaves were confident that a Union victory would bring them their liberation, and they wanted to serve in the Union forces to help make freedom a reality. Northern blacks, too, were anxious to enlist in the Union forces, believing not only that a Union victory would speed up the process of slave emancipation but also that the victory would lead to increased social, political, and economic opportunities for themselves.

Blacks played a pivotal role in helping the Union defeat the Confederacy in the Civil War. When the war ended in a Union victory, the slaves received their long-awaited day of liberation. Four million formerly enslaved black people were now free. The institution of slavery had been the foundation of the social, political, and economic system in the South. With its demise, Southern society was in disarray, and many questions about the new status of blacks were yet to be answered. The answers to these questions would have a profound effect on its future status.

This study does not address how blacks responded to white racism and discrimination. Rather, it recognizes blacks as the central actors in their own lives and not as passive objects of a white-dominated society. It is essentially a history written "from the bottom up," which means that it focuses on those from the lower strata of society and not on the rich and powerful. It emphasizes to a large extent the crucial undertaking of the Reconstruction period: the rebuilding and reinvention of patterns of life and social and economic interaction. Former slaves struggled tenaciously from the moment of emancipation to become independent of white control. They attempted to construct a solid economic base for themselves and their families. Freedmen pooled meager resources to establish and maintain their own schools and churches. They struggled to rebuild shattered families and to legalize marital relationships in order to protect them. Freedmen also risked their own lives, at times, to protect family members from white violence.

Too often scholars write about the historical past as if it has no relevancy for the present. This is a grave error and one of the main reasons why many contemporary Americans regard history as bland, boring, and insignificant for contemporary society. But history must be seen as a process of inquiry and discovery, depicting how the present is shaped by the past. In this book I show how U.S. society of the 1990s was affected by the momentous events of Civil War and Reconstruction. The Union victory gave rise to the enactment of the Thirteenth, Fourteenth, and Fifteenth Amendments to the U.S. Constitution. It also led to passage of the Civil Rights Acts of 1866 and 1875 and the Enforcement Acts of 1870 and 1871, which formed the pretext for much of the Civil Rights legislation enacted in the 1950s and 1960s. Furthermore, on the basis of the Enforcement Acts of 1870 and 1871, President Dwight Eisenhower sent Federal troops to Little Rock, Arkansas, in 1957 to protect black children while they attended a predominately white public high school, and President John F. Kennedy in 1962 sent Federal troops to the University of Mississippi to ensure the safety of James Meredith, the first black to attend that college. Only by examining the history of blacks during the Civil War and Reconstruction can we begin to understand why issues such as equality and justice for blacks that were heatedly debated by Americans during the 1860s and 1870s are still debated and remain unresolved today.

In relating the story of the Civil War and Reconstruction years, I have supplemented my own research with what I believe is the best and most significant recent research. I would like to acknowledge my debt to the numerous scholars of African-American history upon whose fine works I have drawn. The bibliography at the end of the book represents the extent of my reliance on them. At the same time, however, I have drawn from an array of primary documents such as slave narratives, diaries, journals, personal letters, autobiographies, newspapers, travelers' accounts, census reports, and Freedmen's Bureau papers and letters.

This book has been both a joy to write and painful as well. I have been brought to tears by some of the sufferings of people who appear in these pages but also inspired by their courage and perseverance. Although I have admired some of the characters and disliked others, I have always tried to evaluate their behavior within the proper context, which is the historian's primary task. Still, I believe that any scholar is entitled to infuse some passion into his or her work if so moved. And, in a book of this kind, I doubt that anyone could remain unmoved in some sort by the events.

The chapters that follow attempt to bring meaning to the African-American experience during the Civil War and Reconstruction. The first chapter reassesses the role that Abraham Lincoln played in emancipating the slaves. Issues such as the First and Second Confiscation Acts, Militia Act, Emancipation Proclamation, colonization, and the Thirteenth Amendment are covered here. Chapter Two highlights the struggles of African Americans to enlist in the Union armed forces. The trials and tribulations that these soldiers and their families went through are also discussed. In addition, the contribution of African-American women to the Union war cause is emphasized as well as the controversial issue of rape during the war. Finally, some attention is given to the impact of the war on African-American children and the contributions of African Americans to the Confederate cause.

Chapter Three discusses the initial reactions to emancipation of rural and urban slaves, who left the premises of former owners, went to towns and cities, and organized emancipation celebrations. An in-depth discussion of the reactions of African Americans to Lincoln's assassination is also provided. Chapters Four through Eight record the efforts of freedpeople to reunite and provide for their families, educate themselves, build and support churches, and participate in the political process. The role of women in each of these endeavors is highlighted. Some attention is also given to those African Americans who lived among Native Americans. These chapters too describe the end of African-American hopes and the beginning of crushed dreams as the "counterrevolution" reared its ugly head. Nevertheless, many of the positive changes wrought by emancipation and Reconstruction could not be obliterated. They would have a profound impact on American society.

CHAPTER ONE

ABRAHAM LINCOLN
A Reluctant Friend

THE OUTCOME OF the presidential election of 1860 was anathema to most Southern whites. They reasoned that the Republican Party, which was based in the North and opposed the further extension of slavery into the territories, would destroy the whole system of slavery now that it had captured the White House with the election of Abraham Lincoln. From the early years after the country's inception until 1860, Southerners had either occupied the White House or had had sympathetic friends who did. But this state of affairs had all changed. Of course, the anguish and frustration felt by most Southern whites over Lincoln's election was expected by the Republican Party. In fact, even before the election, the party took great pains to distance itself from the antislavery movement and to destroy any perception that Lincoln's election posed a threat to slavery. In an effort to reassure Southerners that he had no intentions of eradicating the institution, Lincoln asserted, "Wrong as we think slavery is, we can yet afford to let it alone where it is, because that much is due to the necessity arising from its actual presence in the nation."[1]

Despite the numerous assurances uttered by Lincoln and other Republicans that slavery would be safe with their party in office, throughout the campaign, Democrats linked them to the cause of antislavery. They also argued that the Republican Party promoted racial equality for blacks, which was a subtle way of saying that they supported black men having access to white women—a position meant to inflame racial hatred, as it was certain to work on the psyche of white men. Others maintained that a Lincoln victory would serve as a catalyst for slaves to escape to the North and compete with whites for jobs. However, in response, the Republicans proudly proclaimed themselves to be the "White Man's Party."[2] This proclamation was one that most Southern whites did not buy, and Lincoln's election represented their darkest nightmare. Their whole world was now turned upside down. Indeed, it was imperative that the Southern states devise strategies to deal with this new state of affairs.

Although most free blacks who could vote in 1860 supported Lincoln's candidacy, outspoken abolitionist, writer, and orator Frederick Douglass and others did not. Their rationale for not backing him, however, was interesting. Whereas most Southern whites regarded Lincoln as a friend of blacks, some free blacks, Douglass among them, did not trust Lincoln and the Republican Party and looked upon him as being against the abolition of slavery. The party of the 1850s was haunted by the question of how to attract a large number of conservative whites while still projecting a humanitarian image of concern for the downtrodden by occasionally addressing their needs. This was a tough tightrope to walk, and Douglass and a few of his cohorts exposed its tenuous nature. They believed that in the election of 1860 the Republican Party would be no better than either wing of the Democratic Party in respect to working toward the abolition of slavery. As a consequence, although they realized that Gerrit Smith, the Radical Abolitionist Party nominee, stood no realistic chance of winning the presidency, they voted for him nonetheless. They were attracted to his candidacy because the party he represented supported the emancipation of all slaves. Douglass spoke passionately in defense of his vote and those of others for Smith, when he wrote, "Ten thousand votes for Gerrit Smith at this juncture would do more, in our judgment for the ultimate abolition of slavery in this country, than two million for Abraham Lincoln, or any other man who stands pledged before the world against all interference with slavery in the slave states, who is not pledged to the abolition of slavery in the District of Columbia, or anywhere else the system exists, and who is not opposed to making the free states a hunting ground for men under the Fugitive Slave Law."[3] Thus, while the election of Lincoln was hailed by most blacks, some prominent African-Americans looked upon it with suspicion and apprehension. Regardless of how they personally felt, however, most blacks took a wait-and-see attitude toward Lincoln. Southern whites, however, could only envision a dark and gloomy existence under Lincoln and the Republicans.

A little more than a month after the Republican victory, the South Carolina legislature ordered an election of delegates to a convention to decide the state's future course. The convention voted unanimously to secede from the Union on December 20. Six other states of the lower South had followed suit by February 1, 1861. A provisional government of the Confederate States of America was established one week later at Montgomery, Alabama. Although Virginia, Tennessee, North Carolina, and Arkansas chose not to leave the Union at this time, they announced that they too would secede if the federal government attempted to use force against the new Confederacy. Thus, by the time of Lincoln's inauguration in March 1861, the nation was rapidly falling apart. Most U.S. property in the Deep South had been seized by the Confederacy. The new president announced that he had no intention of forcibly reclaiming federal property, but he vowed to keep Fort Sumter, in the harbor at Charleston, South Carolina, and Fort Pickens, in Florida, under Union control and ordered them to be resupplied with arms and munitions. In response, the Confederates attacked Fort Sumter on April 14 and forced its commander to surrender. Lincoln regarded this action as a blatant disregard of federal authority. The Confederacy's aggression had to be restrained. Northern whites responded enthusiastically to Lincoln's call for 75,000 volunteers, enlisting in such large numbers that many men had to be turned away. At this point, Virginia, North Carolina, Arkansas, and Tennessee seceded from the Union. The Civil War, which would last for four long, extremely bloody years had begun. Lincoln made it clear that his primary objective in the war would be to preserve the Union, not to abolish slavery.

This objective would consistently guide many of the policies that Lincoln would endorse throughout the war. In fact, as late as mid-1862, in a letter written to Horace Greeley, the New York newspaper editor, Lincoln reiterated his position. As he passionately explained,

> My paramount object in this struggle is to save the Union, and is not either to save or to destroy slavery. If I could save the Union without freeing any slave I would do it, and if I could save it by freeing all the slaves I would do it; and if I could save it by freeing some and leaving others alone I would also do that. What I do about slavery, and the colored race, I do because I believe it helps to save the Union; and what I forbear, I forbear because I do not believe it would help save the Union—I shall try to correct errors when shown to be errors; and I shall adopt new views so fast as they shall appear to be true views.[4]

Lincoln might have regarded the Civil War as a struggle to preserve the Union, but from its beginning some blacks, Frederick Douglass among them, were confident that the emancipation of the slaves must be a prerequisite for preservation. In fact, Douglass was certain that "any attempt now to separate the freedom of the slave from the victory of the government,—any attempt to secure peace to the whites while leaving the blacks in chains—will be labor lost. The

American people and the Government at Washington may refuse to recognize it for a time; but the 'inexorable logic of events' will force it upon them in the end; that the war now being waged in this land is a war for and against slavery; and that it can never be effectually put down till one or the other of these vital forces is completely destroyed."[5] As a result of this belief, Douglass wholeheartedly threw himself into the recruitment of blacks into the Union armed forces. Indeed, it was of paramount importance that blacks militarily contribute to a war that could ultimately lead to the emancipation of all slaves. Douglass's belief proved to be prophetic. In addition, some blacks thought that if Lincoln were elected they would be freed even without a war. For example, Allen Williams remembered that "when Abe Lincoln was running for President, they said, if 'Lincoln is elected the Niggers will be freed.' "[6] Again, this proved to be prophetic.

FREE BLACKS OFFER THEIR
SERVICES TO THE UNION

Believing that the Civil War was being fought over the issue of slavery, Northern free blacks were confident that a Union victory would lead to the emancipation of slaves. And any improvement in the status of the enslaved was certain to benefit all blacks. Free blacks hoped by fighting on the Union side to demonstrate that they were loyal and patriotic, deserving of acceptance into American society on equal terms with whites. But laws and the resistance and prejudice of whites kept them from taking up arms. Nevertheless, in city after city free blacks offered their services. They formed a military club in New York and drilled regularly until the police stopped them. Other blacks in the city tried to persuade the state governor to organize three regiments by promising him that blacks in the state would pay all of their own expenses for arms and equipment and even their salaries.[7] Two regiments were formed in Philadelphia and drilled at Masonic Hall. Several Philadelphia blacks even proposed to go South and organize slave revolts, which they hoped would disrupt the Southern economy and wreak havoc. In Pittsburgh the all-black Hannibal Guards offered their services, pointing out that as American citizens they were anxious "to assist in any honorable way or manner to sustain the present situation."[8]

A group of Boston blacks met at the Twelfth Baptist Church and pledged their lives and fortunes to President Lincoln. A black company in Providence, signifying its determination to engage in conflict, offered to march with the First Rhode Island Regiment as it left for the front. In Cleveland, blacks met at National Hall and offered their prayers, money, and manpower to help defeat the Confederacy as well as declared their allegiance to the government of Abraham Lincoln.[9] Captain O. C. Wood of Detroit and the thirty-five members of his Detroit Military Guard tried to enlist, and Dr. G. P. Miller of Battle Creek, Michigan, sought permission from local authorities to raise 5,000 to 10,000 black soldiers. In addition, J. Sella Martin, a black clergyman, wrote to Lincoln: "If I can be of any manner of service here, should your excellency ever think it best to employ my people, I am ready to work or preach or fight to put down this rebellion."[10] Some free blacks offered their services directly to Union officials in Washington. Jack Dodson, a Senate attendant who had been with General John C. Frémont when he crossed the Rockies during the Mexican-American War, gathered three hundred blacks for the defense of the nation's capital.[11] In every Northern state, free blacks hastened to aid the Union cause, underscoring the depth of their commitment to achieving freedom and equality for blacks and their confidence that a Union victory would be a huge step in this direction.

Unfortunately, in the first months of the conflict, Northern free blacks' proposals to serve were consistently rejected by local, state, and federal officials.[12] They all declared that they had no intention of using black soldiers. Why was there so much Northern white opposition to the idea of arming blacks? Some of the opposition was rooted in traditional beliefs and practices. After the Revolutionary War, which ended in 1783, blacks had been customarily barred from service. This custom became law with the enactment of the National Militia Act of 1792, which stated that only whites could enroll. State laws were also passed prohibiting blacks from joining militias at that level.[13] Some whites also claimed that blacks lacked the qualities of good fighting men and would be more of a liability than an asset. In their opinion, blacks were neither intelligent enough nor brave enough to be good soldiers. Yet, blacks had fought in every colonial war in the 1600s and 1700s and on the sides of both the British and the Americans during the Revolutionary War and the War of 1812. Names such as Peter Salem, Salem Poor, Caesar Brown, Barzillai Lew, Alexander Ames, and Prince Hall show up on the rosters of black soldiers who died fighting in the Revolutionary War. And legends have grown up around the name of Crispus Attucks, a runaway who, although a member of the unruly group who taunted British soldiers

stationed in Boston and as a result became a casualty of the melee in
March 1770 that became known as the Boston Massacre, was, nonetheless, the first American to die for the Revolutionary cause.[14]

Another group of whites feared that arming blacks would be an
admission that white soldiers were somehow lacking, unable to get
the job done without the help of blacks. And since most whites
thought that blacks were innately inferior, the mere notion that they
needed their help was alarming. Others feared that arming blacks
might lead to slave insurrections, and still more whites simply did
not like the idea of blacks serving alongside them. To these white
men, racial equality meant social equality between the races, and
social equality meant that black men would have access to white
women. Miscegenation, the mixing of the races, was a likelihood that
could not be tolerated. For all of these reasons, whites remained firmly
opposed to arming blacks in the first months of the war. Not until
the summer of 1862 did Union officials reverse themselves on the
issue. This reversal took place out of necessity, because the war was
going badly for the Union. Thus, Northern whites began to support
the arming of blacks, slave and free alike.

LINCOLN AND BLACK FREEDOM

Even though Lincoln repeated that the Civil War was being fought
to preserve the Union and not to end slavery, from the beginning of
the war there was speculation about whether or when the slaves
would be emancipated. Lincoln had believed in the gradual emancipation of slaves, but he held a mixed record on the issue of black
freedom when he assumed the presidency. According to the legend
of "Lincoln the Emancipator," one day at a slave auction in New Orleans in 1830, he made an eternal vow against slavery. Witnessing
the sale of a beautiful mulatto girl, he was sickened by the manner in
which she was handled and inspected by prospective buyers. As he
walked away, Lincoln was alleged to have remarked, "If I ever get a
chance to hit that thing I'll hit it hard."[15] Since the story was told by a
man who did not accompany Lincoln on either of the two trips he
made to New Orleans, it cannot stand up.[16] Furthermore, although
Lincoln intended to use his 1860 autobiography for campaign purposes and could not reveal any abolitionist convictions, he made no
mention of slaves or the slave trade in it. He did, however, speak of a
previous trip to New Orleans and recalled an incident in which he
and one of his companions "were attacked by seven Negroes with

intent to kill and rob them"; "hurt some in the melee," they "succeeded in driving the Negroes from the boat."[17]

Lincoln was also alleged to have become incensed over seeing some slaves in shackles on the Ohio riverboat while a young man in his twenties. But, years later in a letter to Mary Speed dated September 27, 1841, he philosophically described the scene on board as exemplifying "the effect of condition upon human happiness."[18] Apparently, it did not bother Lincoln that one dozen slaves were shackled together like animals, separated from their families, and sold off to a place where slavery was regarded as being the harshest. Nevertheless, in his opinion, "they were the most cheerful and apparently happy creatures." Thus, he concluded that God "renders the worst of human conditions tolerable, while He permits the best to be nothing better than tolerable."[19] Moreover, as late as 1847, he accepted a slaveholder as a law client and argued against one of the man's slave's claim to freedom. Lincoln lost the case.[20]

As a young congressman, Lincoln introduced a bill to abolish slavery in the District of Columbia, but he seemed to take a yes-and-no attitude toward the institution. His bill was carefully worded so as not to offend slaveholders. Furthermore, it called, not for the immediate emancipation of slaves, but for gradual emancipation and monetary compensation to the owners. This bill could go into effect if a majority of whites in the District voted for it in a referendum.[21] Consequently, Lincoln placed himself in a no-lose situation since whites in the District would have the final say in the matter. If they approved it, his star might rise; and even if they did not, he would not be damaged politically. During the 1850s it should be borne in mind that Lincoln consistently opposed the spread of slavery into the territories, but he never advocated its termination in the Southern states.[22]

As noted earlier, Lincoln's position as president on the issue of emancipation remained consistent. As Union troops penetrated deep into Southern territory, the Confederacy began to employ slaves in their war effort. Contrabands, as they were called, were making such a substantial contribution that it became necessary for Union officials to devise strategies to counter it. Liberal Republicans threw their weight behind the first Confiscation Act, which was designed to deal with the problem of contrabands. The bill eventually garnered unanimous Republican support and Congress passed it on August 6, 1861, and sent it to Lincoln for his signature. The most controversial provision was one that authorized the seizure of Rebel slaves actively employed in the Confederate war effort. Not surprisingly, John J.

Crittenden of Kentucky and other Border state Democrats were livid. They argued that the provision was nothing less than a general emancipation act. In addition, Midwest Democrats were even more aggressive with their criticism, arguing that the bill would bring several million "wooly headed, thick-lipped" Southern Negroes into the North and "Africanize" the region.

Republicans countered with the argument that since confiscated slaves would be carefully controlled, Southern blacks were not going to flood into the free states. Moreover, they argued that owing to the fact that a war was going on, the government had every right to seize enemy property—including slave property—as legitimate contraband. Finally, Republicans maintained that since the bill affected only those slaves used for rebel war purposes, it was hardly a general emancipation bill, which eradicated slavery as a state institution. Instead, it was an entirely legal war measure designed to weaken Confederate military forces and help terminate the rebellion. Apparently, Lincoln was persuaded by the arguments of the Republicans, as he elected to sign the bill into law. The first Confiscation Act was, to a large extent, similar to General Benjamin Butler's contraband policy, which Lincoln had already upheld. Nevertheless, when racial antagonisms flared up in the wake of the act, Lincoln reiterated his position that emancipation was not a goal in the war.[23] Clearly, events beyond the president's control had moved him to sign the first Confiscation Act. He sincerely believed that it would help him accomplish his overall objective, the preservation of the Union.

Throughout 1861 in particular, Lincoln's chief concern was to maintain a united coalition of war Democrats and Border state Unionists as well as Republicans in support of the war effort. In order to accomplish this goal, Lincoln deemed it imperative to define the war as being solely for the Union and not a war against slavery. Defining the conflict as one to preserve the Union would unite his coalition, while describing it as a struggle against slavery would fragment it. Accordingly, on August 30, Lincoln rescinded General Frémont's emancipation edict in Missouri,[24] which placed the state under martial law and ordered that the slaves of rebels there be seized and "declared freemen."[25] Lincoln could not allow the emancipation edict to stand because it would jeopardize his political and military efforts to prevent the Border states of Kentucky, Maryland, and Missouri from seceding. Moreover, efforts were also under way to garner the support of Unionists in western Virginia and eastern Tennessee.[26] Given the circumstances under which Lincoln operated early in the war, it is easy to understand his reluctance to support Frémont's edict. At the same time, however, his decision to rescind the order did not cause him great grief, as it was consistent with his principal war aim.

As the spring of 1862 emerged, Lincoln and the Republican Congress collaborated on ways to battle at the outer defenses of slavery. The president was sent a bill by Congress that forbade Union officers from returning fugitive slaves to the Confederacy. Lincoln signed it. While the bill represented on the surface a progressive attack against the institution of slavery, this was not entirely why Lincoln supported it. Uppermost in his mind was Confederate defeat, which would equal preservation of the Union. By denying the Confederates the return of fugitive slaves who in turn could be used in their war effort, Lincoln was striking a blow against the Confederacy's chances of survival. He also signed a bill, sent to him by Congress, that outlawed slavery in all federal territories. Thus, in one fell swoop Lincoln reversed the Dred Scott Decision and implemented the Republican goal of slave containment. Shortly thereafter, Washington would witness something scarcely dreamed of when the war began—black diplomats strolling about the streets of a slaveless capital city.[27]

Nonetheless, Lincoln remained adamantly opposed to military emancipation in the rebel states. In fact, Lincoln's reaction to news that General David Hunter had issued on May 9, 1862, a military order that applied to slaves on Union-held islands off South Carolina, reminiscent of Frémont's emancipation edict in Missouri, underscores this point. Because slavery was inconsistent with a free country, Hunter declared, the slaves inside his lines were "free forever."[28] When Lincoln found out about the order, he revoked it at once. Although he believed "that all men everywhere could be free," he thought that only the president alone could decide when military emancipation was necessary to save the country.[29] In time, Lincoln would reach this conclusion, but events had not moved him to this point by the spring of 1862.

In the summer of 1862, Congress began to intensify its attacks against slavery and also increased its efforts to persuade a reluctant Lincoln to follow suit. Radical Republicans, led by men such as Representative Thaddeus Stevens of Pennsylvania, wanted to punish rebels by confiscating their property, including their slaves. In an effort to accomplish this objective, the Republican-controlled Congress on July 17 passed the second Confiscation Act, which defined the rebels as traitors. Not surprisingly, Lincoln voiced concerns about many of its provisions. He was troubled the most by one that declared that after a period of sixty days, the slaves of rebels should be "forever free of their servitude, and not again held as slaves." The

president simply did not believe that Congress had the right to free a
slave within a state. Lincoln did not sign the bill until he had secured
modifications of some of the more stringent provisions, and even then
he took the unprecedented step of placing before Congress his statement of objections to the bill that he had just approved.[30] Why, specifically, did Lincoln feel the need to go to such an extraordinary
length to sign into law the Second Confiscation Act? Was it because
the act was truly a revolutionary measure?

Since the act provided that the slaves of rebels could be made
free if they came under the control of the army, one might conclude
that this would mean emancipation for all the slaves whom victory
by Union forces could guarantee. Therefore, whenever Union soldiers
appeared, slaves could conceivably obtain their freedom. However,
while the goal was revolutionary, the means to reach it were not. Indeed, actual freedom would be difficult to obtain because of the red
tape involved. For example, freedom could only be acquired by appearing before a federal court on a case-by-case basis. There were
estimated to be 350,000 slave owners in the South when the Second
Confiscation Act became law. Thus, if their individual slaves were to
seek freedom under this act, there would have to be one case for every owner. These cases would tie up the courts for several years and
render them useless in terms of dealing with other legal matters. It is
little wonder that Lincoln could say as late as September 13, 1862, "I
cannot learn that that law has caused a single slave to come over to
us."[31] Historian David H. Donald was correct when he wrote of the
Second Confiscation Act, "it had little effect except as an expression
of opinion."[32]

Nevertheless, one ought not completely to minimize the importance of the act. It did, in fact, represent another example of slavery
being undercut by the force of military necessity. There was a provision in the bill that authorized the president to "receive into the service of the United States, for the purpose of constructing
entrenchments or performing camp service, or for any other labor or
any military or naval service for which they may be found competent persons of African descent." The law even provided pay for that
service. On the day that the measure passed, Lincoln informed Congress that he was ready to let military commanders "employ, as laborers, as many persons of African de[s]cent, as can be used to
advantage."[33] As had been the case earlier, he was still concerned
about the political implications of military emancipation, but he had
no major problem in endorsing the utilization of blacks as laborers to

assist the Union war effort. Again, Lincoln's primary concern was the defeat of the Confederacy and the salvation of the Union. He realized that his actions would inevitably lead to the emancipation of slaves, and he had concluded at this time that emancipation was a military necessity. Thus, it is little wonder why Lincoln would sign the Militia Act into law on the same day that he signed the Second Confiscation Act.

The Militia Act empowered the president to call 300,000 nine-month militiamen, ages eighteen to forty-five, from the states, based on their population. Lincoln had the authority under the act to fill the necessary quota if the states did not supply the men. Although recruitment and surreptitious conscription were the main elements of this measure, it also expedited the evolution of black military service. Blacks could now be accepted as soldiers to fill the state quotas. Moreover, as a consequence of the Militia Act, Lincoln had the authority to emancipate any slaves who enlisted, along with their families, if their masters were rebels. Therefore, some blacks who fought in the armed forces were freed even before the Emancipation Proclamation was issued.[34] By signing the bill, for the first time during the war, Lincoln had endorsed a limited form of military emancipation. In the coming days his support for military emancipation would steadily grow as it became tied to the preservation of the Union.

While Lincoln had reached the conclusion by the summer of 1862 that military emancipation was a necessary prerequisite for Union victory, throughout 1862 he continued to promote his colonization scheme that he had unveiled early in his presidency and that he hoped would lead to the peaceful, gradual liberation of blacks. Lincoln's plan for emancipation was twofold: compensation for the slaveholders and colonization for blacks, slave and free. First, he proposed a plan aimed at freeing slaves gradually, over a 30-year period, and compensating their masters out of the national treasury. In order for his proposal to be carried out, Lincoln had to solicit the cooperation of Congress and the particular states involved. He sent Congress a message in March 1862 urging gradual emancipation and proposing that the Federal government assist states initiating such a plan. Congress sided with the president, and on April 10 passed a joint supporting resolution, which specified that federal financial aid should be given to any state that adopted a plan for the gradual abolition of slavery. But spokesmen from the Border states on Capitol Hill responded negatively. They argued that the cost of the program would be $478 million and that their constituents would vote down the proposal even if this sum were appropriated beforehand. This response was a setback for Lincoln, who had hoped that an offer to compensate slaveholders might tip the balance in favor of his plan.[35]

Lincoln's state-run compensated emancipation scheme contained several weaknesses. Fundamentally it was far more sensitive in its appeal to whites to accept the process than it was in foreseeing the consequences for blacks. The prospect of civil and political rights for blacks would surely have been limited had states and the existing white leadership of 1862 retained control over emancipation. Since it would have been implemented before blacks proved their capacities and earned national obligation by their service in the war, it is likely that state-controlled emancipation would not have advanced the course of black rights very much. No national power would have been able to checkmate local oppression of blacks under Lincoln's state-controlled emancipation scheme, since no Fourteenth or Fifteenth Amendments would have been on the horizon.[36]

The second part of Lincoln's plan was a proposal to ship slaves and free blacks out of the country. Deportation would rid the nation of slavery and all African Americans along with it. Again, Congress supported the president. In spring 1862 it voted to appropriate $600,000 for the purpose of colonizing slaves and free blacks.[37] Afterward, Lincoln began to launch a campaign to persuade free blacks to agree to be colonized and endeavored to find somewhere for them to settle. On August 14 he met with a delegation of five free black men, led by Edward M. Thomas, and tried to persuade them that all blacks would be better off if they were to leave the United States and resettle in Liberia, Central America, or the Caribbean.[38] Like Thomas Jefferson, Lincoln believed that blacks were innately inferior to whites and that it would be impossible for blacks and whites to live together in the United States as equals.[39] Thus, Lincoln had come to believe that colonization was the only viable solution to the race problem in America. He expressed the sentiments of many whites, as few of them could contemplate a situation where all blacks were free. One of the most ardent defenders of the white South and its institutions, Senator Henry Clay of Kentucky, expressed the view in 1830 that it "would be unwise" to liberate the slaves "without their removal or colonization." One Mississippi farmer believed that "the majority would be right glad [to abolish slavery] if we could get rid of the niggers. But it wouldn't never do to free 'em and leave 'em here. I don't know anybody hardly, in favor of that."[40]

Most black leaders, however, were furious with Lincoln for suggesting that they should abandon the only country they had known.

They were adamantly opposed to all colonization schemes, believing that blacks, as productive members of society, had just as much right to live in the United States as did whites. Like whites, their ancestors had helped build America into what it now was—a powerful, though divided, nation. Their forebears had fought, bled, and died for the country in all the wars that the nation had been engaged in. Furthermore, some free blacks believed that if they left the country, their brothers and sisters who were held as slaves in the South would be left even more vulnerable to white oppression. They expressed their anguish in open letters. Frederick Douglass, for example, in the pages of his newest publication, *Douglass Monthly*, in September 1862 asserted that "Mr. Lincoln assumes the language and arguments of an itinerant Colonization lecturer, showing all his inconsistencies, his pride of race and blood, his contempt for Negroes and his canting hypocrisy."[41] Free blacks in various cities held protest meetings condemning the president's colonization scheme. The general sentiment of these gatherings was expressed as an "Appeal" sent to Lincoln by free blacks in Philadelphia: "Many of us have our own house and other property, amounting in the aggregate, to millions of dollars. Shall we sacrifice this, leave our homes, forsake our birthplace, and flee to a strange land, to appease the anger and prejudice of the traitors now in arms against the government?"[42]

Not all free blacks were opposed to colonization. Alienated by discrimination and abuse, some grasped at the opportunity. Hundreds emigrated to Haiti during the first year of the war. By 1862, promoters were touting Central America as a new destination, and some free blacks petitioned the U.S. government in efforts to acquire financial backing to emigrate there. The Reverend Henry M. Turner, a prominent clergyman in the African Methodist Episcopal Church, was among the signers of one of these petitions. Free blacks in support of colonization, however, represented a small minority.[43]

Without the support of Northern free blacks, it was unlikely that any colonization scheme would succeed. Lincoln's efforts to locate a place where blacks could create a new life for themselves proved as fruitless as his efforts to persuade them to leave America. Although representatives from the government of Liberia had assured the president that black Americans would be welcome in their country, Lincoln did not regard Liberia as the most feasible place for black resettlement because it was so far from the United States. He preferred somewhere closer. Chiriqui, a province of Colombia (now in Panama), appeared to be satisfactory to him. In attempting to make the necessary arrangements, however, Lincoln allowed himself to

FREDERICK DOUGLASS, THE CELEBRATED ABOLI-
TIONIST, UNION RECRUITER, FEMINIST, AND SOCIAL
ACTIVIST.

Library of Congress

negotiate with members of a fraudulent land company. As a consequence, the project collapsed. Moreover, Colombia's neighbors in Central America had protested vigorously against the proposal. Once Lincoln had abandoned the Chiriqui scheme, he tried to persuade the European powers that owned territories in Latin America to provide a place for blacks to be colonized. But these powers saw no political dividends therein and were not responsive to his overtures. By October 1862, Lincoln had nearly exhausted all his options for colonization in the Western Hemisphere. His last remaining one was Haiti, but, here again, he made the mistake of dealing with land speculators of questionable honesty. Late in December, Lincoln signed a contract with Bernard Kock for the settlement of five thousand blacks on Cow Island in Haiti but was saved from further embarrassment by Secretary of State William H. Seward, who was suspicious of Kock's integrity and refused to certify the contract. Thus, by the fall of 1862 neither of Lincoln's plans for compensation and colonization had caught on.[44]

THE EMANCIPATION PROCLAMATION

During the summer of 1862, while Lincoln tried to work out a plan for the colonization of blacks, he was facing increasing pressure from black and white abolitionists and from the more progressive elements of his party for a commitment to end slavery. Furthermore, it had become clear to the president and other government officials that the war would be long and bloody. Lincoln was confronted with Confederate resistance that was more massive and effective than he had thought possible. He had believed that the Union was on the verge of victory in the spring of 1862, but any hope of success at that time was shattered by General Robert E. Lee's successful counteroffensives in the Seven Days. As he wrestled with the problem of emancipation, he also worried how he could meet the spiraling demands on Union manpower for both combat and logistical duties. By linking emancipation with arming the former slaves, he found a solution. As a war measure, he would issue a proclamation freeing the slaves. He first mentioned this possibility to his cabinet in the summer of 1862, knowing that he had to move cautiously. Politically and strategically, he was restrained by the fear that forced emancipation would turn the loyal Border states of Missouri, Kentucky, and Maryland against the Union. The loss of these states' vital industry and manpower would hurt the Union cause. Furthermore, Lincoln did not want to do anything that would provoke the lower Southern states to launch a war of total resistance—something they were likely to do if he were to free the slaves in that section of the country.[45]

In the end, Lincoln recognized that the Confederate war effort that to date had resisted Union advances was vulnerable at one major point: it rested on an economy and a social structure that depended on slave labor. The only way to combat it effectively was to undermine it by removing that base. Thus, Lincoln argued in July 1862 that a proclamation of emancipation "was a military necessity absolutely essential for the salvation of the Union." Furthermore, "we must free the slaves or be ourselves subdued."[46] And so, on September 22, 1862, just five days after the Union victory at Antietam, Lincoln decided to act, proclaiming that on January 1, 1863, "All persons held as slaves within any State, or designated part of the state, the people whereof shall be in rebellion against the United States, shall be then, thenceforward, and forever free."[47] The Emancipation Proclamation stipulated that freed slaves would be accepted by the Union military "to garrison forts, positions, stations, and other places, and to man vessels of all sorts in said service."[48] In this document he also revived the possibility of compensated emancipation and said that he would continue to encourage the voluntary colonization of blacks "upon this continent or elsewhere."[49] Lincoln, therefore, either continued to believe that white hostility would be too massive for emancipated blacks to live in the same vicinity with whites, or still thought that blacks were inferior to whites and could never live as equals in society. Perhaps he was also trying to placate Northern whites, many of whom were fearful that emancipated blacks would settle in the North. If they were to be colonized somewhere in Central America, there was no need to worry.

RESPONSE TO LINCOLN'S PROCLAMATION

When news of Lincoln's preliminary proclamation reached the South, slaves by the thousands responded by fleeing plantations and rushing into the lines of the Union army. Years later, Mary Crane, a former slave, recalled the event in Larue County, Kentucky: "When President Lincoln issued his Proclamation, freeing the Negroes, I remember that my father and most all of the other younger slave men left the farms."[50] Most slaves were illiterate, but the news of emancipation reached them through an oral network called the "grapevine telegraph."

PRESIDENT ABRAHAM LINCOLN, WITH CABINET MEMBERS, ISSUING THE EMANCIPATION PROCLAMATION.

Library of Congress

Gabe Butler, for example, found out about the Emancipation Proclamation in this way: "I didn't hear much talk 'bout de war, but slaves wud cum frum udder plantations an' dey wud tell how old man Abe was going to sot us free."[51] Thomas Rutling learned about it from his master's son, a medical doctor who did not support slavery. Rutling was sitting in the slave quarters waiting for breakfast when the young doctor came along and spoke to his brother and sister at the front door. His siblings "jumped up and down, and shouted, and sang, and then told me I was free."[52] Benjamin Holmes, a slave in Charleston, South Carolina, read Lincoln's entire Proclamation to a group of slaves who reacted with loud rejoicing. [53] In Louisiana, *L'Union*, a French-English journal started by free blacks in New Orleans in September 1862, spread the news and urged all black men in the state to make the best of their new opportunities "in freedom."[54] Blacks in Union-held territory such as the Sea Islands of South Carolina were informed by Union officials. The Sea Islands blacks were so overcome with joy at services held to celebrate the Proclamation that they began to sing, "My Country, 'tis of thee, sweet land of liberty, of thee I sing!"[55] In addition, Susie King Taylor, on hearing it read, described January 1, 1863, as a "glorious day."[56] Pierce Harper was also in Union-held territory when the news reached him. Union officials "read it to all de colored people who went to town an' had men go 'round an' read it to de ones dat didn't get to town." Once all the blacks returned to the plantation, the celebrating began. Harper remembered "how dey stayed up half de night at Mr. Harper's after de men had read de 'mancipation to us, singing an' shouting. Dat was all dey did, jus' sing an' shout an' go on."[57]

Despite these efforts because of the effectiveness of white owners in withholding information from their slaves, a large number did not know of the Proclamation for several months after it was issued. In fact, one former slave recalled not having heard of it as late as 1864: "De White folks nebber talk 'fore black men, dey mighty Free from dat."[58] Lincoln had earlier predicted with great enthusiasm that the Proclamation would immediately lead to a mass exodus of blacks to Union lines. This did not happen, causing Lincoln to say with concern a few months after the Proclamation was announced that "the slaves are not coming so rapidly and so numerously to us as I had hoped."[59] Thus, August 1863, Lincoln proposed a daring, even revolutionary, secret plan to remedy the problem. This plan called for Frederick Douglass to organize a band of black "scouts" to pass through Union lines into the plantation South "and carry the news of emancipation, and urge the slaves to come within our boundaries." Although Douglass agreed with Lincoln's goal of informing the slaves about the Proclamation, he thought that the president's secret plan was suicidal, akin to the original plan of John Brown at Harpers Ferry. A few days later Douglass offered a counterproposal calling for the employment of agents who would infiltrate the South "to warn [the slaves] as to what will be their probable condition should peace be concluded while they remain within the Rebel lines; and more especially to urge upon them the necessity of making their escape."[60]

At the tender age of fifteen, George Washington Albright was employed as one of the agents who carried from plantation to plantation the news that the Emancipation Proclamation had been signed

Library of Congress

in Washington. Albright explained the nature of this process: "I traveled about the plantations within a certain range, and got together small meetings in the cabins to tell the slaves the great news. Some of these slaves in turn would find their way to still other plantations—and so the story spread. We had to work in dead secrecy; we had knocks and signs and passwords."[61] As a consequence of this successful plan, Albright maintained thousands of slaves were apprised of the Proclamation. The black men and women who served as agents showed great courage, as this was a dangerous enterprise. Detection was possible at anytime. All it would take was the confession of a nervous or loyal slave to the owner that an outsider was disseminating such news and encouraging them to run away. Certainly, if caught, the punishment would be death.

Northern free blacks so anxiously awaited Lincoln's Emancipation Proclamation that in many cities they arranged celebratory meetings of prayer and thanksgiving on the eve of its announcement. One such meeting took place in Boston and was attended by such prominent black leaders as J. Sella Martin, William Wells Brown, and Frederick Douglass.[62] When the actual document was proclaimed on January 1, 1863, these meetings grew in number and intensity. On New Year's Day, hundreds of blacks gathered in Washington, DC, outside the White House and cheered the president, calling out to him, as the black pastor and future Reconstruction politician Henry M. Turner recalled, that "if he would come out of the palace, they would hug him to death."[63] A Pennsylvania gathering declared that "we, the Colored Citizens of the city of Harrisburg, hail this 1st day of January, 1863, as a new era in our country's history—a day in which injustice and oppression were forced to flee and cower before the benign principles of justice and righteousness."[64] Echoing the sentiments of most abolitionists and Northern free blacks who thought that the Proclamation was only a stride toward freedom and complained that Lincoln had not gone far enough, the black Pennsylvanians further declared, "We would have preferred that the proclamation should have been general instead of partial, but we can only say to our brethren of the 'Border States,' be of good cheer—the day of your deliverance draweth nigh."[65] Frances Ellen Watkins Harper, a black leader, regarded the announcement as "a day for poetry and song."[66] And Frederick Douglass was almost overcome. "We shout for joy that we live to record this righteous decree," he wrote.[67] Northern and Southern white reaction to the Emancipation was varied.[68]

THE SIGNIFICANCE OF LINCOLN'S PROCLAMATION

On the day that the Emancipation Proclamation was issued, it did not free one slave. Technically it freed slaves in the South, but the U.S. government could not make this act binding until after the Confederacy was defeated. The Proclamation did not even claim to free the slaves in the Border states of Missouri, Kentucky, Maryland, and Delaware. Likewise, it exempted those working on plantations in areas occupied by federal forces, such as the Mississippi Valley and the Sea Islands, where many owners had taken an oath of allegiance and pledged their "loyalty" to the federal government. It was the Thirteenth Amendment, approved by Congress in February 1865 and ratified the following December, that actually emancipated all the slaves.

The Emancipation Proclamation was of critical importance, however, in meeting Lincoln's manpower goals for the Union military by encouraging slaves to escape and take up arms. Although the first black troops were mustered into service in the fall of 1862, recruitment did not begin in earnest until the spring of 1863, after the proclamation had been issued. In the occupied areas of the South where enlistment drives were launched, many slaves responded enthusiastically.[69] As Solomon Bradley of South Carolina put it, "I used to pray the Lord for this opportunity to be released from bondage and to fight for my liberty, and I could not feel right so long as I was not in the regiment."[70] And in the North, blacks welcomed the chance to fight for their freedom and for that of their families. The Proclamation also strengthened the moral cause of the Union at home and abroad. It rallied the North by adding the idealistic appeal of a war being fought not only to preserve the Union but also to free the slaves. Before Lincoln issued the Proclamation, there was a real possibility that European powers, led by Britain, might formally recognize the Confederacy and intervene militarily on its behalf. But that all changed with the stroke of a pen. The Proclamation turned out to be a shrewd diplomatic move. Thousands of English and European laborers who were anxious to see workers gain their freedom throughout the world perceived that the Union was fighting to free black workers, while the Confederacy was fighting to keep them in bondage.[71]

Lincoln remained undaunted in the face of relentless attacks against the Proclamation. The president stood foursquare behind it. The pressure from his numerous critics got to him; he wavered but did not buckle. Instead, he told weakened Republicans that "no human power can subdue this rebellion without using the emancipation lever as I have done." Lincoln was also quick to dismiss any suggestions that he return to slavery those blacks who had fought for the Union. To the whites who dared propose this, Lincoln passionately replied, "I should be damned in time and in eternity for so doing. The world shall know that I will keep my faith to friends and enemies, come what will!" Lincoln made this statement in the midst of strong political opposition to his emancipation policies on the eve of the 1864 presidential election, which he clearly expected to lose. In effect, he was saying that he would rather be right than president. As matters turned out, of course, he was both right and president,[72] and the nation as a whole benefited from his dual triumph. First, issuing the Emancipation Proclamation was an excellent moral and ethical decision of paramount importance to humanity. Despite any strategic and political dividends that might come to him, the fact that Lincoln stood forthright behind it is noble. And, second, he certainly deserved the opportunity to lead the country to the successful completion of the war. At this point in the nation's history, no other person was better equipped than Lincoln to guide the country through its national nightmare. That the country fully understood this, and reelected him to the presidency in 1864, was indeed a triumph for the nation.

THE THIRTEENTH AMENDMENT

Realizing that preservation of the Union was tied to black emancipation, Lincoln endorsed the Thirteenth Amendment abolishing slavery even before the election of 1864. When Lincoln and the Republicans won large majorities at the polls, the president moved immediately to get Congress to pass the emancipation amendment. In fact, he began pressuring Congress to act in December 1864, only a few days after the election. As Lincoln viewed it, the large majorities that the Republicans won at the polls, including Democratic votes, had dampened the morale of the Confederacy. And, passage of an emancipation amendment, Lincoln believed, especially by the slave states, would further erode its morale. As he told Missouri Democrat James Rollins, "I am very anxious that the war be brought to a close at the earliest possible date. I don't believe this can be accomplished as long as those fellows down South can rely on the border states to help them; but if the members of the border states would unite, at least enough of them to pass the amendment, they would soon see that they could not expect much help from that quarter." Lincoln believed that he was now operating from a position of strength and insisted that the national election had given him a mandate for permanent emancipation. Perhaps the current political climate would help shift the necessary votes in the House in his direction. If not, the next House would surely provide enough votes.[73]

Momentum seemed to be on the president's side in the days just prior to the vote, but a last-minute rumor threatened to stop it. A rumor swept through the Capitol that Southern commissioners were on their way to Washington for peace talks. If this was true, some who had announced their intentions to support the amendment might recant, particularly those representatives from the Border slave states. From their vantage point, why emancipate slaves to save the Union if one could save the Union without emancipation? In a last-ditch effort to hold the votes in line, James Ashley, who was in charge of the measure on the floor of the House, asked Lincoln to issue a direct denial of the rumor. Lincoln readily assented with a one-sentence response: "So far as I know, there are no peace commissioners in the city, or likely to be in it."[74]

There was considerable suspense on January 31, 1865, the day of the vote. No one could be certain of the outcome. Spectators filled the corridors and galleries of the Capitol to observe history in the making. The Thirteenth Amendment abolishing the institution of slavery passed with the necessary two-thirds votes. All 102 Republicans, joined by seventeen Democrats, voted for the amendment. Some fifty-eight Democrats voted no on the measure, and eight Democrats helped out by abstaining. The final tabulation represented just three votes more than the required two-thirds majority.[75] Success, at long last Lincoln's, had taken all of the resources at his disposal to make the Thirteenth Amendment a reality. Indeed, the president lent his talents of eloquence to this effort as well as his political skills, engaging in secret patronage negotiations. As expected, blacks greeted news of the passage of the amendment with unbounded joy. They gathered in mass meetings and clapped and sang: "Sound the loud timbrel o'er Egypt's dark sea, Jehovah has triumphed, His people are free."[76] In the White House, Lincoln pronounced the amendment "a great moral victory." And, beaming, he pointed south across the Potomac and remarked, "if the people over the river had behaved themselves, I could not have done what I have."[77]

Sadly, within three short months after this "crowning achievement," Lincoln would be dead, the victim of an assassin's bullet. Although his voice was silenced, his contributions to humanity would live on. The Emancipation Proclamation and his subsequent efforts on behalf of the Thirteenth Amendment represented the pinnacle of his heroic legacy: the substance of his image as the Great Emancipator. However, although Lincoln had been an indispensable player in the black liberation drama, his primary concern was for the Union. Therefore, as Frederick Douglass noted, Lincoln's image as the Great Emancipator was somewhat exaggerated. Nevertheless, in spite of his shortcomings, he was a vital agent in an inexorable progression of circumstances that would result in the total abolition of slavery.[78]

Lincoln's presidency ushered in a period of symbolic advancement for blacks. For example, on the very day that the House passed the Thirteenth Amendment, the chamber's galleries were packed with cheering blacks—one of the first times that they were allowed to sit in the galleries. Blacks had been denied entry until 1864. And, on February 1, 1865, history was again made. For the first time in the country's history, a black lawyer from Boston, John S. Rock, was admitted to practice before the U.S. Supreme Court.[79] Yet prior to these events, Lincoln had begun to show more sensitivity and respect in his attitude toward blacks. For example, as no president before him had done, Lincoln opened the White House to black visitors; four black men were in attendance at the New Year's Day reception in 1864. Frederick Douglass met him several times at the Soldiers Home, paid at least three calls at the White House, and made his last visit as a guest at the reception on the night of the second inauguration.[80] Accompanied by her fourteen-year-old grandson, Sammy Banks, Sojourner Truth went to Washington in the fall of 1864, where on October 20 she met the president. Lincoln also complied with a request from a delegation of black clergymen to meet with him at the White House. The clergymen sought and were granted permission to preach to black soldiers.[81]

Frederick Douglass, who had more contact with Lincoln than any other black, summed up the legacy of his presidency in regard to black freedom in his "Oration in Memory of Abraham Lincoln" given on April 14, 1876, at the unveiling of the Freedmen's Memorial Monument in Washington, DC. Douglass gave Lincoln due credit for eradicating slavery. Nonetheless, he saw the president as primarily pro-Union and pro-white and only unwittingly pro-black. Douglass maintained that "Abraham Lincoln was not, in the fullest sense of the word, either our man or our model." Further, Douglass asserted, "in his interests, in his associations, in his habits of thoughts, and in his prejudices, he was a white man." White Americans were "the children of Abraham Lincoln," but black Americans were at best only his stepchildren, children by adoption, children by forces of circumstance and necessity.[82] In the end, therefore, Lincoln ought to be best remembered as a reluctant friend of blacks.

CHAPTER TWO

UNWANTED PARTICIPANTS
Service in the War

ONCE BLACKS WERE finally permitted to enlist in the Union army, they reacted with enthusiasm. Popular black leaders such as Frederick Douglass, William Wells Brown, Charles L. Remond, Martin Delany, John M. Langston, Henry Highland Garnet, John S. Rock, Mary Ann Shadd Cary (the only woman officially commissioned as a recruiting agent), and others were called upon to serve as recruiters in the North. In Boston, New York, Philadelphia, and other cities, rallies were organized where speakers urged blacks to enlist, and blacks responded by appearing in huge numbers at recruiting stations. Mary Ann Shadd Cary, who was working as a teacher in Canada to support her two children, was encouraged by her dear friend Martin Delany to become a recruiter and secured soldiers for Connecticut, Indiana, and Massachusetts regiments. That she succeeded in this effort came as no surprise to her contemporaries. William Wells Brown wrote that "she raised recruits with as much skill, tact, and order as any government recruiting officer and that her men were always considered among the best recruited."

Although Shadd Cary was the only woman officially commissioned, she was by no means the lone woman recruiter. As the war progressed, many of the black male recruiters expanded their work into Canada and Union-held territory in the South. In these endeavors they were aided by black women such as Josephine Ruffin in Boston, who had recently married, and Harriet Jacobs, who wrote from Alexandria, Virginia, "I hope to obtain some recruits for the Massachusetts Cavalry, not for money, but because I want to do all I can to strengthen the hands of those who battle for freedom."[1] Indeed, the rationale given by Jacobs expresses the sentiments of most black recruiters. Douglass, Garnet, Wells Brown, Langston, Remond, Delany, Shadd Cary, and others had devoted a lifetime of energy and sacrifice to eradicate the institution of slavery and promote racial justice. Thus, their efforts to secure black soldiers represented their ongoing commitment to excise the cancer of racial oppression from American society. In their minds, the recruitment of a large black liberation force was of paramount importance.

In the South, where the situation was more tenuous, some blacks did not see any need to fight as long as they were winning their freedom without doing so,[2] but many in this region did enlist. Some plantation owners lost nearly all their enslaved field workers. When Admiral David D. Porter visited a plantation twenty miles above Vicksburg, Mississippi, late in 1864, for example, he found only one black out of a former population of nearly four hundred. "Uncle Moses," with whom he had conversed on a previous visit many months earlier, informed him that all the young "bucks" had gone to join the army or enlist on board "Mr. Linkum's gunboats."[3] George Washington Albright asserted that "like many other slaves, my father ran away from his plantation in Texas and joined the Union forces."[4] And Julius Jones recalled, "when the war came on, I must have been fourteen years old. All the men on the place run off and joined the Northern army."[5]

Moreover, March Wilson, of Sapelo Island, Georgia, walked several miles north to Port Royal Island, South Carolina, to enlist in the Union army on December 2, 1862. He became a member that day of the South Carolina Volunteers, the first Union regiment composed of former slaves.[6] Wilson was certainly only one of many blacks from his area to enlist at the earliest opportunity. Indeed, black recruitment efforts were so successful that by the end of the war more than 186,000 had enrolled in the Union army. Ninety-three thousand came from the seceded states and 40,000 from the Border slave states, with the other 53,000 from the free states.[7] Among these black soldiers were several who had emigrated to Canada and then returned to the United States to fight on the Union side during the war.[8] Perhaps the total figure was even higher because some contemporaries insisted that many mulattoes, the offspring of black and white unions, served in white regiments without being designated as blacks.[9]

Black troops were organized into regiments of light and heavy artillery, cavalry, infantry, and engineers. To distinguish them from white soldiers, they were called "United States Colored Troops." They were usually led by white officers with the aid of some black noncommissioned officers. Since most whites in the Union army were opposed to having blacks in the service, it was difficult at first to secure white officers for black outfits. Nevertheless, among those who distinguished themselves as fine leaders were Colonel Robert Gould Shaw of the Fifty-fourth Massachusetts Regiment and General N. P.

Banks of the First and Third Louisiana Native Guards.[10] Thomas Wentworth Higginson, colonel of the First South Carolina Volunteers, spoke proudly about the ability of his men. After a successful raid in Florida in 1863, he stated with passion, "Nobody knows anything about these men who has not seen them in battle. There is a fierce energy about them."[11] By the end of the war, black men had fought courageously in so many engagements that it was no longer difficult to solicit whites to command them.

PRIVATES AND NONCOMMISSIONED OFFICERS AT FORT STEVENS, WASHINGTON, DC.

Library of Congress

A few blacks held commissions in the Union army. Two regiments of General Benjamin Butler's Corps d'Afrique were staffed entirely by black officers; among them were Major F. E. Dumas and Captain P. B. S. Pinchback. Captain H. Ford Douglass and First Lieutenant W. D. Matthews led an independent battery at Lawrence, Kansas. Major Martin R. Delany and Captain O. S. B. Wall were officers in the 104th Regiment. Among the commissioned officers were black chaplains, including Henry M. Turner, William Hunter, James Underdue, Williams Waring, Samuel Harrison, William Jackson, and John R. Bowles, and black surgeons, including Alexander T. Augusta of the Seventh Regiment, and John V. DeGrasse of the Thirty-fifth. Other black surgeons who served but were not commissioned included Charles B. Purvis, Alpheus Tucker, John Rapier, William Ellis, Anderson Abbott, and William Powell.[12]

BLACK SOLDIERS CONFRONT WHITE RACISM

The fact that such a small number of blacks held commissions in the Union army greatly upset many black soldiers, who regarded this as a blatant example of racial injustice. They reasoned that only the color of their skin was the deciding factor, as they knew deserving competent blacks who would make outstanding officers. Many black soldiers, therefore, were quick to launch protests in writing regarding the army's failure to commission blacks as officers in significant numbers. An anonymous soldier in the Fifty-fourth Massachusetts

Infantry wrote about the outstanding performance of a black doctor in saving the life of a captain in his regiment. So many people were impressed that there was a petition circulated in support of his promotion. In fact, all the officers signed the petition except three, and even they admitted that "he was a smart man and understood medicine." Nonetheless, in their opinion, "he was a negro and they did not want a negro doctor, neither did they want negro officers." As a consequence of this prejudice among his officers, the colonel felt compelled to destroy the document.[13] In a letter filled with hurt and disappointment, an anonymous soldier in the Fifty-

An unidentified Black Union soldier. Courtesy of N.C. Division of Archives and History

fifth Massachusetts Infantry asked, "If we have men in our own regiment who are capable of being officers, why not let them be promoted the same as other soldiers?" He was sickened by the army's tendency to take sergeants from white regiments and make them captains or lieutenants, and then place them in charge of blacks.[14] A sergeant in the Fifty-fourth Massachusetts Infantry wrote, "We want black commissioned officers; and only because we want men we can understand and who can understand us. We want men whose hearts are truly loyal to the rights of man." He deemed it necessary to have ample black representation in case of courts-martial, where many blacks would undoubtedly end up. Speaking for many black soldiers, he explained: "We want to demonstrate our ability to rule, as we have demonstrated our willingness to obey." And, zeroing in on the racism of white officers in his regiment, the sergeant concluded, "Can they have confidence in officers who read the *Boston Courier* and talk about 'Niggers'?"[15]

Notwithstanding all these grievances, black soldiers did not lose perspective. Even with the white racism and discrimination that they had to endure, most were quick to point out, "we prefer the Union rather than the rebel government, and will sustain the Union if the United States will give us our rights." Furthermore, they maintained, "we will calmly submit to white officers, though some of them are not as well acquainted with military matters as our orderly sergeants."[16] In other words, they would carry out their duties in a disciplined and dignified way despite their concerns. Although the tenor of most of their letters was forceful, they were also respectful, with one man concluding, "I hope sir, that you will urge this matter, as I am well aware that you are on our side, and always have done for us all in your power to help our race."[17]

Black soldiers were on target in their thinking that if more black men were commissioned as officers, a more harmonious atmosphere would ensure in the army, and the end result would be equal justice for all. In most cases, however, not only were they unable to increase substantially the number of black commissioned officers, but the intense racism of many white officers also drove some of the few commissioned officers from the army. For example, Robert H. Isabelle, a lieutenant in the Second Louisiana Native Guards, one of only three black regiments led by men of color, resigned from the army. The reason was racism: "I joined the United States Army—with the sole object of laboring for the good of our country," he wrote, "but after five or six months experience I am convinced that the same prejudice still exist[s] and prevents that cordial harmony among officers which is indispensable for the success of the army."[18] Unfortunately, Isabelle's resignation was soon followed by those of other black officers.

The fervent racism that forced Isabelle and others out of military service took various forms. Black soldiers were often served barely adequate food that had earlier been rejected by white troops and then sent to them. Benjamin Williams, a young private in the Thirty-second U.S. Colored Infantry, claimed that the rations served to them were "moldy and musty and full of worms, and not fit for a dog to eat." When the men returned to camp for dinner, "there is nothing to eat but rotten hard tack and flat coffee without sugar in it."[19] In addition, racism sometimes took the form of derogatory language. Such was the case involving a white officer in the Fifty-fifth Massachusetts Infantry, who called one of the regiment's soldiers a "nigger." As expected the black solider was offended and threatened to retaliate. The white officer then hid on a nearby ship. Just when it appeared that a group of black soldiers would force the white man off the ship and beat him, Colonel Fox, the commanding officer, arrived on the scene. The colonel assured the men that justice would be done and then ordered the officer to "come out and give a reason why he should call a soldier a nigger." When he failed to respond satisfactorily, Colonel Fox "ordered him under arrest, and sent him, accompanied by at least two files of good brave colored soldiers, to report to the Provost guard."[20]

Cases of racism involving poor food and the use of derogatory language paled in comparison to the random violence wreaked upon black soldiers by white officers. Many of these officers, once enlisted men in white regiments, occupied the very positions of leadership that several blacks continued to argue rightfully belonged to competent members of their race. A private in the Forty-third U.S. Colored Infantry, for example, wrote a letter condemning their actions: "Our officers must stop beating their men across the head and back with their swords." And, he warned, if they do not, "I fear there will be trouble with some of us. There are men in this regiment who were born free, and have been brought up as well as any officer in the 43d, and will not stand being punched with swords and driven around like a dog."[21] The most notorious case of mistreatment involved Lieutenant Colonel Augustus W. Benedict of the Seventy-sixth U.S. Colored Infantry, whose conduct could be ruthless. Benedict tied an alleged guilty soldier with his arms and legs spread apart to stakes driven into the ground and smeared molasses on his face, hands, and feet to attract insects. The man was left there for an entire day, and the entire process was repeated the next day. On two other occasions, Benedict struck one soldier and severely whipped two drummer boys. He was ultimately court-martialed and dismissed from the service.

In another case, authorities were forced to press charges against a lieutenant who abused his troops, usually for trifling reasons. During his short tenure, the lieutenant had tied up four soldiers for prolonged periods of time, one of them for complaining to the regimental commander that he had no rations. He clubbed a private with his revolver three times and punched him once; he also struck another man during battalion drill. In addition, in the Thirty-second U.S. Colored Infantry, abuse occurred so often that one of its black sol-

diers threatened to eliminate the officers in his company: "I know
that some of us have left our homes, only to be abused and knocked
about; but one consolation is left us, we have their own clubs that
they gave us, to break their own heads with; and, in short, they are
making a trap to enslave themselves in."[22] Retaliation was a common
response to white violence, as black soldiers often refused to accept
injustices without a fight.

There was no theater of operations during the Civil War in which
blacks did not see action. They fought in 449 engagements, thirty-
nine of which were major battles. They were at the siege of Savannah
in Georgia, at Vicksburg in Mississippi, at Olustee in Florida, and at
Milliken's Bend in Louisiana. They fought in Arkansas, Kentucky,
Tennessee, and North Carolina, and when General Lee surrendered
to Ulysses S. Grant at Appomattox Court House they were there too.
Decatur Dorsey was awarded a Congressional Medal for gallantry
while acting as color-sergeant of the Thirty-ninth U.S. Colored Troops
at Petersburg, Virginia, on July 30, 1864. Private James Gardner of
the Thirty-sixth was awarded a medal for rushing in advance of his
brigade to shoot a Confederate officer who was leading his men into
action. Four men of the Fifty-fourth Massachusetts Infantry earned
the Gillmore Medal for gallantry displayed in the assault on Fort
Wagner in South Carolina in which their commanding officer, Colonel Robert Gould Shaw, a trusted and respected friend of black soldiers, was killed.[23] When the Fifty-fourth Massachusetts was called
upon to raise $1,000 to help erect a monument in his honor, they
readily agreed, but they were opposed to the proposed site at the
foot of Fort Wagner, facing Fort Sumter. Many members of the regiment thought that this location was inappropriate: "even when peace
reigns supreme, it may be desecrated by unfriendly hands." And
"why place a monument where most of those who want to view it
would have to make a long pilgrimage in order to do so?" The regiment "would rather see it raised on old Massachusetts soil. The first
to say a black was a man, let her have the first monument raised by
black men's money, upon her good old rocks."[24] The tribute to Colonel Shaw and the Fifty-fourth Massachusetts stands today in Boston.

Blacks served gallantly also in the Union navy. When the navy
adopted a black enlistment policy as early as September 20, 1861,
because of a manpower deficit, blacks, barred from service in the
Union army, rushed to enlist. Of the 118,044 enlistments in the navy,
30,000 were blacks and most of them were freedmen from Massachusetts. Blacks were kept in the lowest ranks, where they were discriminated against and segregated by their commanders. None became

petty officers, yet four black sailors won the Navy Medal of Honor. Joachim Pease, cited by his superior officer as having shown the utmost in courage and fortitude, is probably the best known of the four. He was the leader of the number one gun on the *Kearsarge* as well as one of the fifteen blacks on board this warship when it met the most famous Confederate raider, the *Alabama*, and engaged it in battle. Although Robert Smalls, a slave from Charleston, South Carolina, was not awarded the Congressional Medal of Honor, his escape with the Confederate *Planter* was perhaps the most dramatic incident involving a black at sea during the Civil War. Smalls waited until the vessel's officers were asleep on shore; then he and a crew of seven slaves loaded their wives and children on board and on the morning of May 13, 1862, piloted the *Planter* safely to Union lines. For his actions, Smalls was awarded an appointment in the Union navy. He went on to become one of the Reconstruction era's most prominent politicians.

FURNEY BRYANT, A FORMER SLAVE WHO ARRIVED IN NEW BERN, NORTH CAROLINA, AS A REFUGEE IN RAGS AND LATER BECAME A SOLDIER IN THE BLACK FIRST NORTH CAROLINA REGIMENT.

Courtesy of the North Carolina Division of Archives and History

John Lawson, a black from Pennsylvania, also distinguished himself in combat. He served on board the USS *Hartford*, whose job it was to take control of Mobile Bay on August 5, 1864. It was of paramount importance to the Union to knock out Mobile Bay because it was the last Confederate port on the Gulf of Mexico. There, blockade runners shipped out cotton and brought in cannon, ammunition, medicine, and other supplies needed by the rebels. Fort Morgan had to be taken out because its guns allowed the Confederate port to continue to function. As the guns of the *Hartford* fired on Fort Morgan on that somber August day, the fort's guns answered. Many of its shells found their mark, killing several sailors and severely wounding others who were tended by the surgeons below deck. One shell hit where Lawson and five other men were loading and firing. Lawson was badly injured, but refused to go below. He quickly resumed firing. Shortly thereafter, other shells began to land on target, blowing off men's arms, legs, and heads. Nevertheless, Lawson stayed at his post until the fleet had passed the fort and the minefield, sunk most of the rebel gunboats, and captured the ironclad *Tennessee*. The great battle ended by ten o'clock, and Lawson could now have his wounds dressed. The captain of the *Hartford* commended him for his bravery in action, and Lawson ultimately received the Congressional Medal of Honor.[25]

At first, black soldiers did not receive the same pay as white soldiers of equal rank. According to the Enlistment Act of July 17, 1862, whites with the rank of private would be paid thirteen dollars per month salary and $3.50 for clothing; blacks of the same rank would be paid seven dollars and three dollars.[26] If Union officials thought that blacks would accept this discrimination without complaining, they were mistaken; black soldiers and their white officers protested vigorously. "We have come out like men and we expected to be treated as men but we have bin treated more like dogs then men," one black soldier complained to Secretary of War Edwin Stanton.[27] The Fifty-fourth Massachusetts boldly displayed its opposition by serving a year without pay rather than accept discriminatory wages.[28] When Colonel Littlefield suggested to the regiment that they accept ten dollars per month now, with the promise of the additional three dollars per month later, not one man accepted his offer. A little irritated by their behavior, Littlefield insinuated that if they turned the money down, then they "might not receive any money till after the convening of Congress." To this threat, members of the Fifty-fourth replied "that we had been over five months waiting, and we would wait till the Government could frame some special law, for the payment of part of its troops."[29] The regiment marched into battle in Florida in 1864 singing, "Three cheers for Massachusetts and seven dollars a month."[30]

The refusal of black troops to accept unequal pay placed a heavy strain on their wives and children. Over and over again, black soldiers poured out their concern for family members because the government refused to pay them the same as white soldiers. A soldier in the Sixth U.S. Colored Troops cried out, "it almost tempts me to desert and run a chance of getting shot, when I read her [his wife's] letters, hoping that I would come to her relief. But what am I to do?"[31] He noted, "it is the case all through the regiment. Men having families at home, and they looking to them for support, and they not being able to send them one penny."[32] Another soldier in the Fifty-fifth Massachusetts lamented that "although we have been in the service, ten months we have not received one cent of pay, and many of our families are suffering for the aid we must render them if we could only get our hardearned and just dues."[33] Still another member of the Fifty-fifth Massachusetts recalled an emotional scene involving a comrade's anguish over his inability to support his wife: "I have seen a letter from a wife in Illinois to her husband, stating that she had been sick for six months, and begging him to send her the sum of fifty cents." The soldier then asked, "Was it any wonder that the tears rolled in floods from that stout-hearted man's eyes?"[34]

The most likely reason that many black soldiers would not take the ten dollars per month was because to do so would be an affront to their manhood. Black men wanted to be recognized and appreciated by the federal government the same as white men were, and the only way was for them to receive the same amount as their white counterparts: thirteen dollars. One soldier underscored this point: "To say even, we were not soldiers and pay us $20 would be injustice, for it would rob a whole race of their title to manhood, and even make them feel, no matter how faithful, how brave they had been, that their mite towards founding liberty on a firm basis was spurned, and made mock of."[35] It was no wonder that when the Fifty-fifth Massachusetts refused to accept the ten dollars, members of the regiment remarked, "We will stay our three years out, and then go home like men to our homes, and go to work."[36] Furthermore, too much was riding on the issue for black men to budge even an inch on the matter. Although the suffering of their families greatly pained them, they were involved in a struggle that called for short-term sacrifices. Had they given in and accepted unequal pay, it would have disgraced their children and brought shame on the race. This point was eloquently made by a soldier from the Fifty-fifth Massachusetts: "I thank God that we did not take it, for if we had our children would blush with shame to think their fathers would acknowledge their inferiority by taking inferior pay to that of other soldiers." Moreover, the soldier noted, if they had, "the whole civilized world would look on us as being a parcel of fools, not fit to enjoy our freedom."[37]

The persistent efforts of black soldiers and their white supporters did not come to naught, for Congress passed an equal pay law in July 1864. However, victory was far from complete, since it gave back pay only to January 1, 1864. Whereas those blacks who were free at the time of enlistment were to be given back pay from the day on which they joined the army, the enslaved blacks only got six months of back pay. And, since nearly 70 percent of black soldiers were from either the seceded Southern states or Border slave states, the equal pay law would eventually lead to the so-called Quaker oaths: many blacks would declare that they were free by God's law if not by man's. Thus, it would take further protests before Congress would finally yield and on March 3, 1865, pass a law that granted full retroactive pay to all black soldiers.[38]

Sergeant John C. Brock of the Forty-third U.S. Colored Infantry captured in a letter the excitement felt by the men in his regiment when the paymaster handed their money to them in August 1864, when the army began to issue to all black units their back pay. Brock wrote that "yesterday was a joyful day in our brigade on account of the presence of the paymaster. The boys fell in the ranks with more alacrity than they ever did on any other occasion. They were paid at the rate of $16 a month."[39] The Fifty-fifth Massachusetts Infantry organized a celebration on October 10, described by James M. Trotter, a soldier in the regiment: "The men were paraded in companies; commanded by their 1st Sergts. A procession was formed which was marched to some distance from camp headed by our excellent brass band, and then back to the stand where [there] was to be speeches by the sergeants, music, vocal and instrumental."[40] Resolutions were drawn up by Sergeant Gabriel P. Iverson, which were then adopted by the men of the Fifty-fifth, who renewed their commitment to the Union and their race, forgave those who had criticized them for protesting their low pay, and thanked their friends at home who had worked for equality.[41]

As expected, when black soldiers received their back pay, many of them first sent money to their wives and families. For example, the Fifty-fourth Massachusetts sent $64,000 and the Fifty-fifth Massachusetts $65,000 home by Adams Express.[42] One soldier in the Fifty-fifth sent his mother $125 of the $167.10 paid to him. Still, he found the need to apologize. "I should of sent more but from all probability we won't be paid off very soon again, so, mother, I did the best I could."[43] Not surprisingly, there were other demands on their money. In one unit, a soldier reported, "the sutler, patent jewelry venders, watch pedlars and many other kinds of pedlars are reaping a rich harvest."[44]

THE CONFEDERATES' "NO QUARTER" POLICY

The Civil War ultimately had a devastating effect on black soldiers, who suffered a far higher mortality rate than white troops. At least 38,000 black soldiers lost their lives in the war, a rate of mortality estimated to be nearly 40 percent greater than that among whites. For example, the largest number of deaths in any outfit in the Union army occurred in the all-black Fifth U.S. Heavy Artillery, where 829 men died. Disease alone killed more than 600 men in the Sixty-fifth Colored Infantry; and, more often than whites, they were given inferior equipment and inadequate medical care.[45] Higher casualties among black troops were also the result of inexperience. Veteran troops learned to conserve their own lives to fight the next day. But this approach ran counter to the main objective of black soldiers, whose primary aim was to prove to whites that they were not inferior to anyone. Accordingly, as historian Joseph Glatthaar notes, "they consciously took on extra risks, and lost many lives because of it, in hopes that their labors on the battlefield would reap benefits to the survivors, their families, and future generations."[46] Moreover, they were targeted by Confederates' "no quarter" policy.[47] Under this policy, black soldiers were regarded as insurrectionists, and Confederates fought them with heightened intensity. The sight of black men armed, many of whom were runaway slaves, was appalling and frightening to most Southern whites.

The Confederacy sometimes refused to treat captured black soldiers as prisoners of war, thus denying them the opportunity to be exchanged. Moreover, their white officers were looked upon by the Confederates as instigators of slave rebellions. Local Confederate commanders decided the fate of captured black soldiers and their officers in the first year and one-half of the war and often chose to execute them on the spot. President Jefferson Davis, however, in December 1862 ordered the black captives delivered to civil authorities in "the respective [Confederate] States to which they belong to be dealt with according to the laws of said States"; their officers were also to be remanded to state authorities. Under these laws, the soldiers faced punishments ranging from reenslavement or sale into slavery to execution, and officers convicted of inciting slave insurrection

were subject to execution or imprisonment. Although many Northerners were infuriated by the Confederate policy toward black prisoners of war, the Lincoln administration was slow to respond.[48]
Lincoln's caution, however, did not prevent other Federal officials
from taking up the challenge. General David Hunter, for example,
who had played a leading role in early efforts to recruit black soldiers in coastal South Carolina and Georgia, issued a prompt and
stern response to Davis's order: "I now give you notice, that unless
this order is immediately revoked, I will at once cause the execution
of every rebel officer, and every rebel slaveholder in my possession."[49]
Despite Hunter's warning, Davis's order remained in effect. And, as
the war progressed, other high-ranking Confederate officials, such
as secretary of war, promoted the killing of some black prisoners to
set an example. Colonel W. P. Shingler told his subordinates in 1864
to kill all the blacks in battle to prevent any from having the opportunity to surrender.[50]

     These were not empty threats. The Confederates did, indeed, of-
ten refuse to capture black soldiers and instead slaughtered those
offering to surrender. Strong evidence points to the charge that some
wounded blacks left on the battlefield at Olustee, Florida, on February 20, 1864, were murdered instead of taken prisoner.[51] Had the
Confederates abided by the international rules of war, this outrage
would not have occurred. However, black soldiers were quick to assert that if Confederates offered them "no quarter," then they would
offer "no quarter" in return. A soldier in the Fifty-fifth Massachusetts Infantry wrote forcefully, "as far as this regiment is concerned
we will ask no quarter, and rest satisfied that we will give none. We
are compelled to take this in our own hands. The Johnny Reb will
find out that Niggers won't die so fast."[52] Another member of the
Fifty-fifth Massachusetts warned: "Should Jeff. Davis enforce his
threat of treating us as servile insurgents, there will be but little quarter shown to rebels who fall into our hands; every man shall die who
has not the power to defend himself, and then we will hear what Jeff
has to say about enslaving or butchering black soldiers." The soldier
concluded, "It must be one thing or the other—liberty or death."[53]

     The Olustee debacle would be only one of many involving charges
of Confederate atrocities against black soldiers and their white officers. Undoubtedly, the most notorious was the Fort Pillow massacre
of 1864 in Tennessee. On April 12 of that year, the fort fell to Confederate forces under the command of General Nathan Bedford Forrest,
a former slave trader who would later play a major role in organizing the white-supremacist Ku Klux Klan.[54] When the firing concluded,

nearly 300 of the estimated garrison of 600 men suffered death or mortal wounds. The black units lost 64 percent, while the white troops lost 31 to 34 percent.[55] An army investigating committee interviewed thirty-five witnesses, many of them eyewitnesses, who claimed that Forrest's men repeatedly shot unarmed blacks who had their hands raised, desperately trying to surrender—even those alleged to have been on their knees begging for mercy when their lives were taken. Witnesses charged that wounded blacks were either burned or buried alive. Moreover, five men, all members of the Thirteenth Tennessee Cavalry, testified that they had heard during the final assault such cries as "Kill the last God damn one of them," and "Kill them, God damn them."[56]

How much blame for the massacre should be placed directly on Forrest himself? Did he on this occasion plan to carry out his threat of "no quarter," a threat that he had made several times before? And did he actually order his men to do it? Current research tends to suggest that Forrest did not order the killings; in fact, he was lightly injured and remained at his post four hundred yards away. It is very likely, however, that even with Forrest's injury, had he planned the massacre, he would have led the charge and been a willing participant in the bloodletting. Even if we accept the conclusions of those who argue that Forrest did not order the killings, we can still suppose that his inaction may have been just as dubious. Once he lost control of his men, they were free to do as they pleased.[57] And, in all likelihood, what they did was not a source of great concern to him, since he knew that his men shared the same intense hatred of fighting armed slaves and Tennessee Unionists as he harbored. In his written report just three days after the capture of the fort, Forrest boasted about the massacre. Referring to the large numbers of Union soldiers killed after they jumped into the Mississippi, Forrest wrote, "the river was dyed with the blood of the slaughtered for 200 yards."[58]

Not surprisingly, blacks were not caught off guard by the Fort Pillow massacre. A black soldier wrote from South Carolina, "I do not wonder at the conduct and disaster that transpired at Fort Pillow, I wonder that we have not had more . . . Fort Pillow massacres."[59] If Confederates thought their "no quarter" policy would demoralize black soldiers, they were badly mistaken. Indeed, the massacre had the reverse effect. For the remainder of the war, blacks would fight with an intensity never before imagined. Shortly after the Fort Pillow engagement, units of black soldiers met at Memphis, got down "on their knees," and pledged to avenge the loss and to show Confederate troops "no quarter." Their battle cry became, "Remember Fort Pillow.["60] Thereafter, black troops fought with no idea of surrendering. This was the case even where Union forces suffered huge losses. For example, at Brice's Cross-Roads in June 1864, where Union disaster struck the Union troops, reports show that black soldiers engaged there kept firing until their ammunition was spent. Afterward, they fought with bayonet and clubbed musket; finally they either picked up weapons and ammunition from the road along which the rest of the Union forces were fleeing or died.[61]

The desperation with which black troops fought put fear in the hearts of Confederate soldiers. Commenting on this fear, one Federal soldier wrote in a letter to his family, "the Jonnies [Johnny Rebs, or Confederates] are not as much afraid of us as they are of the Mokes [black soldiers]." He added, "when they charge they will not take any prisoners, if they can help it."[62] Afraid of reprisals, Confederate troops avoided surrendering to black troops or fled at their approach. Late in the war, a white Union soldier at Fort Blakely, Alabama, reported that Confederate soldiers were "panic-struck." Rather than confront blacks, the soldier noted, "numbers of them jumped into the river and were drowned attempting to cross, or were shot while swimming. Still others threw down their arms and ran for their lives over to the white troops on our left, to give themselves up, to save being butchered by our Niggers[;] the Niggers did not take a prisoner, they killed all they took to a man."[63]

Nevertheless, Confederate troops continued to employ the "no quarter" policy in dealing with black troops. In fact, just six days after the Fort Pillow massacre, Confederates shot, captured, and wounded black soldiers in the Battle of Poison Spring in Arkansas. Reports revealed that the First Kansas Colored had suffered staggering losses, amounting to 117 dead and 65 wounded. Confederates cut off and subsequently cut up a large foraging party of white and black troops.[64] Although not of the magnitude of atrocities waged against blacks at Fort Pillow, the ruthlessness displayed by Confederate troops at Poison Spring was horrifying. "The surprise of the enemy was complete—at least 400 darkies were killed," wrote Lieutenant William M. Stafford, a Texas artilleryman, in his journal. "No black prisoners were captured."[65] An Arkansas cavalryman appeared to exult in the fact that a large portion of the Union dead were blacks: "We almost exterminated the troops that had the train in their charge." When they were ordered to remove the captured wagons to a safer place, the Confederates drove over the dead and dying blacks, competing to see who could crush the most "nigger heads."[66] Several boasted that they had left six hundred Federal dead rotting at Poison

Spring, "primarily Negroes who neither gave or rec[eived] quarter."[67] Choctaws fighting with the Confederates were among some of the most vicious attackers of black and white Union troops. In fits of rage, the Choctaws seemed to thoroughly enjoy themselves as they scalped and stripped the bodies of Union soldiers.[68]

The response of black troops to the Union disaster at Poison Spring was similar to that after Fort Pillow: they vowed to get revenge. The Second Kansas Colored, the sister regiment of the hard-hit First Kansas Colored, resolved to take no prisoners. Only twelve days after the Poison Spring slaughter, the Second Kansas Colored would take full advantage of an opportunity to exact revenge. On April 30, 1864, Colonel Samuel F. Crawford, the commanding officer, led his troops against the Confederates at Jenkins Ferry, on the Sabine River in Arkansas. Crawford ordered his men to charge, and charge they did, overrunning the rebel battery with shouts of "Remember Poison Spring!" The Confederates paid a huge price, losing about 150 killed or mortally wounded. At the same time, Union casualties were light: the Second Kansas Colored lost only fifteen men killed, and fifty-five others were wounded.[69] Confederate casualties were so high because vengeful blacks drew no distinction between able-bodied or wounded foes in the fury of their charge. One white Union soldier observed a small black boy "pounding a wounded reb in the head with the but of his gun and asked him what he was doing. [T]he negro replied he is not dead yet!" The soldier concluded, "I tel you they won't give them up as long as they can kick if they can just have their way about it."[70] Black soldiers were also seen slashing the throats of wounded Confederates.[71]

Black sailors were also victims of the Confederacy's "no quarter" policy. For example, a sailor recalled, "the rebels captured a colored man, and put twelve bullets in his body and left him in the road. This is the way they treat us when they take us prisoners."[72] Just as this policy had failed to demoralize black soldiers and instead caused them to fight more fiercely, it had the same impact on black sailors. When President Davis issued an order authorizing Confederate forces in the vicinity of Richmond to hang sailors belonging to the Potomac Flotilla whenever they captured them, it "made the officers and men more eager to fight and destroy their property than ever."[73]

Responding to news of the Fort Pillow massacre and other executions of black soldiers by Confederates, President Lincoln announced in July 1864 that the United States would give "equal protection to all its soldiers"; for every Union soldier killed, he directed the execution of a rebel soldier; and for every black Union soldier enslaved, a Confederate soldier would be put to hard labor until the end of the war.[74] Yet, despite the "no quarter" orders of some high-ranking Confederate officers, many captured black troops were not executed but were held as prisoners of war in the South. General Butler reported, for example, that 3,000 black troops were prisoners of the Confederates; moreover, nearly 1,000 black prisoners worked on Confederate fortifications at Mobile, Alabama, late in 1864.[75]

If black soldiers survived as prisoners of war, they led a horrendous existence. Both black and white Union captives were often treated in inhumane ways, but the intense racism of Southern whites added an extra dimension of brutality to the care of black prisoners. Confederates placed them in harm's way by forcing them to work under fire in the trenches near Fort Gilmer, on the James River in Virginia. General Butler, with General Grant's permission, ordered an equal number of Confederate prisoners put to work in his own trenches. As a consequence, the black prisoners were withdrawn from the hazardous and illegal activity. Butler rescinded his order and restored his Confederate prisoners to safety.[76]

No form of degradation was beneath the Confederates. For example, one black soldier wrote that "they give them [black prisoners] nothing but corn-meal and rice, and allow them no tobacco." If any civilians brought them something to eat, continued the soldier, "the guards would take it from them, and trample it under foot."[77] Several parents of black prisoners wrote to President Lincoln addressing this matter. One of these letters was a heartfelt plea from Hannah Johnson, whose son was a member of the Fifty-fourth Massachusetts Infantry: "I know that a colored man ought to run no greater risques than a white, his pay is no greater his obligation to fight is the same." In a straightforward manner, she wrote: "Will you see that the colored men fighting now, are fairly treated. You ought to do this, and do it at once, Not let the thing run along meet it quickly and manfully, and stop this mean cowardly cruelty." She concluded, "We poor oppressed ones, appeal to you, and ask fair play. Yours for Christ's sake."[78]

The Confederacy's prison camp at Andersonville, Georgia, was a death trap for both black and white Union prisoners. Several thousand died there from disease and malnutrition. At one point, there were 8.5 deaths per hour. At the conclusion of the war, those lucky enough to have survived were released by Confederate officials. The testimony of some of these soldiers reveals the magnitude of their suffering at Andersonville. One of them told W. B. Johnson of the Third U.S. Colored Infantry "that there are 250 acres of land, filled with our Union dead, that died completely from starvation." Another said he "subsisted on the coarsest of meal, and was glad to grind up the cob with the corn."[79]

CHARGES OF DRUNKENNESS, GAMBLING, DESERTION, AND MUTINY

In addition to harsh treatment if captured, black soldiers had to deal with the biases of Northern whites, who often argued against enlisting black soldiers due to preconceived ideas that they were either drunkards or cowards. Yet few discipline infractions arose among black troops. In fact, drunkenness was not recorded as a problem among black troops. Thomas W. Higginson, for instance, could not recall intoxication in his regiment ever being an issue, in spite of the trauma of war and the men having money to purchase alcohol. In fact, Higginson wrote, "I have never heard of a glass of liquor in the camp nor of any effort either to bring it in or to keep it out."[80] James Shaw, an officer in the Seventh U.S. Colored Troops, agreed: "The regiment seldom, if ever, had a man drunk."[81] Officers in black units in the Department of the Gulf were relieved that black volunteers showed self-control, since army commanders had soon discovered that "no stimulant was more demoralizing than Louisiana rum."[82] Only one black commissioned officer, Lieutenant John O'Brien of the Thirty-sixth U.S. Colored Troops, was released from the military for drunkenness. While O'Brien was found guilty of drunkenness on duty, he was also charged with disobeying orders, conduct unbecoming an officer, and breach of arrest.[83]

Gambling among black troops was almost as rare as drinking. In one of the few reported instances of gambling, all of the players lost. The captain of the Fourteenth Rhode Island Heavy Artillery, J. M. Addeman, surprised the group by sneaking up on them and then scooped up both cards and stakes. One of the players ruefully remarked that "it was no use to play against the captain, for he got high, low, jack and the game."[84]

The rate of desertion from the military was also much lower for black troops than for whites. However, there were a few reported cases. For example, Joseph Haskins and Robert Beasley, members of the Fifth U.S. Colored Troops, deserted to the enemy, and Warren Hamelton, a young soldier from Louisiana in the Seventy-third U.S. Colored Troops, deserted. In the cases of Haskins and Beasley, the reason may have been mistreatment on the part of officers, or the two may have lacked the necessary discipline to remain in service. In the case of Hamelton, a plausible explanation is concern for the well-being of his mother. Only seventeen years old when he enlisted, Hamelton apparently thought that the government would take care of his mother. When it did not, he deserted.[85]

Many charges of mutiny were brought up against black troops, although the incidents in question were usually nonviolent protests for legitimate reasons. Nonetheless, punishments were harsh, ending in lengthy jail sentences or execution. Although fewer than one in every thirteen Union soldiers was black, nearly 80 percent of those prosecuted for mutiny were black. In one regiment, members passively resisted because their company commander had searched and discarded their belongings when they were on duty.[86] In another case, a brief mutiny occurred in December 1863 at Fort Jackson, Louisiana, where black troops were being brutally treated by racist and incompetent white officers.[87] In still other cases, several units of black soldiers stacked arms and refused any further military service until the government paid them the same as white troops. Most of the participants in these events were prosecuted, some severely. For instance, Sergeant William Walker of the Third South Carolina Regiment was court-martialed and shot for leading his men in stacking their arms at the captain's tent and refusing to fight until they received equal pay.[88]

As expected, black soldiers who assaulted their superiors paid the ultimate price, but these cases were rare. Private Wallace Baker of Company I, Fifty-fifth Massachusetts Infantry, was executed for disobeying orders and violently assaulting his superior officer. A member of Private Baker's regiment sadly wrote, "Private Baker met his death with stoical indifference. The firing party was from our regiment, seven bullets struck the doomed man, and he died instantly, without a struggle." The soldier also noted, "This had been the first execution of the kind in ours, and I sincerely hope it will be the last."[89] In another example, Samuel Mapps, a soldier in the Twenty-eighth U.S. Colored Infantry, was convicted of trying to murder his captain and was sentenced to die. The job of preparing Mapps to make peace with his God fell on the shoulders of Garland H. White, the regiment's chaplain. Just minutes before his execution, White had an emotional conversation with Mapps:

> "Do you feel that Jesus will be with you?"
> "Yes," he replied.
> "Do you put all your trust in him?"
> "I do," was the answer.
> "Do you believe that you will be saved?"

"I do, for though they may destroy the body, they cannot hurt the soul."

"Let us pray," I replied. "Eternal God, the Master of all the living and Judge of all the dead, we commit this our dying comrade into thy hands from whence he came. Now, O my Lord and My God, for thy Son's sake, receive his soul into thyself in glory. Forgive him—forgive, O thou blessed Jesus, for thou didst die for all mankind, and bid them to come unto thee, and partake of everlasting life. Save him, Lord—save him, for none can save but thee, and thee alone, Amen. Good-by, My Brother, good-by."

The order was then given: Ready! Aim! Fire! "It was the saddest spectacle I ever witnessed, and I hope never to witness another the longest day I live," White concluded. "He was the first colored man shot in this army, to my knowledge, during the war."[90]

Why were there so few cases of drunkenness, gambling, desertion, and mutiny among blacks? In the cases of drinking and gambling, black churches may have played significant roles. It was common practice for black churches to condemn drinking, gambling, card playing, and other vices among their members, who might then be socially ostracized and expelled. Moreover, since whites had more money than blacks and more access to alcohol, they developed more of a taste for alcoholic beverages than did blacks. And, of course, with the pressures of war, they would tend to drink even more. For instance, because many white soldiers were better off than their black counterparts, their army status sometimes represented a demotion in life. To blacks, on the other hand, the army represented a promotion. The possibility of a Union victory offered hope to those from Southern states who had until recently been slaves. Some blacks may have also been conservative with their money. After all, they had fought a long and difficult battle to achieve the same pay as white soldiers. Why should black soldiers risk losing their money by gambling?

Some of these reasons also explain why so few blacks deserted and engaged in acts of a mutinous nature. Black soldiers were fighting for more than the freedom of slaves; they were also fighting for the country, for citizenship rights, and for the race. Black soldiers had too much to prove to white society to engage in humiliating and embarrassing activities. Whites had earlier argued that black men should not be allowed to become soldiers because they were cowards and lacked discipline. If they deserted, consumed too much alcohol, or mutinied, would this not confirm what many whites had already been saying about them and were still thinking? It is no wonder why black Civil War correspondent Thomas Morris Chester wrote shortly after Joseph Haskins and Robert Beasley deserted, "The 5th was recruited in Ohio, and to the credit of the loyal colored population of that state, it should be understood that these deserters did not come from that state."[91] Certainly, the views on desertion and mutiny put forth by a soldier in the Fifty-fifth Massachusetts Infantry express those of most blacks: "Would it add to the splendid discipline which characterizes this regiment? Would it alleviate the sufferings of our wives and children at home, or increase or hasten our chances of relieving them? Finally, would it elevate us either mentally, morally or socially, or hasten the time when we shall get our rights under this government?"[92] The answer to all these questions was "no."

NORTHERN FREE BLACKS AND MILITARY PARTICIPATION IN THE WAR

It is easy to discern the reasons why enslaved individuals of African descent would don the "Union blue" and fight, but it is more difficult to ascertain why free blacks, particularly those in the North, would take up arms against the Confederacy. After all, although they led a tenuous existence, at least they enjoyed some of the basic privileges of free men and women. They were stationed in the safety and security of the North, several hundred miles out of harm's way. What difference would it make to them if the Confederacy won the war and retained the institution of slavery? The answer was that in the minds of free black Union soldiers, it would indeed make a difference. Although most were not formerly slaves themselves, some had escaped from slavery and had left family members and friends still in bondage. And since they thought that slavery was morally unjust and an indignity that no race deserved to have thrust upon it, many of these black soldiers believed that they had an obligation to fight for emancipation. Furthermore, most also were of the opinion that freedom for the slaves and citizenship rights for free blacks in the North were connected; one could not have the latter without the former. Therefore, freeing the slaves would promote the interests of free blacks.

Many blacks reasoned that if this opportunity to remove the shackles from slaves was missed, there would be a real likelihood that life would get worse for them. Thus, Sergeant Charles W. Singer of the 107th U.S. Colored Infantry would passionately write," I sincerely and candidly think that every man in the North should, to the fullest extent of his abilities, aid and further the cause of freeing the slaves now held in bondage by Southern tyrants." And, reminding his audience that the emancipation of the slaves and citizenship rights for Northern free blacks were linked together, and painting a bleak picture in the event of a rebel victory, Singer asserted, "We should not forget the fact that the free colored man's elevation is at issue, as well as the slave's." He then posed the following question: "Suppose the rebel army was as far North as the Union army is South; what would be the result?"[93] In his estimation, the homes of blacks would be burned down, and elderly and defenseless parents of black soldiers would be barbarously treated.[94] Echoing similar sentiments, Corporal James Henry Gooding of the Fifty-fourth Massachusetts Infantry exclaimed: "Slavery will not die without the aid of our race to kill it—language cannot depict the indignity, the scorn, and perhaps violence, that will be heaped upon us, unthought of law will be enacted, and put in force, to banish us from the land of our birth."[95] Therefore, Northern free blacks had a moral obligation to help avoid this impending catastrophe by taking up arms against the South. In fact, Gooding believed so strongly in this racial obligation that he wrote, "Let the young women drive all those young loungers off to the war, and if they won't go, say 'I'm no more gal of thine.' "[96]

It should not come as a surprise that black soldiers also considered themselves as role models. They were determined to exhibit positive attitudes and character so as not to bring shame upon the race. In most cases, they refused to be openly critical of one another, fearing that to do so would reflect negatively. However, on one occasion, some black soldiers apparently suggested that the Fifty-fourth Massachusetts Infantry fought courageously, while the Fourteenth U.S. Colored Infantry was disorganized and lacking in direction during battle. In a passionate letter, an anonymous soldier implored all blacks in the armed services to "bear in mind that the brave deeds of one colored man or any one colored regiment, reflects credit on the race and goes in the balance. Let us rejoice, therefore, in each others successes."[97] Blacks were being granted a golden opportunity to stand up and be counted as real men. If one black man succeeded, then the whole race made great strides. But if one failed, so too did the entire race.

If black soldiers were fighting for citizenship rights in addition to the defense of their race, then they must have believed fervently in the Union cause and thus thought that a Union victory would ensure these rights. They certainly did, and some to the extent that they regarded themselves as "soldiers of God." For instance, First Sergeant

Isaiah H. Welch could remark with a clear conscience: "I pray God the time will soon come when we, as soldiers of God, and of our race and country, may face the enemy with boldness." And "for my part, I feel willing to suffer all privations incidental to a Christian and a soldier."[98] In fighting for the Union cause, black soldiers were fighting for their country, and that country had to be saved from ruin by ruthless pro-slavery forces. Welch called upon family members whose sons had been killed in battle to acknowledge that they had perished for a just and noble cause.[99]

Although black soldiers were willing to make sacrifices for the Union and believed that they would receive equal rights for their efforts, they were not bleary-eyed dreamers. Some were aware of pitfalls, such as how whites defined citizenship rights, for a large number regarded equal rights as meaning social equality. And, to them, social equality meant that black men would have access to white women, and vice versa. Indeed, many whites throughout the country were obsessed with the notion of black male sexual potency and reasoned that black men desired white women. Since black soldiers were keenly aware of this white obsession, they took pains to point out the beauty and desirability of black women when they spoke of equal rights. For instance, James Henry Hall, a soldier in the Fifty-fourth Massachusetts Infantry declared: "We do not covet your wives nor your daughters, nor the position of political orator. All we ask is the proper enjoyment of the rights of citizenship, and a free title and acknowledged share in our own noble birthplace."[100] The sad reality is that not only would they be denied these rights to some extent in the post-Civil War period, but in the present day blacks are still no more than second-class citizens. They are first-class citizens only in the most superficial way.

HARSH REALITIES FOR RECRUITS IN THE SOUTH

Although large numbers of blacks continued to join the Union army in the South throughout the war, enlistment was often fraught with great danger. That so many were willing to take tremendous risks in order to enroll and fight attests to their inner strength and determination to gain freedom for themselves and their families. Understandably, the masters of slaves often did not want them to enlist since it would make them free men, and owners employed various measures to prevent them from enlisting. First and foremost, slave-owners in Union-occupied Missouri wanted mobile recruiting parties banned because they made prevention measures less successful.

When General William S. Rosecrans, who replaced General John M. Schofield, banned mobile recruiting parties, this change forced interested blacks to walk long distances to enlist, thereby rendering them more vulnerable to slaveowners and vindictive whites. Often armed patrols awaited them; if captured, they faced either a brutal beating or execution. For example, Aaron Mitchell, a slave in northeastern Missouri, and his comrades were captured by a patrol while attempting to reach Hannibal to enlist. Mitchell and three others were arrested, retained for the night, and the next day taken home and severely whipped. One of his group, Alfred, was shot dead. Alfred's owner had offered ten dollars to any member of the patrol who would kill him, and one man stepped forward and shot him in the heart.[101]

So many blacks who were desirous of enlisting were mistreated and murdered that more than one hundred citizens in a northeastern Missouri county felt compelled to send a petition to General Rosecrans detailing the methods of local slaveholders. To stop blacks from enlisting, owners either used violence or the threat of violence, locked up their slaves' clothing, or, if all else failed, offered rewards or bounties. The situation of those blacks in Kentucky who wanted to enlist in the summer of 1864 was no better than it was in Missouri. In Kentucky, the commanding officer, General Stephen G. Burbridge, banned armed mobile recruiting squads, which had been used to ensure those blacks interested in enlisting a measure of safety. Now, however, as in Missouri, they were susceptible to white retaliation. But, even if mobile recruiters were not banned, armed patrols often followed these men into the camps and threatened the recruiters themselves.

A report by a provost marshal vividly describes the horrendous conditions under which recruits and recruiters labored. As they left a recruitment center, a mob of young men followed seventeen black men who had just been furnished with passes to return home, along with notes to their owners asking that they be permitted to enlist, and "seized them and whipped them most unmercifully with cowhides" before they could reach their houses. One black man trying to enlist was seized by a mob and was "tied to a tree and subjected to the most unmerciful beating." Another black man was captured, badly whipped, and confined in jail as a runaway. Some others were not so fortunate and lost their lives attempting to enlist. When white Union officials tried to intervene and prevent the continual occurrence of these atrocities, they, too, were either beaten or threatened. A deputy provost marshal was subjected to a terrible beating with gun butts and chased from his home. A special agent who enlisted slaves "was caught, stripped, tied to a tree and cow-hided" by local whites. Moreover, when the provost marshal arrested a group of young whites for abusing some potential black enlistees, a mob threatened to lynch him, and shortly thereafter, local whites even tried to kill him.[102]

As expected, since family was dear to the hearts of most black enlistees, slaveholders often sought retaliation against members who were left behind to dissuade other blacks from enlisting in the future. They were subjected to arduous workloads, whippings, evictions, and sales. Martha Glover of Missouri, whose husband had enlisted in the Union army, wrote in despair to her husband about her sufferings at the hands of her owner: "I have had nothing but trouble since you left. They abuse me because you went and say they will not take care of our children and do nothing but quarrel with me all the time and beat me scandalously the day before yesterday."[103] Another wife of a black enlistee was evicted along with her children by her master. Hiram Cornell contacted Union officials to inform them of her horrendous circumstances. Traveling with her youngest child who was two years old, she had left her two older children at home. She was trying to find some work, as her master had told her never to return because "he could not and would not support the women."[104] News of this mistreatment had a negative effect on the morale of black troops, who constantly worried about the physical and emotional well-being of their families. They complained bitterly to Union officials. Martin Patterson of Company H, Second Missouri Volunteers, maintained that his wife was compelled "to do out door work—such as chop wood, husk corn and that one of his children has been suffered to freeze, and has since died."[105] And William Brooks of the same company noted that his family were "required to do the same work that he used to do, such as chopping wood, splitting rails & c."[106]

It is not surprising that the efforts of slaveholders and their supporters to stop black men from enlisting, by penalizing the families of those who did, had a terrible impact on the lives of enslaved women and children. With about 50 percent or more of the adult black male population in military service, it was extremely difficult for most black families to survive. Forced eviction further complicated the problem. In addition, the more strenuous work contributed to more health problems, and a reduction in medical care by their owners certainly did not help. As a result, black women and their children were often homeless, hungry, and vulnerable to various diseases and, in some cases, to the lure of prostitution. Many became no more than beggars.

Why did black men leave them in this predicament? Was it because they did not realize what would happen if they left home and enlisted? Much of the correspondence suggests that black men and women were well aware of what could happen, and in the end the decision to enlist was often made by both husband and wife. For the man to become a member of a liberation force that would help eradicate the institution of slavery was of paramount importance. [107] However, these men had left a region dominated by an intense support of slavery along with ardent racist beliefs, and they certainly worried about the well-being of family members who remained behind.

In spite of the huge obstacles placed before them, black men continued to enlist in the Union forces in staggering numbers. No wonder that Henry M. Turner, a Union recruiter and chaplain, could write that his recruiting effort in Smithville, North Carolina, late in the war "goes on finely." He added that "we have enlisted several hale, stalwart-looking fellows, whom we think will fill their places nicely. One man wants his gun now, so he can get to killing right off."[108] And in the closing days of the war, blacks in Charleston, South Carolina, responded overwhelmingly to the recruitment efforts of Martin Delany, a black major in the Union army. When General Lee surrendered to General Grant at Appomattox Court House on April 9, 1865, formally ending the war, many of the new recruits clung to the hope that their camp would continue training them to do battle.[109] Indeed, this undying belief that they had to do their own part in order for liberation to be truly theirs sustained them through many trials and tribulations. But black soldiers could not have endured without the support of their women, who provided their men with emotional and moral support and took care of their families to the best of their ability while they were away fighting. Not only were black women behind their soldier-husbands, but so also were entire black communities. The mere sight of black soldiers inspired pride in most blacks; and, as historian Reginald Hildebrand notes, "Black soldiers brought liberty and they were the first dramatic symbols of the empowerment of a people who had once been slaves."[110]

Notwithstanding the commitment of most blacks to the Union cause and the high regard held for black soldiers throughout their communities, some men did not voluntarily enlist. Many were kidnapped by Union officials and forced into military action by the army of liberation. Others were utilized as laborers. According to Nelson Dorsey, who served in the Federal army for eight months, "They came out to our place one October and picked me up and made a soldier out of me."[111] Noah Rogers was returning to Mississippi with mules from Arkansas when he "was captured by Yankee soldiers, and placed in the Union army where he served until the surrender."[112] And Noah

Perry recalled that "the Yankees come along and took all the able-bodied Colored men to the army."[113] Federal officials became so hungry for manpower that they sometimes kidnapped those blacks who earlier had been sympathetic to the Confederate cause, some having even seen combat. For example, Nathan Best described his own situation: "One day a soldier fighting for the South and the next a soldier, but firing cannon for the North!" He further boasted, "Yassuh, I'se the one what fought on both sides, but I neber fought for de Yankees till dey captured me and put me in a corral and said, 'Nigger, you fought for de South, now you can fight for de North.' "[114] Echoing similar sentiments, Henry Henderson asserted: "I use to be a fighting man and a strong Southern soldier, until the Yank's captured me and made me fight with them."[115] In another example, William Baltimore served as a servant for the Confederacy until 1863, "when he was captured by the Yankees who took him to Little Rock, where he was sworn in as a Union soldier."[116] Free blacks were just as much a target of Union recruiters as were slaves. Edmond Bradley, a free mulatto, was seized by Federal officials in New Orleans. "De Yankees pick me up dere," he explained, "an' say I have to jine de Army, an' if I don' jine, den dey will conscript me anyways. So I jine under Capt. Walker, Company H, 96th Louisiana Colored Regiment."[117]

Unfortunately, as the Union commitment to black troops increased, the black family again suffered the consequences. And, sadly, although most of the recruiting parties consisted of black soldiers, these squads still could have total disregard for the families of the men whom they took off the streets and out of the fields and forced into the army at bayonet point. Regrettably, it was common practice to refuse the men even the time to notify their families. As was the case with black men voluntarily enlisting, their kidnapping sometimes led to either the disruption or destruction of established households. A letter of Jane Wallis of York County, Virginia, whose husband was seized by a recruiting squad, underscores this point. She made it clear to Federal officials that her husband was taken against his will. But, most important, she explained, "he is verry delicate, and in bad health, in the Bargin, and I am not healthy myself, but if they, keep him, they leave me, and 3 children, to get along, the best we can, and one of them is now verry sick."[118]

In addition, John Banks, a black man who was forced to enlist in the Union army, vividly described his ordeal in a statement in early January 1864. As Banks was cutting wood on December 2, 1863, a few miles from his house, he was confronted by an armed group of ten black soldiers who asked him to enlist. Banks informed them that

he could not afford to enlist and leave his family to fend for themselves. The men responded by telling Banks to go to Newport News
to see their commanding officer, Captain Montgomery. Banks did so
and pleaded with the captain to either release him or at least allow
him the courtesy of going home a few minutes to see his family. However, Montgomery replied that he "had orders" to take all colored
men and make them enlist. The following day Banks was escorted to
Craney Island, where he heard horror stories about what happened
to those blacks who refused to enlist. Some had to "tote" cannon balls,
and others were confined to the guardhouse with only hard bread
and water. But, even before his arrival there, a soldier in Newport
News had threatened to shoot Banks and another black, George Mar-
row, if they did not join the army. As a consequence, Banks yielded.
When his enlistment papers were made out, he "did not dare to re-
monstrate but accepted the five dollars bounty and my uniform and
clothing and performed the duty of a soldier."[119] Banks was forced to
leave behind a wife and mother who depended on his support.

Not only did the army need soldiers, but they also needed laborers. When volunteers could not be found, Federal authorities seldom
hesitated to seize black men and assign them to labor far from their
homes. Impressment, therefore, also had a catastrophic impact on
black families since it separated men from their wives, children, and
other kin. Moreover, it subverted the economic foundation on which
a stable family life rested. In some cases, even when the necessary
laborers were found, Federal officials refused to pay them wages.
This was an underhanded and unscrupulous practice. A group of
black laborers in coastal North Carolina working on Federal fortifications was thus victimized and sent to Virginia on a similar assign-
ment. Forty-five of these laborers petitioned the commander of Union
forces in Tidewater Virginia and North Carolina to address a number
of their concerns. First, they implored him to make sure that their
families were provided for. In their view, they had honestly earned
money that the government had withheld from them which could be
used to support their families. Believing adamantly in the Union
cause, the petitioners seemed hurt and humiliated by their treatment
by superintendents of contrabands. They exclaimed: "Had we been
asked to go to Dutch gap a large number would have gone without
causeing the suffering that has been caused." Furthermore, they
added, "we are willing to go where our labour is wanted and we are
ready at any time to do all we can for the government at any place
and feel it our duty to help the government all we can."[120]

Black soldiers may have had problems with the mistreatment of their families by white Southerners, but they fully understood this retaliation for enlisting in Union forces. However, when Federal authorities treated their wives and children with little regard for their well-being, as in the case of evicting several hundred of them from Camp Nelson, Kentucky, and refusing to let wives visit them at camp, black soldiers were angry. How could the very government that they were fighting and dying for be racist and insensitive? Most responded to the despicable actions of the U.S. government by either writing letters to military authorities or giving sworn affidavits outlining the behavior of white military personnel. Unlike in the Confederacy-occupied South where the enlistment of black soldiers entailed separation from their families, in Union-occupied parts of the Confederacy, parents, wives, and children often lived in contraband camps near the soldiers' quarters. As a consequence, they enjoyed a measure of security. Nevertheless, Federal commanders still sometimes refused sanctuary to the soldiers' families and at times would even expel them from army encampments.

Joseph Miller, a Union soldier, has provided a heart-wrenching account of his family, who for a time lived in Camp Nelson, Kentucky, until they were evicted. Since his master stated that if Miller enlisted, he would no longer sustain his wife and children, Miller brought them along when he first went to Camp Nelson to enlist in October 1864. The couple had four children who ranged in age from four to ten. The lieutenant in command at that time granted permission for his family to stay at the camp, where they remained until November 22 when a mounted guard informed his wife that she and her children would have to vacate the premises the next morning. They had no place to go, and the seven-year-old boy was very sick. Although Miller pleaded with the guard on the next day to let them remain, it was to no avail. The guard told Miller's family that if they did not get into his wagon, he would shoot them all. Miller's wife and children were taken away. A few hours later, Miller went in search of them and found his wife and children six miles from camp in an old meetinghouse belonging to blacks. Unfortunately, by this time, his son was dead. Miller wanted to spend the night with his family but doing so would have compromised his military obligations. Thus, he went back to camp that night but returned the next morning to bury his child.[121]

The family of John Burnside, a Union soldier in Company K, 124th U.S. Colored Troops Infantry, was also evicted from Camp Nelson in November 1864. Like Miller, Burnside had brought his family along to protect them from a vindictive master who had already threatened them for giving aid to Union forces. Moreover, like most soldiers, black and white, Burnside wanted his wife nearby for moral support, and his daughter was ill. Just five days after Miller's family was evicted, an armed guard forced Burnside's wife and daughter into a wagon and drove them seven miles from camp to a wooded area of land owned by a Mr. Simpson. With a degree of despair, Burnside wrote, "while they were in the wood [sic] it rained hard and my family were exposed to the storm."[122] Fortunately, the efforts of soldiers such as Joseph Miller and John Burnside, who wrote affidavits detailing the expulsion of several hundred family members from Camp Nelson, were not futile. The Northern press published many of the affidavits, which became a public relations disaster for the Union army. This publicity, in addition to protests through military channels, resulted in the establishment at Camp Nelson of a "refugee home" for black soldiers' families.[123]

It should come as no surprise to learn that efforts were also made to prevent black women from visiting their men at many army camps, and these measures were employed at the same time that wives of enlisted white soldiers were allowed visitation privileges. George Buck Hanon, a black Union soldier in northern Alabama, wrote a moving letter to the commander of the military division complaining about these injustices. Hanon reached deep into his heart: "a colard man think jest as much of his wife as a white man dus of his if he is black they keep us hemd up here in side the guarde line and if your wife comes they hav to stand out side and he in side and talk across they lines that is as near as they can come." But for white soldiers, Hanon notes, "evver offiscer here that has a wife is got her here in camps and one mans wif feel jest as near to him as anurther."[124] Echoing the same sentiments, an anonymous Kentucky Union soldier wrote about visitation: "When our wives comes to the camp and see us they are not allowed to come in camp and we are not allowed to go and See them they are drumed of[f] and the officers Says go you damned bitches." With frustration and anguish the soldier continued, "you know that it is to much they are treated So by these officer they ought to be a friend to us and them to."[125]

White Federal officials may not have respected the wives of black soldiers or valued black family life, but black soldiers from the North and South certainly did. In fact, two of the top priorities of many black soldiers upon getting settled in camp were to inform their loved ones of the events that had transpired in their lives since leaving home and, of course, to find out about the physical and financial status of

family members. In order to do so, illiterate blacks had to have someone write letters for them. Humphrey, for example, a former Kentucky slave stationed at Camp Nelson, found a friend to write home
for him on a weekly basis. In many of the letters, Humphrey depicted
army life as superior to slavery. A high proportion of those writing
letters at Camp Nelson for black soldiers were white ministers. In
fact, one army chaplain wrote 150 letters to soldiers' families in a
single month, and troops crowded around John G. Fee each evening
with requests. It is estimated by Sanitary Commission authorities that
its representatives at Camp Nelson wrote five thousand letters for
black soldiers. As expected, literate blacks were also besieged by requests for letter writing. Elijah P. Marrs was known as "that little
fellow from Shelby County" who could write. When off duty, he could
be found "surrounded by a number of men, each waiting his turn to
have a letter written home."[126]

Sometimes they were frustrated in their efforts to obtain letters
from the homefront. The following letter of John Posey of the Fifty-
fifth Massachusetts Infantry illustrates the disappointment felt by
many black soldiers over the lack of letters from home. With sorrow,
Posey wrote: "You all appear to be dead, and whether you be [so] or
no, I can not tell. If you are not dead you are very careless about
either friends or relations, and for writing you do not give a damn
whether you all write or not." Furthermore, "though I might write
often, which I do every two or three days, and sometimes every [day],
and to get [a letter] once a month—I care not [for] it." Posey concluded, "I think it is the height of contempt."[127] An anonymous soldier in the Fifty-fifth Massachusetts Infantry lashed out at family
members: "I give you to know that a letter from home is quite con-
soling to a soldier that can not get the news of the day. As for Uncle
James I have not received the scratch of a pen, though I honored him
with two [letters], and Aunt Sarah [says she] wrote three, but I never
got one of them."[128]

That blacks often found entering the military to be a traumatic
experience was even more reason why they relied heavily on the
emotional support of their loved ones. Elijah Marrs, for example,
wished he "had never heard of the war" after his first night in the
barracks. Shortly after being inducted, Marrs and his fellow recruits
marched to Taylor Barracks on Third Street in Louisville, Kentucky,
where they were routinely issued uniforms and weapons and assigned bunks. However, night would usher in a horrid accident. Marrs
was fast asleep on the top bunk when the recruit in the middle, sleep-
ing with a cocked revolver, inadvertently discharged his weapon and

killed the man on the lowest bunk. The dead man had collected $300 as a substitute. As he lay bleeding in his bunk, recruits descended upon him, stealing the money. In spite of the trauma of his first night in the service, reveille awakened Marrs to a new day and a new attitude. Thus, when an officer called his name and he stepped forward for his rations, Marrs "felt freedom" in his "bones," and he thought to himself, "Pshaw! This is better than slavery."[129]

NON–MILITARY ACTIVITIES IN THE FIELD

Many of the black recruits spent most of their days in camp engaged in the routine. Marching to and from battle and actual fighting consumed very little of their time. For those recruits with few interests, boredom took over. For the energetic recruit, however, military life could offer opportunities. For instance, religion played a key role in the lives of black soldiers. The Rev. Sandy Bullitt preached to them on their night in the Louisville barracks; at Camp Nelson, preachers kept the dining hall busy almost nightly, and on Sundays from "sunrise to taps."[130] Having to cope with the real possibility of death, most soldiers, black and white alike, used religion as an anchor. They adopted the view that God would repay them for their sacrifices and hardships on Earth with rewards in Heaven. No wonder that a soldier in the First South Carolina Volunteers uttered the following prayer: "I hab lef' my wife in de land o' bondage. My little ones dey say ev'ry night, Whar is my Fader? But when I die, when de bressed mornin' rises, when I shall stan in de glory wid one foot on de water an' one foot on de land, den, O Lord, I shall see my wife an' my little chilen once more."[131] Many black soldiers also came to believe that God would protect them; and, if they died, God had decided to summon them home. Indeed, some of the most moving scenes in Civil War history are those involving the singing, testifying, and praying of black and white soldiers prior to going into battle.

Military camp also offered black soldiers an opportunity to improve their minds. Since education had been denied them as slaves and many black soldiers recognized the practicality of education, they had a thirst for it. Sometimes the wives of white officers served as teachers. For example, Frances Beecher, wife of Colonel James Beecher, commander of the Thirty-fifth U.S. Colored Infantry, taught many of his men to read and write while they were stationed at Beaufort, South Carolina, and Jacksonville, Florida.[132] Moreover, countless numbers of soldiers, both black and white, took it upon themselves to teach reading and writing to individuals and groups of blacks at Federal encampments. In most cases, however, chaplains had the responsibility of educating soldiers and their families in the regular army. Northern benevolent associations or officers' families provided materials such as books and blackboards.[133]

At the conclusion of the war, when the final tabulations were in, it was seen that black soldiers had made remarkable progress in education. It mattered little whether the teachers had been chaplains and their wives, officers' wives, civilians, or black or white soldiers. For example, Frances Beecher reported that when the men of the Thirty-fifth first enlisted, only two or three of them could sign their names, but when they "mustered out each one of them could proudly sign his name to the pay-roll in a good legible hand."[134] In another case, a chaplain was able in a mere two days to teach a totally illiterate soldier to write his own name, and in only five months the same soldier was preparing company reports and reading the Bible and the Infantry tactics manual. His case was not exceptional but fairly typical. More than five hundred former slaves in a brigade could "read and write very well" after only six months of instruction. Only nine men in Company C, Forty-fourth U.S. Colored Infantry were literate when they enlisted, yet all of them could read and write by the time that they were mustered out. And the Forty-third U.S. Colored Infantry, composed of Northern blacks and freed slaves, had only seventy men who could read, and few of them could do that well. After seven months of work, over one-half could read and many "attend to their own correspondence."[135] In all likelihood the reading and writing skills of black soldiers were more advanced than the black populace overall when they left the service.

Camp life also accorded black soldiers recreational opportunities. At Camp Nelson and other Federal encampments, music classes were taught and taken by many blacks. Instruction was given in playing the drums, the fife, and the bugle, and there were glee clubs as well as occasional classes in vocal music. Moreover, soldiers played games, engaged in wrestling matches, held regimental picnics, and used weekend passes to "visit the ladies."[136] Holidays such as Thanksgiving were sometimes considered as festive occasions by the Union army. For example, the Fifty-fourth Massachusetts Infantry was treated to a wholesome Thanksgiving celebration in November 1863. The men had a delightful dinner of cakes, oranges, apples, raisins, bread, and turkey. Several contests such as greasing the pole and wheelbarrow races were organized, with prizes ranging from two to thirteen dollars. The regiment was "alive and full of fun."[137] One year later the Fifth Massachusetts Cavalry took a break from guarding prisoners in Maryland to celebrate Thanksgiving with a dinner of oysters, turnips, onions, bread without butter, and turkey. The winners of foot races, jig dances, wheelbarrow races, greasing the pole, sack races, a pig chase, and a turkey shoot vied for prizes ranging from a few dollars to a box of cigars, a pair of Mexican spurs, a pig, a plug of tobacco, and turkeys.[138] These celebrations allowed the soldiers, at least for a couple of hours, to take the troubles of war off their minds.

EFFORTS TO ASSIST THE UNION CAUSE
SHORT OF FIGHTING

Black women were as loyal as black men in the Union war cause. Union officials often used both sexes as spies and scouts because they knew the Southern countryside better than most white soldiers and could pass themselves off as just another slave. Jim Taylor, a seventeen-year-old slave, eagerly identified the camps of several Confederate regiments, which greatly assisted Union officials in mapping strategy. Likewise, Dick Williams, a slave, gathered valuable information while working on Confederate military projects. He subsequently escaped to report the disposition of 5,000 Confederate soldiers encamped around Leesburg, Virginia.[139] Former slaves Lucy Carter and Elizabeth Bowser, working as house servants, provided valuable military intelligence to the Union. Bowser, a servant in the household of Jefferson Davis, secretly eavesdropped as the Confederate president and his generals discussed strategy.[140] Mary Louveste's employment at the Gosport Navy Yard in Norfolk, Virginia, placed her in a prime position to be privy to Confederate intelligence. Accordingly, she was able to supply valuable information to Gideon Welles, Union secretary of the navy, about Confederate plans and ships. Mary Catherine Windsor was on board a ship to New Orleans when she saw Confederate forces hiding in the bushes on shore and ready to attack the craft. She passed the information along to Union navy officers, who promptly cancelled the landing. Throughout the remainder of the war, Windsor regularly engaged in similar reconnaissance activities.[141]

Harriet Tubman, one of the most famous nineteenth-century black women and black abolitionists, acted as both a spy and scout for the Union army. Under the command of Colonel James Montgomery of the Second South Carolina Volunteers, Tubman headed a corps of local black men, most of them river pilots. Her attire as a plain freed-

HARRIET TUBMAN, A PROMINENT MEMBER OF THE UNDERGROUND RAILROAD, AND UNION NURSE, SPY, AND SCOUT.

Library of Congress

woman allowed her to travel all over the South without arousing suspicion. Tubman and her scouts were highly adept at pinpointing the location of cotton warehouses, ammunition depots, and slaves who were waiting to be liberated. Montgomery, noted as a guerrilla fighter, made numerous expeditions along the coastal areas of South Carolina, Georgia, and Florida based on information from Tubman and her squad. In fact, Tubman led the way on his most celebrated raid up the Combahee River in June 1863.[142] Sojourner Truth, equally famous, was also a spy for the Union army. For blacks to engage in espionage was particularly risky, and this willingness to do so underscores their commitment to defeat the Confederacy and overthrow the institution of slavery regardless of the costs. Indeed, both the Union army and navy depended on intelligence provided them by black spies and scouts. Union officers praised their service and were impressed by their devotion to duty in the face of danger. Furthermore, even General George B. McClellan, a fierce racist, admitted that his most reliable intelligence about the enemy came from blacks. [143]

Several black women assisted the Union cause by serving as nurses and laundresses. For example, Susie King Taylor was both a nurse and laundress for the First South Carolina Regiment. She also taught eager soldiers how to read and write and cooked for the regiment as well.[144] Elizabeth Keckley, a confidante of First Lady Mary Todd Lincoln, also served as a nurse for the Union army. In addition, when Union officials searched frantically for nurses to tend the wounded on the battlefield, Rose Russell, a slave, volunteered to go. At first, however, she was refused; Union officials thought that she was too delicate a person to handle such a demanding job. Nevertheless, Rose persisted and became a registered nurse in the army medical corps. Several years after the Civil War, Rose still carried a slight scar near her throat where a bullet had grazed her when she got in its path. Rose remembered "bullets falling around her feet like hail."[145] Finally, Lydia Penny served as a nurse with the Fifth U.S. Colored Infantry. A former slave in Memphis, Tennessee, she escaped to the Union lines, where she met and married Thomas Penny, and became a cook. Thomas was serving in the army as a servant in the three months' service. When his term expired, he reenlisted and joined the Fifth U.S. Colored Troops at Camp Delaware, Ohio. Owing to her love

BLACKS SERVING AS SCOUTS FOR THE UNION.

Vincent Colyer, *Report of the Services Rendered by the Freed People*, p. 28

for Thomas and her country, Lydia decided to go along with her husband. She developed such an outstanding reputation as a devoted and caring nurse that she was affectionately called "the mother of the army."[146]

Indeed, black men and black women served the cause of freedom in any way they could. One way was by helping escaped Union prisoners. Blacks in Richmond, Virginia, used the Van Lew mansion, the center of Union espionage in the city, to conceal escaped Union prisoners. Some 109 Federal prisoners were hidden there in a secret room after escaping from Libby Prison, only a short distance from the mansion.[147] A black soldier wrote from Wilmington, North Carolina: "Almost, or I may say, all of the colored people have been engaged in the business of hiding Yankee prisoners. Almost every house in the city occupied by colored people has done this favor for our prisoners."[148] In Savannah, Georgia, Georgiana Kelly and a female friend also hid a prisoner in their homes for four or five months. They fed and cared for him, moving him between the two houses to avoid detection. Francis Keaton, also of Savannah, reported that he "stowed away eleven prisoners that came down from Andersonville." Southern whites, however, discovered Keaton's act and locked him in the guardhouse with the intention of selling him as a slave. Fortunately, Keaton got a break when the keeper fled with the Confederates and left the keys. Keaton took them and freed all the prisoners. Last, another black Savannahian, Joseph Sneed, provided lodging for two escaped prisoners in his home, giving them food and clothes. Subsequently, he instructed his eighteen-year-old son to pilot them to a Union gunboat. The teenager "guided them around through the marsh to past the steamer *Water Witch*, then directed them on the course for escape."[149]

Another covert way of supporting the Union cause was through prayer. Throughout most African-American communities, blacks prayed for a Federal victory, hoping that it would effect their ultimate freedom. In most instances, prayers for freedom were secret and never detected. If masters, overseers, and patrols sometimes heard them, those who prayed were usually brutally whipped. In Alabama a man named Ned was tied to four pegs in the ground and whipped for his freedom prayers "twell de blood run from him lack he was a hog." But, undaunted, he refused to stop his freedom prayers. Shortly thereafter, Ned "slipped off an' went . . . to jine de Union Army."[150] Some blacks were not as discreet as others, and were bold enough to pray aloud for a Union victory, as did Toliver, a Virginia slave. As a result, the aged slave was summoned by two young sons of his master to the barnyard. When they ordered Toliver to get down on his knees and pray for the Confederates, he instead prayed as loud as he could for a Yankee victory. Furious, the two sons lashed him the whole day, taking turns. Toliver finally collapsed, but he prayed to the very end. Only seconds before his death, he mumbled "Yankee."[151]

While some blacks showed support for the Union cause through prayer, others, particularly black women, formed "bread companies" that carried bread to the Union army in violation of policy. In Savannah, Georgia, black women were especially kind to the Union soldiers who had been captured and brought to the city. Sarah Ann Black, for instance, baked bread and potatoes for the Union prisoners and gave them tobacco. Moreover, Georgiana Kelly supervised an operation that collected as many as three hundred loaves of bread baked in black homes throughout the city for the Union prisoners. Small black boys generally threw the loaves of bread to the prisoners. Not surprisingly, such activity was not risk free. One free black female was incarcerated.[152]

Black women in the North contributed to the war effort by forming groups to raise money for the families of black soldiers. They also collected money to purchase flags and banners for the regiments and to buy food for soldiers who were sick and recuperating. Once Federal forces began to occupy areas of the South, slaves ran away in considerable numbers to the camps of Union troops or headed North.

Most were poor, and their presence placed a heavy strain on government resources. Organizations were formed to assist these destitute blacks, and funds were sent to aid former slaves still in the South. For example, the Colored Ladies Sanitary Commission of Boston sent five hundred dollars for the suffering freedmen of Savannah. Furthermore, forty black women from the District of Columbia established the Contraband Relief Society to help runaway slaves who found their way to the capital.[153]

SEXUAL RELATIONS BETWEEN
AFRICAN AMERICANS AND WHITES

Regardless of racial, cultural, ethnic, religious, and class differences, people sometimes cross these boundaries to engage in sexual relations. This was certainly the case during the Civil War. For example, Northern white women feared that their husbands in the Union army would be seduced by black women, despite the fact that white men repeatedly claimed that black women were unattractive. Their wives knew better, however, for they were aware of their men's attraction to black women, particularly to mulattoes. Catherine Hopley, a Northern white, wrote, "There is a sort of gipsy beauty in the nearly white Negro. The large dark eyes retain their brilliancy, while their form is improved; a rich glow in the cheeks, a well-formed nose and full rosy lips, with glossy black ringlets . . . full of feeling, with a smile lingering about the mouth ready to burst forth at a word of encouragement."[154] Colonel Robert Gould Shaw, the commander of the Fifty-fourth Massachusetts Infantry, attended a tea party given by Northern teachers near Charleston, South Carolina, in July 1863. He singled out a light-complexioned black woman as the most attractive of the hostesses: "The interesting member of the Family is Miss Lottie Forten, from Philadelphia, a niece of Mr. Purvis, and a quadroon [of one-quarter black ancestry]. She is quite pretty, remarkably well educated, and a very interesting woman. She is decidedly the belle here, and the officers, both of the army and navy, seem to think her society far preferable to that of the other ladies."[155] Some black women were sexually drawn to white Union soldiers and made their interest known. Candace, a twenty-one-year-old Virginia slave, married Jim Lee of the Fourth Massachusetts Infantry. Another black woman bluntly told a youthful Union officer upon meeting him, "You is a right nice-lookin' man, I declare." The soldier reacted as if she had been a member of one of the finest families: he blushed.[156]

Confederate soldiers sought the company of black women. Many of these men were already accustomed to sexual gratification from black women, and now that they were away from their wives and from the social constraints of their communities, such relationships could flourish. Elijah Parker and John L. Sutherlin were arrested in 1862 after being caught in the house of Jordina Mayo, a free black woman. George Norton was arrested for walking down a Richmond street "arm in arm with a negro wench named Hannah." One free black woman, Millie Rawls, was involved in a common-law marriage with a white Confederate soldier, George W. Jameson, which began in 1861. The couple had five children whom Jameson faithfully supported. He transferred all of his property to Rawl's name. Such interracial couples were viewed with disdain by Southern whites as threats to the status quo.[157]

Sexual liaisons in the South between black men and white women did not cease in wartime. For example, in western North Carolina in 1862, a white man named Jesse Black assaulted his white wife, Tamsey, after discovering her affair with a black man. Jesse was initially found guilty of assault, but a higher court later overturned the decision. In its opinion, since the husband was "responsible for the acts of his wife," Jesse was permitted to use force to make Tamsey "behave herself." Martha Smith, a white woman in Alabama in 1865, was charged with "adultery or fornication" with one of her former slaves, Joe. Smith had to face the charge in court, where witnesses testified that the two had been caught in bed together in Martha's room in the house where she boarded.[158] In all likelihood the liaison between Martha and her former slave had existed for several years. These relationships were fairly typical of the nineteenth-century South and have been well documented by scholars.

Some of these liaisons between black men and white women blossomed into long-term romances. For black men, it was extremely risky to cohabit with white women in the Civil War South. Under most state laws they could either be lynched or executed. Nevertheless, in Virginia, for instance, Richard, a Richmond slave, took up residence with Delia Mack, a white woman. Until Delia's sister Caroline reported them to the police, the couple lived happily together. Richard was subsequently convicted and sentenced to 117 lashes administered over a three day period. Another white woman and her black husband, Jackson, rented a house from the University of Virginia until the faculty chairman suddenly demanded their eviction in 1863. And John P. Anderson, another free black man, married a white woman, and they resided together for the duration of the war and during Reconstruction.[159]

Scholars have failed to adequately address the issue of rape. Most of the alleged victims were white women. Although white men were brought to trial and executed for rape, black men suffered this fate much more than did their white counterparts. Thus, white men got away with rape more often than black men. Members of the Thirty-sixth U.S. Colored Infantry were accused of raping twenty-five or thirty white females in June 1864, after a raid near Richmond and Petersburg.[160] In all likelihood, the soldiers were executed for their alleged crimes. Dandridge Brooks and John Shepperd of the Thirty-eighth U.S. Colored Infantry were also accused of raping two white women. The evidence against them was strong, and their only defense was that they were "not in the house" that night. Both men were hanged.[161]

Local authorities dealt harshly with male slaves accused of raping or attempting to rape white women. For instance, in July 1863, a Virginia slave was hanged amid allegations of rape.[162] Sometimes black men accused of rape were mutilated. In 1864 in Georgia's cotton belt a slave was sentenced to be castrated and two doctors carried out the punishment. Even when local authorities tried to intervene on behalf of accused slaves, their efforts were usually futile. When a slave named Elias was convicted of attempting to rape Martha Burton, a white woman, his master sought a pardon, proposing that he would "put him in the army" if the man were allowed to live. Elias was executed. And after a slave was arrested for attempting to rape a white woman, he was lynched despite pleas from white citizens.[163]

Although fewer men were convicted and executed for raping black women than white women, black women were the victims of the majority of the war's rapes. As such, they were raped by both white and black Union soldiers, Confederates, and the general populace. Often black women were raped in the presence of their family members and friends to indicate a lack of respect for blacks in general and for black women in particular. Both Northern and Southern whites regarded black women as sexually promiscuous and thus prime targets of their sexual advances. In their view, one could not rape a black woman since she was always willing to engage in sexual relations. As expected, white Union soldiers took black women at will. In April 1862 a Yankee raped one of B. E. Harrison's slaves in Prince William County, Virginia. Of the event, Harrison wrote, "As she saw him approaching her she ran, . . . but he caught her and forced [her] to a Brutal act, in full view of my dwelling and wife and two of her nieces."[164] During July 1862 four white Union cavalrymen raped two black women in Newport News. Two of the soldiers took turns unmercifully violating a black female in the yard of a friend whom she was visiting while the other two stood guard with pistols and swords. Shortly thereafter, the soldiers entered the house, and the two who had earlier stood guard now raped another black woman found inside "after a terrible struggle" in front of her father and grandfather.[165] Not surprisingly, Confederates, too, sexually assaulted and raped black women. For example, a Confederate marine, Archibald Wilkinson, was arrested and transferred to the custody of the provost marshal for raping Margaret Willis, a free black Richmond woman, in November 1862.[166] All blacks did not just stand back and allow their women to be sexually abused by white men. They formed vigilante groups and sometimes took revenge on white rapists. In Yorktown, Virginia, in 1863, for example, black vigilantes shot a white sailor to death for the attempted rape of a young black girl.[167]

THE IMPACT OF THE WAR ON SLAVE CHILDREN

From the outset of the Civil War, slaves expended a great deal of effort to learn as much about the war as possible. Children, in particular, became adept at gleaning information from conversations they overheard among both black and white adults. For example, one former slave, who was a small child when the war erupted, recalled: "We colored chaps knew when the war commenced, though we didn't clearly understand what it was all about, but occasionally we got a hint from the older slaves, who had better opportunities for getting news, that somehow, we were the cause of the misunderstanding— the 'unpleasantness' as somebody called it." As a consequence, slaves "understood in a vague way, that our friends at the North were doing battle for us, or, at least, were on our side—and all our sympathies were with them."[168] Likewise, Lizzie Davis, a former slave from South Carolina, became aware of the Confederate attack on Fort Sumter because "my parents en de olden people speak bout dat right dere fore we chillun."[169] A former slave in Tennessee recalled how during the war she and the other children "would go round to the windows and listen to what the white folks would say when they was reading their papers and talking after supper."[170] Most slaves, including children, learned about the war and its progress through the "grapevine telegraph." Young Booker T. Washington would sit up late at night with his mother and the other slaves and listen attentively to the whispered discussions about the progress of the fighting. He maintained that "every success of the Federal armies and every defeat of the Confederate forces was watched with the keenest and most intense interest."[171]

Despite the often successful efforts of slave children to solicit news, Southern whites still tried to prevent them from learning about the war. But as the conflict progressed, it became virtually impossible to keep it from the children. How could this information be concealed when they could observe Southern whites enlisting, drilling, and marching off to war? Rachel Harris, a young slave in Mississippi, recollected, "I went with the white chillun and watched the soldiers marchin'. The drums was playin' and the next thing I heerd, the war was gwine on. You could hear the guns just as plain. The soldiers went by just in droves from soon of a mornin' till sundown."[172] The situation was so serious that even some of the very

NEGROES PLAYED AN IMPORTANT ROLE IN OBTAINING SUPPLIES FOR GENERAL GRANT.

Courtesy of the North Carolina Division of Archives and History

youngest were aware of what was going on. Ann Nettles, for example, a four-year-old in Georgia at the outset, explained, "Dey was sad times, honey; all de people was goin' to war wid de drums beatin' all aroun' and de fifes blowin'."[173] The reality of death also brought the war home for many slave children. For instance, Mary Williams, a ten-year-old at the time who lived on a plantation in Georgia, vividly recalled the death of one of her young masters. Her mistress received a letter one day informing her how her son had been "in a pit with the soldiers and they begged him not to stick his head up but he did anyway and they shot it off." In Mary's words, "Old mistress just cry so."[174]

As expected, when many white men went off to fight for the Confederacy and slave men abandoned the plantations in large numbers to enlist in the Union army, slave children's workload had to be expanded. James Henry Nelson, a ten-year-old when the war concluded, declared, "You know chillun them days, they made em do a man's work."[175] James Gill longed to return to the antebellum summers when as a slave child in Arkansas, he spent most of his time fishing and swimming. Now, he had to work around the clock.[176] Moreover, Eliza Scantling, fifteen years old in 1865, recalled how she "plowed a mule an' a wild un at dat. Sometimes me hands get so cold I jes cry."[177]

AIDING THE CONFEDERATE CAUSE

Slaves and free blacks also assisted the Confederacy. The Confederate and state governments obtained slave laborers by impressment, a means of legal seizure at a fixed price, and by contract with their masters for their use for a limited time. Because of the acute labor shortage in the South, by the fall of 1862 most states had authorized the impressment of slaves. In the following year a desperate Confederate government passed a law, which it put into practice in 1864, calling for the impressment of 2,000 slaves. President Davis encouraged the impressment of slaves throughout the war, but the results were not gratifying. Owners did not like the principle of impressment, even though they were compensated, and most slaves disliked it because the work they were doing for military authorities was more strenuous than the work they were accustomed to doing for their masters. Nonetheless, Confederate and state governments were able to secure the services of thousands of slaves who carried out important tasks. In the Confederate army, slaves served as cooks, teamsters, mechanics, hospital attendants, ambulance drivers, and common laborers. Much of the labor in the construction of fortifications was done by slaves, and gangs of slaves and free blacks repaired the railroads and bridges wrecked by invading Union armies. They worked in factories that manufactured gunpowder and arms. Blacks constituted 310 of the 400 workers at the naval arsenal in Selma, Alabama, in 1865.[178]

In addition, many affluent Confederates brought their black body servants to war with them. These men cut hair, ran errands, secured rations, cleaned the quarters, washed clothes and groomed uniforms, and polished swords, buckles, and spurs. They also took care of the wounded, served as mule and horse tenders, mail carriers, water carriers, and even entertainers; they dug trenches and erected breastworks. For example, William Johnson, the servant of Major Cooke, could affix his signature to the articles of surrender. Of his war experiences in an interview in January 1938, only days before his death, Johnson recalled, "They kept me busy there. Whenever there was fighting, all of us Negroes had the camp to look after and when the shooting was over we had to help bring in the wounded." He continued, "In between battles we had to keep all our masters boots polished, the horses and harness cleaned, and the rifles and swords spic and span. Sometimes, too we were all put to digging trenches or throwing up breastworks."[179] Susanna Metts was one of a few slave women who accompanied their masters to war as cooks, laundresses, or nurses. In Susanna's case, she served Captain M. A. Metts, and his regiment, as a practical nurse.[180] A slave, Howard Divinity, was so outstanding as a forager that he became known throughout the rebel army as the "chicken provider of the Confederacy."[181] At the tender age of eleven, Juda Dantzler acted as a mail carrier for the rebels,[182] and Wash Ingram served as water carrier for the Confederate soldiers in the battle of Mansfield, Louisiana.[183]

Unlike those slaves who were impressed and therefore forced to assist the Confederacy against their will, a large number of the body servants regarded it as a badge of honor to be selected by their masters. For instance, of his master's decision to have him accompany him, Elodga Bradford remembered, "I never will fo'git de day he lef' fo' de war. I was de proudest nigger on de plantation. Doctor Charles was takin' me to de war wid him."[184] Army Jack, a former slave, loved to recount his war experiences and to dwell on the period he served his master during the war. Indeed, he seemed to think that it gave him a certain prestige.[185] George Washington Chiles served so faithfully for four years that once, when his master was slightly wounded, he "exposed himself to the fire of the enemy and carried him from the battlefield to a place of safety."[186] John Gregory was so devoted that when his master was killed in action, he accompanied the body home.[187] Although many slaves served diligently as body servants, such a post was sometimes fraught with danger. After a train collision in 1861, for example, a black cook was killed and another had to have his leg amputated below the knee. And a Virginia cook employed by the Forty-fourth North Carolina Infantry was accidentally killed during a manual-of-arms drill in 1863.

Body servants sometimes fought for the South, if given an opportunity, and occasionally replaced white troops. On the few occasions when they encountered black Unionists on the battlefield, black Confederates generally treated them with contempt. In some cases, they seized the servants of Union officers as their personal prisoners. During the battle of Brandy Station in Virginia on June 11, 1863, a Union officer's black servant was captured at gunpoint by body servants with the Twelfth Virginia Cavalry, Tom and Overton, who shared him as their slave. Nonetheless, his fate proved to be better than that of another male Union servant who was captured by Confederate servants. He escaped but was swiftly recaptured. As an expression of their loyalty to the Confederacy, the black servants promptly executed him.[188]

According to a white Confederate soldier, when his regiment went into battle, so too, did their servants. They seemed to delight in picking off Federals, particularly black ones. On one charge it was reported that a half-dozen blacks had actually preceded the white troops and had each brought back a black Federal prisoner. They kicked and abused the Federals, saying:

> "You black rascal you! — does you mean to fight agin white folks, you ugly niggers, you? Suppose you tinks yourselves no 'small taters' wid dat blue jacket on and dem striped pants. You'll oblige dis Missippi darkey by pulling dem off right smart, if yer doesn't want dat head o' yourn broke" said one of our cooks to his captive; "comin' down Souf to whip de whites! You couldn't stay 't home and let us fight de Yanks, but you must come along too, eh! You took putty good care o' yourself, you did, behind dat ole oak! I was alookin' at yer; and if you hadn't dodged so much, you was a gone chicken long ago, you ugley ole Abe Lincolnite, you!"[189]

Indeed, an abundance of evidence points to the fact that on numerous occasions, body servants of the Confederacy actually fought. For instance, one Confederate officer wrote that William, his servant, "fought by my side in more than one affair."[190]

While body servants found their way into combat as circumstances dictated, other black Southerners enlisted, some officially and some surreptitiously, in regular units. Bart Turner, Nat Turner, Dick Berry, and Milt Wiseman all joined the First Arkansas Volunteers, a regiment organized at Helena, of which Patrick R. Cleburne was colonel. They fought at Shiloh, Murfreesboro, Ringgold Gap, Atlanta, and Franklin. In fact, Turner, Berry, and Wiseman were killed in the battle at Franklin.[191] Holt Collier enlisted in a Tennessee regiment and fought his first battle at a bridge over Green River; he eventually served with the Texas Cowboys, Ross's Brigade, and concluded his service under Colonel Dudley Jones.[192] Two black regiments—one slave, and the other composed of free blacks—took part in the Battle of Bull Run.[193] Another, Rube Witt, enlisted in the Confederate army in Alexandria, Louisiana, but by the time his regiment was prepared to fight, the war was over.[194]

Whereas some slaves volunteered their services to the Confederacy, an even larger number of free blacks volunteered to help. A company of free blacks, for example, in Nashville, Tennessee, offered their services to the Confederate government. Free blacks in Savannah, Georgia, voiced their undying loyalty to the Confederacy in the following letter:

> The undersigned free men of color, residing in the City of Savannah and County of Chatham, fully impressed with the feeling of duty we owe to the State of Georgia as inhabitants thereof, which has for so long a period extended to ourselves and families its protection, and has been to us the source of many benefits—beg leave, respectfully, in this the hour of danger, to tender to yourself our services, to be employed in the defense of the state, at any place or point, at any time, or any length of time, and in any service for which you may consider us best fitted, and in which we can contribute to the public good.[195]

In Richmond in 1861 a company of sixty-three free blacks offered themselves for service,[196] as did free blacks who were members of the New Orleans Native Guards. The Native Guards were composed of proud Creole blacks whose predecessors had served in a free black regiment during the War of 1812, winning the praise of Andrew Jackson for their role in the Battle of New Orleans.[197] Moreover, eighty-two free blacks in Charleston petitioned the state through the mayor "To be assigned any service where we can be useful."[198]

Some blacks, free and enslaved, also served in the Confederate navy. Edward Weeks was a sailor on board the CSS *Shenandoah*, and at least three free blacks served as sailors aboard the CSS *Chicora*, which was used in the defense of Charleston. The CSS *Alabama* had one black crewman, and the Savannah squadron had several blacks. Moses Dallas was the most famous among those in the Savannah squadron. Initially, Dallas enlisted in the Federal army but later deserted and joined the Savannah squadron, where he became "the best inland pilot on the coast." He led a party of 132 Confederates on a successful attack against a Federal gunboat. Shortly thereafter, he guided the raiders up to the USS *Water Witch*. Military records reported that Dallas was killed in the ensuing battle, but he reappeared three months later as a Union soldier, having joined the 128th U.S. Colored Infantry.[199]

A small number of pro-Confederate free blacks and slaves spied for the South under the supervision of Confederate spies such as Belle Boyd or officers such as Colonel John Singleton Mosby. Black Confederate spies often were very proficient in tracking Union troop movements throughout the South. Had Southern whites not displayed so much racial prejudice, in all likelihood they could have garnered even more intelligence information. Like many Union officials, racial prejudice caused many white Confederates to judge blacks as untrustworthy or lacking in the patriotism, brains, skills, and nerve required for the dangerous task of wartime intelligence. Moreover, the efforts of Confederate officials to solicit support from blacks as spies or scouts were hampered by the fact that a significantly larger number of blacks preferred to assist Unionists.[200] As was the case for black Union spies and scouts, the work they engaged in was fraught with danger. If detected, they were executed.

Some free blacks and slaves who did not fight, act as personal servants, or provide intelligence information assisted the Confederate war effort in other ways. For example, Anthony Odingsells, the largest black slaveholder in Savannah, Georgia, sold fish, oysters, meat, and other commodities to Southern troops even after Confederate currency became greatly devalued. With General William Tecumseh Sherman's army swiftly advancing upon the area around Savannah, Odingsells sent his slaves to Fort McAllister to help build fortifications for the impending battle.[201] Likewise, Francis Sasportas, a free black butcher in Charleston, sold meat at reduced prices to the Confederate government to feed the soldiers. One issue of the *Charleston Mercury* reported that "Free Colored men . . . contributed $450 to sustain the cause of the South." The elite Brown Fellowship Society of Charleston voted to donate fifty dollars to defray medical expenses for sick and injured Confederate soldiers, and a group of free black women in the same city collected $450 and presented it to the YMCA for the Confederacy.[202] A black-sponsored ball at Fort Smith, Arkansas, raised money for Confederate soldiers. A Petersburg, Virginia, free black, Richard Kinnard, gave $100, and Jordan Chase, a Vicksburg, Mississippi, free black, donated a horse to the Confederate cavalry and pledged an additional $500. A New Orleans free black real estate broker gave $500 to the war effort.[203] Even though money was in short supply for most slaves, some among this group contributed to the Confederate cause. William, a Virginia slave, patriotically invested $150 in Confederate state bonds, and another Virginia slave donated twenty dollars in cash.[204] Certainly, a lack of money did not prevent those free blacks and slaves who wanted to contribute from doing so. The free black women of Savannah made uniforms for Southern soldiers, and an Alabama slave gave a state regiment a bushel of sweet potatoes.[205] John Jasper, a slave preacher residing in Virginia, ministered to wounded troops in Confederate hospitals.[206]

It is not surprising that some black women who assisted the Confederacy were forced to do so, as was the case for many black men. Calvin Moye recalled that his master "had de women folks on de plantation to makes up lots of clothes for de soldiers. I has seed several wagon loads of clothes hauled off from dar at one time."[207] Kate Crawford, a white owner, remembered that even the youngest of her slaves made sandbags. Another slaveholder recalled the efforts of slave women for a wartime sewing circle that produced only fourteen pairs of drawers in one week.[208] Other black women were forced to work in the hospitals nursing and attending sick soldiers. Whether they were making uniforms, looking after the wounded, or working in any other support role, most black females generally displayed the same lack of enthusiasm for their tasks as did most black males.[209]

Free blacks offered their services to the Confederacy for many reasons. Some, fearing enslavement or reenslavement, may have volunteered in the hope that by showing their loyalty to Southern whites, they would allay whites' fear. Most Southern whites viewed free blacks with suspicion, believing that they had a negative influence on slaves and could not be trusted. Apparently, some free blacks also hoped that their loyalty would lead to an improvement in their everyday condition and to a relaxation of some of the political and legal restraints against them. Indeed, they envisioned increased privileges and rights in the post-Civil War South as the end result of white gratitude. Moreover, free blacks, particularly mulattoes in and around Charleston, New Orleans, Savannah, and Richmond, supported the Confederacy for economic reasons. Many were substantial slaveowners themselves, often having inherited a portion of their wealth from white relatives. If the Confederacy lost, they, too, would lose. Further, many of the free mulattoes aligned themselves with whites against slaves. In their eyes, the degradation of slavery elevated their own status just as the degradation of blacks elevated the status of whites.[210] Most free blacks, however, aligned with slaves culturally, and therefore supported the Union war effort.

Answering the question of why some slaves would support the South is more difficult. Undoubtedly, as did free blacks, a number of slaves developed genuine friendships with Southern whites and sympathized with the Confederate cause. After all, they had grown up around their masters and mistresses who materially provided for them. Some also may have hoped that their loyalty would lead to freedom and some degree of acceptability from whites. A few were certainly committed to the struggle, as a letter from a South Carolina servant to his sister illustrates:

> I've bin havin' a good time ginerally . . . see a heap of fine country and a plenty of purty gals . . . I have also bin on the battlefields and hear the bullets whiz. When the Yankees run I . . . got more clothes, blankets, overcoats, and razors than I could tote. I've got an injin rubber cloke with two brass eyes keeps the rain off like a meetin' house. I'm a made man since the battle and cockt and primed to try it again. If I Kin Kill a Yankee and git a gold watch, and a pair of boots, my trip will be made. How other niggers do to stay at home, while we soldiers are havin' such a good time is more than I can tell.[211]

Perhaps another reason why some slaves sided with the Confederacy was the way they were treated by Yankee troops. Although many Union soldiers treated slaves humanely, often informing them of their freedom and sometimes making their masters and mistresses cook lavish meals for them, others mistreated them. For example, General Sherman's troops in Georgia pillaged slave cabins as well as the planters' big houses on their march to the sea. A former slave described Sherman's men as "hungry wolves who didn't say howdy."[212] Union soldiers also destroyed food and livestock that blacks needed for survival. Finally, most Federal soldiers were straightout racists rather than abolitionists.[213] Especially during the first year and one-half of the war, Union soldiers returned so many runaways to their owners that a number of slaves came to regard Yankees as their enemies. In their minds, Union men were "little better than secessionists."[214]

THE CONFEDERATE DEBATE ON ARMING AFRICAN AMERICANS

The Confederate and state governments consistently refused the offers of free blacks and slaves to join the war effort as soldiers. Above all, they feared that arming blacks would lead to insurrections. Even worse, some whites believed that accepting blacks for military service would imply that racial equality existed between blacks and whites. Win or lose, if black men fought for the Confederacy, they would expect increased social and economic opportunities or envision being admitted to first-class citizenship in Southern society. Such a move would have devastating consequences for a system built on the notion of black inferiority. Nonetheless, despite stern opposition from Southern leaders, agitation in favor of enlisting blacks continued throughout the war. In fact, in its early months, a few voices urging the arming of slaves against the Northern enemy were heard. For instance, a Georgia planter, John J. Cheatham, wrote the Confederate secretary of war in favor of arming a few slaves against the Union. Cheatham reasoned that since some of the slaves clearly thought that President Lincoln would free them, the best way to counteract this idea would be to arm them and make them assist in defeating the Federal forces. By placing only ten or twenty blacks in each company, "there number would be too small to do our army any injury, whilst they might be made quite efficient in battle," he wrote.[215] Cheatham's proposal was regarded by most Confederates as ludicrous. Early Southern victories had convinced many of them that the South's strategy—arming a larger proportion of their white male population than the North as well as utilizing slave labor to keep the Southern economy afloat—was and would continue to be successful. Thus, at this point, it was not necessary to arm the slaves.

Confederate military setbacks in the summer of 1863, however, would change this optimistic outlook. The surrender of Vicksburg, Mississippi, and the costly defeat at Gettysburg, Pennsylvania, especially caused slaveholders to fear for the worst. Now, the calls for arming the slaves grew louder and more numerous. Letters began to pour into Jefferson Davis's office pleading with him to arm the slaves. One planter from eastern Mississippi wrote in despair: "Visburg is gone and as a consequence Mississippi is gone and in the opinion of almost every one here the Confederacy is gone. I can myself see but one chance, but one course to pursue to save it, and I fear it is now too late for even that to check the tide that is overwhelming us." He implored Davis "to call out every able bodied Negro man from the age of sixteen to fifty years old." If the Confederate president did not act promptly, "the negro men will all go to the enemy."[216] But Davis would not budge on the issue, since opposition was still too great. Nevertheless, it would be only a matter of time before this opposition would decrease because the year 1864 brought another string of Confederate losses. In addition, the Southern army witnessed thousands of desertions as many rebels began to doubt that they would ever defeat the Yankees. Heartfelt letters to these men from home underscored the desperate plight of their families. Their wives and children were starving and had to beg for food in order to survive.[217] Meanwhile, the Northern economy was producing war materiél at an unprecedented rate. Thousands of black men were fighting for the Union army, and thousands more were preparing to join their brothers on the battlefield. The Confederates were in trouble and knew it.

The year 1865 brought more gloomy news for the Confederacy. Union forces raced through the South racking up one victory after another. Charleston fell, Columbia was captured, and Richmond was taken, to name only a few. These defeats and others would begin to tip the balance by February in favor of those advocating the arming of slaves. Yet with the Yankees thundering at the gates, the arguments of those opposed became almost fanciful. We can win without black help, they said, if only the absentees and stragglers return to the ranks and the people rededicate themselves to the cause. "The day that the army of Virginia allows a negro regiment to enter their lines as soldiers they will be degraded, ruined, and disgraced," roared Robert Toombs, a prominent Georgian. Howell Cobb, a fellow Georgian, concurred: "If slaves will make good soldiers our whole theory of slavery is wrong."[218]

The secessionist *Charleston Mercury*, moreover, asserted that "it would be the most extraordinary instance of self-stultification the world ever saw" to arm and emancipate slaves.[219] Thus, although the group opposing the arming of slaves and their emancipation was now in the minority, it still represented a significant and vocal segment of Southern white opinion. In mid-February, however, Lincoln shocked many Confederates when he announced at Hampton Roads that he would accept nothing short of unconditional surrender. Clearly, in the event of a now-likely Union victory, the institution of slavery would be abolished. Desperation began to set in as petitions as well as thousands of letters from Confederate soldiers in the trenches of Petersburg were sent to President Davis endorsing the idea of fighting alongside blacks.[220]

Undoubtedly, General Lee's position on the issue also helped to swing the pendulum toward those who favored arming the slaves. In February, he broke his public silence with a letter to the sponsor of a Negro soldier bill: "I think we could, at least do as well with them as the enemy. . . . Those who are employed should be freed. It would be neither just nor wise to require them to serve as slaves." The general's prestige carried the day—but just barely. After much debate, on March 13, 1865, less than a month before Lee's surrender at Appomattox, the Confederate Congress passed a bill authorizing the enlistment of twenty thousand blacks and promising their emancipation if they remained loyal throughout the war.[221]

It is interesting to speculate about what course the war would have taken if time had not run out on the Confederacy after it reached a decision to use black troops. What was the black response to the rumors that the Confederate Congress was debating the issue of arming the slaves? According to at least one source, some black men in the South were prepared for possible recruitment. Scores of anxious black men were said to have been roaming the streets of cities and towns in wild fits of Confederate patriotism. Surely, there were some ready to serve,[222] but, the vast majority of African-American men and women were adamantly opposed to the measure. Black Civil War correspondent Thomas Morris Chester was on the mark when he wrote, "When this question was first broached to the public, it was as evident to the most ignorant slave of the South as to Davis himself that it was dictated by rebel necessity." Moreover, "The idea was so repulsive to these poor, humble people that they immediately began to devise ways and means to escape to our lines."[223] In the midst of the Confederate congressional debate, secret associations, whose purpose was to deliberate upon the proposal of taking up arms, were organized in Richmond and rapidly spread throughout Virginia. These associations agreed that black men should promptly respond to the call of the rebel chiefs, whenever it should be made. On the field, if placed in front of the white Confederate troops, "as soon as the battle began the Negroes were to raise a shout for Abraham Lincoln and the Union, and, satisfied there would be plenty of support from the Federal Force, they were to turn like uncaged tigers upon the rebel hordes." If placed in the rear, the black troops were to fire on the white Confederates in front of them. This two-pronged attack would disastrously defeat Lee's army and might even result in its total annihilation.[224] This brilliant plan sent a resounding answer of "no" to the question of whether blacks would fight for the South in significant numbers at this stage of the war.

Even in the early years of the conflict, most slaves had already made up their minds about which side of the white forces on the Southern battlefields was Pharoah's army. Despite Lincoln's reluctance to approve the enlistment of black soldiers at the beginning of the war and his snaillike pace in abolishing slavery, most slaves believed that a Union victory would lead to their emancipation. A Southern victory, by contrast, would mean a continuation of slavery. Given the intense racism of Southern whites, the brutality of the institution of slavery, and blacks' adamant dislike or mistrust of whites, it is inconceivable that the South would have persuaded blacks to fight for the Confederate cause in any significant numbers. Thomas B.

Wester, a soldier in the Forty-third U.S. Colored Infantry, spoke for most blacks in his response to the question, Will the slave fight against the North? "No, Never!" he answered. "He will turn his back upon the traitors, and leave them to their ignominious fate."[225] The outcome for the South was its worst nightmare, the destruction of slavery. Thus, to argue that blacks would somehow embrace the Confederacy in its final days defies logic and historical reality. As already noted, most blacks stood steadfast against the South from the start of the war to its conclusion.

In one of the many ironies of the Civil War, black participants in both the Union and Confederate causes were unwanted. Both governments, pathetically racist, allowed a number of needless deaths to occur before they actively recruited blacks into their armed services. Two years of fighting transpired, with a string of Union defeats, before Federal officials became convinced of the practicality of employing black troops. Had they recruited blacks at the start of the war, the balance may have tipped in the North's favor at least a year and one-half earlier than it did. By contrast, although there are serious doubts that the South could have ever recruited enough blacks to turn the tide of war in its favor, if the perceived threat were there, perhaps the North would have been more amenable to some form of reconciliation. Instead of at least entertaining the notion of recruiting blacks, however, Southerners could not bring themselves to enlist them as soldiers until it was too late. In an eerie way, the nation benefited from Southern white racism. Had Southern whites not been so racist, they would have been more open to some kind of compromise short of the abolition of slavery. Wanting all or nothing, in the end they got nothing. Fortunately, this led to the monumental liberation of four million slaves.

Black men demonstrated resourcefulness and courage in escaping from plantations and fighting in the army. They were proud of their participation in the war and proud of their role in winning their own liberty. Indeed, military service was of the upmost importance to most blacks, for as Frederick Douglass noted, "liberty won only by white men would lose half its luster."[226] Thomas Long, a black corporal in the First South Carolina Regiment, asserted, "If we hadn't become sojers, all might have gone back as it was before. But now tings can never go back, because we have showed our energy, and our courage and our naturally manhood."[227] A slave from Tennessee who visited his owner while on furlough after the Union victory in the Battle of Nashville found her glad to see him but disappointed that he was fighting for the Union. "You remember when you were sick," she reminded him, "and I had to bring you to the house and nurse you? And now you're fighting me!" Unmoved and with a clear vision, the slave replied, "I ain't fighting you. I'm fighting to get free."[228] From the moment that blacks proudly donned the Union blue, it was clear what they were fighting for—freedom!

CHAPTER THREE

"FREE AT LAST"
The Shackles Are Broken

WHEN UNION TROOPS began to steadily advance into Southern territory, many planters fled into the interior or beyond, taking their slaves
with them to safer ground. Slaveowners were particularly concerned
about the real possibility of their slaves running to Union lines or
being negatively influenced by Northern troops. Thus, slaves had to
be moved as a precaution: "We was all taken down to DeSoto, a place
near Vicksburg, for safe keeping," recounted James Brittian.[1] George
Washington Miller explained the fact that his owner, Dr. P. W. Miller,
"got so uneasy about the Yankees" when the Northern Army got as
near as Memphis, "that he sent us children, the Miller and Youngs,
back to South Carolina in wagons trying to keep the Yankees from
stealing us."[2] Henry Butler and a number of slaves were transported
to Arkansas by their master in 1863 to prevent their capture by Federal soldiers.[3] And Allen Manning recalled that his owner "tried to
evade the Northern army during the war. . . . When we would be
going down the road we would have to walk along the side all the
time to let the wagons go past, all loaded with folks going to Texas."[4]
Owners also took steps to reduce the opportunities that slaves would
have to run to Union lines. In Charleston, South Carolina, for example, municipal officials prohibited slaves from fishing in certain
parts of the harbor, rigorously enforced the curfew, and required pass-
ports for anyone wishing to get in or out of the city.[5]

Such efforts were futile, however, for slaves continued to abandon their masters in alarming numbers. The sweet taste of freedom
proved too alluring. Having convinced themselves that genuine affection was felt for them by most slaves, owners were appalled by
these desertions. Many were embittered and felt betrayed when their
slaves continued to run away to join the Yankees. In fact, they became so angry at the loss of their property that they sought reprisals.
The frequency with which slaves were whipped dramatically increased, and others were brutally murdered. Still, many of the blacks

remained undaunted. As more and more Northern troops appeared, slaves became more aggressive in their attitudes toward Southern whites. They organized insurrections, set fire to houses, and beat and murdered their masters.

FUGITIVE SLAVES COMING INTO UNION LINES AT NEW BERN, NORTH CAROLINA.

Harper's Weekly, February 21, 1863

An uprising was plotted in June 1861 in Monroe County, Arkansas. According to the plan, blacks would murder all white males; and, if they encountered resistance, women and children were also to be killed. Fortunately for the whites, the plot was discovered and several slaves were arrested; two men and one girl were subsequently hanged.[6] During the spring and summer of 1863 in Mississippi, where the slave population was particularly dense, there occurred new outbreaks of violence.[7] And a *New York Times* reporter commented on the surge of black unrest in the parishes of southern Louisiana during the summer of 1862: "There is an uneasy feeling among the slaves. They are undoubtedly becoming insubordinate, and I cannot think that another sixty days can pass away without some sort of demonstration."[8] The same reporter wrote three weeks later that the slaves in two nearby parishes were in a state of "semi-insurrection."[9] The correspondent of the *New York Herald*, writing from New Orleans, concurred: "There is no doubt that the negroes, for more than fifty miles up the river, are in a state of insubordination." He concluded that "the country is given to pillage and desolation," for "the slaves refuse obedience and cannot be compelled to labor."[10]

Indeed, some of the reports of black insubordination may have been baseless, the result of white fear and anxiety. However, black retaliation against whites was often very real. For instance, slaves in Yazoo City, Mississippi, in June 1864 burned a section of town that encompassed fourteen houses and the courthouse. Commenting on the incident, a reporter from the *Mississippian* remarked that "it was with great difficulty that the negroes were kept from burning it [Yazoo City] when the enemy were there before."[11] Whites in New Orleans were especially disturbed by the frequency with which police arrested blacks for insulting and even assaulting their owners. According to the *Picayune*, "a savage old nigger named Ben, forgetting all past benefits conferred upon him, was brought into court for insulting his mistress."[12] Slaves on a plantation in Choctaw County, Mississippi, in 1864 inflicted five hundred lashes on their master. Not far from this thrashing, David Pugh, a planter, and his overseer were assaulted by slaves who refused to work. But at least the two men shared a better fate than did General Dillard, a planter in Lynchburg, Virginia, who was murdered by five of his slaves, who were put to death by hanging.[13] In another Virginia case, in Alexandria, slaves killed an overseer who had a reputation for abusing young slave girls. Again, Southern whites made certain that those accused paid the ultimate price, as all six of the assailants were put to death. White Alexandria was particularly shocked by the heinous nature of the crime. Stephen Williams, a former slave, vividly described it: "One night they slip out and catch de overseer and kill him and tie a plowshare to the body to weight it down and throw him in the river."[14]

This aggressive behavior toward Southern whites did not emerge out of thin air. Rather, it represented a degree of continuity in slave behavior dating back to the colonial period. Rumors of insurrections were in abundance in the 1600s and 1700s throughout what was then English America. An uprising of serious proportions took place in New York City in 1712, and another near Charleston, South Carolina, in 1739. The 1800s witnessed slave insurrections led by Gabriel Prosser in Richmond in 1800, Denmark Vesey in Charleston in 1822, and Nat Turner in Southampton, Virginia, in 1831. There were also individual cases of blacks murdering whites. For instance, Lewis Bonner's father became a legend to a large number of blacks near Palestine, Texas, because he allegedly killed twenty-five whites before he was captured and put to death.[15] Once Northern troops began to appear in the South in large numbers, circumstances were much more conducive to black retaliatory action. Thus, the frequency of black violence dramatically increased. Blacks had tasted the sweetness of freedom, and they ultimately would be able to digest it once the Union Army triumphed and their shackles were broken.

Slaves freed by the Emancipation Proclamation and Union victory did not all rejoice and leave their homes spontaneously. Most slaveowning families in rural areas determined when and whether to announce the news of emancipation to their slaves. Thus, many of them remained unaware of their new status long after they were legally free. "Massa didn't tell us we's free till a whole year after we was," remarked one former slave.[16] Union troops passing through rural areas or stationed in the cities and towns confirmed and helped to enforce black freedom. "We's diggin' potatoes," a former slave from Louisiana and Texas recalled, "when de Yankees come up with two big wagons and make us come out of de fields and free us. Dere wasn't no cel'bration 'bout it. Massa say us can stay couple days till us 'cide what to do."[17] Some rural slaves learned of their freedom when they accompanied their master to town on some errand and carried the news back to the plantation. Often body servants of Confederates returning from the war would spread the news. One such servant recalled, "All de slaves crowded 'roun me an' wanted to know if dey wus gonna be freed or not an' when I tol' 'em dat de war wus over an' dat dey wus free dey wus all very glad."[18]

Most rural slaves, though excited by the news, did not hastily leave the plantations. Instead, they waited until they could make concrete plans and then either left or remained on their own terms. With emancipation, they themselves now had the right to choose what they wanted to do with their lives. On the Elmore Plantation near Columbia, South Carolina, six days after the initial announcement of freedom, slaves made plans to depart. "Philis, Jane and Nelly volunteered to finish Albert's shirts before they left," Grace Elmore recalled. "Jack, the driver, will stay till the crops are done."[19] On David Harris's plantation in the Spartanburg district, only one man left immediately, on August 15. The others decided to remain until New Year's Day.[20] Some rural slaves may have moved cautiously out of fear. Once Union soldiers left an area, Confederate troops would often return, bringing masters and overseers with them. Thus, slaves learned not to rejoice too quickly or too openly. "Everytime a bunch of No'thern sojers would come through," recalled one slave, "they would tell us we was free and we'd begin celebratin'. Before we would get through somebody else would tell us to go back to work, and we would go."[21] Another slave recalled celebrating emancipation "about twelve times" in one North Carolina county.[22] Before long, the uncertainty of when to claim freedom evaporated.

SLAVES ESCAPING TO FREEDOM BY BOAT.

Harper's Weekly, April 19, 1864

Although their timing varied, most rural blacks ultimately chose to leave the farms and plantations of their former owners. These places were constant reminders that they had had no freedom of mobility. As slaves, blacks could not travel without a written pass and were restricted to a nine-o'clock curfew. If they were caught in violation, they were usually sent to the workhouse and whipped. With emancipation, blacks now possessed the ability to come and go as they pleased, and one of their first actions was to test this new freedom by traveling around the South. "I's want to be free man, cum when I please, and nobody say nuffin to me, nor order me roun'," one Alabama black told a Northern journalist after Appomattox.[23] "Right off colored folks started on the move," a Texas freedman recalled,[24] and Mississippian Charles Moses declared, "I didn't spec' nothin' outten freedom 'septin' peace an' happiness, an' the right to go my way as I please."[25]

Former slaves were so adamant in their determination to test their new freedom that even those with supposedly kind owners left the plantations. For example, a Virginia planter reported that some of his former slaves "came up with tears in their eyes to shake hands with me and say good-bye." When he reminded them that he had always treated them well and asked why they wanted to leave, they replied politely, "we bleege to go, sah—, we bleege to go, Massa." Of his 115 slaves, all but four or five departed when they heard that they were free. Only those who were either old or sick remained.[26] When a family in South Carolina with a reputation for kindness offered their cook higher wages than she would earn at her new job, she still decided to leave. "I must go," she said. "If I stays here I'll never know I'm free."[27] In Florida a black preacher advised all the slaves of a kind owner to leave: "So long as the shadow of the great house fall across you, you ain't going to feel like no free man and no free woman." Furthermore, he added, "you must all move to new places that you don't know, where you can raise up your head without no fear of master this and master the other." They all chose to go.[28]

Sometimes former slaves, against the determined efforts of owners to prevent them from leaving, left nonetheless and scoffed at predictions that they would return. One man, determined to keep his slave against his will, whipped him "till de blood come." He then said, "Now you change yo' mind and give up?" But the slave said no and left with his family.[29] One woman, realizing that her freed slaves were all going, predicted, "Ten years from today, I'll have you all back 'gain." But sixty years later, one of her former slaves noted happily, "Dat ten years been over a mighty long time, an' she ain' got us back yet, an' she is dead an' gone."[30]

Compared to field hands, rural domestics or house servants were said to have had easy chores and to have enjoyed congenial relations with their masters. But they, too, departed at an astonishing rate, a fact that puts to rest the myth of the faithful old family servant who remained loyal throughout the Reconstruction years. The myth is based on only a few recorded incidents. Patty's story is one. A black woman who served the John Berkeley Grimball family for thirty-six years before emancipation, Patty stayed with them after the war for several months, sometimes feeding the now-impoverished family with her own food. To do so, she often went hungry herself. When she eventually decided to leave, she made sure that all the clothes were washed, gave presents to the young ladies of the house, and left two of her younger children to wait on the family.[31]

Some whites were deeply hurt when slaves who they thought were faithful or for whom they felt great affection suddenly departed. "I have never in my life met with such ingratitude," a South Carolina mistress exclaimed when a former slave ran off.[32] "Something dreadful has happened dear Diary," a Florida woman wrote in May 1865. "My dear black mammy has left us. . . . I feel lost, I feel as if someone is dead in the house. Whatever will I do without my Mammy?"[33] The mass defection of rural domestics threw many white households into disarray. Eliza Andrews, a Georgia woman, complained that it seemed to her "a waste of time for people who are capable of doing something better to spend their time sweeping and dusting while scores of lazy negroes that are fit for nothing else are lying around idle."[34] Even more disturbing, as a North Carolina woman put it, was their "impudent and presumin' " new manners.[35] Did this rude behavior mean that blacks wanted social equality? Former slaves perceived the situation differently. Their newfound freedom gave them the right to come and go as they pleased—and also the right to act disrespectfully toward whites. It was a new day.

For many blacks, particularly women, clothing took on a larger social significance during the Reconstruction period. Black women, even those who had never attended school, gave up their old plain and drab dresses and wore more colorful and stylish garments. A perceptive statement on the role of women's clothes during the transition from slavery to freedom is offered by Rossa Cooley, a New England white woman who taught on the Sea Islands in the early twentieth century. According to Cooley,

> Slavery to our Islanders meant field work, with no opportunity for the women and girls to dress as they chose and when they chose. Field workers were given their clothes as they were given their rations, only the clothes were given usually as a part of the Christmas celebration, "two clothes a year," explained one of them as she remembered the old days. With the hunger for books very naturally came the hunger for clothes, pretty clothes, and more of them! And so with school and freedom best clothes came out and ragged clothes were kept for the fields. Work and old "raggedy" clothes were . . . closely associated in the minds of the large group of middle-aged Island folk.[36]

When freedom arrived, black husbands took pride in buying fashionable dresses and silk ribbons, pretty hats, and delicate parasols for their womenfolk. When a white landowner in Louisiana scolded one of his tenants for spending the proceeds of his cotton crop on clothing, which the landowner regarded as "the greatest lot of trash you ever saw," the black man stood his ground. He told his employer that "he and his wife and children were satisfied and happy. What's the use of living if a man can't have the good of his labor?"[37]

Since "insolent" behavior and stylish clothing defied the traditional code of Southern race relations, many whites were deeply concerned about the freedwomen's more expressive dress. For example, a Freedmen's Bureau officer stationed in Wilmington, North Carolina, in the fall of 1865 remarked to a Northern journalist that "the wearing of black veils by the young negro women had given great offense to the young white women, "who consequently gave up this form of apparel altogether."[38] The connection between insolent behavior and elaborate dress was often made, particularly by white city dwellers. Henry W. Ravenel, a white Charlestonian, described a typical street scene in the mid-1860s. In his opinion, it was "so unlike anything we could imagine." He went on to imply that there was more than a casual connection between the two: "Negroes shoving white persons off the walk—Negro women dressed in the most outré style, all with bells and parasols for which they have an especial fancy—riding on horseback with Negro soldiers and in carriages."[39] The forsaking of deference plus the presence of black troops signaled an imminent struggle over "social equality" in the minds of apprehensive whites. This was a battle that could prove costly to fight and devastating to lose.

BLACK EFFORTS TO ALLEVIATE THE SUFFERINGS OF FREED PEOPLE

With emancipation, many rural blacks headed for Southern towns and cities in the belief that freedom was "free-er" there. They were drawn to numerous schools, churches, fraternal societies, and other black social institutions. Also in the cities were the Freedmen's Bureau and occupying Union soldiers, offering blacks a measure of protection from the violence of whites that pervaded much of the rural South. Moreover, some blacks migrated to cities and towns in search of relatives from whom they had been separated during slavery as well as in search of jobs that they believed would be plentiful. Not all these black migrants, however, experienced a significant improvement in their economic and social life but instead were witness to disease, starvation, poverty, and death.[40] And, not surprisingly, they were often subjected to white racism and racial discrimination. Still fervently believing in black inferiority, whites throughout the South were incensed over the black migration. One young white asserted in 1865 that he would leave the country before he would "live in a city where I have got to mix with free niggers." A white woman declared: "My old Mama who nursed me is just like a mother to me; but there is one thing that I will never submit to, that the Negro is our equal. He belongs to an inferior race."[41] As expected, black migration also heightened racial tensions and increased the economic problems facing both blacks and whites since there already existed an overabundance of labor. Blacks arriving barefoot, with ragged clothes on their backs, congregated in sections of cities that were rife with unsanitary conditions and disease. As a result, thousands of freedmen perished, and the death rate among them was staggering. A Freedmen's Bureau agent in Charleston vividly described a neighborhood occupied by poverty-stricken blacks: "Much suffering prevails among the old and infirm Freedmen. They have been suffered in some circumstances to congregate in abandoned buildings, where they are dragging out a miserable existence, suffering extremely from lack of food, clothing, fuel, proper quarters and medical attention."[42]

As concern for the suffering of black migrants rose, black men and women working through their own initiative or through northern freedmen's aid societies worked tirelessly to alleviate the suffering. As early as 1862, Elizabeth Keckley, a confidante of Mary Todd Lincoln, helped start the Contraband Relief Association. This organization became the Freedmen and Soldiers Relief Association of Washington after black men were enrolled in the army. Owing to many contributions throughout the war, it was able to continue providing food, clothing, housing, and medical attention to the needy.[43] Working on his own initiative, the Reverend Richard Cain, a future member of the U.S. House of Representatives from Charleston, played a leading role in obtaining health care for freedmen arriving in Washington, DC, and also helping them to secure employment.[44] In addition, Harriet Jacobs and her daughter Elizabeth expended much time and energy to relieve the suffering of freedmen in Arlington, Virginia, and Savannah, Georgia, through the New York Society of Friends. Harriet Jacobs was so adamant in her determination to improve the status of freedmen that in 1868 she went to England to solicit funds for a home for orphans and aged blacks in Savannah. She hoped to eventually build an asylum on about fifteen acres of land, which would give the freed people the opportunity to grow their own vegetables and fruit and keep poultry. Jacobs thanked British friends for their contributions in an appeal published in the *Anti-Slavery Reporter*. In her opinion, their support was "noble evidence of their joy at the downfall of American slavery and the advancement of human rights."[45]

Library of Congress

Both Sojourner Truth and Frances Ellen Watkins Harper were deeply concerned about the plight of black people and worked long hours for the benefit of their race. In an effort to assist freedmen in Washington, DC, Truth opened an employment office. She also sought to put pressure on city officials to stop spending huge sums on imprisoning vagrants. Instead, she noted, "officials could use the funds to provide adequate money and education for Freedmen."[46] The intensity of Truth's efforts to uplift her race was matched by Frances Ellen Watkins Harper. While acting as an ambassador to the white South, Harper spent most of her time with freed blacks. She informed William Still that "I meet with a people eager to hear, ready to listen."[47] Sometimes Harper would speak twice per day at no charge, and part of her lectures were directed to women. She particularly preached against men who physically and emotionally abused their wives. It was necessary for black men to treat their women with the utmost respect and with sensitivity because they had been ill treated under slavery, Harper insisted. Perhaps the following statement expresses the sentiments of numerous blacks such as Elizabeth Keckley, Richard Cain, Harriet and Elizabeth Jacobs, and Sojourner Truth on the need to promote the interests of the race. Harper noted: "I belong to this race, and when it is down I belong to a down race, when it is up I belong to a risen race."[48] Indeed, this commitment represents long-standing traditions of solidarity and self-help among North American blacks. It also epitomizes a shining moment in the struggle of blacks in the post-Civil War period for dignity and self-respect.

THE BLACK MIGRATION OF THE SOUTH

Despite the efforts of blacks and Northern white Freedmen's Aid societies, however, the mass sufferings of black migrants continued.

The response of Federal officials to this migration often ran counter to the interests of blacks. In Richmond, for example, U.S. Army officers adopted the strategy of forcing freedmen to return to work on the plantations. In return the government would provide rations to the farmers who employed them. The ranking commander in the area, Major General J. Irvin Gregg, was instructed by his superior to "do all in your power to prevent the able-bodied men from deserting the women and children and old persons." When practicable, migrants also should be sent back to plantations. Moreover, sentinels who were posted on the roads to Richmond were ordered to turn back all freedmen attempting to reach the city. The head of the Freedmen's Bureau in Virginia directed "all destitute persons, white and colored, who have come in from the country . . . to return to their homes where there is abundance of work and where work will provide food."[49] Owing to the fact that the military controlled distribution of the rations, it was able not only to encourage but also to virtually compel blacks to reenter the workforce by returning to their families and former owners.

Military officials repeated this strategy in cities throughout the South. For instance, in Charleston, freedmen were mistreated by those whose protection they had sought. Some were arbitrarily arrested and brutalized by occupation troops; others had their food rations suspended by the Freedmen's Bureau. In June 1865 the commander of Charleston's occupation force, Colonel William Gurney, issued a warning to the large number of freedmen who had congregated in the city: they must return to the farms. When they failed to take his advice, "he asked ward committees to report the names of all able-bodied idle-persons so that they might be put to work on the streets." Any unemployed freedmen whom Bureau officials found at large were designated as vagrants, denied food rations, and removed from Charleston. In this way the Bureau hoped to stem the overwhelming tide of black migration to the city.[50] Apparently, most officials considered this the most plausible way of dealing with an overabundance of urban labor coupled with massive hunger and disease. From their perspective, the government simply lacked the resources to materially provide for all the black migrants; and to do so ran against the basic tenets of capitalism. It would give rise to a lazy and dependent group of freedmen. Since, in the minds of many, most freedmen already possessed these deplorable characteristics, why should government policy make matters worse?

If Federal officials thought that their efforts would lead to a significant reduction in the number of black migrants, they were badly mistaken. The exodus of blacks from rural areas to cities and towns continued unabated. After emancipation, the black population of Southern cities and towns increased substantially. For example, Memphis's black population rose by 450 percent between 1860 and 1865. In addition, by 1866, Charleston had a black majority; and from 1860 to 1880, Savannah's black population grew so substantially that it constituted 51 percent of the city's total population. Other cities also experienced dramatic increases in their black populations. By 1870, Atlanta, Richmond, Montgomery, and Raleigh had black populations totaling close to 50 percent. Overall, during the 1860s, the urban black population increased by 75 percent, and the number of blacks in small rural towns grew as well. The case of Demopolis, Alabama, illustrates the latter trend. In 1860, Demopolis had only one black resident. However, at the conclusion of the war it became the site of a regional Freedmen's Bureau office; as a result, blacks began to trickle into the town. They came in such large numbers that by 1870, Demopolis had a black population of nearly one thousand.[51]

Although most freedmen migrated to either Southern cities or towns, some rejected the region entirely. Instead, they sought their fortunes in the North. While it is true that the North was not yet the beacon of Southern black hopes and aspirations that it would become in the first decades of the twentieth century, 68,000 blacks relocated to these states during the 1870s.[52] Why did freed people not migrate to Northern cities in more significant numbers? Apparently, most of them regarded migration as neither feasible nor desirable. Regardless of acute white racism and racial discrimination, the South was home to most blacks, and they were determined to remain there. Furthermore, they were now free and no longer had to steal away to the North to achieve their freedom.

While large numbers of rural blacks took to the road in pursuit of "real freedom," many former slaves, such as Charlie Davenport and a woman named Adeline who was scolded by other blacks for not leaving, stayed at the homesteads of their former owners, often for several years after the war.[53] For example, Daddy Henry proved faithful to his owner, Edward J. Thomas of Georgia. As he was getting ready to depart for battle, Thomas told Henry that everything was being placed in his care. Daddy Henry replied, "Mas' Ed, fore God I won't betray you." He protected Thomas's family and helped them take refuge in Savannah when the fighting came too close. He lived with the Thomas family for several years after the war.[54] In a similar case, Captain W. M. Davidson, leaving Savannah in the December evacuation, asked his slave, who would be free the next day,

"Take care of my wife while I am gone, will you?" The slave agreed
and resided with the Davidson family for many years after the war.[55]
Some of those who left eventually returned, but not out of affection
for "Old Massa." They may have been driven by "an instinctive feeling that the old cabin in which they had labored so long ought by
right to belong to them," or they hoped to find some means of liveli-
hood among familiar people. Most who returned settled on neighboring plantations rather than on those of their former owners.
Freedom was the major goal, and most did not believe that they could
be free and still work under the supervision of their former owners.
Freedom had to be held apart from them.

JOY OVER THEIR NEWFOUND STATUS

The arrival of Union soldiers in rural areas witnessed much excitement among freedmen. Colonel Thomas W. Higginson, a white
officer in the First South Carolina Volunteers, the first slave regiment
mustered into the service of the United States, described the reaction
of blacks on Edisto Island to the arrival of his regiment. "What a sight
it was! With the wild faces, eager figures, and strange garments, it
seemed, as one of the poor things reverently suggested, 'like notin'
but de Judgment Day.' " Higginson noted that "presently they began
to come from the houses also with bundles of all sizes on their heads."
Old women trotting down the narrow paths would kneel to say a
little prayer "still balancing the bundle. . . . Then they would suddenly spring up, urged on by the accumulating procession behind."
Higginson continued: "They would move on till they were irresist-
ibly compelled by thankfulness to dip down for another prayer." But,
as he perceived it, the most moving scene occurred when the freedmen reached the soldiers, for at this point "our hands were grasped
and there were exclamations of 'Bress you, mas'r,' and 'Bress de
Lord.' " Women brought children on their shoulders. "Small black
boys came, carrying on their backs their little black brothers whom
they gravely deposited on the ground, then turned to shake our
hands."[56] Indeed, in the minds of these rural blacks, this was their
long-awaited day of deliverance.

Like former rural slaves, most former urban ones left the houses
where they had been enslaved when they first received news of their
freedom. They departed because these dwellings symbolized slavery
and they wanted to remove themselves from any reminders of the
institution. They were also motivated by the constant desire to assert
and test their newfound freedom. One black cook, though satisfied

in her position, resigned because "it look like old time to stay too long in one place."[57] A native white Charlestonian who lived in a household just north of the city reported incredulously in the spring of 1865 that most of the servants "say they are free and went off last night." These even included "one Uncle Henry trusted most."[58] Widespread desertion by urban former slaves was particularly true of domestics, a group that had constituted the bulk of urban slaves prior to the Civil War. In fact, they deserted in such large numbers that one contemporary newspaper described domestics as "perfect nomads" who seldom remained in a family's service for any appreciable time.[59] White owners saw only that their former slaves were leaving material security for uncertainty. Apparently, most whites did not grasp the nature of the anger, frustration, and anxiety experienced by urban domestics. Their every move was watched by white owners, they often had to work long hours, and, in addition, they had to answer their master's every beckon and call. They were essentially on the job for twenty-four hours per day. Moreover, despite the fact that their work was usually less arduous than that of the field hands and that close proximity to owners bred relationships based on genuine affection, there was a negative side. Domestics were often in a position to observe on a firsthand basis the huge discrepancies between slaves and whites in terms of food, shelter, clothing, and personal belongings. They knew the enemy all too well.

Many of the former slaves who migrated to cities and towns arrived there with conquering Federal troops and shared in the excitement of the Union triumph with former urban slaves. On the morning of December 21, 1864, soon after the Confederates evacuated Savannah, Union forces led by General William Tecumseh Sherman marched into the city accompanied by their corps of black laborers and followed by a long train of more than ten thousand former slaves. Most were cheering and dancing. The city's blacks gave Sherman a welcome that was "singular and touching," greeting his arrival, wrote George Ward Nichols, "with exclamations of unbounded joy." One elated black woman grabbed the general's hand and made a short thank-you speech.[60] John Gould noted that when Sherman's troops entered Savannah, "swarms of black children followed his troops through the city." Another Union soldier spoke to a freed black woman who summed up her emotions by exclaiming, "It is a dream, sir—a dream!"[61] Spotted outside the window of a white woman was a young black girl jumping up and down and singing as loudly as she could, "All de rebel gone to hell, now Pa Sherman come."[62]

Union troops liberating the city of Charleston inspired similar jubilation. Black soldiers were among the first Union units to enter Charleston after the Confederate evacuation, and their arrival ignited an explosion of adulation among the black population. As the all-black Fifty-fifth Massachusetts entered the city, "shouts, prayers, and blessings came from the former slave population," according to a contemporary observer, who also noted a touching scene. One black soldier, holding aloft a banner proclaiming "Liberty," rode a mule down Meeting Street at the head of an advancing column. A black woman shouting "Thank God! Thank God!" dashed over to hug him but missed her mark and hugged the mule instead. Several other blacks were so overcome with emotion that they wept.[63]

Black Union soldiers liberating slaves in North Carolina.

Harper's Weekly, January 23, 1864

To white Charlestonians the presence of black troops was unsettling, particularly since the Third and Fourth South Carolina regiments that joined the Twenty-first U.S. Colored Troops and the Fifty-fourth and Fifty-fifth Massachusetts black regiments in liberating the city were made up of former slaves from the Charleston area. The liberation by black troops of Charleston, the bastion of the secession movement, was a deliberate ploy by the Federal government to psychologically and emotionally wreak as much havoc as possible. Indeed, the city had to pay a heavy price for its role in bringing on the Civil War. Wendell Phillips, a white abolitionist from Massachusetts, captured the sorrow felt by most white Charlestonians when he asked: "Can you conceive a bitterer drop that God's chemistry could mix for a son of the Palmetto State, than that a Massachusetts flag and a colored regiment should take possession of Charleston?"[64]

For whites in Charleston it was a novel experience to have blacks not give them "the inside of the [side]walk" and to have a black man address them without first doffing his hat. The sight of black sentinels stationed at public buildings to examine the passes of all who would enter was especially depressing to whites. Black soldiers made up the provost guards, charged with maintaining law and order and quartered at the Citadel, and "whoever desired protection papers or passes, whoever had business with the marshal or the general commanding the city, rich or poor, high-born or low-born, *white or black*, man or woman," wrote Charles Coffin, "must first meet a colored sentinel face to face, and obtain from the colored sergeant permission to enter the gate."[65] Having lost the war, it now appeared to injured white Charlestonians that the North was rubbing salt in the wound.

Mrs. Frances J. Porcher, a prominent white South Carolinian, described the changed situation in a wry letter to a friend: "Nat Fuller, a Negro caterer, provided munificently for a miscegenat dinner, at which blacks and whites sat on an equality, and gave toasts and sang songs for Lincoln and Freedom. Miss Middleln and Miss Alston, young ladies of colour, presented a coloured regiment with a flag on the Citadel green, and nicely dressed black sentinels turn back white citizens, reprimanding them for their passes not being correct."[66] To freedmen, it was a day that they had prayed for and long awaited.

As in Charleston, black troops were among the first Union soldiers to enter the city of Richmond. The gallant 36th U.S. Colored Troops, under Lieutenant Colonel B. F. Pratt, was the first to arrive. The regiment's drum corps played "Yankee Doodle" and "Shouting the Battle Cry of Freedom" amid the cheers of the boys and the white soldiers who filed by them.[67] The all-black Fifth Massachusetts Cavalry next rode in with two white regiments, followed by Companies C and G of the Twenty-ninth Connecticut Colored Volunteers and Ninth U.S. Colored Troops. And here, too, the black residents of the city were ecstatic, running along the sidewalks to keep up with the troops, while other residents stood gasping in wonder as the Union soldiers marched through the streets.[68] Thomas Morris Chester, the

Northern black war correspondent, captured the moment: "Some waved their hats and women their hands in token of gladness." According to Chester, newly freed blacks in Richmond expressed their joy and appreciation to the Union army in such phrases as: "You've come at last," "We've been looking for you these many days," "Jesus has opened the way," "God bless you," "I've not seen that old flag for four years," "It does my eyes good," "Have you come to stay?" and "Thank God."[69] Shortly before this electrifying scene took place, however, another emotional scene transpired. Chaplain Garland H. White, who had been born and raised nearby as a slave, was among the first troops entering Richmond. He was asked to make a speech, to which he complied. As he wrote, "I was aroused amid the shouts of ten thousand voices, and proclaimed for the first time in that city freedom to all mankind."[70]

A few hours later, a large crowd of black soldiers and residents assembled on Broad Street near Lumpkin Alley, where the slave jails, auction rooms, and offices of the slave traders were concentrated. Encouraged by the presence of black troops, the slaves held in Lumpkin's jail began to chant: "Slavery chain done broke at last! Broke at last! Broke at last! Slavery chain done broke at last! Gonna praise God till I die!" When the crowd outside took up the chant, the soldiers opened the cells and the prisoners came pouring out, some praising God and "Master Abel" for their deliverance.[71]

The highlight of the first day of the Union occupation of Richmond was the visit to the city of President Abraham Lincoln. As soon as he arrived on April 3, 1865, the news quickly spread. Some free blacks shouted that the president had arrived. But the title "president" was associated with Jefferson Davis in the South, so initially most blacks did not realize that Lincoln was in the city. Rumors had circulated that Davis had been captured and was being brought to Richmond for punishment. As they approached the visitor, they cried out in anger, "Hang him! Hang him! Show him no quarter!"[72] Davis represented to most blacks the embodiment of the pro-slavery South. Indeed, one of the most popular tunes sung by both black civilians and soldiers went something like this: "Hang Jeff Davis on a sour apple tree, Hang Jeff Davis on a sour apple tree, Hang Jeff Davis on a sour apple tree, As we go marching along."[73]

When blacks discovered that the visitor was Lincoln and not Davis, they were thrilled. In only a few minutes, there were thousands of freed people trying to catch a glimpse of Lincoln. Later, as the president was preparing to depart, one contemporary, overtaken by emotion, asserted that "there is no describing the scene along the route. The colored population was wild with enthusiasm. Old men thanked God in a very boisterous manner, and old women shouted upon the pavement as high as they had ever done at a religious revival."[74] Foreshadowing what would be the gloomy fate of Lincoln in only a few days, as his ship sailed off amid the cheering of the crowd, a black woman cried out, "Don't drown, Massa Abe, for God's sake!"[75]

The Union occupation of Richmond represented the beginning of freedom for blacks, but it was a nightmare for the city's whites. It was bad enough that the conquering Union troops were patrolling the streets, but worse still that black soldiers were among them. For most whites, it seemed as if the victorious North had conspired to make the occupation as distasteful as possible. The sight of long lines of black cavalry sweeping by the Exchange Hotel, raising their swords in triumph and exchanging cheers with black residents, was intolerable.[76] The anguish felt by Richmond whites and those throughout the South over the changed state of affairs is illustrated by a confrontation between a black Union soldier, who had earlier been a slave in the area, and his former owner. The black man was one of several guards escorting through the streets a large squad of rebels, which happened to include the white master. When he spotted his former slave, he stepped a little out of ranks and called, "Hello, Jack, is that you?" The black guard stared at him with a look of blank astonishment, not unmingled with disdain. The rebel captive still was determined to be recognized and asked, "Why, Jack, don't you know me?" "Yes, I know you very well," was the sullen reply, "and if you don't fall back into that line I will give you this bayonet." This reply, of course, terminated any attempts at familiarity.[77]

After the first, spontaneous celebrations of freedom, urban former slaves staged parades and organized formal events. Rural freed slaves flocked to the nearest town or city to participate in these emancipation celebrations that continued throughout the years of Reconstruction. Perhaps the most impressive parade was the one held in Charleston on March 29, 1865, and organized by the black leaders of the community, when four thousand marchers moved through the streets cheered on by a crowd of thousands. About two weeks later black Charlestonians, freedmen from outlying areas of the city, and Northern white dignitaries assembled at Fort Sumter to witness the ceremonial raising of the U.S. flag. Since the Confederates' successful attack against the fort had ushered in the start of the war, now the raising of the U.S. flag over it signaled the Union's triumph in the conflict. Some of the best-known participants in the celebration included Major Robert J. Anderson, the commander of Fort Sumter at the time of its capture, Judge Advocate General Joseph Holt, Supreme Court Justice N. H. Swayne, Senator Henry Wilson, Henry Ward Beecher, William Lloyd Garrison, Theodore Tilton, Judge William D. Kelley, George Thompson, General E. D. Townsend, Captain Robert Smalls, and Major Martin Delany and his son Toussaint L'Ouverture Delany of the Fifty-fourth Massachusetts. When Major Anderson hoisted the flag, "the bay thundered with the roar of cannon from ship and shore, every band burst into full-throated sound, every drum came alive, and the thousands of keyed-up celebrators shouted and screamed for joy."[78]

Other urban black communities were not long in following the example of Charleston. Just four days after the entry of Union troops into Richmond, the city's blacks assembled at the First African Church on Broad Street for a Jubilee meeting. More than 1,500 blacks, including a considerable number of soldiers, sang hymns and shouted their joy.[79] In South Carolina, blacks in Columbia organized an emancipation parade on July 4, 1865,[80] and in Aiken, on the same date, blacks held a picnic, prayer meeting, and dance at a hotel.[81] Former slaves in Athens, Georgia, sang and danced around a liberty pole to celebrate freedom until white residents cut it down.[82] An emancipation celebration was witnessed by Sergeant William A. Warfield, a black soldier from Company D, 119th U.S. Colored Infantry, at Fort Nelson, near Lexington, Kentucky, also on July 4, 1865. Present were several regiments of black soldiers and thousands of blacks from Fort Nelson and the surrounding areas. "Such an assemblage of colored people on the 'sacred soil of Kentucky' was never before beheld," wrote Warfield. The "exercises consisted of martial music, songs, speeches, and declamations, with an interlude of a good dinner." He concluded that "almost boundless enthusiasm prevailed throughout."[83]

THE IMPACT OF LINCOLN'S ASSASSINATION

Many of these celebrations were greatly tempered, however, because news of the assassination of President Lincoln only a few weeks earlier by John Wilkes Booth had a devastating impact on black communities. The day that witnessed Lincoln's death, April 14, 1865, would long be remembered by blacks as one of profound sadness. They associated Lincoln with their newfound freedom. Scholars can continue to debate the merits of the Emancipation Proclamation and argue over the president's true intentions in issuing it, but it is an undeniable fact that former slaves held Lincoln in the highest regard.

Indeed, the testimony of many former slaves underscore this point. Turner Jacobs maintained that "we all thought Abraham Lincoln was a young Christ come to save us."[84] Lewis Jenkins captured the view of many when he said, "I think Abe Lincoln was next to Jesus Christ. The best human man ever lived. He died helpin' the poor nigger man."[85] The stature most befitting Lincoln from the standpoint of the majority of freedmen was the one accorded to Moses in the Bible. As Frank Hughes said, "What do I think about Abraham Lincoln? I thinks about him jes like I did about Moses. I think it was de will of de lawd to talk to Abraham Lincoln through de spirit, to work out a plan to set the niggers free. I think he carried out God's Plan."[86] Echoing similar sentiments, Julius Jones wrote that "Mr. Lincoln was sure a wonderful man. He did what God put him here to do, took bondage off the Colored people and set them free."[87]

Given the fact that Lincoln represented the personification of freedom to most blacks, it should not be surprising to learn that many freedmen feared that his death meant their return to bondage. On St. Helena Island, South Carolina, a freed black asked schoolmistress Laura M. Towne if it were true that the "Government was dead";[88] and in Mississippi, James Lucas recalled that "us all got skaired . . . fear us hab to be slaves agin."[89] The uncertainty about their future persuaded some freedmen, particularly those in cities such as Mobile, Alabama, and Charleston, South Carolina, to seek revenge on Southern whites for Lincoln's death and at the same time to ensure the maintenance of their newfound freedom. The black threat of violence against whites was so real that whites in Mobile became alarmed and urged Thomas W. Conway, the general superintendent of the freedmen in the Department of the Gulf, to use his influence to keep blacks in the area under control. It is also possible that violence would have broken out in Charleston had it not been for the calming influence on the black population of Major Martin Delany. [90]

As expected, blacks throughout the country participated in large numbers in the funeral services held for the slain leader. And they were present from beginning to end. Many of the 25,000 people who filed through the East Room of the White House on April 16, 1865, to view the body of Lincoln were black. On the following day when the coffin was carried to the Capitol, thousands of blacks followed the procession. "Wearing a dejected aspect and many of them in tears," wrote *Harper's Weekly*, these colored marchers bore a banner inscribed, "We mourn our loss." Indeed, blacks were prominent among the 60,000 spectators who lined the sidewalks and filled every roof and window along the mile of the march. On the morning of April 21, the funeral cortege left Washington and headed for its destination in Springfield, Illinois, the final resting place of Abraham Lincoln. At every stop on the journey, the train was met by thousands of people who wanted to pay their respects to the fallen president. A crowd of nearly 350,000 in Philadelphia filed past the mahogany coffin. Among this number was an elderly black woman in tears who laid a wreath on the casket and cried, "Oh, Abraham Lincoln, are you dead? Are you dead?" At New York 2,000 blacks showed up to pay their respects, many of them dressed in army blue.[91]

Blacks in the South joined in the grief. Typical of the Lincoln memorial exercises in the coastal regions was that held in Beaufort, South Carolina. The mourners assembled in a schoolroom draped in black. Some emblem of sorrow was worn by everyone—a black headband, or a black bow on a topknot.[92] One young black woman "begged us for some strips of black cambric, which she basted around the bottom of her gown and up and down the front with white cotton," wrote Elizabeth Hyde Botume. A girl tied a black band around her head, and another made a bow of black cambric and wore it as a topknot. One man had turned his coat inside out to show the black lining. Those in attendance listened attentively to prayers and chants, one leader ending with: "Massa Linkum! Our 'dored Redeemer an' Saviour an Frien'! Amen!"[93] Blacks in Michelville, South Carolina, wore crepe on their left arms until the end of April.[94] And the Reverend Richard H. Cain held a memorial service for Lincoln at Emanuel A.M.E. Church in Charleston, where there was not a dry eye.[95] Black drapes in memory of Lincoln were left hanging from the walls and pulpit at Zion Presbyterian Church in Charleston for an entire year.[96] Moreover, on the day of Lincoln's burial, hundreds of blacks in the pews of the First African Baptist Church in Richmond prayed in silence for their deliverer. Throughout the city, black streamers and banners darkened freshly whitewashed shacks, and those who had no black cloth are said to have dipped flour sacks in chimney soot as a substitute. Indeed, mourning was in every heart and on every face.[97]

In the days and weeks following Lincoln's assassination, black organizations in the North and South passed resolutions honoring his memory. The Colored Men's Convention of Michigan, held in Detroit in early September 1865, spoke of "the noble, patriotic, philanthropic and humane deeds of our much beloved and ever to be praised late Chief Magistrate." At the first annual meeting of the Equal Rights League, held in Cleveland in mid-October, the delegates expressed joy that Heaven permitted "so good and great a man to live so long among us."[98] Mourners at the Third Street African Methodist Church in Richmond passed a series of resolutions on the sorrow of the city's black community at Lincoln's untimely death, and they offered their condolences to his bereaved family.[99]

The largest observance by blacks of Lincoln's death took place in New Orleans one week after his assassination. It was sponsored by the city's one hundred benevolent organizations, which pooled their resources and called a mass meeting. Ten thousand blacks paraded down the main streets of the city—Rampart, Canal, St. Charles, Poydras, and Camp—to assemble at Congo Square. Here they drew up resolutions expressing their indebtedness to Lincoln and vowing to wear mourning bands for thirty days. A line in the *Black Republican*, the city's black newspaper, summed up the sentiment of those who signed the resolutions: "in giving us our liberty, he has lost his own life."[100]

Not only did blacks hold services and pass resolutions to show their respect for Lincoln, but, although many were nearly penniless, they also eagerly contributed whatever they could to help finance monuments in his memory. In an open letter written a few days after the assassination, Martin Delany, who had recently been commissioned an army major, asked blacks throughout the nation to each contribute one cent toward a memorial for the president.[101] They did not need Delany's urging. Charlotte Scott, a newly freed woman from Campbell County, Virginia, declared that she would "give five dollars of her wages," an astronomical amount. Donations began to come in at a rapid rate, and enough funds were secured to build the memorial paid for entirely by blacks. It was unveiled in Lincoln Park in Washington, DC, on the eleventh anniversary of the martyred president's death. Blacks were estatic about their accomplishment, and they had every right to be. A group of people, many of whom were only a few years removed from slavery and were living on the brink of poverty, had nevertheless, financed a magnificent statue. It reveals the Great Emancipator as the freedmen envisaged him: holding the Emancipation Proclamation in one hand, with his other hand outstretched above a slave whose face, "lighted with joy, . . . anticipates the full manhood of Freedom."[102]

Black regiments also gave $8,000 of the total of $27,682 contributed by the U.S. armed forces to build a Lincoln monument at Oak Ridge. In fact, the greatest single contribution, except for those of the states of Illinois and New York, was given by the Seventy-third U.S. Colored Troops in the amount of $1,437. Even among the white regiments, a black giver occasionally could be found. For example, in one Illinois company the last name on the list was "Anthony E. Carter—Captain's cook, colored man—$10.00."[103] That black men, women, and children would make sacrifices to honor the memory of Abraham Lincoln is understandable. In their eyes, he had given his own life to deliver them from slavery.

EMANCIPATION CELEBRATIONS THROUGHOUT
THE RECONSTRUCTION PERIOD

Not surprisingly, blacks throughout the South continued to hold emancipation celebrations well into the post-Civil War period. Sometimes on an annual basis they would honor the day that Union troops liberated their town or city, or they would choose either January 1, June 19, July 4, or August 4 on which to stage commemorations. While the dates of January 1 and July 4 are understandable, it is difficult to ascertain why blacks would select either June 19 or August 4. These celebrations were festive occasions, attended by hundreds or even thousands of freedmen. For example, on April 3, 1866, blacks in Richmond celebrated the anniversary of that city's fall to Union troops. A huge parade, organized by secret societies, took place in which the marchers walked together in ceremonial garb. Observers noted "a banner with a concentric tobacco plant and an eccentric inscription"; one group wore striped sashes; another group was decked out in broad black scarves tipped with white, carrying a banner inscribed: "Union Liberties Protective Society, organized February 4, 1866— Peace and Goodwill Toward Men." The parade, two thousand strong, proceeded to Capitol Square, on the grounds of the former Confederate capital. The message was clear: Out with the days of the Old South of slavery, and in with the days of the New South of freedom. At Capitol Square the marchers were joined by fifteen thousand observers. Amid songs, dancing, games, food, speeches, and prayers, the celebration continued well into the evening.[104]

Disgruntled whites often did more than stand by quietly or merely complain about the noise while celebrations took place. Sometimes they expressed their opposition in violent ways. For instance, on the eve of the Emancipation Day celebration in Richmond in April 1866, the Second African Baptist Church burned to the ground in a mysterious blaze, certainly the handiwork of whites determined to undermine black plans for the celebration.[105] They failed to do so; as noted above, the celebration took place and was a resounding success. Moreover, the attitude of the church's congregation was clear: you have burned us down, but we will not be deterred. As further evidence that white violence would not sway them, Richmond blacks again took to the streets on July 4 in a massive emancipation celebration. Blacks wholeheartedly enjoyed themselves, but whites stayed off the streets. [106] The celebrations that took place in Richmond—and the whites' response—were typical of those that occurred in Charleston, Memphis, Raleigh, Atlanta, New Orleans, Savannah, Wilmington, Baltimore, Vicksburg, Louisville, Columbia, and other towns and cities throughout the South during the post-Civil War period.

Although there is no evidence that Chickasaw freedmen observed Emancipation Day during the Reconstruction period, an abundance of evidence suggests that the Cherokee, Creek, and Seminole freedmen did observe it. For example, about five hundred people attended the Emancipation Day celebration held by Cherokee freedmen in Tahlequah (in present-day Oklahoma) on August 4, 1876. A well-anticipated event, preparations went on for several weeks. The parade participants, all fashionably dressed, assembled in the morning and marched about two miles north of town, where a large crowd had assembled. Barbecued beef was offered, and people came in wagons with boxes of delicacies. Speeches were given by prominent Cherokee politicians and several freedmen. The large crowd continued to enjoy themselves until five in the afternoon.[107] Not to be outdone by the freedmen of Tahlequah, those of Delaware and adjoining districts also held a massive celebration on August 4, 1876. This event was billed several days in advance as "a grand horseback tournament together with speaking and a barbecue." Among the speakers were Arthur William and Joseph Rogers, who both spoke against colonization and encouraged the blacks to demand their birthright. To the tune of "John Brown's Body" and "Rally 'Round the Flag, Boys," groups marched and countermarched around a red piece of bunting set on a pretty knoll, which symbolized the tree of freedom.[108]

THE STRUGGLE TO HOLD ONTO THEIR RIGHTS

That blacks valued freedom immensely would prove to be beneficial in their struggle to combat white racial violence, which was designed to take away that freedom. Indeed, they would need all the determination they could muster to withstand the massive onslaught of white violence launched against them. Having lost the war, whites were embittered and in a state of shock. How could this have happened? they asked. How could their way of life have been destroyed? How was it possible that lowly and inferior blacks were now truly free? And how could they tolerate blacks as free individuals? The answer was that under no circumstances could they accept blacks as their equals. The only alternative was to convince blacks that while the U.S. government might recognize them as being free, Southern whites never would, even if it meant the annihilation of freedmen—a mission that roaming gangs of former Confederate soldiers would be happy to carry out.

In some areas, violence against blacks reached staggering proportions in the immediate aftermath of the war. In Louisiana in 1865 a visitor from North Carolina wrote, "they [whites] govern . . . by the pistol and the rifle." "I saw white men whipping colored men just the same as they did before the war," testified freed slave Henry Adams, who claimed that "over two thousand colored people" were murdered in 1865 in the area around Shreveport. The Freedmen's Bureau was not able to establish order in Texas, and blacks there were especially vulnerable to white violence. Blacks in the state, according to a Bureau official, "are frequently beaten unmercifully, and shot down like wild beasts, without any provocation." A freedwoman from Rusk County named Susan Merritt remembered seeing black bodies floating down the Sabine River and said of local whites, "There sure are going to be lots of souls crying against them in Judgement."

It was not unusual for whites to wipe out whole black communities on fabricated allegations. For example, in 1866, after "some kind of dispute with some Freedmen," a group near Pine Bluff, Arkansas, set fire to a black settlement and rounded up the inhabitants. A man who visited the scene on the following morning described it as "a sight that apald me 24 Negro men woman and children were hanging to trees all round the Cabbins."[109] Moreover, whites sometimes would take advantage of starving freedmen by offering them poisoned food. Annie Day explained: "I wuz told by some older niggers dat after de war and de slaves had dere freedom, de niggers was told to go to Millican. A lot of 'em went down dere. Dey wuz awful hungry, and de storekeepers dere give 'em barrels of apples to eat and de apples had been poisoned, and dey killed a lot of de Colored people."[110]

Regardless of the obstacles they faced, some blacks refused to take the random violence meted out to them by whites without a fight. They employed two strategies: blacks sought to use the judicial system; and, in some cases, they took the law into their own hands. On one occasion, a poor white woman hit a black woman for no apparent reason other than the color of her skin. At first, the black woman did not complain. However, when her white neighbor struck her a second time, she retaliated. In response, the white woman had her arrested, but the black woman had already contemplated filing charges against the white woman for violating her civil rights. The judge ruled in favor of the black woman. As a result, the case was thrown out of court, and the white woman was assessed the court costs. Utilization of the judicial system, however, was often long and taxing and yielded few positive results.

Even if they banded together and took the law into their own hands to suppress crimes committed by whites against them, blacks tried to work within the system. For example, when a group of armed blacks in 1866 in Orangeburg, South Carolina, apprehended three whites who had been terrorizing freedmen, instead of lynching them, the blacks delivered them to the county jail. And when a white man was found guilty of the cold-blooded murder of a freedwoman in Holly Springs, Mississippi, blacks formed a posse to hunt him down, although there is no record of their having caught him. Some whites who assaulted blacks were, however, not so fortunate. In the Newberry district of South Carolina, two former Confederate soldiers attacked a black Union soldier. While he was struggling with them, one of the rebel soldiers stabbed him so severely that the wound was thought to be fatal. News of this confrontation quickly spread, and both rebel soldiers were apprehended by black soldiers of the regiment to which the injured soldier belonged. Within three hours the Confederate who had stabbed the Union soldier was tried, found guilty, shot, and buried.[111] Certainly, the second rebel would have undergone a similar fate had he not managed to escape.

Many blacks in the South looked to the Cherokee Nation as a haven. Although racism existed among the Cherokees, blacks were treated in the Nation better than they were in the American South. Unlike the Southern whites who often indulged in mob violence, the Cherokees did not. In fact, there is no record of a lynching among them. Freedmen there did not fear for their personal safety, and they were assured of a hearing before a properly constituted tribunal.[112] Moreover, the Choctaws and Chickasaws had few difficulties with their freedmen, as cases of violence involving them were relatively few. Ironically, the racial tension that existed in both Nations was the result of confrontations between freedmen from Southern states and their white counterparts who moved to the Choctaw and Chickasaw Nations after the war. Of course, the Southern whites who moved into the Chickasaw Nation brought with them their old bigotry. Ardmore and other towns in the Indian Territory became the home of active Confederate veterans' organizations. As expected, racial prejudice against blacks ran high among the white population of the region that later would become known as "Little Dixie." Indeed, if crimes were committed, blacks were looked upon with suspicion. Visitors were asked to leave town if they could not convince local whites that they had business in the area. Not surprisingly, fist-fights were common on the streets. If the fight was between two blacks, it became a spectacle, as people gathered and began to cheer for one or the other. However, if the fight was between a black and a white, racial tensions ran high and the fight would likely spread to onlookers.[113]

Despite the many trials that blacks had to endure during the early years of emancipation, they remained undaunted. They were determined to enjoy the fruits of their newfound freedom to the fullest. Whites could continue to employ whatever measures they devised to deny them full autonomy, but it would be to no avail. At long last savoring the sweetness of liberty, the black people could now shout, "Free at last; Free at last; Thank God Almighty, we are free at last."[114]

CHAPTER FOUR

A "WORKING CLASS OF PEOPLE"
The Struggle to Gain Economic Independence

THE WARTIME PROSPERITY continued into the postwar years in the North, but in the South towns and cities lay in ruins. Plantations were wrecked, and neglected fields were overgrown with grass, weeds, and wildflowers. Bridges and railroads were destroyed. White Southerners had lost much of their personal property in the war, including, because of emancipation, about $2 billion worth of slaves. Furthermore, Confederate bonds and currency were now worthless. These losses were a huge blow to the economic future of Southern whites. Many of them faced the prospect of starvation and homelessness. Even some of those who had earlier been counted among the wealthy would now be able to survive only on government rations.[1]

While conditions were bad for Southern whites, they were even worse for Southern blacks. Four million black men and women were now emerging from slavery. They and their ancestors had been held in bondage for nearly two and one-half centuries. Once they were emancipated, many left the plantations in search of a new life in freedom, walking to the nearest town or city or roaming the countryside and camping at night on the bare ground. Most of these people had no more possessions than the clothes they wore, and often these were merely old sacks tied together and socks instead of shoes. The new freedmen were overwhelmingly unskilled, illiterate, and poor. Moreover, since responsibility for their well-being had always been assumed by the master, they had little knowledge about how to survive on their own.[2] Now that blacks were no longer under the direct supervision of whites, the nation looked in 1865 at its now-large free black population in the South and wondered: Will they work to provide for themselves and their families? Will they rely on government handouts? Will they become parasites or beggars? Will a large number of them become criminals? The answers to these questions proved that the former slaves had definite ideas about how free men and women should conduct themselves.

WORKING TO PROVIDE FOR THEMSELVES
AND THEIR FAMILIES

Contrary to the belief held by most Southern whites that blacks would not work without being forced to, most freed slaves were willing under emancipation to provide for themselves and their families. The editor of a black newspaper declared in 1865 that black people need not be reminded to avoid idleness and vagrancy. After all, he concluded, "the necessity of working is perfectly understood by men who have worked all their lives." For example, at Augusta, Georgia, a convention of freedmen discountenanced vagrancy and encouraged every one of their group to obtain employment and labor honestly.[3] Blacks had established a remarkable work record under slavery, and as free men and women they were determined not to blemish that record. A resolution was passed at a convention of freedmen in Hampton, Virginia, asserting that they were capable of maintaining themselves in their new situation. They argued that any one advancing a different viewpoint was either purposely misrepresenting them or was ignorant of their capabilities.[4] Furthermore, if any class could be considered lazy, they stated, it would be the planters who had lived in idleness and on forced labor all their lives. One scholar posits that "blacks brought out of slavery a conception of themselves as a 'Working Class of People' who had been unjustly deprived of the fruits of their labor."[5]

The efforts of blacks throughout the South to secure employment during Reconstruction lends credence to their claim of being a working class of people. Of course, many toiled on farms and plantations. Some found jobs in factories and on railroads, and as janitors, porters, stevedores, tailors, longshoremen, painters, carpenters, blacksmiths, tanners, firemen, and even law enforcement officers. Others went into service, performing such tasks as washing clothes, cleaning, cooking, and sewing. Still others worked as nannies and midwives. In addition, due in large part to poverty, prostitution flourished in many of the South's towns and cities, and black as well as white women supported themselves in that way. Since prostitutes generally made more money than farm workers or domestics, they were willing to risk violence, arrest, disease, and early death. Prostitution was generally segregated but not always. For example, it was rumored that Celia Miller in Galveston, Texas, in 1867 kept a nondiscriminatory "disorderly house" where both white and black women lived and worked.[6] In general, not only were blacks working, but it also was a universal observation among Southern whites that they worked well when paid. One hotelkeeper, for instance, informed Sidney Andrews, a Northern white traveler, that he was doing well with his black labor. He asserted, "I treat 'em just as I would white men; pay them fair wages every Saturday night, give 'em good beds and a good table, and make 'em toe the mark. They know me, and I don't have the least trouble with 'em."[7]

Former slaves undertaking farm work in the South.

Courtesy of the North Carolina Division of Archives and History

The Federal government gave some help to blacks in their struggle to survive as free men and women. In March 1865, Congress created the Freedmen's Bureau to help oversee what it hoped would be the peaceful transition of blacks from slavery to freedom. The Bureau was intended to function like a primitive welfare agency, providing food and clothing to freedmen and to white refugees. It was also authorized to distribute up to forty acres of abandoned or confiscated land to black settlers and loyal white refugees and to draft and enforce labor contracts between freedmen and planters. The Bureau cooperated with the Northern voluntary associations that sent missionaries and teachers to the South to establish schools for former slaves, and it achieved a measure of success in the area of black education. Its record in other areas was mixed, however. It distributed virtually no land to former slaves. Indeed, Bureau officials would often collaborate with planters in expelling blacks from towns and cities and forcing them into signing contracts to work for their former masters.[8]

Although Southern whites accused freedmen of relying on government assistance, in some places more whites than blacks benefited from this aid. In fact, it was far more easy for whites to accept government help than it was for blacks. Many freed people, embarrassed by their needs, disdained such handouts in favor of providing for themselves if at all possible. After emancipation, needing the assistance of whites may well have been too reminiscent of the time under slavery when they had to take whatever food and clothing was allotted to them by their masters. As free men and women, they felt obliged to provide for their families and themselves to the best of their abilities. It is no wonder that Sarah Chase, a Northern white schoolteacher, wrote from Richmond in May 1865 in reference to freedmen that "most of these people will not beg." In order to bring her point home, Chase told a story about a black woman with several small children who asked her for a job: "for something, missus—anything to be earning a little something."[9] Given the fact that the Freedmen's Bureau usually would not supply rations to freedmen unless they were old or decrepit, it proved beneficial to blacks to display independence and self-reliance.

Freedmen tried to take some control of the conditions under which they labored. As free men and women, they refused to continue working in gangs under the direction of whites as they had done during slavery. They also demanded that their employers give them time off to devote to their own chores. Convinced that working at one's own pace was part of freedom, they simply would not labor as long or as hard as they had in slavery.

THE STRUGGLE TO ACQUIRE LAND

"The ex-slaves seemed to see in land ownership, the symbolic and actual fulfillment of freedom's promise," according to one contemporary historian. The slogan "forty acres and a mule" epitomized the longing of former slaves to acquire land and, through it, economic independence and the certainty that they could provide for their families.[10] Without land, most freedmen believed that they would always be slaves. One elderly freed black posed a heart-felt question to journalist Whitelaw Reid in 1865: "What's de use of being free if you don't own land enough to be buried in?" The old man then answered his question: "Might juss as well stay [a] slave all yo' days."[11] "Gib us our own land and we can take care ourselves, but widout land, de ole massas can hire us or starve us, as dey please," said one South Carolina black.[12] And a Mississippi black remarked, "All I wants is to git to own fo' or five acres ob land, dat I can build me a little house on and call my home."[13] That blacks would have a passion for the land should come as no surprise. They had worked the soil—planting, cultivating, harvesting, tending gardens—and raised livestock for generations. Like most rural people, blacks respected the land and its bounty. Although their owners legally owned the property on which slaves had their garden plots, some blacks had felt a certain proprietorship over these plots.[14] Moreover, the passion for owning a small piece of land shown by North American blacks is not unusual when compared to the experience of other postemancipation societies. In the aftermath of slavery, freedmen throughout the Western Hemisphere in Haiti, the British and Spanish Carribean, and Portuguese Brazil all saw ownership of land as crucial to ensuring their economic independence.[15]

Former slaves toiling on the land, location not known.

Courtesy of the North Carolina Division of Archives and History

In early 1865 many former slaves believed that, having set them free, the Federal government would now give them forty-acre plots taken from the plantations on which they had previously been confined. Lizzie Norfleet remembered that "the report came out after the war that every family was going to get forty acres and a mule to start them out." However, the government did not make good its promise because "I ain't never seed nobody what received nothing."[16]

Charlie Holman stated that "dey said they was gonna give us so much land an' a mule but we never did get that."[17] Sally Dixon maintained that "we was told when we got freed we was going to get forty acres of land and a mule. Stead of that we didn't get nothing."[18] Echoing similar sentiments, Berry Smith asserted, "Dere was a heap of talkin' after de war, about every nigger was goin' to git forty acres an' a mule, an' had us all fooled up, but I ain't seen my mule yit. I never did see nobody git nothin!"[19]

Why did so many former slaves expect the government to give them forty acres of land and a mule? General Oliver O. Howard, the commissioner of the Freedmen's Bureau, argued that the myth of land redistribution in the South probably arose from the wording of the law establishing the Bureau. This might have been the case, but, if so, it appears that the government purposely misled the freedmen. As noted, the Bureau was authorized to distribute up to forty acres of abandoned or confiscated land to black settlers. In General Howard's opinion, land speculators should have been blamed for spreading the rumor. The intention of the speculators, he argued, was to lower the value of the land.[20] Elizabeth Hyde Botume, a Northern white teacher among Sea Islands blacks, maintained that white and black Union soldiers convinced many freedmen that they would be given the land of their former owners.[21] Indeed, Andrew Boone recalled that "shortly after the Union troops arrived in his community . . . a story went round an' round dat de marster would have to give de slaves a mule an' a years' provisions an' some lan', about forty acres."[22] Moreover, some Southern white civilians and Confederate soldiers believed that land would be given to former slaves and thus helped spread the rumor. For example, a prominent white Georgian, James T. Ayers, wrote in his diary in early February 1865: "I really think this whole South, or that part called South Carolina with a large portion of Georgia and Florida will be gave to the niggers for a possession."[23]

Freedmen thought that they had a moral right to the land. This sentiment is expressed in a statement issued by freedmen in Virginia in protest against their removal from a contraband camp there in 1866: "We has a right to the land where we are located. Our wives, our children, our husbands, has been sold over and over again to purchase the lands we now locates upon; for that reason we have a divine right to the land. . . . And den didn't we clear the land, and raise de crops ob corn, ob cotton, ob tobacco, ob rice, ob sugar, ob everything? And den didn't dem large cities in de North grown up on de cotton and de sugar and de rice dat we made? . . . I say dey has grown rich, and my people is poor."[24]

Emancipation would usher in a new economic order as compensation for their years of involuntary work on the land, they believed. A black preacher in Florida told a group of fieldhands, "It's de white man's turn ter labor now . . . whites would no longer own all the land, fur de Gouvernment is gwine ter gie ter ev'ry nigger forty acres of lan' an' a mule."[25] One confident Georgian offered to sell to his former master his share of the plantation that he expected to receive after the Federal redistribution.[26] Eli Coleman told his reviewer in the 1930s that "it looks like the Government would have give us part of our Maser's land cause everything he had or owned the slaves made it for him."[27] Agreeing with this view, William Coleman remarked, "They should have give us part of Maser's land as us poor old slaves we made what our Masers had."[28]

While it appeared initially that the government would grant land to freed blacks in the South, for the masses of them, this never happened. As early as January 1865, General William Tecumseh Sherman responded to the large numbers of freedmen who flocked to his lines by designating all the Sea Islands south of Charleston and all abandoned rice fields along rivers up to thirty feet deep as areas for black settlement. Black families were to be settled on 40-acre plots and given "possessory title."[29] Given Sherman's negative racial attitude and the fact that he allowed his white soldiers on at least one occasion to kill black recruits, it is ironic that he would issue an order granting land to freedmen. Apparently, Sherman hoped by such an order to get rid of the thousands of blacks who followed his army, to keep black males out of the Union army, and to grievously injure the morale and material fortunes of his enemies. Southern whites, he reasoned, would be humiliated and publicly insulted by the very thought that their former slaves would own their land.[30] What could better demonstrate the powerlessness of Southern whites before their enemy?

Special Field Orders No. 15 thereafter was the principal topic of conversation in black communities throughout the South. For example, blacks in Savannah held a meeting on February 2, 1865, at the Second African Baptist Church attended by General Rufus Saxton, whom Sherman had placed in charge of the land distribution program, and his staff. The meeting attracted so much interest that the building was packed to capacity, and hundreds of freedmen were turned away. When Saxton said, "I have come to tell you what the

President of the United States has done for you," the audience responded with emotion, "God bless Massa Linkum." Hymns were sung, tears were shed, prayers and thanks were given to God, and men began preparing for a life on their own land.[31] Once assured of the legality of General Sherman's Special Field Orders No. 15, General Saxton, an assistant commissioner of the Freedmen's Bureau, proceeded to implement the Bureau's program of land redistribution. These early government policies were never carried out because President Andrew Johnson's Amnesty Proclamation of May 1865 pardoned former Confederates and restored all their property rights to them, except the right to own slaves.

In October 1865, Johnson instructed General Howard to inform Sea Islands blacks that they would have to return the land they occupied to white planters. Howard, who considered himself a friend of blacks and fully understood the importance they attached to land ownership, reluctantly obeyed Johnson's order. When he told freedmen that they must give up their land, some of them wept, protesting, "Why do you take away our lands? You take them from us who have always been true, always true to the Government! You give them to our all-time enemies! That is not right." Union soldiers forced them to leave or stay on and work for their former masters.[32] But they were not removed without a fight. Sea Islands blacks and freedmen throughout the South, determined to hold onto land whatever the cost, battled with plantation owners and local and Federal law enforcement officials. For example, a dozen or more freedmen were living on Celey Smith's farm in Elizabeth City County, Virginia, where they had built homes and were supporting themselves by their crops. They met the sheriff with loaded muskets when he came to oust them and informed him that they would "yield possession only to the U.S. Government." In spite of sheriffs, deeds, or writs, black settlers in Norfolk County, Virginia, also refused to give up their land. Ultimately, Governor Gilbert Walker instructed county officers to intervene as the freedmen fought a pitched battle with county agents until overcome by superior numbers. Moreover, near Richmond, 500 freedmen armed themselves and defied authorities to put them off the land. Federal forces forced them to vacate and then burned to the ground the houses that they had built.[33]

Although black women played a significant role in the struggle to hold onto the property of white slaveowners, it has largely gone undocumented. In South Carolina's Low Country, for instance, Charlotte and Sarah, two among more than 260 former slaves who had occupied and cultivated the Georgetown plantation Weehaw for over a year on their own, opposed the owner when he returned in 1866. Charlotte, Sarah, and Fallertree attacked him and tried to take control of the plantation. Charlotte's role in the attack must have been especially egregious, for while Sarah and Fallertree received lesser sentences, Charlotte was sentenced to thirty days in the Georgetown jail. A critical part in the defense of Keithfield plantation against restoration was also played by eight or ten freedwomen, who in March 1865 drove away the white overseer. As a consequence, the 150 freed people were able to work the plantation on their own for the remainder of the year.[34]

This luxury came to an end at the beginning of the new year, when Keithfield's absentee owner, a widow, asked a neighboring planter to help her retake control. The neighbor was no other than Francis Parker Sr., probably the white man most hated by blacks in the region. During the war, Parker had served as the local Confederate provost marshal and had helped carry out the public execution of recaptured fugitive slaves. He hired Dennis Hazel, the former slave driver, as overseer. With the employment of these two men, the potential for conflict escalated. There was absolutely no way that the freedmen and women would relinquish Keithfield without a battle, especially with Parker and Hazel as their antagonists. Thus, when Parker sent his son and Hazel to the plantation to resume control, the work gang turned their tools—"Axes hatchets hoes and poles"— into weapons and attacked Hazel, threatening to kill him.[35]

Hazel was fortunate to escape with his life but returned to the plantation a few hours later with Parker's son and two soldiers. They would have been better off not to have appeared, for the blacks assaulted them with their tools and pelted them with bricks and stones. Armed with heavy clubs, Sukey and Becky entered the fray. Aided by Jim, they exhorted their fellow laborers to join the fight, "declaring that the time was come and they must yield their lives if necessary—that a life was lost but once." Eight to ten "infuriated women" now swelled the crowd. Among this group were Charlotte Simons, Susan Lands, Clarissa Simons, Sallie Mayzck, Quahuba, and Magdalen Moultrie, armed with heavy clubs and hoes and backed by four or five men. They focused their attack on Hazel, and, as a result, the soldiers' efforts to defend the slave driver from their blows were "entirely ineffectual." The women continued to beat Hazel, Parker, and the two soldiers. Parker, followed by Hazel, made the only escape he could, by jumping into the river and swimming away "under a shower of missiles." The soldiers, bloodied and disarmed, made their own escape by foot.[36]

The incident was settled a few days later when an armed guard of U.S. soldiers arrested several of the ringleaders. Not wanting to acknowledge the leadership capabilities of women—and particularly black women—local authorities charged three of the freedmen with inciting the women to violence. Five of the women served sentences in the local jail. Although Freedmen's Bureau officials tried to play down incidents such as the one at Keithfield plantation and insisted that they were aberrations, they happened throughout the South on a frequent basis.[37] The freed blacks were determined to hold onto land that they believed rightfully belonged to them, whatever the cost. Possession of land represented economic independence.

Unfortunately for most freedmen, the Federal government would not support a full-scale plan to confiscate the land of Southern white plantation owners and redistribute it. Although some white Republicans, such as Representative Thaddeus Stevens of Pennsylvania and Senator Charles Sumner of Massachusetts, two champions of black rights, supported such a move, a majority of their party did not. Most Republicans believed that a more practical way to promote the economic interests of freedmen was through the ballot box. In their estimation, there were few things that former slaves could not accomplish with political power, and thus they concentrated most of their efforts on acquiring the vote for freedmen. Moreover, far too many Republicans, black and white, believed that the right to own property was sacred; therefore, supporting any plan to redistribute the property of Southern white plantation owners to blacks could set a dangerous precedent.[38] The *New York Times* underscored this view when it warned, "An attempt to justify the confiscation of Southern land under the pretense of doing justice to the Freedmen, strikes at the root of all property rights."[39]

Since Southern whites realized that the best course to keep freedmen in an economically dependent position was to deny them the acquisition of land, they mounted a determined campaign to make it extremely difficult for most blacks to either rent, lease, or own land. Accordingly, in 1865, Mississippi prohibited "any Freedman, Free Negro or mulatto" from renting or leasing "any land or tenements" except within the limits of "incorporated titles or towns" where local authorities could control and oversee "such rental and lease agreements."[40] Furthermore, many white landowners in various parts of the lower South refused to sell or lease them land.[41] Whitelaw Reid noted during his travels that in many sections of the Mississippi Valley if a white man or woman sold land to a black, he or she might be physically attacked. He added, "Every effort will be made" to prevent negroes from acquiring lands, "even the renting of small tracts to them is held to be unpatriotic and unworthy of a good citizen."[42] Another contemporary who toured the South noted that whites preferred to let a "no-account white man" have a plantation rather than rent it to negroes.[43] And yet another contemporary remarked, "In some parts of the country there is a social prejudice against selling to them; that is, in localities where white people prevail, they do not always like to have negroes coming among them."[44] Of course, whites were not reluctant to use force against those blacks defiant enough to attempt to either purchase or rent land. For example, in the early part of 1869, the *New Orleans Tribune* reported the murder of three black men who dared to live by themselves on rented land.[45]

In spite of these obstacles, a small number of freed people became property owners during the 1860s and the 1870s. Most accomplished this feat as a consequence of their own efforts. For example, A. M. Moore recalled that he and his brother saved their money and "bought and paid for 500 acres of land after emancipation."[46] William "Red" Taylor was able to acquire 150 acres of land through his own efforts,[47] and Tob Davis pointed out that his father went to work and "in two yeahs, he had 'nough money to pay down on a piece of land, an' weuns moves onto it."[48] In 1866, moreover, one black man in Norfolk County, Virginia, was able to purchase 1,000 acres at a total cost of $10,000; and in 1868 another black Virginian, Tom Sukins of Charlotte County, purchased 1,500 acres of farmland at $2 per acre.[49] Many former slaves pooled their meager resources and formed cooperatives. Blacks in Hampton, Virginia, established Lincoln's Land Association under the direction of a local Baptist minister and acquired several hundred acres that was worked collectively by a group of families.[50] Several freedmen in Charleston, South Carolina, formed a society for buying land and building homes of their own. At a sale they bought a plantation of 600 acres on Remley's Point, opposite the city, for which they agreed to pay $6,000 or $10 per acre.[51] In addition, several discharged black soldiers invested their bonuses and back pay individually in small farms or collectively in plantations. One regiment stationed in Louisiana accumulated $50,000 for this purpose.[52]

A few former slaves were able to acquire land through the assistance of Federal authorities and former plantation owners. Congress passed the Southern Homestead Act in 1866, which set aside land for freed persons. As a consequence, by 1869, although much of the property available was of poor quality, about 4,000 persons had applied to take advantage of the act. In an effort to guarantee a workforce and relieve themselves of some Federal taxes, a few planters divided their lands among their former slaves and gave their lifelong workers homes and a few acres for their own. The following case noted by a Freedmen's Bureau agent is an example: "Some of the old aristocratic planters are acting splendidly toward their former slaves." One rich planter who owned over 5,000 acres of land had "bestowed a certain number of acres to each of his former slaves who are now working for him."[53] Moreover, Laura Thompson recalled that "Master Strader gave our Father some land and a shack, and he farmed and gave the Master about half what he made to pay for the land."[54] Amy Else remembered that "most all the old generation stayed on and bought farms from Marster. He let them pay him out by the year."[55] An even smaller number of owners handed over land to their former slaves with no strings attached. Although his master did not give him anything when emancipation came, Lewis Mundy noted, "I remember the Bowans give their slaves eighty acres."[56] And John Sneed's mother's former master "willed every last one of his slaves something." His mother got "two cows, a pair of horses an' wagon an' 70 acres of land."[57]

A small number who had been slaves to Native Americans were able to acquire land. Treaties that the U.S. government signed with the Creeks, Cherokees, Choctaws, and Chickasaws in 1866 all had provisions regarding land for freedmen. Richard Franklin's mother, who had been a slave under the Creeks, was accorded 160 acres of land near Canada at the end of the Civil War.[58] Mollie Barber's family members, who also had been held by the Creeks, received sixty acres.[59] Chaney McNair remembered that "after the war was over we colored folks all had to go back to prove up; tell where you come from, who you belong to, you know, so we get our share of land." McNair returned to the Cherokee nation in 1866 and "drawed some money once and some land too."[60] Moreover, Irena Blocker recalled that when the McCarty family proved that Patsy Rogers and her mother had been stolen as slaves, the Choctaw Nation provided both women with forty acres and also awarded each one of their descendants forty acres.[61]

Unfortunately, some freedmen became victims of false sales. In Albemarle County, Virginia, for example, an elderly black man who could neither read nor write purchased some land and a shack from a white man, who allegedly gave the old man a deed. Not long thereafter, the county sheriff visited the black man's shack and informed him that he had to vacate the premises since the property was not legally his. The freedman implored the sheriff to examine the deed, but the "deed" read: "And as Moses lifted up the serpent in the wilderness, so have I lifted fifty dollars out of this old nigger's pocket."[62] Jack and Rosa Maddox bought a piece of land and were doing well for three years. However, upon the death of the man who had owned it, "We found out the place didn't b'long to us. The children of the first wife of the man who sold us the land took it away from us."[63]

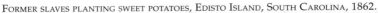

Former slaves planting sweet potatoes, Edisto Island, South Carolina, 1862.

Courtesy of the North Carolina Division of Archives and History

Although the masses of former slaves in rural and urban areas of the Deep South remained landless, there was an increase in the number of black landowners. The value of their holdings also increased significantly after the war. Blacks accomplished this remarkable feat despite the generally hostile attitudes of whites, the rise of the Ku Klux Klan and other terrorist groups, and the refusal of some whites to sell them land. It is also significant because it took place despite economic problems such as general indebtedness among freedmen, scarcity of money and capital, and "unsettled conditions."[64]

Since most freedmen lacked the resources to buy even a small farm or a town lot, the vast majority of them found it easier to acquire a few personal items. Black men and women purchased horses, mules, cattle, wagons, carts, plows, machinery, tools, furniture, and clothing, and sometimes carriages, watches, and jewelry. In 1865 in Augusta, Georgia, one observer was surprised to discover that freedmen and women were anxious to begin the ascent toward property ownership: "A Government sale of horses and mules brought large numbers to the city to-day." He went on to point out that freedmen comprised about two-thirds of the 10,000 persons who attended, and they bought a good deal of property at this sale. Mississippi and Georgia, the two Deep South states with the largest antebellum slave (and among the smallest free black) population, led all states in the total number of property owners by 1870. Mississippi had 23,665, and Georgia had 17,739. Some 63,846 freedmen and women had become property owners in the other states of the Lower South with $100 worth or more, for a regional total of one family in five.[65]

EFFORTS TO ACHIEVE ECONOMIC SECURITY

Believing that they held the key to their own economic progress, freedmen in large numbers invested their savings in the Freedmen's Savings Bank when it was established during the early years of Reconstruction. On March 3, 1865, Congress passed a law creating the National Freedmen's Savings and Trust Company whose function was "to receive on deposit such sums of money as may . . . be offered . . . by or on behalf of persons heretofore held in slavery in the United States, or their descendants, and investing the same in the stocks, bonds, Treasury notes and other securities of the United States." Those who created the institution hoped that it would do for the freedmen "that which savings banks have done for the workingmen of the North."[66] Throughout the South, blacks began to deposit their money—often brought in bundles of paper, rags, and old stockings—in the various local branches.[67] Many thought that if they put their money in the bank, they would show whites that blacks were thrifty and industrious and not lazy. Moreover, they were adamant in their support of the bank, believing that it was the duty of every black person who had a dollar to spare to deposit it because the bank was doing much to advance the cause of black people. The Freedmen's Savings Bank was a morale booster and a source of inspiration for blacks. The distinguished and much-admired Frederick Douglass was at one time president of the national branch. Whenever former slaves went into a local Freedmen's Bank, they would see finely dressed blacks working as tellers.

Freed blacks struggled against great odds to save money and deposit it in the Freedmen's Savings Bank. A reporter for the *New York Tribune* told his readers: "I know of one colored washerwoman, who has a family to support, that has in one of these banks over $260 in gold and silver. I know an old black man—all his life a slave—who deposited at one time, soon after the branch was established, $380 in gold and silver. He said he earned it while a slave by working at night by the light of a pine-torch, after he had done all the overseer demanded of him." Another freedman brought $700 in gold to deposit, which he had kept concealed for twelve years. But large deposits were rare. Most freedmen had very little money. What was important to many of the poor, however, according to one scholar, "was the idea of saving toward a better life." Having a savings account meant freedom and advancement, a chance to "get on in the world."[68] Louisa Anderson, a thirty-five-year-old former slave and widow with three children, managed to save $16 from her meager earnings as a servant. An illiterate teamster named Oscar Gibbs, who guessed his age as between thirty and forty and had to provide for a family of nine, had a bank account, although it contained only $4.50. One depositor later recalled: "I can remember that I used to walk up to the bank and put in the few pennies that I could scrape together." Indeed, freedmen saved money by the penny, nickel, and dime—the average amount deposited at one of the 890 branches in July 1874 was only ninety-two cents. These small sums should not be dismissed too lightly. In 1869 the average wage for a farm laborer was $15.50 per month. In 1870, $60 would buy several acres of land, three head of cattle, or ten hogs. It might represent one-third of a farm laborer's yearly income, excluding board.[69]

Freedmen used the wealth acquired through savings to engage in business as individuals and as groups. Mary Barbour's father was a successful shoemaker after the war near New Bern, North Carolina.[70] Blacks organized the Chesapeake Marine Railroad and Dry Dock Company in Baltimore, Maryland, in 1865. It would remain in operation until 1883, providing employment for over 300 black mechanics. Its success was due, in no small part, to the skillful leadership of Isaac Myers. The company was founded as a consequence of the pressure placed upon black caulkers by white caulkers. Due to either unfair competitive methods, prejudice, or force, blacks were driven out of the shipyards. Fortunately for black carpenters, the white carpenters finally agreed among themselves not to work in those yards where black carpenters were employed. The result was the organization of a shipyard owned and controlled by freedmen where their fellow workmen might labor. Railways were built, and furnaces and workshops were erected. Now, the black carpenters and caulkers could begin their work.[71]

Not to be outdone, some freedwomen also became entrepreneurs. They ran boardinghouses and opened restaurants and grocery stores. Hager Ann Baker, for example, a waitress during slavery, opened a grocery store in Savannah after the Civil War.[72] Another Georgian, Annie L. Burton, was a domestic in the North when her sister died and left an eleven-year-old son. In an effort to start a new life, Burton and the youth moved to Green Cove Springs, Florida. "My idea was to get a place as chambermaid at Green Cove Springs through the influence of the head waiter at a hotel there, whom I knew. After I got into Jacksonville, the idea of keeping a restaurant came to me. I found a little house of two rooms where we could live, and the next day I found a place to start my restaurant." It was nothing fancy. Burton purchased a stove and then secured second-hand furniture and other things she needed from a dealer.[73] In Dallas County, Texas, Jane Johnson Calloway, who had been a slave, opened one of the county's largest and most profitable coal businesses.[74]

Unfortunately, a number of these black businesses folded. For a people only recently freed from slavery and desirous of demonstrating their thrift to whites and serving as role models for young blacks, failure sometimes proved devastating. Of course, since most freedmen had little business experience, they fell prey to unscrupulous promoters. At Savannah, for example, $50,000 was invested in a venture that proved worthless, and $40,000 was invested in a land and lumber enterprise that failed.[75]

Labor unions were another means to obtain economic advancement. Former slaves, once organized, could use their near-monopoly over certain trades to force concessions from employers. Even before the longshoremen, destined to become the most powerful black union in Charleston, organized officially in late 1868, they had already engaged in two successful strikes.[76] Other black urban laborers such as the stevedores in Richmond, longshoremen in New Orleans, stevedores in Savannah, mechanics in Columbus, coopers in Richmond, and unskilled dockworkers in New Orleans also struck for higher wages.[77] In most cases, however, a combination of an overabundance of labor, a lack of black-and-white labor solidarity, and the use of law enforcement officials against strikers contributed to the failure of strikes. For example, in Richmond, despite community support, black stevedores and coopers' strikes failed in April and May 1867 because strikebreakers were found among the large number of unemployed blacks and whites.[78] In December 1865 black and white dockworkers in New Orleans struck for higher wages. In this case, black-and-white labor solidarity would not become a reality. White crewmen marched along the levee, "knocking down every black man who would have gladly worked for less than that high tariff," the black *Tribune* reported. White workers repeatedly drove off a number of freedmen toiling along the docks at the lower rate with threats and assaults. When it became obvious that the shipmasters intended to request Federal military protection for black strikebreakers, white workers grew alarmed and began to fraternize with blacks in an effort to get them to not work. Their actions were not sincere, for they had no intention of promoting solidarity with black workers. When police were called in to quell the disturbances, they generally targeted black strikers and let white strikers do as they pleased. Thus, police arrested six blacks but allowed several hundred whites to parade along the levee for several hours.[79]

That black dockworkers failed in their bid for higher wages and white dockworkers succeeded illustrates not only the sharp limits of interracial collaboration but also the distinct positions occupied by blacks and whites in the waterfront's occupational hierarchy. Unskilled blacks were easily replaced; all it took was police protection of strikebreakers. Consequently, black dockworkers were forced to return to the job at their original wage of $2.50. By contrast, skilled white crewmen eventually won their wage demands of $6 for gang members and $7 for foremen per day. Despite the failure of black dockworkers to secure their wage increase, they did succeed in imposing a greater degree of order upon the chaotic system of employment and payment by May 1867.[80]

Black women throughout the South were also cognizant of the value of their labor and refused to work for unfair wages without protest. For example, washerwomen in Jackson, Mississippi, struck for higher wages in June 1866. They requested $1.50 per day, $15.00 per month for family wash, and $10.00 per month for individuals.[81] Whether or not the strike was successful is not known. In the summer of 1877 twenty-five black laundresses struck for higher wages in Galveston, Texas. They marched through downtown Galveston demanding $1.50 per day and shutting down steam and Chinese laundries. Crying out, "We will starve no longer," they insisted that other laundresses stay away from work. The women caught a Miss Murphy and carried her out into the street when she insisted on going to work anyway, and they tore off the clothes of Alice because they thought that she had "gone back on them." Moreover, the black laundresses locked up Mr. Harding's laundry and demanded that Chinese owners "close up and leave this city within Fifteen days, or they would be driven away."[82]

The failure of many labor strikes by blacks must be placed in the proper historical context. Their failure reflected a national trend. Strikes throughout the nation were largely unsuccessful, particularly in the last three decades of the nineteenth century. The influence of management was growing while the influence of labor was steadily declining. Both black and white workers held little clout in a country ravaged by depression, where work was often difficult to find and labor was overabundant. After the Panic of 1873, union membership fell nationwide by 90 percent, and by 1880 fewer than one in one hundred workers belonged to a union.[83] Once Radical Republicans were driven from power in the South, the threat of any significant labor strike succeeding all but vanished. Political support from conservative legislators now reinforced the control that industry had over labor. Law enforcement officials were used in ever-increasing numbers to protect strikebreakers and quell labor disturbances.

Forming labor unions and engaging in strikes was just one of many battles that blacks would have to wage. To escape the racism and racial discrimination of Southern whites and provide better social and economic opportunities for themselves, some blacks in the closing years of Reconstruction either migrated to the West and Southwest or emigrated to Africa. Three of the best-known black proponents of emigrationist movements in the late 1870s were Benjamin "Pap" Singleton, Henry Adams, and Bishop Henry M. Turner.[84] However, before this time, some blacks were already living in the West and Southwest, having moved to these areas either before or during the early years of Reconstruction. In these regions, black men found employment as railroad workers and miners. In San Francisco, black men who often were young and single worked as sailors and railroad laborers. Other black men joined cattle drives in Kansas, Texas, and Oklahoma as cooks and cowboys. Nat Love, for example, earned the nickname "Deadwood Dick" by winning a roping contest in Deadwood, Arizona. Still other black men in the West became farmers, taking advantage of the Homestead Act, which offered free land to those who agreed to cultivate it. Although it was difficult for black women in western cities to find employment other than domestic work, some secured jobs as laundresses.[85]

Not only did black men and women in the West demonstrate a great deal of determination to prosper, but some also succeeded. For instance, in 1865, blacks in San Francisco owned tobacco and soap factories as well as laundries and real estate offices. A small number of mining companies, such as the Colored Citizens of California, were organized by black men. In Nevada, Montana, Colorado, and Utah a

few blacks owned silver mines. In addition, as a result of her thrifti-
ness, Clara Brown, who cooked and washed for miners, became the
first black member of the Colorado Pioneer Association in 1870.[86]
Anna Graham ran a successful beauty parlor in Virginia City, Nevada. And Sarah Miner built her deceased husband's express and
furniture-hauling venture into a successful business.[87]

THE TRIALS OF THE BUFFALO SOLDIERS

The vast majority of black men who enlisted in the U.S. Army
went to the West and Southwest to serve in the many military campaigns against Native Americans. Black men were attracted to the
army for many reasons. Regimental chaplains usually taught the soldiers, who displayed a keen desire for education, to read and write.
The military also provided one of the few semblances of equality for
blacks, since the prosperity of the post-Civil War years did not otherwise extend to them. It also represented a steady job in an overabundant labor market. The package deal for a recruit included food,
clothing, shelter, and salary, with an annual increase of one dollar
per month and a reenlistment bonus at the end of five years. While
black regiments had more applicants than positions available, white
regiments had difficulty in finding and retaining volunteers. Moreover, as noted earlier, black volunteers viewed military service as an
elevation in status and an opportunity to improve themselves.[88] In
fact, lithographs of black soldiers in action often hung in the homes
of blacks as "symbols of hope for a better day." Indeed, historian
Rayford Logan captured the feelings of most blacks toward soldiers
from their own community when he said, "We Negroes had little, at
the turn of the century, to help sustain our faith in ourselves except
the pride that we took in the Ninth and Tenth Cavalry, the Twenty-
fourth and Twenty-fifth Infantry."[89]

Black soldiers participating in the military campaigns in the West
and Southwest against Native Americans numbered 12,500, about
20 percent of the total of U.S. soldiers deployed in these areas.[90] Yet,
until recently, very little was known about these men. Throughout
the latter half of the twentieth century, Hollywood produced one
movie after another on soldiers who fought Native Americans in the
post-Civil War period without devoting much attention to the role of
black soldiers. For better or worse, black soldiers played an integral
role in winning the West for America. Although black soldiers were
involved in their share of Native American firefights between the
late 1860s and World War I, much of their duty in the West revolved

around the mundane and the unglamorous. They built telegraph lines, escorted stagecoaches and government supply trains, protected supply lines, and chased bandits and hooligans.[91]

These black soldiers came to be called "Buffalo Soldiers," a name given to them by Native Americans. Why Native Americans gave them this name is unclear. Perhaps it was due to their tenacity in battle,[92] since buffaloes were regarded as tough and nearly impossible to subdue. It also may have been the similarity between the curly black hair of blacks and that of the buffalo or the dark brown skin of both.[93] Whatever the reason, black soldiers, appreciating the comparison to the stoic animals considered sacred by the Native Americans, adopted the name. The Tenth Cavalry even added the image of a buffalo to their unit insignia.[94]

The Ninth and Tenth Cavalry and the Twenty-fourth and Twenty-fifth Infantry served throughout the West and Southwest against Native Americans for twenty-eight years. More than two hundred battles and skirmishes were fought by these regiments during that period. The Buffalo Soldiers won fourteen Congressional Medals of Honor, nine Certificates of Merit, and twenty-nine Orders of Honorable Mention between 1870 and 1890.[95] Sergeant Emanuel Stance, a native of Charleston, barely five feet tall, became the first black to earn a Medal of Honor in the Native American wars in May 1870.[96]

In spite of the military accomplishments of the Buffalo Soldiers, they were regularly subjected to white racism and racial discrimination by U.S. Army officers. Not only were they forced to live and work in separate quarters, but they also had to endure inferior quarters, inferior food, inferior clothing, and even inferior leadership and training. An inspector at Fort Clark in Texas in 1872 wrote of the conditions that black soldiers there were being forced to endure: "The quarters are wretchedly [constructed]. All except two companies of cavalry are in huts." He added that the officers' quarters were also inadequate, "the guard house is cramped: the regimental Adjutant's office is in a tent. There is no place for divine service or instruction." The situation was even worse for those units on the move, as in the case of a black infantry regiment serving on the Mexican border in Texas, which had not slept under a roof for several years. It was customary for commanders at military installations to force black units traveling on assignments throughout the West to sleep outside the fort's walls if segregated facilities were not available inside.[97] Their obvious vulnerability to Native American attacks while they slept apparently did not concern most army officials.

The Buffalo Soldiers not only had to contend with the racial discrimination of army officials but also with civilian hostility toward them in the towns and territories to which they were assigned. Notwithstanding the fact that they were protecting the settlements, black soldiers could not depend on equal justice from white sheriffs. Local police sometimes targeted black soldiers suspected of some violation and subjected them to unrestrained abuse. Adam Paine, a black Seminole scout and Medal of Honor winner, for example, in January 1877 was shot from behind and killed by a Texas sheriff.[98]

Despite racism and racial discrimination, the Buffalo Soldiers amassed an impressive record of service. Their desertion rate was the lowest in the frontier army although their posts were often in the most godforsaken places. In the post-Civil War era, more than one-third of white enlisted men went AWOL each year. The white Seventh Cavalry in 1876, for example, had seventy-two deserters, the Third had 170, and the Fifth had 224, but the black Ninth only had six deserters and the Tenth eighteen.[99] Moreover, although alcoholism was often a problem among white soldiers, black soldiers escaped chronic alcoholism, "the scourge of the West."[100] Many factors contributed to the superior morale and performance of the black regiments. As had been the case with black Civil War troops, the Buffalo Soldiers regarded themselves as representatives of an entire race whose performance would determine its future treatment both in and outside the military. Many were determined not to confirm whites' negative perceptions of them as shifty, lazy, cowardly, undisciplined, and prone to alcoholism. Furthermore, given the fact that a black deserter would stand out anywhere he went in the predominantly white Western territories, his color would limit the likelihood of desertion.[101] And, certainly, a black soldier roaming alone would be vulnerable to a white population that was racist and had no love for blacks.

The fact that the Buffalo Soldiers helped subjugate Native Americans while their own people were being oppressed in American society is a tragic irony. It is all but certain that some of the Buffalo Soldiers were aware of this contradiction and concerned about it. In order to decipher the magnitude of their concern, however, more in-depth studies of Buffalo Soldiers are necessary. At this time, the literature seems to suggest that most black soldiers agreed with the U.S. government's genocidal policies toward Native Americans, for they carried out their orders.[102] To many blacks, fighting Native Americans was simply a job—one that they were determined to do to the best of their ability.

African Americans did all they could to carve out a place in American society and to build an economic foundation. Contrary to the claims of many Southern whites, freedmen and women worked at whatever jobs they could find to provide for themselves and their families. Believing that property ownership represented economic independence, many blacks struggled tenaciously to acquire land. To improve their economic situation, they formed labor unions, engaged in strikes, and migrated to points North and West;[103] some even emigrated to Africa. That they failed to accomplish their objective in large measure is not due to a lack of effort on their part. They simply could not overcome the huge obstacles placed in the way of a "Working Class of People."

CHAPTER FIVE

"WE CAN NOW LIVE AS ONE"
The Reunification of the Family

THE BLACK FAMILY was vulnerable to disruption during slavery, but strong family ties existed nonetheless. Slaves fervently believed in the sanctity of the marriages that regularly took place among them. And although these marriages were not recognized by the state, they were sometimes sanctioned by owners who reasoned that these unions would make their slaves less likely to run away. The owners, however, broke up families at their own discretion. The grief and pain caused by forced separations were much more than any human ought to have to endure. Edwin Walker recalled a relatively peaceful family life "till one day Sis Julia wuz sole away from us. Her new Mars' took her plum off to South Carolina away from us an' her husband. We mourned an' grieved fer her."[1] On the auction block, slaves cried out in anguish at witnessing the sale and separation of family members. James Brown asserted, "Ise see dem cry like deys am at de fune'al whens de am parted, dey has to drag dem away."[2] "When one of them buyers bought a slave you never did hear such bawling and hollering in your life that would take place because they did not want to leave each other," explained Dave Byrd.[3] Similarly, when Charlie Cooper observed several slaves being auctioned, he noted, "when they put them on the auction block you never heard such bawling and going on in your life. For 3 or 4 days they would bawl like a cow does when she is in a strange place."[4]

Northern white travelers' accounts of the trauma experienced at the auction blocks are even more graphic than those given by former slaves. One contemporary recorded a scene in which a slave girl named Lucy was sold as her mother stood by, brokenhearted, "with tears streaming down her face." At the same auction, Harry, a fifteen-year-old lad, was sold while his mother was waiting for her turn. When she realized that Harry had been sold, she began to scream, "O, my child! my Child!" Her irritated slaveholder warned her, "Ah, my girl! if you do not stop that hollering, I will give you something to holler for." The mother's efforts to suppress her grief proved fruitless. As Harry left with his new owner, the children cried out, "Good by, Harry, good by." His mother joined in, sobbing, "Farewell, my boy, try to meet me in heaven."[5] Another contemporary recorded a scene in which a white minister bought the mother of a young slave girl. "With eyes swimming in tears, and with loud, dolorous heart-rending cries, she approached the minister who had bought her mother and said, 'pray, massa, please do, massa, buy me too.' " Although he was touched by her cries and tears, the reverend replied, "I can't buy you, I am not able to keep you both."[6] Their only solace was one final embrace before they parted.

The psychological and emotional toll of forced separation was high. For example, Elizabeth Hyde Botume, who taught slaves to read and write on the Sea Islands of South Carolina, came across one young slave woman whom forced separation had psychologically and emotionally damaged. Botume described the woman as the "saddest person I ever saw," who always kept to herself. Initially, she had been sold to a trader to pay a gambling debt; then she was sold to her third owner and was forced to leave her child behind in Virginia. As a result, she told Botume, "I cannot sleep nights. Every time I shut my eyes I hear my baby cry, 'Take me wid you, mammy, take me wid you!' " In despair, the woman continued, "I put my fingers in my ears, but all the time I hear him just the same, crying, 'Take me wid you, mammy, take me wid you!' "[7]

THE IMPORTANCE OF MARRIAGE AMONG SLAVES

In most instances, the wedding of slaves would be simple, particularly when field hands were involved. On plantations where there were overseers or strict masters, the ceremony would be held before or after work or at noon in the row of slave cabins at the home of the bride. All would walk in, the bride and bridegroom in the center, with their attendants close beside them. Very solemnly someone would lay a broomstick across the middle of the floor. Arm in arm the two would step across, and that was all there was to it. Ella Booth remembered, "When my mammy and daddy got married, dey jest 'jumped over de broom'—den dey wuz married."[8] When an interviewer in the 1930s asked Rena Clark how slaves were married, she responded, "Dey just jumped over de broom stick and some of dem didn't have dat much ceremony."[9] Henry Lewis McGaffey noted, "I seed Marse marry his slaves an' all I seed wus he wud hold a straw broom out an' make dem jump over it frontward an' den backward, an' sed dey was married."[10] Similarly, Cynthia Erwing recalled, "Ol' Marster would make them jump over a broom stick, and then they would be married."[11]

Weddings of house slaves were sometimes more elaborate than those of field hands. Although house slaves also customarily jumped over the broom, a much larger number of them were married by either black or white preachers. James Bolton remembered, "Effen the slaves gittin' mahied was house servants sometimes they mahied on the back porch or in the back yahd at the big 'ouse." However, with respect to "plantation niggers," Bolton said, "whut was fiel' hands, mahied in their own cabins. The bride an' groom jes' wo' plain cloes, kyazen ['cause] they diden' have no mo!"[12] Squire Irvin also recalled field slave couples getting married in "them pretty colored clothes," and house slave couples dressing more elegantly for their ceremony, with the brides being "given lilly white dresses to wear."[13]

Various accounts of weddings of house slaves told by Northern white travelers and former slaves demonstrate the detailed nature of these ceremonies. Fredrika Bremer was invited to attend the weddings of two couples of house slaves owned by a white professor. She described both brides as being fashionably dressed in white, with beautiful bouquets. The preacher married both couples, and dancing followed. Bremer was impressed by the attire of the black women at the weddings, who were "dressed and decked out in gauze and flowers, altogether like our ladies." She also found the dinner table to be so splendidly covered with flowers, fine cakes, and an abundance of meats that it seemed almost to bend under the weight.[14] Henry Lewis vividly recounted his wedding several years later: "I had a nice hat and a nice suit of black close," and his bride was dressed in white. His father, a shoemaker, made him a pair of new shoes. He and his bride were married by a white preacher. There were some whites in attendance, and "some of 'em give us presents and some give us money."[15] Phoebe Henderson and her bridegroom had "de weddin' dere in de house." They were married by a black Baptist preacher. Phoebe wore a white cotton dress. As wedding gifts, her mistress gave her a pan of flour and her master gave the couple a house of their own.[16]

The wedding of Tempie Durham was no doubt one of the most elaborate involving a slave couple. Tempie and her bridegroom were married on the front porch of the big house. Her master killed a shoat for the event, and her mistress had the cook prepare a large wedding cake, "all iced up white as snow wid a bride an' groom standin in de middle holdin' hands. De table was set out in de yard under the trees,

an' you ain't never seed de like of eats." With delight, Tempie recalled that she "had on a white dress, white shoes, an' long white
gloves dat come to my elbows, an' Mis' Betsy done made me a
weddin' veil out of a white net window curtain." They were married
by the black preacher from the plantation church. The newlyweds
spent a one-day honeymoon in a cabin that Tempie's mistress had
decorated.[17]

That slaveowners would sometimes exhibit favoritism toward
their house slaves is not surprising. A disproportionate number of
these slaves were mulattoes, many of whom were related by blood to
their owners. As such, they often were emancipated in larger numbers than their brothers and sisters of a darker hue, and sometimes
their white fathers would leave them property in their wills. Bestow-
ing better treatment on house slaves, as was the case with respect to
wedding ceremonies, could also have the advantage of dividing the
slave population, thereby making it easier to control.

Most slaves esteemed their marriages even if the unions were
not recognized by the state. For example, Jennie Hill, a freedwoman
from Missouri, declared: "I was proud of my marriage, performed
by the 'educated nigger' and I sure got mad when anybody said anything about us not being married."[18] The vast majority of husbands
and wives were loyal to each other and demonstrated a fierce attachment to family. Millie Ann Smith's father belonged to a different
master in Mississippi than did his wife and three children. When his
family's master moved them to Texas, Smith remembered, "Pappy
run off and come to Texas and begged master into buying him so he
could be with his wife and chil'ren."[19] When some fathers were sold
away from their wives and children, the experience was so painful
that it was almost unbearable. When Hannah Chapman's father was
sold away from them, she recalled, "My pa sho' did hate ter leave us.
He would often slip back ter us' cottage at nite." His affectionate
children would crawl onto his lap. But he paid a heavy price for it.
"When his Mars missed him he would beat him all de way home,"
Chapman maintained. "Us could track him de nex' day by de blood
stains."[20]

Because of their devotion to family, some escaped slaves who were
able to live as free individuals put themselves back in bondage. For
instance, Wash Ingram's father escaped from a plantation in Richmond and secured work in a gold mine. Freedom was sweet as long
as his family remained in the vicinity. However, his wife died. When
he heard of his three sons' master's plan to sell them to a planter in
Texas, he became distraught. Ingram overtook them before they

reached Texas and put himself back in bondage alongside his sons under their new master, Jim Ingram. Wash's father simply could not stand the thought of being separated from his children.[21]

Not all slave husbands and wives were faithful. Some took advantage of the lax rules governing marital relations. Former slaves tell of semi-legendary "travellin' men," "married" to several women, each on a different plantation. Israel Massie remembers adventurous Tom, who died "befo' he oughter." It seems that "Tom woulda been in a mess of trouble, ef he'd lived. But he died. An' dere come to mourn over his grave four women, Jenny, Sarah, Nancy, and Patience, all four of 'em his wives an' cryin' over dat one man. Do you know, chile, dem women never fought, fuss, or quarrel over who was de true wife of dat man? Guess dat was because he was daid, but dey walk way fum de grave together jus like dey was sisters. Yes, Sir."[22]

LEGALIZATION OF MARRIAGE BONDS
AFTER EMANCIPATION

Once blacks acquired freedom, they were able to affirm and solidify their family connections. Former slaves in contraband camps moved eagerly to legalize marriage bonds. In fact, as early as September 1861, the demand to legalize their marriages was so great among black contrabands at Fortress Monroe that the Reverend Lewis G. Lockwood felt compelled to perform mass marriages for hundreds of blacks.[23] When the Freedmen's Bureau and state governments made it possible to register and formalize slave marriages, blacks would still continue to hold mass marriage ceremonies. General Howard, the general superintendent of the Freedmen's Bureau, boasted to Whitelaw Reid, a Northern correspondent, that weddings among blacks at Beaufort, South Carolina, occurred on a frequent basis. After spending some time in Beaufort, Reid reached the conclusion that the superintendent had not made an idle boast, and he acknowledged that "scarcely a Sunday passes without a marriage."[24] An army chaplain, A. B. Randall, attached to a regiment of black soldiers in Arkansas, reported that he spent much of his time conducting marriage ceremonies among blacks in the area. Randall wrote, "Weddings, just now, are very popular, and abundant among the Colored People. I have married, during the month, at this post, twenty-five couples; mostly, those, who have families, and have been living together for years."[25] J. R. Johnson, a Freedmen's Bureau superintendent of marriages working among blacks in northern

Virginia, recorded similar activity. In a one-month period, he gave out fifteen marriage certificates but seemed disappointed in his work: "Nearly three weeks of sickness prevented me from accomplishing more." Once he recovered, however, he reported, "Yesterday, 31st of May, we gave seventy-nine certificates in Freedmen's Village."[26]

Some of the black couples married on the spur of the moment. Elizabeth Botume, for example, reported from Beaufort that on "one evening four couples came to the schoolhouse to meet 'the parson' who was to perform the marriage ceremony for them." They came straight from the field, "in their working-clothes," she noted.[27] Hattie Austin remembered little or no planning going into her and James Austin's wedding. According to her, "Jim was wukkin' in' come in from d' turpentine wuks. I was cookin' 'n' cleanin', 'n' d' preacher come t' d' house, 'n' us jis' stan up 'n' git marry. Us didn't tek no time t' dress."[28] When Frank Ziegler and his future bride decided to "get hitched," they started out to find a preacher. When they found one, they were married right there in the middle of the road.[29] Similarly, Anna Lee's future husband picked her up on a horse, "and away he went to the preachers and we were married."[30] Orris Harris recalled, "Sam just got de papers en we went to de parson en got married, en dat wus all."[31]

Despite the simple weddings of some blacks, most spent time preparing for the ceremony. Whether they were married at someone's house or in a church, a minister usually performed the service. Much attention was devoted to the clothes worn by the bride and bridegroom. After the wedding, a huge feast would take place, along with music and dancing, that might continue for days and nights. The wedding of Austin Grant and his fiancée is fairly typical. Grant wore a black suit with a nice shirt and a good pair of boots, and his bride wore a pretty white dress. They were married at her house at about seven o'clock in the evening. Shortly thereafter, the eating and dancing commenced. Grant asserted, "Yes 'm, they had a dance. Danced about half the night at her house. . . . Eat? My God, we had everything to eat. Barbecued a calf and a hog too! All kinds of cakes and pies. The men had whiskey to drink and the women drank coffee."[32]

Apparently, some blacks did not grasp when it was time to stop celebrating. For example, when Charlie Sandles and his bride returned home from their wedding, nearly every black person in the vicinity was waiting for them at their house. They had an abundance of food and whiskey and were already eating, drinking, and dancing. Sandles recalled, "Boy oh boy, did we have a time. It lasted us about a month. I've done plum wore out before it was over."[33] Perhaps one of the most elaborate ceremonies held by freedmen was that of Harriet Jones and her bridegroom, who were married under a big elm tree at the house of Jones's former owner. The wedding party included nicely dressed flower girls. As for Jones's attire, "I has on one of my mistis dresses wid a long tram, hit is a white dress an I wear a red sash an' a big bow in de back, den I has on red stockings an a pair of bran new shoes, an a big wide brim hat." The dinner table was laden with barbecued pork, roast sweet potatoes, dumplings, pies, and cakes. Once the large crowd had finished eating, they were ready to dance all night.[34]

Regardless of whether the ceremonies of blacks were simple or elaborate, most were proud of their newly official status. Elizabeth Botume, for example, reported the case of Smart and Mary Washington, who had lived together for over forty years. They were among the first persons to come forward to be married. According to Botume, "They were very happy when they walked away together side by side, for the first time endowed with the honorable title of husband and wife."[35] One freedwoman was so excited about marrying a soldier that "when the minister asked [the groom] if he would have this woman to be his wife, she hastily exclaimed, 'Oh! Yes, massa, I'll be his wife.' And when the irrevocable words were said, the huge veil disappeared with wondrous rapidity before the ardor of the kiss."[36] Marie Aurelia Green boasted, "Dey got my marriage license dere in de chu'ch. You find my name in de big book dere, and at de white house in Washington, D.C."[37]

Many of the former slaves who renewed their vows and those who married for the first time remained together for years. Among these were Israel Jefferson of Virginia, who was married for about thirty-five years;[38] Elbert Head of Georgia, for over forty years until his wife's death;[39] and Cato Carter of Alabama, for forty-seven years until his wife's death. The Carters had thirteen children.[40] Moreover, several marriages lasted well over fifty years. For example, Carey Davenport was married for more than sixty years;[41] Sarah Felder, for about fifty-nine years;[42] Henrietta Gooch, for fifty-seven years;[43] and Wesley Burrell, for fifty-three years until the death of his wife.[44] Numerous children were usually born to these unions.

While many blacks remained married for years, others were married numerous times. Some of these unions were also of short duration and painful. Elsie Ross remembered, "I married a low, no 'count nigger and I don't want to talk about him. I dunno why I evah picked him. I wuz crazy at de time, I guess, and thought dat I wuz in love." She lived with him for about one year, but when he beat her, Elsie

An unidentified black couple during Reconstruction.

Courtesy of the North Carolina Division of Archives and History

"left him on de spot." She never returned to live with him, nor did she marry another man.[45] Similarly, Manda Boggan "uped an' married de sorriest nigger in de whole county." Once he died, she made the mistake of marrying "another nigger who turnt out ter be as sorry as de fust one."[46] Betty Bormer separated from her first husband after five years. She waited twelve years to remarry but then had even worse luck than the first time, for she and her husband separated after only two years. However, persistency paid off. Betty married a third time, and this marriage lasted forty-one years.[47] In reference to her first husband, Annie Coley remarked, "Dat wus the meanest niggah dat ever lived. He would slip up behin' me when I was wukin' in the fiel' an beat me." Annie left him and took her three children to live with her brother. She remained single for a long time but then made the mistake of marrying Charlie Ashmore, "a mean niggah too." After twelve years, Ashmore left her and went to Georgia. However, for Annie, as for Betty Bormer, the third time was the charm. Annie eventually settled into a lasting union with Harry Coley.[48] Sadly, Malindy Smith was even less fortunate than either Bormer or Coley. With much bitterness on the question of marriage, she informed her interviewer, "I's been married four times an separated from all four my husbands. De Devil owed me a debt an paid it off in sorry men. They was so mean to me I couldn't stay with 'em."[49]

Although the vast majority of marital problems occurred because some couples were not compatible, other problems developed due to the failure of some husbands and wives to grasp the real nature of marriage in the early years of freedom. For example, a young couple in Beaufort, South Carolina, went to Chaplain Woodworth, who married them. The groom paid his dollar and got his certificate. How-

ever, only a day or two later, the groom returned, apparently disappointed. He demanded that the chaplain take back the certificate and
give back his dollar, " 'cause he didn't like that woman nohow." When
the chaplain told him that he could not back out and must stick to his
bargain, the man was dumbfounded. In another case, Woodworth
married Mingo and Rachel. It was not long before a concerned Mingo
returned to his office and informed the chaplain that "I want either a
paper to make her come and lib wid me, or to have her pit in jail, or
I wants a pass to marry another wife." When the chaplain asked which
he would prefer, Mingo replied, "Well, you might as well give me
the pass, I reckon." An exasperated Mingo was told that he must go
to the Freedmen's Bureau to get the affair settled.[50] Also, when Mary
Gladdy's grandfather got mad at his wife, he "picked up his feather
bed and toted it all the way from Macon to Lochapoka!" He then told
everyone that "he was done with grandma and was going to live
with [his son] Adam." After only a few weeks, he returned home,
"still toting his feather bed."[51]

Although most freedmen rushed to renew their marital vows,
some instead used the situation to rid themselves of unwanted
spouses. The parents of Mollie Dawson of Tennessee, for example,
separated soon after emancipation, and both married other partners.[52]
George Weathersby recalled, "After de surrender my pa and ma never
tried to live together no mo."[53] "De day when freedom rung out, our
pappy went one way, and our mammy went another way,"[54] Mattie
Williams remembered. When Primus Magee's father found out that
couples who had been married as slaves had to get a license for the
marriage to be considered legal after emancipation, he refused to remarry the woman he had taken in slavery. Furthermore, according to
Magee, "a heap ob 'em quit dat way. I reckon they felt free sho' nuf,
as dey wuz freed from slavery an' from marriage."[55]

Some couples were so determined to separate that not even preg-
nancy or the possibility of a nasty custody battle could prevent them
from doing so. Despite the fact that Rose Williams was pregnant, she
left Rufus, her husband, immediately after freedom. When she was
asked if she ever remarried, Rose replied, "Never! No sar! One
'sperience am 'nough fo' dis nigger." Apparently, Rose quickly ended
the relationship with Rufus because her master had forced her into it
and she had always resented it. The emotional toll of the forced marriage remained with Rose for more than fifty years. She said, "Dere
am one thing Massa Hawking does to me what I can't shunt from my
mind."[56] In another example, Madison Day and Maria Richard had

lived together as husband and wife for seven years and had three children together. However, upon emancipation, they refused to legalize their marriage. Both each claimed the children and an unpleasant custody battle ensued, in which the Freedmen's Bureau heard and rendered a decision. Custody was granted to Madison Day, the father.[57]

AN UNIDENTIFIED BLACK FAMILY DURING RECONSTRUCTION.

Courtesy of the North Carolina Division of Archives and History

Some blacks chose never to marry. Lizzie Atkins, for example, did not marry because her lover was killed during the Civil War. "I'se never did see another man that I ever wanted so I just stayed at home and took care of my old mother and father." Nevertheless, she thought that she would have been better off if she had married "because times sure have been hard on the poor old negro since he was freed."[58] For James Brooks, "women [were] too much trouble. Want too much 'ttention. I couldn't be bothered wid 'em."[59] Lizzie Polk never exchanged marital vows because "I was working too hard to have time to flirt. Anyway, if I had to work, I would rather work for myself than for a man."[60]

Blacks regarded the twin institutions of marriage and family as sacred. Thus, by 1870, a large majority lived in two-parent households.[61] There were several reasons why blacks found marriage appealing. Undoubtedly, many married for love, as was the case for Maggie Jackson: "I didn't marry John 'cause I wanted to leave home. I married him 'cause I loved him and he loved me."[62] Blacks also considered marriage to be morally right. Moreover, it established the legitimacy of children and helped blacks gain access to land titles and other economic opportunities. Black soldiers in particular wanted to formalize marriages because they feared that their women and children would have no legal claims in the event that they were killed.[63] Furthermore, church membership often required legalized marriage. Susan Grant explained that she and Aaron Grant as well as several other couples were living together when their preachers "told them that the[y] must get married and that they, as did many others, got up in church and were married." A friend of Susan and Aaron Grant, Judith Swinton, explained that after the war churches "compelled the members who were living together as man and wife but not married to have these ceremonies performed."[64] In fact, the First African Baptist Church of New Orleans, after the abolition of slavery, declared: "Any persons wishing to become members of this church who may be living in a state of illegitimate marriage should first procure a license and marry."[65]

Since marriage conformed to the laws of civil society, the enforcement of legal marriage was therefore a matter of concern for the entire community. A Freedmen's Bureau agent, J. E. Eldredge, reported from Bladenboro, North Carolina, that "the Colored people of this place are trying to make their colored brethren pay some respect to themselves and the laws of the country by making them pay some respect to the marriage bond." Blacks in Bladenboro targeted one case in particular. A black man had promised on four different occasions to marry a woman whom he had lived with for a year. However, he continually put her off. As a result, the Bureau agent noted, "the colored men of this place appointed a committee to wait on him and see if they could not influence him to do better but no satisfaction could be obtained."[66] In another case, a group of blacks at a contraband camp enthusiastically supported the expulsion of a black minister who refused to marry his mistress from the camp. Shortly thereafter, the couple died of smallpox. Upon their deaths, there was no mourning among blacks at the camp, for their demise, observed the officer in charge, "was looked upon by the Negroes as a direct and swift application of retributive justice."[67]

REUNION WITH LOST LOVED ONES

To the newly freed blacks, the work of emancipation would be incomplete until the families dispersed by slavery were reunited. Some freedmen set out on their own to find lost relatives. One journalist from the North reported encountering a black man in September 1865 who had walked more than six hundred miles from Georgia to North Carolina in the hope of finding his wife and children from whom he had been separated by sale.[68] Sarah Jane Foster, a Northern white teacher of freedmen in the vicinity of Charleston, wrote: "One woman here has exerted herself to find her four children at great expense, though dependent on her own labor altogether."[69] Many advertised in black newspapers in efforts to locate lost loved ones. A typical plea for help appeared in the Nashville *Colored Tennessean*: "During the year 1849, Thomas Sumple carried away from this city, as his slaves, our daughter, Polly and son. . . . We will give $100 each for them to any person who will assist them . . . to get to Nashville, or get word to us of their whereabouts."[70]

Sometimes blacks solicited the aid of whites or other blacks in the hope of tracking down family members. Unfortunately, when giving descriptions, some failed to take into account the fact that many of the lost children were now adults. Such was the case when Elizabeth Botume reported that she came across an old slave woman in Central Georgia who had been sold away from Virginia some thirty or forty years earlier. The woman left a daughter in Virginia whom she had not heard from since their forced separation. Upon learning that Botume had traveled through the region, the old woman wanted to know if she had seen her "little gal." "With tears streaming down her face, she told me what a 'store she set by that little child'," noted Botume. "She begged me to look out for her when I went back. She was sure I should know her, she 'was such a pretty little gal.' " Botume concluded that "it was useless to tell her the girl was now a woman, and doubtless had children of her own."[71]

Unfortunately, a large number of freed blacks were unable to find lost loved ones, although there were some successes. A former slave recounted the stories of dozens of children who searched throughout the South after the Civil War for parents sold "down the river" and of parents who searched equally desperately for their children. Lizzie Baker's family tried to get some news of her brother's and sister's whereabouts after the war, as her mother "kept 'quiring 'bout 'em as long as she lived and I have hoped dat I could hear from 'em. Dey are dead long ago I recons, and I guess dare aint no use ever expectin' to see 'em.'"[72] Another former slave, Mattie Curtis, recalled that after the war her parents "tried to find dere fourteen oldest chilluns what was sold away, but dey never did find but three of dem."[73] Fortunately, others had better luck. Laura Redmoun advertised "roun' in the papers and found my mammy and she came and lived with me."[74] After exhaustive efforts, Kate Drumgold found her children alive.[75] After the war, Charles Maho, a former slave who had been sold away from his wife and daughter in Virginia in the late 1850s to a Mississippi cotton planter, set out for Richmond to find them. When he finally reached the city, he was disheartened to learn that his wife had been dead for years. But he did locate his daughter, and the two shared an apartment while he worked in a tobacco factory to support them. Olmstead Scott, from Virginia, was another former slave who was sold in 1860 to a planter in Florida. After the war, Scott saved money so he could return to Richmond and try to reunite with family members. He arrived there in 1869 and found his grandmother, his aunt and uncle, and his brother and sister, but he discovered that his parents had died before the war.[76] Another freedman who traveled throughout the South for twenty years looking for his wife finally found her in a refugee camp.[77]

One former slave recalled the joyous moment when his mother located him after the war. He couldn't believe it was she. "Then she took the bundle off her hand [sic] and took off her hat, and I saw that scar on her face. Child, look like I had wings!"[78] Equally exciting was the reunion of Chaplain Garland H. White of the Twenty-eighth U.S. Colored Infantry with his mother. White had initially been a slave in Richmond but was sold to Robert Toombs, a lawyer in Georgia, when he was a small boy. After the war began, White's mother came across Toombs in Richmond with troops from his state. When she asked him where his body servant Garland was, Toombs informed her that Garland had escaped to Canada and was probably living somewhere in Ohio. The mother continued to inquire about one Garland White of Ohio until some of the soldiers in her son's regiment overheard her. Shortly thereafter, the soldiers found White and told him, "Chaplain, here is a lady that wishes to see you." He turned and followed them until he came upon a group of black women. Of the occasion, White wrote, "I cannot express the joy I felt at this happy meeting of my mother and other friends."[79] Another freedman who ended up in Illinois after the war surprised his family by returning home to Roxboro, North Carolina. His overjoyed parents had not seen him in several years. The father "had a few days previously remarked that he did not want to die without seeing his son once more." The son recalled that he "could not find language to express my feelings. I did not know before I came home whether my parents were dead or alive."[80] In another story, one soldier recalled that some men "cried while others laughed to hide the tears" when they witnessed a black woman reunite with her lost daughter, who had been sold away ten years earlier.[81]

On some occasions the Freedmen's Bureau helped former slaves obtain information about missing relatives. In May 1867, Hawkins Wilson, in Texas wrote to the Bureau seeking assistance in finding his sisters, whom he had not seen in twenty-four years. He sought the aid of the Bureau because "I have no other one to apply to but you and am persuaded that you will help one who stands in need of your services as I do—I shall be very grateful to you, if you oblige me in this matter." He informed the Bureau that one of his sisters, Jane, belonged to Peter Coleman in Caroline County. Wilson also provided the name of his sister's husband, her owner, and his area of residency as well as the names of his sister's three children at the time he left. Next, he did the same for his other two sisters, Martha and Matilda. Finally, Wilson alerted the Bureau about his Uncle Jim and Aunt Adie and their oldest son Buck, who all belonged to Jack Langley. With much emotion and anticipation, Wilson asserted, "These are all my own dearest relatives and I wish to correspond with them with a view to visit them as soon as I can hear from them."[82] In addition, Milly Johnson, a freedwoman in North Carolina, solicited the assistance of the Freedmen's Bureau to locate her five children.[83] And John Allen of Austin, Texas, enlisted the aid of the Bureau in finding his two children, whom he left in Batesville, Arkansas, in 1859. Allen's daughter Rachel was just nine years old at the time, and Benjamin, his son, was two years younger. Despite the fact that Allen had not heard from them since their separation, he was "anxious" to know if they were still alive and wanted them again "under his charge and protection."[84]

As were the cases when black parents searched for family members on their own, placed advertisements in black newspapers, and solicited the aid of individuals, results were often either disappointing or mixed. Hawkins Wilson's kinfolk probably were never found. Likewise, John Allen probably never reunited with his two children. However, Milly Johnson located her daughter Anna, found information about two of her children but received no word about the others.

If freed blacks knew exactly where their family members had relocated, Freedmen's Bureau agents routinely arranged transportation to facilitate reunions. Willis Love, for instance, a black bricklayer "of good character," successfully petitioned the Bureau for assistance. Agents were assured by Love that he would support his children, but he could not afford the fare for their passage to Atlanta to join him.[85] Marcia Johnson was also able to solicit help from the Bureau to rejoin her husband. She had "walked, worked, and scuffed along from West Point, Mississippi" in efforts to reach Tarboro, North Carolina, where her husband resided. She was now in Raleigh, some forty miles away, "but now that all her means and strength are exhausted she can go no further."[86]

Some former slaves experienced complications with the law in attempting reunions, but others experienced complications of the heart when they found themselves having to choose one spouse over another. As slaves, they had started second families after being forced into separations assumed to be permanent, whether because of the sale of one mate or because of an escape. Robert Washington, for example, had escaped to the North from South Carolina before the war. When he returned to Charleston in 1870 to claim his wife, Lucretia, and their children, he found that Lucretia had taken another husband. He went to court to win her back, but the magistrate who heard the case, T. J. Mackey, ruled against him. In Mackey's opinion, Washington should have had enough interest in Lucretia to have returned to Charleston long before he did.[87]

A more complicated story involved a Virginian, Philip Grey, and his wife, Willie Ann. Philip and Willie Ann had married before the war and had one child, Maria. Willie Ann and Maria were then taken to Kentucky. Philip never remarried, but Willie Ann married a Federal soldier who was killed in battle; three children were born to this union. After the war, Philip searched for his wife and daughter. It was obvious that Philip wanted his daughter back, but he was less sure about Willie Ann, although she still loved him and wanted to return to him. In an impassioned letter to Philip, Willie Ann wrote, "I know that I have lived with you and loved you then and I love you still . . . every time I hear from you my love grows stronger." Nonetheless, Willie Ann insisted that Philip accept her now-fatherless other three children: "You must not think my family to large and get out of heart for if you love me you will love my children and you will have to promise me that you will provide for them all as well as if they were your own." [88] It is not clear whether Philip and Willie Ann Grey ever lived again together as husband and wife.

Cases involving two spouses and two sets of children were especially troubling and difficult to settle. James McCullum of North

Carolina married again four years after his wife and two children were sold. Two children were also born to him and his second wife. When the war ended, McCullum's first wife and children returned to him, and he now had two wives and two sets of children to choose from. Although he believed that only his first marriage was valid, McCullum sought a ruling from the Freedmen's Bureau in Lumberton, North Carolina.[89] Similarly, Elizabeth Botume reported the case of a woman whose husband was first sold away and then went into the army. Since she was again single, the woman took a second husband. Once the war concluded, the regiment of husband number one disbanded, and he returned to claim his wife. The woman had given birth to two boys with him, and a girl with husband number two. Both men wanted their own children. The poor woman was in a quandary.[90] Even more heart-wrenching was the experience of Laura Spicer and her slave husband, who had been separated for many years. The husband, assuming that Laura was dead, remarried and established a new family. After the war, he was shocked to learn that Laura was still alive. Although he decided to stay with his second wife, Anna, and refuse Laura, he reached that decision with great difficulty. In a series of letters to Laura, he wrote out his feelings:

> I would come and see you but I know you could not bear it. . . . You know it never was our wishes to be separated from each other, and it never was our fault. . . . I had rather anything had happened to me most than ever have been parted from you and the children. As I am, I do not know which I love best, you or Anna. . . . I do not think I would die satisfied till you tell me you will try and marry some good, smart man that will take good care of you and the children; and do it because you love me; and not because I think more of the wife I have got than I do of you. The woman is not born that feels as near to me as you do.[91]

Sometimes freedmen and women found their relatives without at first knowing it. Since as slaves blacks were often separated from family at an early age, mothers sometimes did not recognize their children as adults and brothers and sisters did not recognize each other. As a result, they might marry each other without being aware of their kinship. William Mathews recalled, "After de war when dey was all free, dey marry who dey want to an' sometime a long time after dat dey find out dat brothers had married dere siters an' mothers had married dere sons, an' things like dat."[92] Richard Carruthers maintained that he knew of many cases where brothers and sisters married. He offered the following scenario of how they usually found out that they were siblings: "One night they gits to talking. She say, 'One time my brother had fight and he git a awful scar over his left ear. It long and slick and no hair grows there.' He say, 'See this scar over my let ear? It long and slick and no sign of a hair.' Then she say, 'Lawd God help us po' niggers. You is my brother.' "[93]

The sad story of Bess, told by Tom Epps, further illustrates the painful consequences of slavery. When she was a little girl, Bess was sold from City Point, Virginia. Her mother was sold to a second trader, and her brother to a third one. Separated by many miles, they were unlikely to meet again. After the Civil War concluded, Bess walked all the way from Georgia to Richmond looking for her mother and her older brother but failed to locate them. While in Richmond searching for her family, Bess met and married a man, and two boys were born to this union. One day, Bess's husband came home extremely happy because he had found his mother. The next day his mother came to live with him and Bess. The older woman knew right away that Bess was her daughter but only said, I am glad to know you. However, it bothered the woman so much that she could not keep it to herself. She "tole 'em dat she was de mother to dem both, an' dey was brother an' sister." Of course, both were very upset, "but dey was really in love so dey 'cided to stay married." This was too much for their mother to bear, and it was not long before she died, " 'cause she couldn't stan' seein' her son and daughter livin' wid each other."[94]

THE QUEST TO FREE THEIR FAMILIES
FROM WHITE CONTROL

Slave families, many of whom were divided because their members belonged to different owners, could now live together without the fear of forced separation. Parents began to assert the right to raise their own children. After the war, one mother reclaimed her child, Sarah Debro, whom the former mistress, Miss Polly, had been rearing in her own house. When the mother came to get her, Sarah did not want to leave, and Miss Polly said, "Let her stay with me." But Sarah's mother was defiant: "You took her away from me an' didn' pay no mind to my cryin', so now, I's takin' her back home. We's free now, Mis' Polly. We ain' gwine be slaves no more to nobody."[95] In most cases, however, black men and black women were not able to reclaim their children on their own and had to solicit the assistance of law enforcement officials or the Freedmen's Bureau. Millie Randall remembered, "After Freedom ol' marster wouldn' 'low my maw to hab us chillen. My maw hatter git de Jestice of de Peace to go mek him t'un us a-loose."[96]

Lucinda Jacoway sought the aid of the Bureau in February 1866 to force William Bryant to release her four-year-old daughter, Jane Ellen. Bryant demanded that he be paid fifty dollars for the child. A Freedmen's Bureau agent in Arkansas, John Vetter, directed a letter to Bryant on Jacoway's behalf: "You are hereby instructed to surrender said child to the complainant." He added, "and that immediately."[97] In late 1867, Mary Brown returned from Canada to claim her two children whom she had left behind when she fled slavery. One of her daughters, Dinah, still lived as a slave in Nicholasville, Kentucky, and the other daughter, Mary Jane, was held in Fleming County in the same state. Brown was forced to seek redress through the Bureau since in each instance the former owner refused to give up the child.[98] Even a woman who was considered insane appealed to the Bureau to force her former mistress to return her child. Mollie Williams's mother had repeatedly tried to get Miss Marguerite to free Mollie, but efforts on her own proved futile. Then, according to Williams, "Nex' time she come, she brung a written letter to Miss Marqurite frum de Free Man's Board an' taken me wid her."[99]

The system of apprenticeship was more threatening to black families than the random refusal, which had no legal basis, of some former owners to release black children. Apprenticeships, on the other hand, were legal. Under the system, some Southern states allowed "responsible" employers to capitalize on the labor of minor children until they reached eighteen or twenty-one years of age, depending on gender. Wholesome food, suitable clothing, and medical care along with training in industry, housekeeping, or husbandry were to be provided to those apprenticed. Moreover, it was also understood that they were to be taught to read and write. Although children allegedly could not be apprenticed without parental consent, they frequently were. Ages were sometimes falsified to retain apprentices for longer periods of time. And, since many parents were not present when slavery ended, many former owners took advantage of their absence by apprenticing the children before parents could return to claim them. Owing to the fact that there was not yet any protection of legal marriages, any child born in slavery could be considered an orphan and subject to apprenticeship. Indeed, postwar apprenticeship laws allowed former slaveholders to salvage much of the old labor system. At the same time, it divested parents of the labor useful to a family's stride toward economic independence.[100]

Understandably, since blacks possessed a fierce attachment to family and were determined to take back control of the lives of kinfolk now that they were free, they waged intense battles against apprenticeship laws. They either defied the system on their own, used legal means through the hiring of lawyers, or sought the aid of the Freedmen's Bureau. When Jane Kamper, for example, learned that her former master regarded her children's apprenticeships as the price of her freedom, she took their recovery into her own hands. Kamper wrote in a letter to the Bureau that her former owner, William Townsend, "told me that I was free but that my children should be bound to me [him]. He locked my children up so that I could not find them. I afterwards got my children by stealth and brought them to Baltimore." Townsend pursued her to the wharf in an effort to seize her children, but Kamper "hid them on the boat." Although she made a successful escape, Kamper had to leave her bedclothes and furniture and requested the aid of the Bureau in retrieving them.[101] In an effort to get his son released from an apprenticeship under W. R. Holt, his former owner, Orange Holt hired a lawyer to represent him and argued that his son had been neglected in W. R.'s care. Orange maintained that his son had become ill because of insufficient clothing. Harriet Holt also hired a lawyer to present her argument against W. R. Holt. Her attorney argued that Harriet's two sons had been apprenticed to W. R. against her will and then contracted to another party. As a consequence of the strenuous efforts made by parents and relatives to regain their children, by January 1867, W. R. Holt asked to be released from his obligation for all but six of the eighteen children.[102] In another case, Henry Walton's father went to court to have his apprenticeship to Mrs. Miller nullifed.[103]

While some Freedmen's Bureau officials were reluctant to interfere with contracts, others showed some sensitivity toward blacks who were concerned about the welfare of their children and relatives. As a result, they sometimes tried to ferret out thinly disguised ruses that were used to reenslave children.[104] Certainly, the Bureau was beseiged by letters seeking help in getting children released from apprenticeships. In Florence, Alabama, Martin Lee asked for assistance in getting custody of his nephew from his former owner, Sebe Burson, in Georgia. Lee could not understand why his family could not have custody of his nephew since "the law in our State is that a childe cannot be bounde when the[y] have mother father brother sistter uncl or Aunt that can take care of them."[105] Sallie Harris, a Virginian, wrote the Bureau requesting that her cousin Wilson, who was apprenticed to Mr. Jefferson, be released from his contract and allowed to come stay with her and her brother Albert. In a letter full of concern, Harris said, "I have a house for him and will take care of him and do all I can for him." She wanted to take Wilson from Jefferson "because he is not treated well and as he is my cousin I think it my duty to see to him."[106] Another Virginian, Wister Miller, wrote to the Bureau asking that Charles Ganaway, his eleven-year-old brother-in-law, who was parentless and without a permanent home, be bound to him: "As I married his sister I feel it my duty to take care of him."[107] Moreover, Penny Barksdale also appealed to the Bureau for the return of her two grandchildren. Bureau officials ruled that Barksdale's grandchildren be sent back to her because the teenagers were nearly old enough to support themselves and could help their aging grandmother.[108] And, if they could, their help would free the government from having to take care of her.

Both those who held young blacks under apprenticeship and those working to nullify contracts claimed to represent the interest of the child. But how did the children themselves feel about apprenticeship? Apparently, many were opposed to the system. Their opposition was expressed through their refusal to return to their employers after visiting their families at Christmas or by fleeing to relatives. For example, Alfred, a twelve-year-old, left his master after two years and made his way to South Carolina. Although Alfred's owner decided not to retrieve him, and to cancel the indenture, in many other cases the Bureau ordered the children returned to their lawful masters. Not only did some children resist apprenticeship for themselves but they fought on behalf of their siblings as well. In March 1867, five brothers filed for a writ of habeas corpus to release their sisters, aged eighteen, sixteen, twelve, and eight, all orphans held as apprentices.[109]

ADDITIONAL STEPS TO PROMOTE THE INTERESTS OF FAMILIES AND COMMUNITIES

Concern for the welfare of family members was also reflected in the attitudes of black soldiers in the post-Civil War period. A large number were not mustered out of service at the conclusion of the war but instead were retained as a part of the army's occupation force in the South. This job fell on black troops to a large extent because they had not been allowed to join the armed services until well into the war, and, of course, many whites had enrolled from the start. Thus, black troops were required to serve out their terms. As expected, many of the black soldiers still on duty after the war were very worried about their families. After all, their relatives often had to depend on them for survival. Black soldiers from a Virginia regiment on garrison duty in Texas were so desperate to return home after receiving discouraging news from their loved ones that they offered to buy their way out of their enlistments. In a candid letter to army officials, the men spelled out their concern: "Wee have been on Dayley fetig [fatigue] from the last of Juli up to this Day without a forlough or any comfort what ever and our wives sends Letters stateing thir suferage saying that they are without wood without wrashions [rations] without money and no one to protect them." Rather than allow their families to continue to suffer without their aid, the men argued that they would "pay for our next years serviss and be turned out then to stay in and no pertecttion granted to our wife."[110] Black soldiers from a South Carolina regiment pointed out that they "was expected to get out at the closing of the war, and then go back over the Rebels lands to look and seek for our wives and mother and father." They were especially concerned because "we hadent nothing atall and our wifes and mother most all of them is aperishing."[111]

Throughout the South, blacks extended bonds of kinship to nephews, nieces, and cousins. For example, Adam Woods of Kentucky rushed home from Kansas to take care of his three nephews when he found out that his brother, who was their father, had died. Woods indicated "that he is married and has an industrious wife and a good manager, and that he owns two houses and lots in Leavenworth and has no children and is well able to raise and educate the children of his deceased Brother." Furthermore, in order to convince Freedmen's Bureau officials that he had access to additional support if he needed it, he added that he "has Four sisters living and they are all doing well" together with two brothers who were doing superbly. All six of them "are able and willing to assist in raising and educating these children," he noted. [112] In Florida, Dave Waldrop invited a female cousin in Montgomery, Alabama, who was struggling by herself to raise her three children, to come and live with him and his family. Waldrop promised her, "if you will come down here to me I will take care of you and your children and you and children shall never want for anything as long as I have anything to help you with . . . it is hard enough for a woman to get along that has a husband to help her and one that has not I do not know how they do to get a living these times." With open arms, Waldrop wrote, "Cousin I want you to be shure and come down if you possibly can and stay here as long as you want to if it is three or four year it will not make a bit of difference to me."[113] Moreover, after the parents of Sally Porter, a former Virginia slave, died, Washington Brown, her uncle, took her into his household.[114]

Many freedmen took it upon themselves to adopt kin and non-kin children, again demonstrating not only a commitment to family but also a determination to protect children. Hannah Allen and her husband had no youngsters of their own but adopted a little boy who was born to her husband's sister. The lad came to live with them when he turned three years of age and remained in their household until the age of nine. Hannah and her husband also adopted the biracial daughter of a black man and a white woman who was not related to them. After the woman and the girl's father separated, the woman remarried, this time to a white man. Her new husband, however, did not want the child since its father was black. This couple went on to help raise about one dozen children.[115] Although adoptions were acceptable to many African-American freedmen and women, some adoptive parents were guarded and sensitive. While Evangeline Banks grew up as the adopted daughter of Anna DeCosta Banks, her grandmother, Elizabeth DeCosta, allowed no one to refer to her adopted status. Anna still had not informed Evangeline when she died in 1930. Nevertheless, Evangeline had discovered her adoption several years earlier, but she refused to allow it to emotionally disrupt the pleasant life given to her by Anna Banks.[116]

Even during slavery, the parents of black children sometimes chose whom their children dated and married, although circumstances might limit their influence. As expected, then, when freedom arrived, they often took it upon themselves to play a major role in determining whom their children were to date and marry. After all, to do so was consistent with their concern for the welfare of the family. Since the position of breadwinner fell on the male, parents were especially interested in the marital partners selected by their daughters. Dicy Windfield, a former slave, recalled, "when I wuz 'bout eighteen years ole I met de boy dat I married. Pa an' ma never would let us chillun run 'bout none so he wuz de onliest boy I ever did court. We wont allowed to go no whars together to 'mount to nothin'."[117] Another freedwoman, Lucy Dunn, remembered that during the whole year of her courtship with her future husband, they were seldom alone. Not only did her mother accompany them when they walked home from church, but she also forbade Lucy to walk her suitor to the gate at the end of his Sunday visits. Lucy, however, finally won a big concession after her future husband proposed to her. She was allowed to walk him to the gate provided that her mother "was settin dere on de' porch lookin."[118] Laura Bell met her future husband when she was only twelve years old. Her parents told her that she was too young to have a male friend, but they gave their blessings to her seeing him at an older age if she still wanted to.[119]

At least in these cases, former slaves were eventually given their parents' blessings to marry. This, however, was not the case for some others. For example, one young woman remarked on the frustrating veto that her mother had held over her marriage plans. "My first husband courted me seven years," she related, "and then liked to have steadled me 'for my mother never did say yes."[120] George Weathersby remembered the problems while trying to date the woman who eventually became his wife of more than fifty years. According to Weathersby, "My love affair wont very smooth as de gals pa did not want us to git married an' did a heap o' interferring." At several points in their relationship, the woman's father was working hard to keep them from getting married. But, since they loved each other so much, "de more he tried to break us up de more us wuz determined." With the aid of his brother Steve and two cousins, Weathersby concocted a plan to steal his future wife from her father. Although the plot did not turn out exactly as planned, his lover did escape from her father and she and Weathersby were subsequently married.[121]

Although enslaved parents had insisted upon respect from their children and were not reluctant to use the rod on them, they would now decide when and how their children were to be punished. One freedwoman became defiant when her former master claimed the right to whip her children, boldly informing him that "he warn't goin' to brush none of her chilluns no more."[122] In another case, Eliza James refused to punish her son because a white man had demanded it. She explained that "she would not whip her child for no poor White folks." For a white person to either claim the right to beat black children or demand their punishment, smacked of slavery to most freedmen and women, and this they would not tolerate.[123]

Once freedom arrived, some black women refused to let their sons and daughters accept clothing donated by whites that they considered ill-fitting or immodest. As free men and women, they might be poor but they were proud. Many regarded it as a badge of honor not to accept hand-me-downs from whites. Freedmen's Bureau officials were sometimes baffled by this refusal. Northern teachers were also taken aback. Mary Ames, a Yankee, recorded in her diary: "One girl brought back a dress she had taken home for 'Ma says it don't fit, and she don't want it.' It was rather large and short, but she was very dirty and ragged, and we told her she must keep it."[124]

Black men and women also took steps to free their families economically from white control now that they had been emancipated. Black men often forbade their wives and children to continue to work in the fields or as domestic servants in white households, believing that such work was a mark of slavery. One freedman told a former master who was attempting to hire his wife as a servant, "When I married my wife I married her to wait on me. She got all she can do right here for me and the children."[125] As the heads of their families under emancipation, black men hoped to be able to allow their wives to remain at home to care for the household. This was seen as important, not just so that black women could have roles similar to those of white women, but also so that black women could be protected from the sexual exploitation that had existed under slavery.[126] In addition, freedmen regarded a nonworking wife as a symbol of a financially successful husband able to support her without her having to work outside the household.[127]

Many black women were happy to stay at home and no longer work in the fields or as domestic servants in white households. They, too, wanted to reduce the chances of sexual exploitation by white men and to devote more time than had been possible under slavery to caring for their children and attending to their own households.[128] Withdrawal from the fields and from the white plantation house was also tied to their insistence on working less and differently than they had as slaves and was part of their strategy to take absolute control over their time and labor. Historian Leslie Schwalm has shown that with respect to freedwomen in the South Carolina Low Country, this strategy may have reflected their efforts to cope with the conditions of life after the war. Owing to the physical devastation of the countryside, the shortage of food, clothing, and the most basic necessities, and the poor harvests of the 1860s, home labor increased after the war.[129] Noralee Frankel argues that freedwomen in Mississippi chose to work in their own households as much as possible because they needed more time for their families. Cooking and clothes-making often ceased to be communal activities as they had been under slavery.[130] Moreover, now that they were free, some black women felt that they should stay at home and be supported by their husbands just as white women were by their men. As one planter learned, "The black women say they never mean to do any more outdoor work;

. . . white men support their wives and they mean that their husbands shall support them."[131]

White Southerners found the withdrawal of black women and
children from wage labor intolerable because it upset the daily operations of many white households. Furthermore, it smacked of social equality for black families to have the same roles and expectations
for their members that white families had. These fears were unwar-
ranted, however, for the shift in the locus of black female labor from
field work and paid domestic service to the unpaid maintenance of
their own homes proved to be only temporary. With the rising cost of
rents and the dire poverty of most black families as a consequence
of the depression of the 1870s, it became necessary for both black
men and women to contribute to the family's income. Therefore, although emancipation did not eliminate wage labor by black women
and children, it fundamentally altered control over it. The family itself, headed now by the black man, not the white owner or overseer,
made the decision about where and when black women and children
would work. Thus, blacks were able to liberate their families to some
extent from the authority of whites.[132] This liberation was to them an
important element of freedom.

Emancipation also transformed the black family itself. Within the
slave family, men were not the breadwinners and their authority was
limited. The dominance of masters was paramount. In a real sense,
both black men and black women were powerless during slavery,
but with emancipation men's new role strengthened their position
within the family and institutionalized the notion that men and
women should inhabit separate spheres. Thus, for the first time, many
black men assumed authority and a sense of superiority over
women.[133]

This evolution was strongly influenced by outside events. Because
black men had fought in the Union army, they had been able to participate more directly than women in the struggle for freedom. Also,
black men assumed the same attitude toward women that they saw
in white men and that was supported by the policies of the Freedmen's
Bureau. The Bureau officially designated the man as the head of the
black household, insisting that men sign contracts for the labor of
their entire families and establishing wage scales that set lower wages
for women than for men doing identical plantation labor. Political
developments also contributed to promoting the notion that black
men should be dominant over black women. Whereas both black men
and women participated in informal mass meetings in the early days

of freedom, only black men served as delegates to organized black conventions. Black men were given the right to serve on juries, vote, hold office, and play a leading role in the Republican Party. But neither black nor white women could vote and play formal roles in political parties. And although militia units and fraternal societies might have female auxiliaries, their memberships were all male.[134]

THE ADOPTION OF NAMES ASSOCIATED WITH FREEDOM

Of all the changes brought by emancipation, perhaps none meant more to the former slaves as a symbol of their new status than the opportunity to choose names and surnames. Most black children were named after their parents, grandparents, aunts, and uncles during slavery, but often slaveholders assigned names from ancient history or mythology such as Primus, Bacchus, Scipio, Orpheus, and Caesar. Biblical names such as Isaiah, Moses, Joshua, and Ezekiel symbolized blacks' new status as free men and women and continued to be passed from one generation to the next. After emancipation, there appeared a host of Anglo-Saxon-sounding names such as Mary, Elizabeth, John, William, Charles, and George, which also were identified with freedom.

Once freedom came, blacks also acquired surnames. Some adopted the surnames of their masters, not out of affection, but because it was convenient and the easiest way to be identified. The slaves on the same plantation with Martin Jackson of Texas, for example, took the name of their owner, Fitzpatrick.[135] George Selman and his parents also adopted the surname of their owner at the time of emancipation.[136] Likewise, Albert Henderson took his owner's name when he was freed.[137] Hundreds took the names of historic or public figures such as Washington, Jefferson, Jackson, Grant, Hamilton, Lincoln, Fillmore, Madison, or Polk—names that were associated with the concepts of independence and freedom. Nelson Polk, for instance, was named after President James Polk rather than any master.[138] And Austin Grant's father took his name from General Ulysses Grant, and his grandfather was named for President Millard Fillmore.[139]

Other blacks adopted surnames because they simply liked the way they sounded or found them to be unique. Some had an emotional or cultural appeal. Aaron Ray recalled, "Me an' my sister us changed our names to Ray case us jes' lak dat name, an' hit wuz anodder name, an' dar didn't seem to be noboddy dat had dat kind ob er name."[140] James Martin took the surname Martin after the man who brought his grandfather from England,[141] and Martin Jackson adopted the surname Jackson because one of his grandfathers in Africa was called Jeaceo.[142] In most cases, however, blacks took the name of the first master in the family's oral history, as far back as it could be recalled.[143] For instance, although William Moore and his parents were owned by Tom Waller when emancipation arrived, they called themselves Moore after their first owner.[144] Similarly, although the family of Mandy Jones was owned by a man named Stewart, the family took the surname of their first owner, named Young.[145] Like their black counterparts living in Southern states, Seminole freedmen adopted the last names of their fathers or former owners. To the citizenship rolls of the Seminole Nation were added the family names of Abraham, Cudjo, Dindy, Primus, and Sandy—names still borne by their descendants today.[146] Regardless of the name, it was important to blacks that they made the decision themselves without the interference of whites.

Along with the symbolic disassociation from whites represented by their taking new names came efforts by freedmen to physically separate themselves from whites, the most visible reminders of slavery. Whitelaw Reid noted that "the more intelligent negroes generally think it would be better for their people to be freed from contact with the whites; but their idea of accomplishing it is, not to remove the blacks, but to have the whites remove from them." Thus, Reid continued, "They believe in colonization; but it is in colonization on the lands they have been working."[147] Apparently, a large number of freedmen and women shared this view. Annie Young, a former slave, recalled that "after the war my stepfather come, and got my mother and we moved out in the piney woods."[148] One freedman's former owner offered him a nice house nearby, but he refused to accept it and moved instead to a shack in "Freetown." He also declined the former owner's offer to grind his grain at no charge because it "make him feel like a free man to pay for things just like anyone else."[149] In an effort to minimize contact with whites, freedmen built all-black communities where they could live among themselves and control their own affairs. All-black communities were established at Princeville, North Carolina; James City, North Carolina, near New Bern; Kendleton, Shankleville, and Board House, all in Texas, to name only a few.[150] Some of these all-black settlements still exist today. Princeville, for example, was a relatively thriving town until Hurricane Floyd devastated it in September 1999.

PROBLEMS WITHIN AFRICAN–AMERICAN COMMUNITIES

Strengthening the bonds of their own community was a major goal of freedmen, but the new black community was confronted with many serious problems. Despite the fact that most black men fulfilled their roles as husbands and fathers admirably, some did not. They beat their spouses, were adulterous, refused to support their families, and broke promises to prospective wives. Black women in the South flooded the Freedmen's Bureau with complaints about these marital problems. Julia Gibson reported that her husband beat her over the head and bit her hand. [151] A woman named Esther was constantly whipped and maltreated by her husband, who also threatened to poison her.[152] Julia Ray complained that her husband, Alec, beat her badly, and a Freedmen's Bureau official noted that "her appearance is such as to indicate a gross assault."[153] Rose Freeman's husband, David, repeatedly beat her and refused to support her. When Rose informed him that she would go to the Bureau to lodge a complaint against him, he replied, "damn the Freedmen's Bureau—I'll cuss you before them."[154] Betty Ann Ellington caught Harry, her husband, in their bed with another woman. When she confronted him, "he seized her by the throat and choked and beat her." He took his belongings and left with the woman, deserting not only Betty Ann but his three children as well.[155] Harriet Buchanan accused her husband, Alfred, of having sexual relations with another woman. Alfred eventually moved in with the woman, leaving the two children behind with Harriet. When Harriet charged him with living with the woman, Alfred beat her.[156] Charlotte Brown complained to Bureau officials that her husband, George, was having illicit sexual intercourse with a white woman, Amelia Tines. After promising to foresake his bad conduct, he was caught by Charlotte at Amelia's house. When Charlotte struck Amelia twice, George intervened and "held her off the woman and put her out of the yard and picked up a stick and struck her with it and put a large hole in her head."[157]

Black women were not reluctant to file charges against the white fathers of their babies if they refused to support their children. Harriet Ogleby, for example, asked the Bureau to assist her in forcing Drew Ogleby, the father of her son, Beauregard, to provide child support.[158] Ellen Nesbit also went before the Bureau to argue that Frank Lumpkin, a white man, was the father of her son Frank, and that he was not providing support.[159]

Sometimes the Freedmen's Bureau rendered decisions favorable to black female complainants. For example, Celia Horn successfully sued her husband for child support. Reese Horn was ordered to immediately pay twelve dollars and then two dollars per month for two years. George Washington Holmes was forced by the Bureau to support Louisa, his former wife, and their children, whom he had deserted.[160] A father in Louisiana was ordered by a Bureau officer to pay four dollars per month for his daughter's upkeep until she was ten years old. Ellen Nesbit and three other women from Athens, Georgia, received lump-sum payments of $50 to $60 from the white fathers of their children.[161] Henry Goaldsby was found guilty of breach of promise to marry Amanda Moore and fined $150. And a man named Simmons lived with Ann Marshall for several years. Even though Ann gave him her savings of almost $400, he refused to marry her. He was heavily fined for using the prospect of marriage to defraud her.[162]

Black men also complained of being physically, psychologically, or emotionally abused. David Fry accused his wife of beating him, refusing to sleep in the same bed with him, and denying him all "matrimonial connections."[163] Jackson Fields of Louisville, Kentucky, swore in an affidavit before a Freedmen's Bureau agent that his first wife, Sarah, had been unfaithful to him, having lived with another man while he was in the armed forces. As a result of Sarah's alleged infidelity, Jackson felt justified in taking another wife. Jackson was so incensed at Sarah that he refused to pay child support. After hearing the case, the Bureau agent gave judgment that Jackson pay fifty dollars to Sarah "to assist in supporting her child of which he is the Father."[164]

During Reconstruction, the black community was confronted with problems such as unemployment, hunger, homelessness, prostitution, drunkenness, and lack of adequate medical attention. In order to solve these problems, however, blacks relied upon a tradition of self-help that they had developed during slavery. They counted on themselves, not on the Federal government or sympathetic Northern whites. Freedmen took great pride in their ability to care for their orphans, widows, widowers, cripples, and those who were destitute through their own mutual-aid and beneficial societies. Beneficial societies required members to pay dues so that funds would be available to provide respectable funerals for their members and to pay death benefits to their widows and children. Mutual-aid societies were organized for the benefit of members but they sometimes would help poor non-members as well. As soon as the war ended, blacks in Nashville, Jackson, New Orleans, Atlanta, Richmond, Charleston, and in many rural areas began the work that would bring them pride and dignity as a community, raising money to establish orphanages, soup kitchens, employment agencies, and funds for relief of the poor. Although not exclusively, most of the beneficial and mutual aid societies were organized by black churches. They will be discussed in detail in Chapter Seven.

Throughout the antebellum period, skin color was a major issue among blacks. It was a problem that black social activism could not solve. Mulattoes looked down on darker complexioned blacks, and blacks of a darker hue ridiculed mulattoes because of their light skin. Dora Franks, for example, a mulatto during slavery, recalled, "The children chased and taunted her with shouts of 'Old Yellow Nigger.' " She added, "Dey didn't treat me good neither."[165] Apparently, some blacks detested mulattoes because they often were accorded positions of privilege among slaves and free blacks, due to their white ancestry.

These ill feelings would spill over into the Reconstruction period. In Charleston, for example, when two well-dressed young mulatto women and their black servant entered a railway car together, one of the young women ordered the servant to stay on the car's outer platform. When the conductor saw the servant and told her to take a seat inside, she replied, "Oh, Lor' bless you, massa, no, missus wouldn't 'low it." But when the conductor made it clear that riding on the outside of the car was not allowed, she reluctantly took a seat by her mistress, who seemed greatly disturbed that "blacks were allowed to ride alongside ladies."[166] In another incident, a visitor to Charleston noted that "a couple of ebony damsels and a mulatto boy are belaboring one another in terms more vigorous than select as to each other's claims to respectability on the ground of color on the walk outside my window."[167]

Although skin color sometimes was interconnected with socioeconomic class and determined whom one might date or marry during the post-Civil War period, this was not exclusively the case. For example, Frances Rollin, a member of the old freeborn mulatto elite in Charleston, married William Whipper, a prominent black politician, over the objections of her father. Despite the fact that her father indicated that he could not approve of the marriage because "it was too soon," he no doubt objected for other reasons. Charlotte, Frances's sister, probably expressed the sentiments of the entire Rollin family over Frances's decision to marry Whipper when she told the *Herald* reporter: "In fact, our family never condescended to notice such small people as Elliott and Whipper, although Whipper married our sister Frances. They are both negroes and our family is french." It is clear that antebellum class divisions among blacks did not suddenly disappear with emancipation. The Rollins and other mulatto elites remained deeply conscious of their status and traditions. Distinguished by culture, "previous condition," and often color, these "colored aristocrats" adhered to a system of value and behavior that separated them from the black masses.[168]

While most blacks lived in wretched misery, the mulatto elite lived in nice houses, wore fine clothes, threw fancy balls, and formed militia clubs, musical bands, and literary and debating societies. The culture of the mulatto elite, materialistic and Victorian, was derived from white culture since it represented the standard against which they expected that they and all blacks would be judged. Having been educated in schools and colleges operated by white churches, many of them were taught the same value system that permeated respectable white society.[169] At a time in which racial discrimination was hardening and white violence intensifying, they stood on the sidelines and did not play an active role in the black struggle for equality. Although they, too, sometimes had to confront white racism and racial discrimination, most members of the mulatto elite apparently did not see the need to join forces with other blacks to combat these injustices. In all fairness to the mulatto elite, however, it should be noted that some among their group did join the black struggle for equality. Nonetheless, the mulatto elite regarded themselves as superior to the black masses and looked down upon them with disgust. The black masses were an embarrassment to them and represented the confirmation of all the negative stereotypes attached to blacks by whites.

Despite the trials and tribulations experienced by blacks in the post-Civil War period, black families emerged from them stronger and with even more determination to prosper in American society. Now that they had control of their families, they were determined not to relinquish it to whites. Freedmen would raise their children as they saw fit, teaching them to love and respect each other and to honor and obey their elders. They would have to accomplish this goal against huge obstacles, as white racism and racial discrimination continued as threats. That they succeeded is a testament to their inner strength as a people. The fortitude shown by them should serve as an inspiration to all of humanity.

CHAPTER SIX

"GET US SOME EDUCATION"
The Efforts of Blacks to Educate Themselves

MOST SLAVEHOLDERS FEARED the consequences of educating their slaves. Since Southern white society was built on the false premise of white superiority, it was in the owners' best interest to keep slaves ignorant and therefore less likely to challenge white authority. Although Julia Frazier's owner did not threaten her with bodily harm, she nevertheless intimidated her. It was not unusual for her mistress to watch her to make sure that Julia did not open any books while she was cleaning the library. But her master went further: he "would close up all de books an' put 'em on de shelf so's she couldn't see 'em."[1] Freedman William Henry Towns recalled that if they were to "talk er' bout learnin' ter reed and rite why ef we so much as spoke uv learnin' to read and rite we was scolded like de debil [devil]." Even worse, "If we was caught lookin' in er book we was treated same as ef we had killed somebody."[2] Indeed, slaves realized both the significance and the harsh realities of learning. Elijah Cox pointed out that if they picked up a newspaper, "they were whipped for that too."[3] "If Missus Betsy caught a nigger wid a piece o' paper up next to his eyes, she'd talk 'bout bustin' his brains out," maintained Frances Willis.[4] Lizzie Williams remembered the severe punishment of a woman named Nancy who could read and write. When her owner discovered her accomplishment, he "whipped her an den slapped hot irons to her all over" her naked body.[5]

While most slaveowners forbade instruction, others actively encouraged and supported the literacy of their slaves. They deemed literacy necessary for Christian salvation and thus permitted Bible reading. Some apparently thought that since instruction would counter ignorance, it was the right course of action to take. Still others taught their slaves to read and write in order for them to carry out certain tasks. Harrison Beckett recalled a school on the plantation where he resided, where "Dey teach 'em manners an' behavier too." Sometimes, he noted, "Dey git a broke-down white man to be de teacher. Dey try not to let de chillun come up so ign'nant."[6] Echoing similar sentiments, Robert Laird said that "Marse Jones had us slaves taught how to read an' write. He didn't want us not to know nothin'."[7] Mariah Synder's master hired a black man to teach the plantation slaves their ABCs.[8] Moreover, the masters of Elige Davison, Minerva Bratcher, and Cornelia Robinson took it upon themselves to teach slaves how to read and write.[9] Davison's owner wanted to be able to send him on errands, and one of the other owners instructed his slave so he could copy the names and addresses of patients.[10] Regardless of the circumstances, it appears that the driving force behind the promotion of literacy to blacks by whites was not humanitarianism but self-interest.

Another means by which slaves could be taught was through the aid of Southern white children. Accounts in the slave narratives reveal that both white children and slave youth were aware of the threat of punishment by white adults, because in describing how they learned to read and write from white children they used words such as "slipped" and "secretly." Susan Merritt recalled that since her young mistress liked her, she tried to teach her. "She would slip to my room, and had me doin' right good. I learned my alphabet." Unfortunately, the young girl's mother discovered what they had been up to. "She lammed me over the head with the butt of a cowhide whip and tell Miss Bessie that she would cowhide her if she caught her learnin' me anything." In her owner's opinion, "Niggers don't need to know anythin."[11] Aware of the dire consequences of discovery, Susie King Taylor's white playmate, Katie, offered her lessons if she would not tell Mr. O'Connor, her father.[12] In this way, Taylor learned how to read and write. She was more fortunate than Susan Merritt, however, since her playmate's mother was aware of what was going on but chose not to interfere.

If white children were unwilling to instruct black youths, then the slaves found practical and creative ways of learning. Lizzie Atkins, for example, began to read and write by observing white children as they were being taught: "I would come and watch while they was telling their children their lessons in their home by the light from the fire-place."[13] When Frederick Douglass was no longer given lessons by his owner's wife, he devised a clever scheme to further his education. When he met a white child who could read and write, he would say that he himself could do so. "The next word would be, don't believe you. Let me see you try." Although Douglass knew only four letters of the alphabet, he wrote them down and challenged the boy to top that. "In this way," he recalled "I got a good many lessons in writing."[14] In another ploy, Morgan Ray tells the story of how his stepfather learned to write his name. When he was a boy, he was sent to carry the books for the white children attending school. "On de way home he would get de chillun to write different things on a slate er on de ground by bettin 'em dey couldn't do it." By the time that his stepfather's trick was found out, he had already learned to spell out his name.[15]

Slaves and free blacks with the ability to read and write often taught other blacks as well as some whites. Frederick Douglass, for example, who had struggled to learn, wanted to enlighten his fellow slaves. Accordingly, he organized a school for blacks and soon had between twenty and thirty eager students. In observing his pupils, Douglass wrote, "it was surprising with what ease they provided themselves with spelling-books."[16] Jerry Cook's father taught his two oldest sons, but Cook never had the opportunity to benefit from his father's literacy.[17] Mark Oliver recounted the way that he and other slaves on the plantation where he resided learned how to read and write. His master purchased some slaves from Cincinnati who had worked in the households of whites. Upon their arrival on the plantation, these literate slaves "passed on to us what they knew."[18]

Because education was forbidden to slaves either formally or informally, it became one of the prizes that freed people struggled hardest to acquire. Through their daily interactions with whites, they had seen the advantages that education conferred.[19] As a community, blacks were proud of those who had learned to read or write in slavery and held them in high regard.[20] Upon emancipation, most former slaves, old and young alike, wanted to learn how to read so that they could read at least the Bible. One elderly freedman, sitting beside his grandchild in a Mobile, Alabama, school, told a reporter from the North that he did not want to "trouble the lady much, but he must learn to read the Bible and the New Testament."[21] Others wanted to be able to defend their newly gained political rights. For instance, if black men could read their ballots, it would be more difficult for whites to manipulate their votes. Moreover, since the Freedmen's Bureau insisted on written contracts between planters and former slaves, these workers needed basic literacy to protect themselves from labor contracts designed to deliberately confuse and entrap them. Thus, when asked why she was determined to learn to read and write, one freedwoman replied, "so that the Rebs can't cheat me."[22] Freedmen did not assume that education would bring them easy riches or equality, but they knew that it could give substance to their liberty.

TEACHING THE FREEDMEN, 1866.

Courtesy of the North Carolina Division of Archives and History

Although some Southern states voiced support for black education, the financial aid given by most governments was considerably less than what was needed. The Freedmen's Bureau provided no funds for the education of freedmen until the summer of 1866, and that support amounted to only $500,000.[23] But the Bureau, along with Northern benevolent societies, did provide valuable services. In the early stages of Reconstruction, they sent more than 1,000 people to the South to teach freedmen and their children, donated books, and contributed thousands of dollars to build schools and pay teachers. Nevertheless, government support and the charitable efforts of Northerners continued to lag behind the actual need. The New England Freedmen's Aid Society, for example, only offered funds to blacks who built, repaired, and cared for schools, furnished board for teachers, and paid small tuition fees. Moreover, the guiding assumptions shared by many who managed Northern benevolent societies were expressed by Edward Everett Hale, who stated that "the policy has not been to make those people beggars—'Aide-toi et Dieu t'aidera' [Help yourself and God will help you] is their motto. The black people know they must support themselves, as they have always done."[24] Consequently, the twin burdens of financing and operating the freedmen's schools fell in some part on the shoulders of the former slaves themselves.

EFFORTS OF FREE BLACKS

Free blacks from the South and the North committed themselves to the education of former slaves. Among those from the South were Francis L. Cardozo, William O. Weston, J. Sasportas, Henry S. Spencer, Francis Rollin, and Harriet and Richard Holloway, most of whom were light-skinned members of Charleston's black aristocracy. Some were teachers who had been educated in antebellum Charleston and had run private schools for free blacks in the pre-Civil War period.[25] Other Southern free blacks included Robert Fitzgerald of Delaware, John Oliver of Virginia, and John Overton of North Carolina. Among those sent down from the North by private benevolent organizations and the federally funded Freedmen's Bureau were Jonathan Gibbs, Virginia C. Green, Blanche Harris, Franklin Randolph, Clara Duncan, Sara G. Stanley, Charlotte Forten, Sallie Daffin, and Edmonia G. Highgate. They, too, were mostly light-skinned and had all been educated in Northern schools.[26]

Black teachers were so strongly committed to advancing the cause of their race that they were willing, as Blanche Harris wrote from Mississippi, "to suffer many things" in order to see their race elevated.[27] Despite their light skin and privileged education, many black teachers were subjected to racism. After it was discovered that Clara Duncan was black during the train ride to her post in Virginia in 1864, she was called a "nigger wench," refused meal service, and forced to ride in a separate compartment.[28] In a letter to the American Missionary Association (AMA), Duncan wrote that despite the hardships she was enduring, she was "prepared to give up everything even life for the good of the cause, and count it not a hardship but an honor and blessing to me."[29] Edmonia Highgate, though in danger of falling ill with yellow fever or even being shot, proclaimed, "I must do or die for my freed brethren."[30] Sallie Daffin turned down teaching jobs near her home in Philadelphia, where wages were higher and facilities better than anywhere in the South. She wrote instead to the AMA that she would "never teach in the North again after realizing the needs of her race in the South."[31] Remembering these efforts, black scholar W. E. B. DuBois wrote in 1920, "After the [Civil] War the sacrifice of Negro women for freedom and uplift is one of the finest chapters in their history."[32] Helping to prepare the newly freed slaves for their new position in society merely reflected the long-standing tradition of self-help maintained by North American blacks.

Some former black officers in the Union army also contributed to the cause of black education. William H. Holland, for example, after his tour of duty, attended Oberlin College and then returned home to Texas to teach school. Holland's interest in politics led to his successful campaign for the state legislature as a member of the Republican Party. As a Texas legislator he helped to establish Prairie View Normal School (now called Prairie View A & M), and the Texas State Institute for Deaf and Blind Black Youth, which he ran for fourteen years. Two black former army surgeons, Alexander T. Augusta and Charles B. Purvis, practiced in hospitals in Washington, DC, that catered to blacks. Both men also taught at the Howard Medical School for many years, remaining there even though they received no pay for their services when Howard fell on hard times. When the local affiliate of the American Medical Association refused to admit them because they were black, Augusta and Purvis formed the National Medical Association for black physicians.[33]

Although many Northern and Southern whites took teaching jobs in schools for blacks in the South during the Reconstruction period, a large majority of black parents preferred black teachers for their children. Underscoring this sentiment, Methodist minister Thomas W. Stringer wrote from Vicksburg, "Our people will not be satisfied until they have colored teachers."[34] In Charleston in 1867 the Reverend Richard Cain underscored the psychological, emotional, and practical benefits of black teachers: "Honest, dignified whites, may teach ever so well, it has not the effect to exalt the black man's opinion of his own race, because they have always been in the habit of seeing white men in honored positions, and respected; but when the colored man, his fellow, comes upon the stage, and does the honorable work, exhibits the same great comprehension of facts, this ocular proof to the mind of that class, is tenfold more convincing, and gives an exalted opinion of the race."[35] Similarly, James Walker Hood paid homage to the "noble, self-sacrificing devotion" of white teachers from the North, but he maintained that he would always work toward "colored teachers for colored schools."[36]

Blacks regarded many white teachers as racists, whether consciously or unconsciously so, and thought their children, only recently freed from enslavement to whites, should have black men and women as teachers and authority figures.[37] Adding more credence to the value of black teachers was the racism and paternalism of white members of Northern benevolent societies. A leading critic of these benevolent societies was Frederick Douglass, who noted in 1865 that "these groups tended to give blacks pity and not justice."[38] The organ of the African Methodist Episcopal Church, the *Christian Recorder*, published in 1865 a scathing editorial on the glaring disparity between the principles and practices of some Northern white missionaries. The *Recorder* condemned those missionaries "who while in the North make loud pretension to Abolition, [but] when they get South partake so largely of that contemptible prejudice that they are ashamed to be seen in company with colored men."[39] Not surprisingly, blacks wanted the schools to encourage racial pride in their children as well as to educate them—that is, freedmen wanted to use education to further liberate themselves from the control of whites. Only black teachers and black school boards could put control of the education of freedmen where it rightfully belonged: in the black community itself.[40]

SACRIFICES MADE FOR EDUCATION

Observers throughout the South were impressed with the freedmen's strong desire for education. "Too much cannot be said of the desire to learn among this people. Everywhere to open a school has been to have it filled," a Freedmen's Bureau official in Alabama noted.[41] Classrooms were often extremely crowded, with as many as fifty or even one hundred students in each of them. In fact, in Louisiana from May 1864 to the end of the war, the student-teacher ratio never fell below an average of sixty to one.[42] When a teacher in Athens, Georgia, tried to limit her primary class to one hundred, black parents implored, "Do let them come if you please, ma'am, and if you can't teach them even a little, just let them sit and hear what the rest learn; they'll be sure to catch it."[43] A witness before the Joint Congressional Committee on Reconstruction testified that the Alabama negroes "have scarcely a leisure moment that you cannot see them with a book in their hand learning to read."[44] White Northern journalist Sidney Andrews noted, "I saw the negro porter of a store laboring at his spelling book in the corner, when no customers were in, and a young negro woman with her spelling book fastened to the fence, that she might study while at work over the washtub."[45]

Northern white contemporary John Trowbridge found the difference in the ages of students striking: "six years and sixty may be seen side by side, learning to read from the same chart or book."[46] Because books were scarce, freedmen "studied their letters in almanacs and dictionaries or whatever was available. They usually sat on log seats or the dirt floor."[47] Despite these conditions, they continued to attend school as regularly as possible throughout the Reconstruction years. In Savannah, for example, approximately 1,200 out of 1,600 black children attended school on a regular basis, and enrollment figures for black school-aged children in Charleston registered nearly

50 percent, with attendance rates varying from 70 to 90 percent.[48] Moreover, James Anderson has shown that blacks throughout the post-Civil War period had remarkably high rates of attendance.[49] Young children whose parents were working brought infant siblings to school with them, and adults attended at night or during the day after the crops were harvested.[50]

Black pupils were soon advancing as rapidly in their studies as many of their white counterparts. Indeed, the principal of Charleston's Morris Street School declared that black children learned "as readily as whites" and that "their thirst for knowledge was much greater than that of whites."[51] A reporter for the *New York Times* wrote that he had seen black students in Charleston working algebra problems, answering questions in ancient and modern history, and reading literature with good comprehension.[52] An AMA instructor declared that in ten years of teaching in the North, he had "never seen greater advancement in the same time."[53] One teacher from a school near Savannah reported that after only eight months of instruction, her 120 students could "read, sing hymns, and repeat Bible verses and had learned about right conduct which they tried to practice."[54]

Not all of the children, however, practiced "right conduct." For example, Sarah Jane Foster, a white teacher employed by the AMA, "kept David standing all day for his fighting."[55] She recalled whipping Mary Smith one day,[56] and noted an episode in which two students started a ruckus in her class. They both ran out of the classroom, but when one returned, she gave him a "severe flogging."[57] The freed children, unaccustomed to sitting for long periods of time and listening to teachers, sometimes allowed their minds to wander, and this lapse contributed to classroom disruptions. And, like white children, they sometimes used implausible excuses for lateness. One teacher in North Carolina became so exasperated that she complained in a letter to the AMA that "you never know at what point you may expect to find them clear or stark blind," because there was "the most free-and-easy defiance of all rules of discipline or self-regulation."[58] Another exclaimed that the children were "too easily amused," laughed "at trifles," and found almost any excuse for not paying attention in class.[59] Given the fact that freedmen had not received any formal education, it is remarkable that discipline was not a bigger problem. That it was not is a testament to their determination to read and write and to the successful efforts of parents in raising their children.

The children as well as their parents made substantial sacrifices to attend school. Parents who did not have enough money to pay tuition offered teachers milk, eggs, butter, chickens, and even pottery as compensation. These contributions were certainly necessary because some black and white teachers were starving. General Scott of the Freedmen's Bureau endorsed the application of a black man who wanted to teach, thereby guaranteeing him a Federal salary. Scott explained that "there are a number of competent colored men here who would willingly devote their time to the education of the young, providing that their support could be insured them while so engaged."[60] Young black pupils sometimes worked at odd jobs to earn money for their tuition. Jennie Armstrong noted that "the students pay for every book and slate with a readiness that is remarkable, the money coming to us in the almost forgotten shape of dimes and quarters."[61] They went ragged, skipped meals, and walked great distances to get to school. The educational inspector for the Freedmen's Bureau, J. W. Alvord, for example, reported the hardships of some young blacks: "At daylight in Winter, many of the pupils in the sparsely populated country places leave their home breakfastless for the school-house, five, six, or seven miles away."[62] Margaret Newbold recalled meeting a "motley assemblage" on her first day in a Freedmen's School. "Cold, dirty, and half-naked but eager to learn," her students were not concerned with what they could obtain in food and clothing, but "[were] anxious to feel sure that they would have the privilege of coming to school everyday."[63]

As they had during the antebellum period, once freed, blacks often taught other blacks, particularly family members and friends. The report of Ellen Stearns, a teacher at Oakdale Farm, North Carolina, makes this point. Stearns wrote, "I have a new scholar. He comes several miles to school, and is never absent, rain or shine." She appeared stunned that this student had learned his letters in three lessons, and in only three weeks was able to spell words of three letters. Moreover, "he has taught his mother and two sisters all he has learned as we went along."[64]

Receiving instruction from their children had both a positive and a negative impact. While many black parents wholeheartedly supported their children's educational pursuits, occasionally they would voice the fear of being outpaced by their youngsters who then would learn to despise their parents' country ways.[65] Elizabeth Hyde Botume observed that parents on the Sea Islands urged their youngsters to school, but the best scholars refused to go back to fieldwork. "This was a serious offense to the old people. 'Do they think I am to hoe with them folks that don't know anything!' exclaimed one of the older boys. 'I know too much for that.' 'Them children discountenance we,' groaned the parents. 'They is too smart; they knows too much.' "[66] In other words, some black parents were afraid that an education would make their children too independent and ultimately they would lose control of them. It is ironic that this fear was also one held by Southern whites about educating blacks.

Although the Freedmen's Bureau and Northern benevolent societies contributed to the efforts of blacks, freedmen often took the initiative in opening, financing, and maintaining their own schools. In fact, before Northern benevolent societies entered the South in 1862, before President Lincoln issued the Emancipation Proclamation in 1863, and before Congress established the Freedmen's Bureau in 1865, blacks had begun to make plans to educate the illiterate among them. They started schools in New Orleans and at Fortress Monroe, Virginia, in 1860 and 1861, and some schools that predated the Civil War simply increased their activities during and after the conflict. One such school was established in Savannah in 1833 and ran until 1865 without the knowledge of local authorities. During all those years, its teacher, a black woman named Deveaux, worked tirelessly teaching blacks to read.[67]

This kind of self-sustaining behavior led to the growth of what John W. Alvord, the general superintendent of schools at the Freedmen's Bureau, called "native-schools."[68] Classes were held in any available building—an abandoned warehouse, a pool room, a former slave market, a church basement, or even a private home.[69] To the freedmen, it mattered little where they were taught as long as they had the chance to learn. Consequently, Freedmen's Bureau officials were astonished to find so many schools organized and operated by blacks when they arrived in the South in 1865. Alvord discovered several of these "native-schools" on a tour of the Southern states in 1865 and 1866. Among those he described was one he stumbled upon at Goldsboro, North Carolina: "Two colored young men, who but a little time before commenced to learn themselves, had gathered 150 pupils, all quite orderly and hard at study."[70] Northern white teachers who were sent to the interior found a school for freedmen at Tigerville, Louisiana, organized by a former slave using books procured by a plantation worker from children's libraries on local plantations.[71] Similarly, when the first AMA missionary, Lewis C. Lockwood, arrived to open a school for blacks at Fortress Monroe in September 1861, there was Mary S. Peake, a prosperous black woman from Hampton, already teaching blacks in a school she had organized.[72] Unlike Peake, many of the blacks who established "native-schools" were not well qualified to teach. For instance, a visitor to James City, a community of freedmen across the river from New Bern, had an opportunity to talk with an elderly man who conducted a "native-school" in the area. Describing his background, the teacher said, "I taught myself."[73] However, in the opinion of most of those who instructed freedmen, credentials or the lack thereof were relatively unimportant. Their top priority was the lowering of the illiteracy rate among blacks.

Financing and maintaining schools were often community efforts. Some communities voluntarily taxed themselves to pay for everyone's education. In others, black schools charged tuition. Children of families who were not able to afford the tuition, however, were allowed to attend without any charge.[74] Black commitment to education was so great that even on the remotest plantations, some freedmen "asked the proprietors to reserve out of their wages enough to hire a teacher for their children."[75] Others refused to sign contracts with planters without a clause stipulating that the planter would supply lumber and a plot of land to build a school. Black artisans sometimes donated their labor,[76] and elite blacks sometimes donated lots. The Rollin family of Charleston, for example, offered to provide a lot if the Freedmen's Bureau would pay for the construction of a school. Subsequently, with the help of James Lynch, a missionary of the AME Church, Charlotte Rollin opened a school for freedmen in Charleston. In fact, one of the reasons why the Rollin sisters appeared before the legislature in Columbia was to secure state support.[77]

In an attempt to raise funds to build their own school, blacks in Wilmington, North Carolina, gave a Bible and a Methodist hymnbook as prizes to those who collected the most money. In response to crowded and poor school facilities, blacks in Beaufort, North Carolina, began a building campaign in January 1866. With over $300, on July 4, 1866, construction of the new school commenced. The actions of Beaufort's blacks did not go unnoticed by contemporaries. Harriet Beals wrote, "men, women, and children are all eager to advance this work, denying themselves every little comfort, that they may pay the money for the schoolhouse." She added, "a woman gave up a dress last week that she greatly admired."[78]

Another contemporary commented on the efforts of other North Carolina blacks to build a new school. By January 1867, freedmen had contributed $800 toward their new building, which was nearly completed. In describing the school and the sacrifices made for it,

S. J. Whiton wrote, "This edifice contains the finest hall for colored people in North Carolina, and the freedmen here are naturally rather proud of it. Many of them have gone without their dinners, and denied themselves in various ways, in order to help along the good work."[79] Moreover, a group of black women in Lexington, Kentucky, launched a successful campaign that culminated in the opening in September 1866 of Howard School, named for General O. O. Howard, the Freedmen's Bureau director. It occupied a large brick building on Church Street known as "Ladies Hall," which James Turner and other black leaders purchased for $3,500. Howard School opened with three black teachers and five hundred enrollees.[80]

Often, despite their poverty, black families offered room and board to teachers to supplement their salaries. Fayetteville, North Carolina, blacks provided a house for AMA teacher David Dickson and agreed to pay for his fuel, lights, books, and assistants. When thirteen teachers were requested from the AMA national headquarters in 1866, at almost every location freedmen had agreed to assume the costs of board and fuel. The AMA had to pay only salary and transportation.[81] In addition, Dudley blacks paid Carrie Scott, a teacher, $15 per month in 1872.[82]

The black thirst for education existed among the civilized nations as well. Indeed, black Indians collected money from poor but ambitious parents, built their own schools, and hired and paid teachers. A government report on black Creeks in 1866 confirmed that "they are anxious that their children shall be educated" and are "determined to profit" from "the school formed at their own advance."[83]

Throughout the South, blacks formed societies to promote education, raising money among themselves to purchase land, build schoolhouses, and pay teachers' salaries. One such society in Georgetown, South Carolina, collected $800 to purchase a lot.[84] In 1866 the Louisiana Educational Relief Association was organized to pay for the education of poor black children. Its board of trustees had the authority to lease or buy school property as they saw fit and to examine and employ teachers.[85] In 1865 black leaders established the Georgia Educational Association to set school policies, raise funds to help finance the cost of education, and supervise schools in districts throughout the state. It was established on the principle that freedmen should organize schools in their own counties and neighborhoods and finance and maintain them as well. By the fall of 1866 the association had helped finance entirely or in part ninety-six of the 123 day and evening schools for freedmen in that state and owned fifty-seven buildings. In Savannah in 1866, sixteen of twenty-eight schools were under the control of an all-black board and had only black teachers.[86] Blacks in Maryland similarly established the Baltimore Association for the Moral and Educational Improvement of the Colored People to advance the cause of black education. It, too, was a smashing success. In 1867 it was able to build sixty schoolhouses and raise over $23,000 for freedmen's education.[87]

Having established a long tradition of self-help, black churches were at the vanguard of the freedmen's educational campaign. In Texas both before and after the Freedmen's Bureau left the state, churches offered their facilities for classrooms. One of the first Bureau schools to open in Galveston, in September 1865, was held in the black Methodist church, and two other black schools that opened in the city by 1867 also utilized church facilities. African Methodists in Houston allowed schools in their churches. And as a consequence of the black community's failure to raise enough money to build a schoolhouse, freedmen in Corpus Christi in 1869 still used one of their churches for regular classes.[88] Also, in Kentucky, the black First Baptist Church of Lexington, pastored by the Reverend James Monroe, opened a school in the fall of 1865, and other churches in the city such as Pleasant Green Baptist, Main Street Baptist, Asbury AME, and the Christian Church followed suit.[89] In these church-based schools, preachers often served as schoolteachers. For instance, D. C. Lacy, an African Methodist minister, taught at one of the three freedmen's schools in Limestone County, Texas, and a black Baptist pastor in Austin, Texas, taught at one of the Travis County schools.[90]

Although many churches that were used as schools were poorly lit and ventilated and furnished with benches rather than desks, they were often the only public buildings owned by the freedmen that could be put to use as schools. Most people were poor, and congregations throughout the South in rural areas and small towns could afford only small, simple buildings that were sparsely furnished. A Northern teacher, G. Thurston Chase, conducted classes in North Carolina in a church that was "made of staves split out by hand."[91] The building was totally inadequate for the large number of students, thus forcing the teacher to cram as many as seventy-five to one hundred children in a room built to accommodate about twenty-five. To make matters worse, rough pine benches served as seats.[92] Nevertheless, some places were even worse. In Marietta, Georgia, a church school was large enough, but soldiers had torn out the pews and broken the windows. As a result, the students had no place to sit, and icy winds and heavy rains blew through the room.[93] The situation did not substantially improve in towns or cities with larger congregations and sturdier buildings. Conditions were still extremely difficult, with classes typically conducted in basements that were dark, damp, and dingy.[94]

Church leaders were meeting their ecclesiastical responsibilities when aiding in the establishment of schools. An important part of the moral training and religious upbringing of children pertained to their learning how to read the Bible. Operating schools would help bring about this goal as well as enable the preachers to care for the spiritual welfare of the members of their communities.[95] As a consequence of their firm commitment to education, their churches would continue to play a leading role in bringing literacy to thousands of blacks throughout the post-Civil War period, in spite of inadequate funds and facilities. By 1880, for example, the AME General Conference reported that it was operating 2,345 Sunday schools, employing 15,454 teachers and other officers, and serving 154,549. It also owned eighty-eight schoolhouses, with 1,983,358 books and pamphlets in libraries. Moreover, the other Methodist organizations and the Baptists also operated regular schools and Sunday schools. Perhaps the following comments of a journalist best express the sentiments held by church members in regard to their commitment to promote education without the help of sometimes paternalistic whites: "The Church and its schools were supported entirely by its members. It was not a 'pampered favorite' of white philanthropists but 'leaned upon itself for brains, money, and Christian sympathy.' White philanthropy was meddlesome and intrusive, and it provided largesse only 'when white men stood at the helm.' "[96]

Given the limited resources of most freedmen, many of whom were homeless and barely clothed, the number of schools built and maintained and the number of teachers supported throughout the South are truly remarkable. Despite their grinding poverty, which was aggravated by the devastation of the whole Southern agricultural economy and by the frequent refusal of planters to pay black workers their wages, freedmen somehow found in excess of $1 million for schools by 1870.[97] Their actions should provide a valuable lesson for present-day blacks. If freedmen of the Reconstruction period accomplished this feat against nearly insurmountable odds, then today's blacks should be willing to help promote the education of their children by becoming actively involved in the process—assist children with homework, attend PTA meetings regularly, and volunteer a few hours each week at school. These efforts to a small extent would pay homage to the great sacrifices made by their ancestors in their struggle to obtain literacy.

SOUTHERN WHITE OPPOSITION TO BLACK EDUCATION

The opposition of Southern whites to black education was a serious threat to the survival of freedmen's schools. Whites feared that education would give blacks the notion that they were equal to whites—an idea that could not be tolerated in a society built on the myth of white superiority and black inferiority. Some whites regarded the teaching of blacks as a treasonous act, and others were afraid that education would prompt blacks to become more aggressive in their dealings with whites. Perhaps the comments made by an elderly white man whom Whitelaw Reid came upon capture the feelings of most Southern whites toward black education. He thought "that education for blacks was positively indecent," and informed Reid: "Sir, we accept the death of slavery, but sir, surely there are some things that are not tolerable."[98] This Southern white opposition to black education could manifest itself in dangerous ways. For instance, a Virginia freedman testified before a congressional committee that anyone starting a school in his county would be killed and that blacks there were "afraid to be caught with a book."[99] Elvira Lee recalled that former slaves from Captain Hall's plantation were given an acre of land on which to build a school, but "prejudice ran so high against the negro school that this was burned after a few weeks."[100] Thirty-seven black schools were destroyed by fire in 1869 in Tennessee alone.[101] Indeed, so many of these schoolhouses were burned down by Southern whites that former slave Pierce Harper told his interviewer that "de gov'ment built de colored people schoolhouses an' de Klu Klux went to work an' burn 'em down."[102] Frequently, freedmen would rebuild because they refused to let anything stand in their way. Education was far too important to allow it to escape their grasp.

White Southerners often attacked the freedmen's teachers, regardless of their skin color, but most of their anger was aimed particularly at black teachers. For example, a mob broke into the home of a black teacher in Delaware and frightened her so badly that she resigned from her position and left the area. White students continually harassed Martha Hoy, a black teacher in Maryland, by tripping her, pushing her off the walk, and throwing dirt and stones at her. Six whites beat a black teacher in Centerville, Maryland, and shot at him as he struggled to free himself. In Savannah, a black teacher known as Mr. Whittfield was murdered in 1866. Another black teacher, in Mississippi, watched his school burn to the ground and later was beaten nearly to death by the Ku Klux Klan. One black teacher was killed in Alabama in 1868, and there were attempts on the lives of two others. Two black teachers at Fisk University were stripped and savagely beaten by a dozen men who forced them to run through the woods as if they were animals while several whites shot at them.[103] But all of this violence would not go unanswered. Sarah Jane Foster, a white AMA teacher, for example, remembered a school meeting that was disturbed by a group of whites. However, "some of the colored people fired a pistol after the intruders, and gave chase and caught two."[104] They discovered the names of two more, who were eventually arrested and taken to jail.[105]

Southern whites ultimately would use whatever means necessary to prevent black literacy. They regularly insulted Southern and Northern white teachers of freedmen, prohibited their communities from boarding or leasing rooms to them, and beat, harassed, and murdered them. Although there was no factual basis, Sarah Foster was accused of having had sexual relations with black men. This charge was used as an excuse by a Mrs. Hoke not to board her.[106] John Trowbridge, a Northern white, noted that "there were combinations formed to prevent the leasing of rooms for schools, and those who would have been willing to let buildings for this purpose were deterred from doing so by threats of vengeance from their neighbors."[107] John Alvord wrote about a Southern white man in Greensborough, Georgia, being "taken out of his house at night and whipped unmercifully" for boarding a white teacher of freedmen, who was run out of town.[108] Although the above-mentioned teachers were at least spared their lives, this was not the case for a Mr. Heather, who, according to former slave Evie Herrin, was tied to a log by a group of whites and shot to death. This assault led to the Clinton race riot.[109]

With the constant and often violent opposition of whites to the education of blacks and with the chronic shortage of financial support for freedmen's schools in the late 1860s and throughout the Reconstruction era, these schools fell on hard times. The condition of the already weakened economy was worsened by the economic depression of the 1870s, and the Freedmen's Bureau and Northern benevolent societies withdrew their financial aid. As a result, many of the schools organized by freedmen themselves were forced to close. But they persisted in their quest for education. There was much work to be done—more qualified teachers had to be hired and retained, school buildings had to be secured and maintained, and supplies had to be found. To these ends, freedmen labored diligently. In so doing, they not only continued the tradition of educational self-help but also became the first Southerners to wage a campaign for universal public education. With the help of the Freedmen's Bureau and Northern benevolent societies, the campaign grew from a meager beginning in 1860 to a school system that was virtually complete in its institutional form by 1870. In other words, the freedmen's schools served as the precursors of the new public schools that were in operation throughout the South by 1870.[110] Indeed, this accomplishment is a fitting tribute to the struggle made by black men and women to become literate.

THE FORMATION OF BLACK COLLEGES
AND UNIVERSITIES

The issue of higher education was the concern of numerous blacks, the Freedmen's Bureau, and Northern benevolent societies. As was the case in regard to creating and maintaining grade schools, the three groups again united their efforts and established and supported several institutions of higher learning for black men and women during the Reconstruction years. Black churches, too, often played a leading role in founding and supporting black colleges and universities. Although the AME Church did not found Wilberforce University, it purchased it in 1863, and Bishop Daniel Payne became the school's president.[111] Northern Methodists founded Claflin College in 1869 in Orangeburg, South Carolina,[112] and Bennett College for black women was opened in 1873 in Greensboro, North Carolina, by Methodists, although the college was the inspiration of newly emancipated slaves who had bought the land on which it now stands.[113]

During the post-Civil War period, black Baptists, with the assistance of their white brethren, helped establish and support Spelman College for women in Atlanta, Benedict College in Columbia, Leland University in New Orleans, Shaw University in Raleigh, and Morehouse College in Atlanta.[114] Saint Augustine's College was opened in Raleigh in 1867 by the Episcopal Church, and in the same year in Concord, North Carolina, the Presbyterian Church founded Barber-Scotia College.[115] The Congregational Church, working through the American Missionary Association with the aid of the Freedmen's Bureau, also founded numerous schools for blacks during the Reconstruction era. Among these were Fisk University in Nashville in 1865; Howard University in Washington, DC, in 1867; Atlanta University in Atlanta (now Clark-Atlanta University) (1867); Talladega College in Talladega, Alabama (1867); Hampton Institute in Hampton, Virginia (1868); and Tougaloo College in Tougaloo, Mississippi

LAURA SPELMAN ROCKEFELLER MEMORIAL BUILDING, SPELMAN COLLEGE.

Courtesy of Archives/Special Collections, Atlanta University Center, Robert W. Woodruff Library

SAINT AUGUSTINE'S COLLEGE

Courtesy of the Archives Division, Saint Augustine's College

HOWARD UNIVERSITY, 1870.

Courtesy of the Moorland-Spingarn Research Center, Howard University Archives

ATLANTA UNIVERSITY, ADMINISTRATION BUILDING, 1934.

Courtesy of Archives/Special Collections, Atlanta University Center, Robert W. Woodruff Library

(1869).[116] Finally, Fayetteville State College was established in Fayetteville, North Carolina, in 1867 through the joint efforts of seven blacks and the Freedmen's Bureau. The black citizens—David Bryant, Nelson Carter, Matthew N. Leary, A. J. Chestnut, Robert Simmons, George Grainer, and Thomas Lomax—paid $140 for a lot on Gillespie Street for the sole purpose of providing education to blacks. In accord with their desire, General Howard of the Bureau erected a building on this site.[117]

The priorities of these institutions varied to some extent from school to school. The goal at Atlanta University, Tougaloo College, Fayetteville State College, and Wilberforce University was the training of teachers to instruct the growing numbers of black students.[118] And, although Howard University, Saint Augustine's College, Lane College, and Fisk University sought to train religious leaders, they, too, had as their priority the training of teachers.[119] Others such as Shaw University and Livingstone College focused primarily on educating religious leaders for black communities.[120] Some of the private schools also concentrated on teaching morality, discipline, and responsibility as the means toward developing good character. Hampton Institute, in particular, under the leadership of General Samuel Chapman Armstrong, adopted this approach.[121] Moreover, while most of the black schools developed a Liberal Arts curriculum that included Greek, Latin, English, French, Philosophy, Astronomy, Chemistry, Geology, Political Economy, History, International Law, Mathematics, Geometry, Trigonometry, Algebra, and Logic,[122] Hampton's curriculum emphasized industrial education and focused specifically on instructing its students in manual labor. Such courses as brickmasonry, printing, cooking, sewing, basket weaving, broommaking, stock raising, dairying, farming, tinning, tanning, blacksmithing, wagon-making, carpentry, painting, barbering, and steam-power sawing were offered.[123]

Most of the black colleges and universities were open to whites, although very few whites were enrolled, and most of them were also coeducational, which fit in with a larger national trend. In 1872, for example, there were ninety-seven coeducational colleges and universities in the United States.[124] The historical record is sparse in terms of how female students were treated in these schools. However, we do know that Mary Ann Shadd Carey withdrew from Howard University's law school because of her gender in 1871. She eventually returned and earned a bachelor of law degree from Howard in 1883.[125] Since teaching was one of only a few professions open to black women, the vast majority of those enrolled sought degrees in education. Most of Atlanta University's female graduates, for example, either taught in Atlanta's public school system or in private schools. Mary Pope McCree, a member of the graduating class of 1880, ran a private school at Big Bethel AME Church until the Reverend Wesley Gaines recruited her to serve as the principal at Morris Brown College. Despite her success, private schools often lacked the funds for current books and teachers aides, and salaries remained meager. Moreover, most public school systems did not hire black men and women as teachers. It was not until 1878, for example, five years after the first Atlanta University teachers graduated, that five of them were hired by Atlanta's Board of Education. They were Indian Clark, Ella Townsley, Julia Turner, Mattie Upshaw, and Elizabeth Easley, all black women.[126]

Although the evidence is limited, it is plausible to suggest that a disproportionate number of the earliest black enrollees at these colleges were from the middle class. When Hampton Institute opened its doors in 1868, for example, most of its fifteen students were drawn from the village's black elite, including the family of the prominent William Roscoe Davis.[127] And, given Atlanta University's stiff admission requirements, it is unlikely that many students from the lower class would have been able to meet these standards. We also know that, like Amanda Dickson and Adella Hunt, many of the students from Hancock and the surrounding counties who attended Atlanta University during its first decade or so either had been nominally free before emancipation or at least shared surnames and other connections with prominent white families from their home county. Among this group were Matilda Rogers and Linton Stephens Ingram from Hancock County, Tolbert Bailey from Warren County, John Wesley Marlow from Milledgeville, and Fannie and Quinnie Stephens from Crawfordville. These individuals were so light-complexioned that they were virtually indistinguishable from most whites. Moreover, unlike the vast majority of people of color in Middle Georgia, many families of the Atlanta University students had also accumulated some personal and real property in the years following the war. Certainly, free status prior to the war, association with prominent families in the white community, and ownership of at least a small amount of money and property combined to create an undeniable advantage in gaining access to a better education during Reconstruction.[128]

We also know that Howard University's admissions requirements were steep in comparison to other black colleges, and that although Howard was not a true university placed up against most white schools, it reigned supreme among the black ones. No other black college offered as comprehensive a curriculum as did Howard. Furthermore, Howard was also opened to white men and women and expected to enroll some of them as well. It was thus unlikely that many blacks from the lower strata of society would measure up to the Howard standard. Indeed, a quick perusal of the historical record seems to bear out this assumption. A number of Howard's earliest students were from the black middle class, and three prominent families in particular—the Wormleys, Shadds, and Shippens—first were represented by these graduates. Two members of the Wormley and the related Shadd families, who have served Howard University and the Washington community in many important positions, were Anna Wormley, Class of 1870, and Eunice B. Shadd, Class of 1872. The Shippens, prominent especially in the public schools of the District of Columbia, were represented by Fannie Shippen, Class of 1870.[129]

Financial support for higher education flowed from various sectors of black communities. It came from religious bodies as well as from the individual and joint efforts of black men and women. Not only did black Baptists support higher education for men and women, but so, too, did the AME Church. Since they viewed women and ministers as important agents of cultural change, their educational status was of great concern to missionaries. Bishop Payne reasoned that since women were mothers, wives, and teachers, they played critical roles in shaping and transmitting the culture of the race. Furthermore, in his opinion, those roles took on even greater significance as African Methodists considered the task of regenerating the freedpeople. Therefore, Payne reached the conclusion that "the future demands educated women, . . . who will give unto the race a training entirely and essentially different from the past." He further clarified the mission of black women as one in which the demands of the new era required them to "descend into the South as educators." Richard Cain, an AME minister, underscored the sentiments of Payne when he asserted: "We need, and must have schools for girls."[130] Although there is no record of the AME Church establishing institutions of higher education for black women, there is no concrete reason to doubt its sincerity in terms of educating them, since schools begun by the AME Church such as Allen University, Morris Brown College, Edward Waters College, Paul Quinn College, and Wilberforce University (which the church purchased in 1863) all enrolled black women.

Black institutions of higher education were psychologically and emotionally uplifting to a people only a few years removed from slavery. Support for these schools was crucial. Cain's account of the significance of the AME Church's purchase of Wilberforce University echoes the sentiments held by most blacks in regard to the importance of black colleges and universities. Cain asked the denomination to support Wilberforce because within its walls blacks would be permitted to study "every branch of useful knowledge." Under the tutelage of a "faculty of distinguished colored gentlemen," students would be shielded from the "Negrophobia" that was "rampant" at other institutions. Cain further argued that blacks who contributed to the cause of Wilberforce were helping to "regenerate and redeem their race."[131] Apparently, many blacks agreed with Cain. When the university experienced a financial crisis two years after its purchase by the AME Church, black soldiers of the Eighth U.S. Colored Infantry regiment representing at least ten different states contributed $241 to Wilberforce.[132]

It was not unusual for blacks to either double or quadruple their fund-raising efforts if their institutions were on the verge of bankruptcy, which unfortunately was often the case. In the fall of 1871, for example, the Fisk Jubilee Singers went on tour to raise money and new supporters for Fisk University, which was in dire financial straits. They toured the Northern part of the country and sang slave spirituals to appreciative audiences. They performed before President Grant in the White House before returning home. The group earned over $20,000 for their university, which enabled it to become financially solvent. Indeed, the tour of the North was so successful that the Jubilee Singers subsequently embarked on a European tour, which netted nearly $50,000. This money was used to build Jubilee Hall on a new and much larger campus.[133]

In establishing and maintaining secondary schools and institutions of higher education for blacks, the Northern benevolent societies, the Freedmen's Bureau, and, significantly, blacks themselves laid a solid foundation that has been used to break down the high rate of black illiteracy and to move the race forward. Notwithstanding the aid of whites, however, the bulk of the credit should be accorded to blacks, who struggled mightily throughout the latter nineteenth century against nearly insurmountable odds to guarantee access of education to blacks. By the dawn of the twentieth century, most of the white philanthropic assistance had ceased, and the Freedmen's Bureau was out of existence. Consequently, then, after initial help from sympathetic whites, the major burden of ensuring the survival of black schools fell on black communities. Although most blacks were living in poverty or near it, they worked feverishly to keep their schools open. That they did so against tremendous obstacles attests to their commitment to education as well as to their inner strength as a people. And, as the twentieth century was being ushered in, the results of their labor became apparent. In fourteen Southern states, for example, the black illiteracy rate dropped substantially from 1880 to 1900, representing nearly a 28 percent decrease. On the national level the black illiteracy rate plummeted from 70 percent in 1880 to about 30 percent in 1910.[134]

Given the fact that acute white racism and racial discrimination permeated American society in the latter nineteenth and twentieth centuries, had it not been for black schools a sizable number of African Americans certainly would not have been educated. These institutions of higher learning represent the bedrock of black progress and have produced a significant number of black professionals, ministers, politicians, and business leaders. Indeed, the list is too extensive to present here. The pioneers of black education sensed the urgency of creating schools, and society as a whole is better off because of their foresight and determination. Their triumph will be everlasting. That is the legacy left by our daring black brothers and sisters.

CHAPTER SEVEN

"OUR OWN HOUSES OF WORSHIP"
Black Churches during Reconstruction

THROUGHOUT THE ANTEBELLUM period, slaves and free blacks attended the Southern white churches of the Baptists, Methodists, Presbyterians, Episcopalians, Congregationalists, and other Protestant sects. A few were also Catholics. In antebellum churches, black members generally were judged by the same standards as white members.[1] Ruhama Baptist Church, for example, disciplined its black and white congregants for stealing, dancing, gambling, adultery, drunkenness, and other moral offenses by excluding them from services.[2] Black marriages and morals were overseen by biracial churches as strictly as those of whites. A charge, for instance, was made in 1849 against Julia Nalen, a black, for leaving her husband and marrying again. After a thirty-day investigation of her conduct that most observers dubbed as fair, Julia was expelled from church. Baptists, whether black or white, were prohibited from dancing on church property. In 1838 a black woman named Minna Rice was accused of this offense. When she refused to stop her evil ways, she was excluded. The only discernible double standard was sexual: only black and white women were charged with fornication. Conversely, black or white men (or couples) were charged with "living disorderly," an offense that required more than a single sexual encounter.[3]

Despite the fact that black and white church members were often disciplined in the same way in Southern antebellum biracial churches, they were usually separated by seating arrangements. Sometimes a partition isolated them, or blacks were seated either in the back of the church or in the gallery. These areas became known as "nigger pews," and many blacks resented them. The separate seating arrangements were designed to send a strong message to blacks: while they were de facto members of the church, at best they still occupied a subordinate position in Southern white society. The voluminous slave narratives give several vivid examples. Polly Turner Cancer asserted: "We went to da white folks church; de black folks wud set on one side ov de partition an' de white folks 'ud set on de udder."[4] Arthur Colson recalled "a place in the back of the church reserved for the slaves,"[5] and Mary Childs remembered going to a Methodist church with whites, where "we'd sit in the back, not upstairs."[6]

Those blacks not subjected to separate seating arrangements attended services held at times different from those of the white members of their congregation. According to Ella Harris, "the slaves didn' have no church er dey own but us used Moster's white church cept us had our service in de evening and day 'un in de mornings."[7] Tillman Bradshaw maintained that "the white people attended church Sunday Morning and colored people in the afternoon."[8] And Martha Everett recalled that "when th' preacher got through preachin' ter th' white fokes they'd leave an' then he'd preach ter us."[9]

Notwithstanding the fact that Southern biracial churches accepted blacks as members, allowed them to worship in the same buildings, and disciplined them the same as whites, black congregants were generally treated as subordinates. They rarely had any responsible voice in church matters. Thus, historians such as John Boles who argue that biracial Southern churches in the antebellum period represented a form of short-lived egalitarianism have missed the mark. In fact, one study of white Baptists and slavery in Alabama found no evidence of any white church having a black deacon, moderator, or correspondent, nor was a black ever a delegate to a denominational meeting or state convention. Although some white slaveowners showed concern for the spiritual welfare of their slaves, no efforts were made to install blacks in positions of equality in churches throughout the antebellum South.[10] Moreover, in some Virginia churches a slave could be expelled for disobeying his or her master.

In the decades preceding the war (1820–1860), most Southern whites had reached the conclusion that blacks should be given religious instruction, albeit the right kind. Scripture was tailored to meet their objective. Slaves were told that if they obeyed master and mistress they would live in eternal happiness. According to Charlie Bell, his minister's text "would always be 'obey yo' marster an' mistress that yo' days may be lingerin' upon God's green earth what he give you.' "[11] The preacher exhorted Andrew Jackson Gill and other slaves to "obey your missus an' marster. When you obey dem you obey God."[12] Julius Jones's preacher told his congregation, "when you serve your master, you is serving God."[13]

The slaves had contempt especially for white ministers whom they regarded as hypocrites. James Sumler recalled that "the ministers used to tell us not to be disorderly on taking the sacrament. However, I thought he was disorderly for he kept slaves." William Humbert, a fugitive slave from Charleston, noted: "I have seen a minister hand the sacrament to the deacons to give the slaves and before the slaves had time to get home, living a great distance from church, have seen one of the same deacons, acting as patrol." Humbert further observed that the deacon flogged "one of the brother members within two hours of his administering the sacrament to him, because he met the slave without a passport, beyond the time allowed for him to go home."[14] In addition, Henry Butler recalled the reactions of most slaves on the Sullivan plantation, where he lived, to Sunday sermons given by a white preacher: "he was very inconsiderate in the treatment of his own slaves, therefore his brotherly talk was not taken seriously by most of the colored folks." Further, he noted, a listener laughed at the minister's remarks during a discourse on kindness. In rebuke, the minister gave "twenty-five lashes to the unfortunate Negro."[15]

Blacks also aimed their condemnation at the Southern white population as a whole in regard to religious hypocrisy. Folktales developed around the theme that since whites were hypocrites, they would never enter the kingdom of Heaven. For example, one anonymous black told some of his friends the story of his having dreamt about Heaven. Not surprisingly, not one single white person was there. Versions of this story continued to flourish for years with its clear message: Heaven would be peopled only by blacks who had led Christian lives.[16] Although whites informed blacks that they should obey the Ten Commandments, they did not always obey them themselves—murder, theft, rape, and adultery were committed by whites while spousal fidelity and family values were ignored. Finally, while maintaining that it was sinful to drink alcohol and gamble, whites were observed by blacks committing these moral offenses at a higher rate than themselves.

Not surprisingly, slaves generally found the watered-down religious instruction they received from whites insufficient to meet their needs. Besides the superficial message of obedience to whites, blacks found the sermons bland, boring, unemotional, and uninspiring. Therefore, whenever possible, slaves would meet either in each other's cabins or at some secluded place in the woods where they could conduct their own religious services. The result was the development of the invisible slave church that historian Albert Raboteau has written so eloquently about. Former slaves described this institution in their interviews during the 1930s. Sylvia Floyd pointed out that "at times de darkies would go off to de woods to preach, shout an' sing praises."[17] Caroline Ates revealed that "lots o' times, durin' the week, we'd slip off by ourselves an' have prayer-meetin'."[18] According to Laura Ford, "We did all ob our real worshiping in de fiel's, out deir we could turn loose in our own way. We would sing, shout an' pray."[19] Precautions had to be taken to avoid detection. As Mary Gladdy explained, "A large iron pot was always placed against the cabin door to keep the sound of their voices from escaping."[20] The biggest threat to these secret services came from slaves patrollers who sought to catch blacks allegedly disobeying laws.

The usual penalty for detection was a severe whipping. To Jake Dawkins, the slave patrollers were "a bunch of de meanest oversees from all de plantations round. De patrollers would coth [caught] dem and give dem thirty nine lashes wid dey whips."[21] A careful slave would always carry a pass, especially if he was traveling from a plantation a few miles away. So as not to admit that they could not read, the patrollers sometimes would accept forged passes from slaves. If detected, the only sensible course for a slave was to run as fast and as hard as he could. The Reverend W. B. Allen's father told him about his experience at a prayer meeting that was broken up by slave patrollers. His father's quick thinking saved all the slaves there from brutal whippings. As the patrollers entered the house through its one door, Allen's father "stuck a big shovel in the fire place, drew out a peck or more of hot ashes and cinders and flung them broadcast into the faces of them patrollers." As a result, "the room was soon filled with smoke and the smell of burning clothes and white flesh." Every slave was able to escape during the confusion.[22] Many others, however, were not so fortunate. Some were caught and nearly beaten to death. For example, Dora Brewer relates the story of a slave who was caught attending a prayer meeting by her master. The "marster" became furious and "beat her within an inch of her life."[23] That blacks risked so much to worship in the way they desired is a testament to the value they placed on religious autonomy.

THE SEPARATION FROM BIRACIAL CHURCHES

Once slavery ended, blacks moved immediately to withdraw from Southern white congregations and establish their own churches. As noted earlier, they were unhappy with their prewar status in white churches and longed to break free of white supervision and control. Reconstruction afforded them this opportunity, and they took full advantage of it. Indeed, they withdrew in staggering numbers and at a rapid pace. On the eve of the war, 42,000 black Methodists worshipped in biracial churches in South Carolina; by the 1870s, only six hundred remained.[24] Cleveland County, North Carolina, counted 200 black members of biracial Methodist churches in 1860, ten in 1867, and none five years later.[25] Overall in North Carolina, from 1865 to 1866, 2,000 blacks deserted the Methodist Episcopal Church South, and during the six years between 1860 and 1866 the number of black communicants decreased by almost 7,000.[26]

Many of the blacks who left the Southern white Methodist churches were claimed by the African Methodist Episcopal Church (AME), the African Methodist Episcopal Zion Church (AME Zion), the Colored Methodist Episcopal Church, or the Northern Methodist Episcopal Church. In South Carolina, for example, the AME membership grew to 44,000 by 1877 because of the efforts of Bishop Daniel Payne, Richard H. Cain, and other energetic ministers. As a result of the labors of the Reverend T. W. Stringer, the AME's chief emissary in Mississippi, the denomination in that state grew from virtually nothing in 1865 to thirty-five churches with 5,000 members by 1870.[27] In North Carolina the AME Church counted fifty ministers and 7,267 members by 1869.[28] Nationally, the AME Church had only 20,000 members in 1856, but twenty years later, in 1876, it had over 200,000. By 1880 the membership numbered 400,000, mostly concentrated in the South.[29] Black membership in North Carolina among the AME Zion Church numbered 7,267 by the end of 1865, with fifty churches.[30] Its national membership increased from close to 27,000 in 1860 to 200,000 in 1870. Moreover, black membership in the Northern Methodist Episcopal Church in South Carolina had grown to 36,000 by 1881.[31]

There are several reasons why the AME and AME Zion congregations were so successful in recruiting Southern blacks. Even during the antebellum period, particularly in Border states such as Maryland and Kentucky, there had existed churches representing these denominations. Thus, they had already planted the seeds of black Methodism. When emancipation came, they quickly moved to establish themselves as the rightful preserve of blacks and spelled out specifically why blacks should desert white churches and embrace them. For example, both groups held statewide conferences in North Carolina for this purpose. Only a few days after the war ended, the AME conveners explained why they were ready to separate from Southern white religious bodies and form their own churches: "[We were] compelled to listen to her ministers till the coming of the Federal Army, now we desiar to dispence with the services of men who fidelity to the government by us is doubted in order therefore that we may be able to worship God according to the dictates of our consciances."[32] A few months later, at the AME Zion conference, the religious brethren articulated their mission: "to organize the army of reserve to carry forth the hallowed crusade of mercy and grace."[33] Certainly, here was the strong message that these objectives could be carried forth only by either the AME or AME Zion Church.

Many black Methodists were undoubtedly attracted to both denominations for racial reasons. These black church organizations promised them the Christian fellowship and leadership that was not possible in white churches. Indeed, without white supervision and paternalism, blacks would be able to express themselves with emotion during services if they desired. In other words, they could let loose and be themselves. Moreover, the African Methodist churches often served as social service agencies for blacks. As a result, many freedmen benefited directly from the missionary, educational, and material assistance rendered by these churches during and after the Civil War. The Contraband Committee of Mother Bethel Church of Philadelphia and the Union Relief Association of Israel Bethel Church of Washington were outstanding among Freedmen's Aid societies. Nearly $167,000 was contributed by the AME Church between 1862 and 1868.[34] In addition, as noted earlier, the AME Church had purchased Wilberforce University in 1863 and embarked upon the mission of educating black ministers, teachers, and leaders. Moreover, although the Methodist Episcopal Church North sometimes employed white clerics to administer to black members in the South, it was essentially an all-black church active in materially providing for freedmen. As a result, it, too, had enormous appeal.

Like the Methodists, black Baptists also saw the number of their members move upward. Data from Baptist associations underscore the extent of the racial separation that took place in North Carolina. In 1870 the Brown Creek Association, encompassing Union and Anson counties, reported 125 black members out of a total of 1,301; however, five years later, there were only twenty-eight black members. The Central Association, consisting of Wake and Franklin counties, reported 337 black communicants in 1866, but that number had dwindled to fifty-five by 1874. The Eastern Association, which covered an expansive area in the eastern section of the state, reported 1,461 black members in 1865 but none in 1870. Finally, although the Pee Dee Association reported 441 black members in 1867, only thirty-eight were counted in 1872.[35] Nationally, black Baptist members increased from 150,000 in 1850 to 500,000 in 1870.[36] Since Baptist congregations were autonomous, allowing members to control their religious affairs, the Baptists had the greatest appeal for the newly freed. The practice of baptism by immersion, reminiscent of some African religions, may also have attracted some adherents. By 1890, Baptists constituted 54 percent of those who attended all black churches in the South.[37] Additionally, a sizable number of blacks left the Episcopal and Presbyterian sects in the aftermath of the Civil War and formed their own churches.[38] The rapidity with which blacks exited from white churches illustrates the urgency felt by most freedmen and free men in disassociating themselves from the churches of the white slaveholders. Once the shackles of slavery were broken, most blacks were determined to enjoy autonomy in every aspect of life, including their religions faith.

Despite the fact that some white members encouraged blacks to remain in white churches after freedom, most made it clear to blacks that they were not welcome. Many white churches continued their paternalism. Blacks were forced to retain their seats in the gallery and were barred from participating in church governance. Sometimes those few blacks who refused to voluntarily withdraw from white churches were threatened with loss of life. For example, although freedmen were allowed to attend Liberty Sylvania Church in Fort Brown, Texas, most blacks, faced with hostility, withdrew by late 1865 with the exception of one former slave who continued to attend services. However, after a group of terrorists confronted him and warned him that he would be killed if he did not leave, he reluctantly pulled out.[39] Consequently, then, the move by blacks to separate from white churches and form their own congregations was met with enthusiasm by most white churchgoers, who had never been comfortable with blacks as members. They expected the same separation from blacks in the religious realm as they did in other realms of life, although they wanted to exercise some control over the churches that blacks organized. The mass exit of blacks from white churches proved mutually beneficial to both groups.

In retrospect, even if whites had invoked more egalitarian policies in efforts to retain their black membership, it is doubtful whether the outcome would have been significantly different. Once freedom came, affiliation with the churches of their former masters was simply too much for most blacks to endure. Long before emancipation, blacks had struggled to achieve religious autonomy, even at the risk of their lives. Now that the opportunity was at hand, the outcome was a foregone conclusion. They would move in masses to withdraw from white churches and establish their own, in spite of the response of Southern whites.

THE STRUGGLE TO ESTABLISH AND MAINTAIN
THEIR OWN CHURCHES

Because most freedmen were poor, they were severely limited in their ability to buy or construct churches and were forced at first to worship in primitive locales. For example, Atlanta's First Baptist Church gathered in a railroad boxcar, and the First Baptist Church of Memphis met in a "bush arbor" in 1865. Blacks in Danville, Virginia, worked tirelessly to secure enough funds to rent an old tobacco warehouse for services, and it became the High Street Baptist Church. Similarly, blacks on an island in the James River initially held services in the home of a worshipper but eventually secured a warehouse in Richmond.[40] In many cases, the homes of worshippers where religious services were held were little more than crude dugouts, as was the case for members of the AME and Baptist churches in Nicodemus, Kansas.[41]

It is noteworthy to acknowledge the role that many black women played in organizing several of these makeshift religious bodies that sometimes grew into large politically and socially active churches. Mary Smith, for example, volunteered both her organizational skills and her home in Austin, Texas, for the Sweet Home Baptist congregation until they secured a permanent church in 1882.[42] Sister Mattie Rainey's log cabin, with her blessing, became the home of New Hope Baptist Church in Dallas in 1873. In addition, the Third Baptist Church in Austin began in the home of Mrs. Eliza Hawkins in 1875, and Matilda Lewis helped organize the Macedonia Baptist Church of Georgetown, Texas, in 1881 in her backyard.[43]

A largely ignored but significant fact is that black women not only played a crucial role in organizing churches but also constituted a majority of the charter members. For instance, women made up six of the seven charter members of the New Hope Baptist Church in Dallas, and eleven of the thirteen charter members of the First Baptist Church in Austin, which was formed in 1867, were women. Black women also constituted 122 of the 174 early members of the African Congregational Church in 1868 in Paris, Texas.[44] That they would play a vital role in the black church should come as no surprise. Indeed, without their overwhelming participation, the church might not have become the central institution that it was in the black community.

After freedom, some Southern whites assisted blacks in organizing, building, and securing places of worship. In Elizabeth City, North Carolina, for example, in 1866 when blacks who had attended the First Baptist Church for whites during slavery decided that they wanted their own church, a group of whites in the city helped them build the Olive Branch Baptist Church.[45] And when freedmen in Jonesboro, Alabama, from the congregation of the white Canaan Baptist Church opted to leave and establish their own church, some white members assisted them in constructing a new building.[46] In 1867 when all thirty-eight black members of the Fairfield Baptist Church of Northumberland County, Virginia, decided to withdraw, they not only received the blessings of their white brethren but were also given two plots of land.[47] Moreover, with the consent of the white members, thirty-seven black members of the Ruhama Baptist Church near Birmingham, Alabama, withdrew in 1868 and formed Mount Zion Baptist Church. The church was built on land donated to blacks by Obadian Woods, formerly one of the largest slaveowners in the area.[48] In each of these instances, it is difficult to discern what, if any, motives whites had in assisting blacks. Perhaps they did so out of genuine kindness or else to ensure that blacks would have their own churches apart from white congregations. If not helping to erect church buildings or donating plots of land, some whites found other ways to aid blacks. For example, from 1865 through 1867, the white Church of Christ in Circleville, Texas, allowed blacks to use its facilities until they could purchase a separate meeting house. Likewise, the Methodist Episcopal Church (South) in Houston allowed the African Methodists there to use its sanctuary until they could secure their own.[49]

Despite the occasional assistance of Southern whites, blacks in most instances had to rely on themselves. Often, freedmen had to wait until they could save enough money to secure adequate facilities. To speed the process, blacks from different denominations sometimes cooperated with one another, raising money as a community to build or rent one building where all denominations could worship. In 1867 in Waco, Texas, for example, black Methodists and Baptists pooled their resources and erected a small church that they used on alternate Sundays. Six years later, they tore it down, divided the building materials between the two denominations, and parted on friendly terms to construct two separate churches.[50] Moreover, in most areas of Travis County, Texas, Methodists and Baptists used a common building. One denomination used the church for morning services and the other for afternoon worship. And freedmen built a community center in a segregated shantytown in the Brenham suburb of Watrousville, Texas, which met the religious needs of all the black denominations and also served as the headquarters of the Loyal League.[51]

Sometimes, however, when such efforts did not bear fruit, freedmen used more desperate means. For example, shortly after emancipation, a group of freedmen in Selma, Alabama, who had worshipped
as slaves at the St. Phillips Street Baptist Church, now First Baptist
Church, attempted to forcefully seize it from whites. They were prevented from doing so when the pastor, the Reverend J. B. Hawthorne,
alerted the white community, who then armed themselves and put
an end to the threat.[52] It is likely that the freedmen did not see themselves as rebels in a conventional sense. They were simply reclaiming what they thought was rightfully theirs. After all, their tireless
labor had contributed to the bulk of the work done on the church,
the few pennies they had as slaves were used for its upkeep, and
their overall labor certainly generated not only the cash flow to build
the church but also to maintain it. Consequently, since Southern
whites had stolen from them all their lives and had engaged in trea-
son against the U.S. government by taking up arms against it while
the slaves remained loyal to the Union, in the minds of several freedmen, then, everything that Southern whites had previously owned
should now belong to them—their land, houses, crops, dairy, poultry, and, certainly, churches. In other words, blacks had a moral right
to all of these things.

In most instances, the members of individual denominations
raised money among themselves to purchase land and erect their own
churches, and some donated property. In addition, various denominations organized successful building-fund campaigns. Black women
as well as black men often gave financially or more commonly donated land for church construction. Former slave Delilah Harris gave
land for the Smith Chapel, African Methodist Church. Double Bayou
built its church on land donated by Martha Godfrey in 1877, Emily
Brown donated land for the St. Emily United Methodist Church in
Chambers County, Texas, and in 1868, Mrs. Annie Blackley gave a
large sum and a church bell to the First Colored Baptist Church, re-
named the Palestine Missionary Baptist Church, in Victoria, Texas.[53]

Despite great poverty, enormous amounts of money were often
raised by blacks to build churches. For example, the Reverend Morris Henderson's congregation in Memphis, Tennessee, raised $5,000
to purchase a lot in October 1866, and three years later built the Beale
Street Baptist Church in the city. Of significance, although largely
ignored by most scholars, is the role played by black women from
Beale Street in raising money to help pay the $5,000 mortgage on the
church lot. On one warm Sunday afternoon in June 1865, several
black church women organized the Baptist Sewing Society, a group

dedicated to securing funds for a permanent church. Through their collective efforts, the women raised more than $500 during the first nine months of the society's existence. Once built, Beale Street Baptist Church spawned several other churches and went on to become Memphis's most famous black church.[54]

Black denominations in Charleston, Macon, and Richmond duplicated the building-fund campaign of the black Baptists in Memphis, even though many of their members were penniless. And, here in Charleston, even schoolchildren contributed coins. It was estimated that Emanuel Church, under the guidance of the Reverend R. H. Cain, would cost about $10,000. As early as the fall of 1865, $1,500 of this amount had been raised. Blacks who could not give money to this venture often provided their own labor instead. In fact, everyone who worked on the building was black, including the architect, Robert Vesey. Subsequently, Emanuel Church, located on Calhoun Street, was completed to serve some 2,500 people. With the rapidly increasing membership of the AME Church, however, it soon became necessary to find an even larger facility, and, once again, members raised money to purchase another church and lot which would cost $8,000. By the summer of 1866 they had already raised $2,000.[55] In Macon, Georgia, during one of his many trips South, John W. Alvord of the Freedmen's Bureau observed the completion of a beautiful black church. He noted, "I saw in Macon a colored church edifice going up, of brick, to cost $10,000. It was planned and constructed by their own mechanics— tasteful in style, and to be paid for wholly by themselves."[56] Black Baptists in Richmond under the leadership of the Reverend James H. Holmes also prospered. Holmes became pastor of the First African Baptist Church in 1867, and in only twelve years, he paid off the huge church debt and increased membership to a staggering 5,000. This church grew so rapidly that it spawned two others, Ebenezer Baptist Church and Sixth Mount Zion Baptist Church.[57]

Despite the success of some blacks in raising substantial amounts of money to erect handsome churches and to retire their debt, however, most blacks could not duplicate this feat. As a consequence, even those in the majority who built small, modest churches for only a few members sometimes could not pay the mortgage. And they were devastated when this failure resulted in the loss of their church. The Freedmen's Bureau was besieged by letters from congregants weighed down by the financial burden. Thomas Allen, a Baptist minister, wrote in 1867 to General Howard that his congregation owed $250 on its building. Local whites had constructed and financed the church, but the members could not pay the mortgage. Facing the cold reality of the situation, Allen acknowledged that "we cannot rase the money til next year if then, and the fact is the church will be taken from us . . . if I can not get the money." In Georgia, in another case, Henry M. Turner wrote to the state superintendent of education about a church struggling desperately against a crushing debt: "I would remark that the people are very poor and I cannot see how they can possibly pay this debt." He found it despicable that the church's white creditors were not only trying to force its sale but also seemed to delight in doing so. With concern for the devastating effect that the sale would have on the congregation, Turner continued, "these poor people have worked hard to get their church and school built. And now to have it sold for half its value, from them, is really discouraging."[58]

SOUTHERN WHITE OPPOSITION TO BLACK CHURCHES

Those blacks able to pay the mortgages on their churches still faced several overwhelming obstacles in day-to-day operations. Black and white preachers, for example, were often attacked for holding services for blacks. Many of these attacks had political implications. Obviously, many whites feared the development of black independence, even in religion. In the churches, blacks were able to hone the organizational, leadership, and oratorical skills needed to produce some of the most vocal and politically active leaders of the African-American community. At a time when Southern whites were determined to halt the rising tide of black political participation, attacks on all aspects of black religion had to be launched. Although both black and white preachers of freedmen were sometimes threatened and assaulted, blacks along with their congregants lost their lives in greater numbers than did whites. For example, a group of whites near Austin, in 1869, murdered George Porter, a black minister. Owing to the fact that Porter provided leadership for local blacks, counseled them on their rights, and complained to authorities about ill treatment of black apprentices, whites had targeted him for assassination. Whites in Grayson County, Texas, also murdered a black preacher who was viewed as a formidable obstacle to white political and economic control of the county. In addition, in Columbia, Texas, a group of whites invaded a black church, called the black minister a "d *** son of a B****" and ordered him to stop preaching. A black congregant tried to protect him when one of the whites drew a gun, but the white shot him dead.[59] Indeed, throughout the South during Reconstruction, so many black preachers were assassinated that Federal officials sometimes assigned them bodyguards. Carl Schurz, a Northern white correspondent, wrote of one of these cases in Mobile, where Major General Woods had assigned a black minister a special guard.[60]

As the physical symbols of black autonomy, churches were especially targeted by Southern whites. Many were burned down. For instance, in North Carolina, in the first few months of emancipation, a black Baptist church in Wilmington was destroyed by fire, and in Cleveland County a black church was "burned to the ground."[61] However, Southern whites were not the only ones bent on destruction. For example, Union soldiers demolished an AME church in Atlanta simply because one of the local white citizens complained that blacks were making too much noise during services.[62] To the dismay of Southern whites, however, when a black church was destroyed, regardless of denomination, the entire community would dedicate itself to rebuilding it. Black churches were too important to the community to not do so. After all, it was the only true institution that blacks could call their own.

VARIOUS RELIGIOUS DENOMINATIONS ATTRACT BLACKS FOR DIFFERENT REASONS

During the post-Civil War period, black churches had an impact on nearly every aspect of African-American life. Membership became a badge of honor. A person was known for whatever church he or she attended as well as the name of its minister. Blacks generally attended church in large numbers. One Northern white correspondent, speaking of black Baptists in Augusta, Georgia, noted: "On Sundays these churches are well-filled with intelligent and well-dressed hearers."[63] In another case, Whitelaw Reid, a Northern white correspondent, commented on the large number of blacks whom he observed one Sunday attending a church on St. Helena Island, South Carolina. He described the scene: "Overflowing all the church-yard, flooding the road, through which our carriages could hardly be driven, and backing up against the graveyard, were the Negroes, gay with holiday attire."[64]

The frequency with which blacks attended services is all the more remarkable given the fact that ministers conducted services as frequently as they could, with three services each Sunday as the norm and prayer meetings on Wednesday nights. Some preachers, however, even eclipsed this schedule. For example, Atlanta's Friendship

Baptist Church held as many as two or three worship services each weekday as well. In cities and towns throughout the South, church services often began in the morning at sunrise. More were held in the afternoon, there were usually evening services, too. It was fairly common for the evening service to turn into a lengthy affair that sometimes lasted well into the night. For instance, William Wells Brown attended a Methodist service in Nashville and noted that "the meetings was kept up till a late hour."[65] Sometimes local residents complained about the noise from late evening services. Not every church kept late hours, however, as Carry Vaughan attended a service among a large Baptist congregation in New Orleans, "but not till late, as the custom is."[66]

Freedmen from the lower class had a strong belief in the presence and power of God in everyday life and therefore emphasized revelations, visions, dreams, and inward expressions of the divine presence. Their services, a mixture of grief and sadness about their weary life on Earth, provided a release for them. Sermons and songs about their bondage and impassioned prayers for divine aid caused the congregations to shout, cry, and raise a joyful noise to the Lord. Notwithstanding the emotion, there existed in the sermons a deep practical theme that usually compared the plight of blacks with that of the Jews as it emphasized the need to protect and expand their freedom.[67]

In contrast, elite congregations sang hymns from standard hymnals, listened to sermons delivered more articulately and less emotionally than those in lower-class churches, and behaved with considerable dignity. Thus, it is not surprising that a visitor to the Fifteenth Street Presbyterian Church in Washington, DC, led by the respected clergyman Francis Grimké, would describe the atmosphere as "serious but restrained." Sometimes, Baptist and Methodist congregations of middle-class blacks exhibited the same qualities. For instance, the sermons of St. James AME Church in New Orleans were listened to "with marked attention and a deep spiritual interest by a very large and intelligent audience." And the *Christian Index* described the Collins Chapel, CME Church of Memphis as a congregation made up of schoolteachers, postal workers, and other middle-class blacks. In the view of the *Index*, Collins Chapel Church was the "most refined and quiet large congregation in the city."[68]

As expected, blacks from the lower class were uncomfortable in middle-class churches, and vice versa. The freedman Ed Barber, for instance, found the worship service at St. Mark's Episcopal Church in Charleston distressing: "How they did carry on, bow and scrape and ape de white folks. I see some pretty feathers, pretty fans, and pretty women there! I was uncomfortable all de time though . . . cause they was too 'hifalootin' in de ways, in de singin' and all sorts of carrin' ons."[69] In mid-1865, Thomas Cardozo, an American Missionary Association teacher and brother of Francis Cardozo, was frustrated with the form of worship found in most of Charleston's black churches, most of which consisted of lower-class congregations. The religious services offered by the black Episcopalians were the exception, however, because, according to him, these congregations "worship intelligently."[70] Thus, he attended St. Mark's.

It made little difference in terms of content, denomination, or social class because most ministers in the independent black churches delivered their sermons in the rousing style typical of Protestant evangelism. Their style was extemporaneous, full of gusto, and embellished with vivid imagery. Preachers did everything they could to make connections between contemporary topics and Old Testament lessons about liberation and the power and justice of God. Illustrating this approach is a sermon delivered by James Lynch, who could hardly be described as an uneducated backwoods preacher, in the AME church in Mitchelville, South Carolina, shortly after Abraham Lincoln's assassination. Lynch compared Lincoln to Moses leading his people safely through the wilderness to the banks of the Jordan River. He then chose to depart from the Scriptures and take a metaphorical approach, depicting John Wilkes Booth as the spirit of rebellion, "creeping up the back stairs" to strike one final blow for slavery and disunion. Indeed, the sermon was well received by the congregation. A Northern teacher, Jane B. Smith, summarized its impact: "The feelings of his excited audience were wrought to such a pitch, that it was impossible to hear from above their sobs, groans, and shouts."[71]

The striking differences in religious services among Baptists, Methodists, Episcopalians, and Presbyterians are still very much in existence today. In both Episcopal and Presbyterian churches, although the sermons are informed and intellectually stimulating, they lack the emotional appeal of those generally delivered by Baptist and Methodist ministers. Although most black churches have witnessed steadily declining numbers among their congregations, one of the many factors contributing to this trend, especially with respect to Episcopalians and Presbyterians, is the laid-back and unemotional format of their religious services. Their services still appeal to the black middle class, while the more emotional ones of the Baptists and Methodists continue to attract a large segment of working-class blacks. This is an ongoing problem for Episcopalians and Presbyterians. While it is true that the black middle class has been steadily growing over the past two decades, it is also true that most blacks are from the working class. Moreover, even those who count themselves among the middle class live on its fringes. Traditionally, they are more working-class in their outlook on life.

AN INSTITUTION CENTRAL TO THE BLACK COMMUNITY

After the Civil War, black churches set down a rigid moral and social code for their black congregants that condemned card playing, swearing, gambling, drinking, and "irregular" relationships and encouraged a monogamous family life. Deacons formed juries to render decisions on family disputes, and anyone who violated the code risked expulsion from the church.[72] For example, Bella Fraser of Morris Street Baptist Church in Charleston was accused of committing adultery and was then investigated by deacons who found her guilty. As a result, she was expelled from the church. [73] Barney Alford recalled that "I jined the Little Tangipahoe Baptist Church when I was a young feller, en dey turned me outen fur stealin'." [74] Under these rules, the divorce rate among church members declined,[75] along with incidents of domestic abuse, alcoholism, and disciplinary problems among children.

Those blacks who engaged in criminal behavior risked not only expulsion from church but social ostracism by the black community as well. A case in point is the story of Noah Wilburn, who was employed for several years as the janitor of a Baptist church. He and his family were members, and Noah was held in high regard. However, when it was discovered that Noah was selling whiskey from the basement of the church, shock waves resounded throughout the community. As a result, Noah was so humiliated that he ran away from his wife, Jane, and his children and never returned. His crookedness brought shame and humiliation to Jane and her family.[76]

Local churches also served as a social and psychological outlet for blacks. In addition to the regular worship services, various activities took place there. Church buildings often functioned as community theaters and concert halls for choral performances and religious and secular plays. An especially festive time of the year was the Christmas season, when programs were offered in abundance, particularly for children. One year the adult members of the Ebenezer Baptist Church in Richmond packed a large box full of gifts and distributed them to excited children on Christmas Day. Black churches also organized picnics and barbecues, parades, carnivals and fairs, emancipation celebrations, baseball games, and boat and train excursions. These events attracted hundreds, if not thousands, of blacks, many of them coming from several miles away.[77] One emancipation celebration sponsored by a church took place in 1881 in James City, North Carolina, a black town just outside New Bern. A New Bern newspaper reported that "from Beaufort and Morehead City a train of four or five cars arrived in the morning bringing some two hundred and fifty or three hundred," and over 1,000 were expected to come to the celebration from the eastern counties. The newspaper noted that "this will necessitate the dispatching of an extra train as far up as Kinston."[78]

MOUNT SHILOH FIRST BAPTIST CHURCH, FOUNDED IN 1866, IN JAMES CITY, NORTH CAROLINA. THE BUILDING PICTURED WAS ERECTED IN 1924.

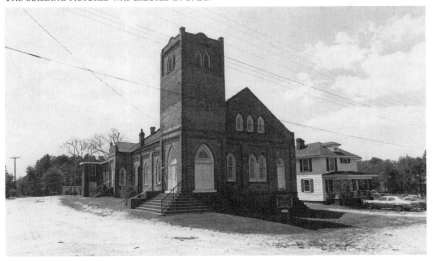

Courtesy of the North Carolina Division of Archives and History

Boat or train excursions were particularly popular with blacks. Usually, excursions included short train or boat rides to nearby beaches or parks for picnics, games, and fellowship. Typical is an advertisement placed in the *Huntsville Gazette* by a Methodist Episcopal church that had organized an excursion in Huntsville, Alabama: "Everyone should enjoy some pleasure, and a trip to the pretty little town of Florence is a good way to pass a day pleasantly." The cost for the day was $1.75. Sometimes churches would sponsor outings with other churches. For instance, in the summer of 1882 the Birmingham

THE REVEREND HURLEY GRIMES, PASTOR OF
MOUNT SHILOH FIRST BAPTIST CHURCH IN JAMES
CITY AND AN IMPORTANT RELIGIOUS AND CIVIC
LEADER IN NORTH CAROLINA DURING EMANCI-
PATION AND RECONSTRUCTION.

Courtesy of the North Carolina Division Ar-
chives and History

AME Sunday school proposed an excursion to a nearby location with other churches to have a "grand time." And when the Bank Street Baptist Church of Norfolk, Virginia, in 1881 organized a trip to Richmond, several whites went along.[79]

Although black women did not serve as ministers, elders, or deacons in the early churches, their impact was nevertheless significant. They organized fund-raising events and social activities, cooked for the church suppers, put on the fairs, and planned the June Tenth celebrations. Moreover, the job of making sure that large crowds attended such events fell on their shoulders.[80] At these church affairs, blacks were able to forget the everyday grind of poverty and the fear and humiliation of their constant confrontations with white racism and violence in the aftermath of the war. By providing blacks with a structured social life in which to achieve status, express their deepest feelings, and perhaps find meaning in their lives, the black churches functioned as a refuge from a hostile world.[81]

The freedmen's campaign to promote education was also supported by the black churches. Most of the funds raised to build and maintain schools were collected in worship services. Whenever a minister called on the congregation to contribute, they gave whatever they could, no matter how small the amount. Black ministers such as R. H. Cain and Jonathan C. Gibbs, both of Charleston, organized schools there. Three schools opened by the Freedmen's Bureau in Galveston, Texas, in 1865 and 1867 used church facilities.

Black churches provided another service crucial to their members' survival: social welfare. Most black benevolent and mutual-aid societies that were established after the Civil War were organized by the churches. Through these societies, church members found homes for the homeless, gave money to the poorest among them, and sent care givers to the sick. Most of the parishioners in the mutual-aid societies were women, a largely ignored aspect of African-American history. The black ladies of Louisville, Kentucky, sponsored fairs and benefits to raise money for clothes, fuel, and furniture for destitute refugees. In addition, black congregants throughout the South also gave food and clothing to the indigent.[82] Charley White, a black preacher in Jacksonville, Texas, worried that winter would give rise to greater hardships, thereby creating a situation in which "lots of children warn't gonna have nothing for Christmas," and he called on several local businessmen to contribute to a Christmas fund. The response was an outpouring of food and clothing for the children and their families.[83]

St. Philip's Church, school for colored children, Richmond, Virginia.

Library of Congress

Throughout the war, black wounded soldiers suffered tremendously, due in large part to the inadequate nursing services of the Federal government. Federal officials also often all but ignored the families of black soldiers who sometimes followed them from one camp to another. With little or no material assistance provided them, black volunteer societies helped fill this void. The Soldiers' Aid Society, for example, was established by Green Street Baptist Church in Louisville, Kentucky, for this purpose. Under the leadership of Mary Lewis, Sally Fretus, and Flusie Pope, the society cared for the sick and wounded black soldiers who had been brought to hospitals in Louisville and New Albany, Indiana. In their mission of caring for the sick and providing for the needy, society members also visited the barracks of black troops. Similar work was done by the Colored

Soldiers' Aid Society of the Fifth Street Baptist Church of Louisville. Moreover, the Sons and Daughters of the Morning and the Daughters of Zion, both Louisville groups, also engaged in efforts to aid wounded and disabled soldiers and assist their families.[84]

Attention to the sick and disabled extended well beyond black soldiers and their families. For instance, with the noble goal of extending medical attention to ailing members, Dr. S. H. Toles, a black man and a native of Ohio, was hired on July 1, 1867, by the Daughters of Zion of Avery Chapel AME Church in Memphis, Tennessee, at a yearly salary of $200. Dr. Tole's annual report underscored the importance of black women's efforts to safeguard the health and well-being of a community denied equal access to public-supported professional health care. Two-hundred and sixty patients were treated by Dr. Toles between July 1, 1867, and June 30, 1868, yet he reported only two deaths. The Daughters of Zion also disbursed $248.50 within a three-month period to indigent members of the congregation, despite the financial burden of supplying the services of a physician. And the 304 dues-paying members were avid fund raisers, sponsoring events such as fairs, picnics, and balls. They pooled their resources and solicited voluntary contributions from the congregation. The Daughters of Zion were so successful in their efforts that despite spending nearly $450 by the close of the 1868 fiscal year, the group still had $140.20 in their account at the Freedmen's Savings and Trust Bank.[85]

Sometimes, black congregants took an even larger step in their determination to provide health care to ailing members of the community. For example, the Fifth Street Baptist Church of Louisville in February 1866 began a movement to establish a hospital for freedmen. The church raised $180, a phenomenal amount, at its initial meeting. Shortly thereafter, other churches made similar pledges, and leaders soon selected a location. In April 1866, with the help of the Sanitary Commission, a hospital was located in Louisville at the corner of Seventeenth Street and Broadway. Although the hospital grew rapidly, with thirty-five patients and four nurses, a lack of funds hampered its efforts.[86] Similarly, black churches in Savannah pooled their resources to establish Lincoln Freedmen's Hospital, and they continued to support it throughout its brief existence.[87] Black parishioners did not forget the social outcasts of society, for they visited inmates of jails and prisons to extend medical attention and comfort to them.[88]

Black churches also established old folks' homes to take care of the aged, materially assisted the infirm, and organized burial associations. For example, in the fall of 1865, blacks in Paducah, Kentucky, organized a Freedmen's Aid Society to support the aged and infirm. Methodist churches in Louisville also opened an old folks' home. Burial associations gave money to those lacking funds to provide decent burials for loved ones. It was especially gratifying for the bereaved to be able to arrange a suitable funeral service. Sometimes church organizations collected and spent several dollars on burial expenses. For instance, the Benevolent Daughters of Zion in Natchez, Mississippi, an AME affiliate, raised and spent $823 in support of the poor and for a burial fund, and Paducah's Sanitary Commission collected and spent $204 for burials. Moreover, following the leadership of black ministers, freedmen in Columbus, Kentucky, in June 1868 organized the Freedmen's Aid Association, with the objective of feeding the starving and burying the dead.[89]

An especially daunting problem confronting black communities was the care of orphans. The decimation wrought by the institution of slavery on the black family further exacerbated this situation. Whole families were sometimes separated by sale, with some members so young that later in life they would not be able to recognize parents, grandparents, uncles, aunts, cousins, or siblings. Moreover, the Civil War gave rise to a fluid situation in which many blacks were constantly on the move in their attempts to gain the freedom that had long eluded them. Many of them perished along the way, the victims of Northern white soldiers or vengeful Southern whites. Other freedmen saw military duty in the war, and nearly 40,000 gave their lives. As a consequence, it should come as no surprise to acknowledge the fact that black communities were besieged by orphans. Of course, black churches formed societies to assist orphans, especially since women, with their nurturing motherly instincts, dominated the mutual-aid societies in terms of activism. Thus, the welfare of orphans was of paramount importance to them. Their welfare also assumed great importance to black communities because children represented the future of the race.

In post-Civil War black America, orphanages often served as daycare centers in addition to their more standard function of housing children who were homeless because of broken households or of deceased parents. Scattered black orphanages did not escape the perceptive observation of whites. General O. O. Howard, the superintendent of the Freedmen's Bureau, for example, commented on the success of one started by blacks in New Orleans. It was so effective that "many of its early residents ended up in homes with parents and friends." A black woman is given credit by John Eaton for starting the first Mississippi Valley wartime orphanage, on President's

Island near Memphis. Similarly, not long after the war, freedmen either helped start or entirely supported orphanages in Beaufort and Charleston, South Carolina, and Mobile, Alabama. The orphanage in Beaufort was "properly officered by the colored citizens." Mobile's blacks held a fair in the summer or fall of 1865 and raised a staggering $1,200 to build an orphanage. A group of black women from a local church in Charleston secured and outfitted an "orphan house" for the children of parents who found employment in the countryside. And when Northern relief officials started a second orphanage for freedmen in New Orleans, the city's "poor," though destitute, contributed $1,500 to support it.[90]

Although the data delineating the socioeconomic backgrounds of most black females who were active members in benevolent societies are sparse, some illuminating documentation does exist for women's benevolent societies in Memphis. The data indicate that not only did the vast majority of members come from the working class, but so, too, did the leaders. For example, almost two-thirds (61.5 percent) of the leadership elite worked as laundresses, ironers, and domestics. Given the dire poverty of most blacks, in all likelihood the socioeconomic profile of the members of women's benevolent societies of Memphis is reflective of most throughout the South in the post-Civil War era. That these societies accomplished so much during the difficult economic times of the 1870s, 1880s, and 1890s makes their achievement all the more impressive. The panic of 1873 and the subsequent depression, which dragged on until 1879, contributed to chaotic financial conditions in areas throughout the South. In addition, when the Freedmen's Savings Bank collapsed and subsequently closed its doors in July 1874, the economic situation further worsened. Many freedmen had their life savings in the bank, and now all was lost. Yet, despite these obstacles, black parishioners—mostly women—persisted in their efforts to help the needy in their communities. And regardless of the size of their congregations, most churches maintained some ongoing program of benevolence.[91]

Today, although its influence has decreased, the church is still a pivotal institution within black communities. Many black preachers continue to deliver moral messages from their pulpits. They emphasize the need to save money for the future, to acquire an education, and to work and support the family as well as raise the children to be respectful and industrious. Owing to its devastating impact on the family, adultery and divorce are regarded as twin evils, and some churches offer counseling services for couples. As noted earlier, such vices as drinking, gambling, prostitution, smoking, dancing, and stealing are frowned upon. Church parishioners continue to visit jails and prisons in efforts to persuade those who have gone astray to straighten out their lives.[92]

THE BLACK CHURCH AND ITS IMPACT ON POLITICS

As expected, many black churches in the South were popular sites for organized political activity among freedmen and their Northern supporters. For example, in Louisville, Quinn Chapel AME Church hosted the states' black teachers' convention in 1870. Quinn Chapel was also the scene of meetings protesting the absence of impartiality for blacks in Kentucky courts, and prominent roles in the city's streetcar segregation demonstrations of 1870 were played by several of its members. Moreover, under the supervision of the Reverend J. C. Waters, Asbury Chapel, also located in Louisville, hosted numerous protest rallies.[93] And throughout the early years of freedom, blacks held mass political meetings at Zion Presbyterian Church and Emanuel AME Church in Charleston, both of which could seat between 1,500 and 2,000 people. These gatherings were held to discuss the state and welfare of the country in general and the condition of newly freed slaves in particular. Committees were organized to devise strategies to deal with the changed conditions wrought by the war.[94]

Clergymen were among the most effective and able black politicians during the Reconstruction period. Black ministers from both the North and South, experienced in the politics of the church arena and used to exerting influence in the black community, successfully won election to legislative seats and took an active part in government at the Federal, state, and local levels. To fully understand the disproportionate representation of the clergy among the political leaders, one need only to look at South Carolina. Of the 255 blacks who served in the state legislature between 1868 and 1876, forty-three were ministers.[95] Among some of the best-known minister-politicians of the Reconstruction era were Bishop Henry M. Turner, Bishop James W. Hood, Holland Thompson, R. H. Cain, and Mansfield Tyler. The careers of Turner and Hood are representative. Bishop Turner of the AME Church, plunging with tremendous energy into recruiting blacks into the Republican Party, became active in Georgia politics after the war. He was eventually elected to the state legislature but later lost his seat when racist Georgians resumed control. Bishop

Courtesy of the North Carolina Division of Archives and History

Hood of the AME Zion Church presided over what may have been the first convention called by blacks after they gained their freedom. He then served as a local magistrate, a deputy collector for the Internal Revenue, and assistant superintendent of public instruction of the state of North Carolina. Interestingly, only two of the twenty blacks elected to the U.S. House of Representatives were ministers, but one of the two blacks elected to the Senate, Hiram Revels of Mississippi, was a preacher.[96] Furthermore, the vast majority of those ministers who were active in politics were Republicans and shared on the whole the conservative political philosophy of the party. In other words, they did not try to upset the existing order. While they did support political and civil rights for blacks, they refused to support the land reform proposals that would have made it easier for freedmen to acquire land and thus build a foundation for economic independence. Black minister-politicians also opposed unionization. If freedmen could not own or rent land, they had to work as sharecroppers or wage earners, and in those positions they wanted fair wages and decent working conditions. One way to accomplish these goals was through unionization, but on this issue most minister-politicians again followed the conservative party line.[97]

Despite their shortcomings, however, minister-politicians as well as the preachers who did not enter politics made a significant contribution to the black community. They helped promote the ideas of racial solidarity and self-help. Under their guidance, the churches provided religious services and functioned as a social, economic, and political institution within the black community. That black ministers accomplished so much under such difficult circumstances is one of the most remarkable triumphs of the post-Civil War period.

WOMEN STRUGGLE TO GAIN ACCEPTANCE
INTO THE MINISTRY

One of the darkest chapters in black church history has been the discrimination against female members by males. Apparently, although the practices of injustice that they heaped upon women paralleled those that had led them to rebel against white churches, men could not see the error of their ways. How did this situation come about? In the process of institutionalizing clandestine religious practices formed during slavery and separating them from white congregations, freed people reserved church leadership positions for men. In fact, women were turned out of the sanctuary "before the men began to talk" about matters of church policy. Perceptive whites on the Sea Islands reported the public censure of freedwomen there who had showed a lack of proper respect for their husbands' authority. Since the reputation of husbands was tied to wives, it was thought that a woman should not engage in actions that would embarrass or humiliate her spouse. To do only as he desired was reinforced by biblical interpretation. In fact, the biblical injunction, "Wives, submit yourselves to your husbands," gave preachers the justification for church-based decisions that seemed arbitrary or unfair to the women involved.[98] The fact that black women had such crucial roles in establishing and ensuring the success of the churches makes the subordinate status assigned to them by men all the more despicable.

Black men, of course, especially regarded the ministry as their domain, and throughout the postwar period they steadfastly resisted the efforts of women to become ordained. For example, as one scholar has noted, "rather than concede the full authority of ordination, the A.M.E. chose to accommodate its organizational arrangements to include positions specifically designed for women—namely, stewardess and deaconess—and under duress would approve the licensing of women as evangelists." However, even before these minimal victories were won, the struggle of black women preachers desirous of becoming ordained by the AME Church would be long and arduous. And despite the structural inclusion of women and their intensive labors for the church, at the conclusion of the nineteenth century, their role had not markedly changed. They were barred from official leadership positions and kept subservient. At the 1844, 1848, and 1864 AME General Conferences, petitions requesting that women be allowed to preach were presented and turned down. But by 1868 the AME Church decided to institute an alternative to ordination: women preachers could now become stewardesses. Perhaps the church made this concession out of concern for the steadily increasing number of women who were publicly preaching.[99]

After 1868 the preaching of AME women openly escalated, although it would be three decades later before the church would again open its hierarchy to women. While the church never turned down prospective female members, it certainly accepted their money and never declined the material support produced by women's benevolent societies. Yet, women were only supposed to be seen, not heard. However, some were being heard, and the response was positive. Amanda Berry Smith, for example, the best known of the AME preaching women, was as early as 1871 credited with having markedly increased the membership of the waning congregation of Mount Pisqah in Salem, New Jersey, during a three-week stay there. Commenting on her work in the *Christian Recorder*, Elder Frisby Cooper wrote that she is "a very useful helper in the vineyard of the Lord, God bless her ever."[100] Elder Cooper's assessment of Smith's ability to save souls was echoed even by some bishops at the 1872 General Conference of the AME Church. After hearing her sing at a session held at Fisk University, they were convinced that Smith was blessed with the spirit of God. As a result, she received several invitations to preach at churches but no appointment as pastor or the rite of ordination.

Given the response of some of the AME brethren to Smith's inquiry into the cost of going to Nashville to attend the General Conference of 1872, the remarks made by bishops concerning her being "of the spirit" appear hypocritical at best. One of the AME brethren wrote back to Smith, "I tell you, Sister, it will cost money to go down there; and if you aint got plenty of it, it's no use to go." Another asked, "What does she want to go for?" "Woman preacher; they want to be ordained" was the reply. Another wrote, "I mean to fight that thing," and yet another said, "Yes, indeed, so will I."[101] These statements illustrate the staunch opposition faced by black women preachers in their efforts to become ordained ministers. Yet, they did not despair. They continued to fight on. In this struggle, Smith was joined by other prominent AME black women such as Margaret Wilson, Emily Calkins Stevens, Lena Doolin-Mason, and Charlotte S. Riley.[102] Although these women sought ordination by the AME Church without success, women striving for ordination in other black denominations such as the AME Zion Church, CME Church, or Baptists did not fare any better. The black church as an institution was male dominated, and there was great resistance to change.[103]

Chapter Eight

"We Intend to Have Our Rights"

Political and Social Activists in Post-Civil War America

In the Reconstruction Act of March 2, 1867, Congress unfolded its design for establishing loyal governments in the South. The former Confederate states, except Tennessee, were to be divided into five military districts administered by a major general who would be charged with the task of preparing his district for readmission to the Union. The process of readmission entailed a series of steps. Loyal voters, defined as all citizens excluding former Confederate leaders, were to be registered. They would then elect delegates to a state constitutional convention. When the new constitution had been approved by the voters and by Congress, the state would have to ratify the Fourteenth Amendment. And only after the Fourteenth Amendment had been ratified by three-quarters of the states and added to the Constitution could the former Confederate states send representatives and senators to the U.S. Congress. A key component of the Reconstruction Act was its requirement that blacks be given the vote, which meant that the electorate who chose delegates to the state constitutional conventions had to include blacks. Furthermore, the new state constitutions were required to codify the same rule of suffrage for the black man. Thus, the former slaves were assured of the right to take part in the reconstructed governments of the Southern states.

Under the new state constitutions, blacks were elected to public office in all Southern states, but although they held some political power and had influence, they were never in complete control. Even in states such as South Carolina, where they constituted a majority of the population, black legislators were still disproportionately underrepresented. Whites always had the majority in the state senate, and a white man always occupied the governor's mansion. But, out of a total of 127 members in the first legislature, eighty-seven were blacks. Two blacks served as lieutenant governor in South Carolina, Alonzo J. Ransier in 1870 and Richard Gleaves in 1872. And two blacks served as speaker of the house there, Samuel J. Lee in 1872 and Robert B. Elliott in 1874. Prominent educator Francis Cardozo was secretary of state from 1868 to 1872 and state treasurer from 1872 to 1876.

In Louisiana there were 133 black members of the legislature, made up of thirty-eight senators and ninety-five representatives, between 1868 and 1896. Most of them in office between 1868 and 1877 were veterans of the Union army and free men of color before the war. Some, however, were former slaves, including John W. Menard, who was elected to Congress but denied a seat. Three blacks, and also former slaves—Oscar Dunn, P. B. S. Pinchback, and C. C. Antonine—held the position of lieutenant governor in Louisiana. Pinchback even served as acting governor of the state for forty-three days in 1873 when Governor Henry C. Warmoth was impeached. Pinchback was the only black to serve in that capacity until Douglas Wilder was elected governor of Virginia in 1990.

P. B. S. PINCHBACK, LIEUTENANT GOVERNOR AND GOVERNOR OF LOUISIANA.

Library of Congress

From 1869 to 1901, twenty-two blacks were active in national politics: two in the U.S. Senate and twenty in the U.S. House of Representatives. The two senators, Hiram Revels, born free in North Carolina, and Blanch K. Bruce, born a slave in Virginia, were elected from Mississippi. Bruce, who was elected in 1874, was the only black who served a full term in the Senate until the election of Edward Brooke from Massachusetts in 1966. The first of the twenty blacks to serve in the House were seated in 1869; eight were from South Carolina, four from North Carolina, three from Alabama, and one each from Georgia, Mississippi, Florida, Louisiana, and Virginia. Two from South Carolina, Joseph H. Rainey and Robert Smalls, each served five consecutive terms, and J. T. Walls of Florida and John R. Lynch of Mississippi each served three terms. Like most other congressmen, many of these men had been in politics at the state level before being elected to the House. Of the twenty-two blacks who served in Congress between 1869 and 1900, ten were members of the old free black elite.

Nevertheless, at both the state and national level, the majority of the black politicians during Reconstruction had been slaves. From among this group the most influential had lived as slaves in cities, working as clerks, carpenters, blacksmiths, or waiters in hotels and boarding houses. A few had been the privileged body servants of aristocratic and powerful whites. Robert Smalls of South Carolina, for example, became

HIRAM REVELS, U.S. SENATOR FROM MISSISSIPPI.

Library of Congress

the most influential and successful Reconstruction politician in the state, and Louisiana's Oscar Dunn and P. B. S. Pinchback had illustrious political careers.[1]

While most black politicians held political bases in the South, at least one, George Washington Williams, served in the Ohio House of Representatives; others sat in both the Massachusetts and Illinois state legislatures. Some held various Federal and state positions, such as former Union army lieutenant James M. Trotter, who was appointed to the lucrative post of recorder of deeds in Washington, DC. Since less than 2 percent of the black population lived in the North, however, their influence was considerably less than that of their Southern counterparts.[2]

Most black politicians supported civil and political rights, public education, jury reform, voting rights, and the expansion of social services, but, like the black minister-politicians, they refused to press for the kind of real economic reform that would allow unionization and give freedmen the land that they needed to build a secure economic foundation. On the issues of land reform and unionization, black politicians let down their constituencies. Far too many of the black politicians, like their white Republican allies, had narrow class-based interests supported by their own wealth. As landowners, they believed in the sanctity of private property and could not bring

Robert C. DeLarge, state representative and congressman from South Carolina.

Library of Congress

themselves to support the confiscation of planters' land for redistribution to freedmen. Furthermore, those among them who were employers were reluctant to support unionization, and some of them had even owned slaves. In truth, their activities in Congress—fighting, for example, for such local issues as river and harbor legislation—did not differ substantially from those of white congressmen.[3]

On the whole, however, black officeholders were able and conscientious public servants. Extensive studies of states such as Mississippi reveal that even at the local level, where politicians tended to be ill prepared, there was little difference in the degree of competence and integrity displayed by white and black officeholders. T. W. Cardozo, the black superintendent of education in Mississippi, was convicted of embezzling funds that had been allotted to Tougaloo College, but other black politicians, such as Dunn and Lynch, had impeccable reputations.[4] Furthermore, any political corruption in the decade after the Civil War, at every level of government and in every section of the country, must be seen in perspective. The big thieves were nearly always white; blacks got mostly crumbs.[5]

THE STRUGGLE AGAINST RACIAL DISCRIMINATION

Most black citizens were unwilling to leave the solutions to their problems to the politicians. Now that they were free, they were determined to eliminate all forms of discrimination. They took particular aim at gaining access to streetcars and horsecars. In 1866, shortly after a group of freedmen in New Orleans blocked the passage of streetcars in the streets, local military authorities ordered the provisional governor to outlaw the separate streetcars, which had meant that the service to blacks was inferior to that provided to whites. The next year saw protests by freedmen in Charleston and Richmond against streetcar segregation. The military commander in Charleston responded by ordering an end to the discrimination; and in Richmond, where the protests had led to violence, the streetcar company gave in and announced that segregation was ended. In Louisville, freedmen embarked on a successful campaign in 1871 to ride the horsecars without discrimination, and in 1872 blacks in Savannah conducted a successful two-month boycott against the local horsecar company.[6]

Black women often played key roles in combating segregation and racism, especially in the area of public transportation. Despite Sojourner Truth's notoriety, she encountered discrimination in Washington, DC, where she worked at Freedmen's Hospital after the war. While in the company of her friend, Josephine Griffing, a white woman, the conductor of a streetcar refused to stop for them. Truth grabbed the iron railing but was dragged for several yards before the streetcar came to a halt. Shortly thereafter, she reported the conductor to the president of the City Railway, who dismissed him at once. The president also told her to notify him if she were ever mistreated again by a conductor or driver.[7] In Charleston in 1867 the captain of a steamboat also picked the wrong black person to offend. He refused to grant a first-class passage to Frances Ann Rollin, one of five sisters who reputedly were among the most influential lobbyists and power brokers in South Carolina during Reconstruction. Frances took the captain to court, and he was found guilty of violating section 8 of General Orders No. 32, issued on May 30, 1867, which prohibited any discrimination "because of color or caste" in public conveyances on all "railroads, highways, streets and navigable waters." As a result of his conviction, the captain had to pay a $250 fine.[8]

Another well-known personality—no other than Ida B. Wells, the famous settlement house worker and anti-lynching advocate—experienced discrimination when she was forcefully removed from a whites-only rail coach in Memphis in 1883. She sued the Chesapeake & Ohio Railroad seeking redress. Although the lower court ruled in Wells's favor, the Tennessee supreme court overturned the decision and questioned her motives in bringing the suit. In its opinion, "her persistence was not in good faith to obtain a comfortable seat for the short ride." Instead, the court explained that "it is evident that the purpose of the defendant in error was to harass with a view to this suit."[9] Notwithstanding the fact that Wells ultimately lost the case, it is important because she and other blacks refused to endure segregation and racism without challenging those twin evils headon.

Lesser known black women willingly stepped up to the fight. For instance, Milly Anderson won a suit in the U.S. District Court, Western

District of Texas, on April 26, 1875, against the Houston & Texas Central Railroad for not allowing her to board a railroad car. The judge ruled that it was illegal to deny a female passenger access to the ladies' car solely because she was of African descent. He rendered his decision on the basis of the Civil Rights Law of March 1, 1875, for which a number of black men and women had openly campaigned.[10] In another example, a Memphis teacher, Sarah Thompson, wrote to Senator Charles Sumner, who was sponsoring the act, as early as February 1872 in an attempt to convey to him the urgency for such a bill. She noted several instances in which blacks were discriminated against on public transportation. Thompson concluded her letter by thanking Senator Sumner: "the Colored people owe you a debt of gratitude which they can never repay. Long may the name of Charles Sumner live in the hearts of the Colored people of America."[11]

In some cities, groups of black citizens purchased their own means of transportation to avoid the discriminatory practices of whites. In 1866 operators of boats that ran from Savannah to Darien, Georgia, refused to take freedmen unless they remained apart from the whites. In response, several blacks, including former soldiers, formed a cooperative and bought a large boat of their own from a company in New York. The boat made two successful trips to Darien and Beaufort, South Carolina, but on its next trip, to Florida, it struck St. John's bar and was torn to pieces. It was later learned that the company had swindled the freedmen by selling them a defective boat. Since it was uninsured, the cooperative lost their whole investment.[12]

Black women protested their treatment at public theaters. In response to being ejected from her seat in the parquet "white ladies' circle" of the Freement Opera House in Galveston, Texas, Mary Miller sued for damages in Federal court, which ruled that the owner, Henry Greenwall, was guilty of depriving her of her civil rights and fined him $500. In the opinion of the racist judge, the fine ought to have been just one cent, and he later dismissed the fine altogether. The black community of Galveston responded swiftly to the judge's decision. A mass meeting of outraged blacks was held to vent their anger. A larger number of the audience were of women "who were doubtless drawn out from sympathy with one of their race."[13]

That black women were active in Reconstruction politics ought not to be surprising. Although they could not vote, they could exercise influence through the secret societies that were often formed as auxiliaries to men's political groups. For example, in Richmond the Rising Daughters of Liberty was affiliated with the Rising Sons of Liberty. These groups were particularly important in generating enthusiasm among blacks during political campaigns, leading fund-raising drives, and getting black men out to vote. The wives of black coal miners from Manchester, Virginia, organized as the politically active United Daughters of Liberty and cooperated with similar groups in the area.[14] Black women in Houston in August 1868 formed two clubs: a Grant and Colfax Club, and a Thaddeus Stevens Republican club. Apparently, black women in Houston also attended black political meetings in considerable numbers. The Houston press reported in June 1869 that "80 negro women and 150 negro men were present at a meeting of Radical Republicans."[15]

THE STRUGGLE FOR THE FIFTEENTH AMENDMENT

One of the most heated debates during the Reconstruction period took place over the Fifteenth Amendment, which endorsed black male suffrage. Shortly after the Civil War concluded, a group of black and white abolitionists and suffragists met in New York City and founded the American Equal Rights Association (AERA) in May 1866. Although social reformers such as Wendell Phillips, Lucy Stone, Stephen Foster, Abby Kelley Foster, Susan B. Anthony, Elizabeth Cady Stanton, Frederick Douglass, George Downing, Sojourner Truth, Hattie Purvis, Robert Purvis, Sarah Remond, and Charles Lenox Remond had worked harmoniously earlier for the abolition of slavery, this cooperation would soon evaporate. Only a few months later, it become apparent that the overall objective of the AERA, whose major architects were Anthony, Stanton, and Douglass, would not be realized. Its purpose was to bring together abolitionists and feminists to agitate for black and woman suffrage. By 1867 it was evident that either group, but not both, would be enfranchised; and, as a consequence, AERA forums became more heated than ever.[16]

The 1869 AERA meeting was a contentious one, resulting in the split of the AERA into two suffrage organizations: the National Woman Suffrage Association, founded by Stanton and Anthony; and the American Woman Suffrage Association, founded by Lucy Stone and Henry Ward Beecher. Douglass and Frances Ellen Watkins Harper, a prominent black political and social activist, argued that black men should be given priority over women in the struggle for the ballot. However, Stanton, Anthony, and Sojourner Truth believed otherwise. They argued that both black men and women should simultaneously receive the right to vote.[17]

The Fifteenth Amendment, which granted black males the right to vote, was passed by Congress in late February 1869, with the steadfast support of black politicians at the state and national levels. It was ratified by the states and became a part of the Constitution on March 30, 1870, just ten months after the AERA dissolved itself. The Amendment stated specifically that the right to vote "shall not be denied on account of race, color, or previous condition of servitude."[18] Some perceptive black leaders, who correctly feared that passage would later open the door to poll taxes, literacy tests, and property qualifications as requirements for voting, preferred language in the Amendment that would explicitly guarantee all male citizens the right to vote. Had this been done, the loopholes that white supremacists used to deprive black males of the vote in the aftermath of Reconstruction would have been closed.

Nevertheless, the majority of black leaders were aware of the monumental step forward that the Fifteenth Amendment represented. For example, Joseph Rainey, who went on to serve four terms in Congress, declared in Georgetown, South Carolina, in 1870 at a Fourth of July rally that distinctions of color had been "to a great extent destroyed by the adoption of the Fifteenth Amendment to our National Constitution—the keystone to the arch of our political structure."[19] But the view of the Amendment's significance put forth by Charles B. Ray, pastor of Bethesda Congregational Church and former editor of the *Colored American*, perhaps best reveals the feelings of most black leaders in its regard. He maintained that "the Fifteenth Amendment fulfilled the revolutionary idea of equality in the same way that the Civil War completed the revolutionary idea of freedom." Without the Amendment, Ray noted, "the nation would not have completed the fabric of government which it commenced to build on the principles enunciated in 1776, as the chief cornerstone of the government, namely, 'All men are created free and equal.' "[20]

As expected, the black population as a whole embraced the Fifteenth Amendment as enthusiastically as did their leaders. With the announcement of its adoption, celebrations took place in black communities throughout the South. Four thousand blacks attended a political rally in Augusta, Georgia, where, in the opinion of a local newspaper, "there must have been a general suspension of farm and other labor within a radius of ten miles square from the city." Several thousand gathered in Macon, Georgia,[21] and Louisville, Kentucky, also witnessed a large celebration. It was agreed by those present to support the Republican Party, which many believed was responsible for emancipation. The adoption of the Fifteenth Amendment was declared a "victory of right over wrong, of liberty over slavery, of freedom over oppression." Moreover, blacks should make "no terms

—with Kentucky Democracy." Ratification was also observed in other areas of Kentucky such as Frankfort, Hopkinsville, and Georgetown.[22] And, of course, many ratification celebrations took place in South Carolina, the state with the heaviest concentration of blacks and where a large number of prominent black leaders resided. There were festivities in Edgefield, Abbeville, Charleston, Columbia, and elsewhere; indeed, every city, town, and county courthouse had a Fifteenth Amendment celebration. Apparently, Robert Brown Elliott was among the most popular speakers.[23]

THE PROGRESS OF NORTHERN BLACKS

As a consequence of the passage of acts by Congress that applied throughout the country and of laws enacted at the state and local levels, the decade following the Civil War witnessed astonishing advances in the political, civil, and social rights of Northern blacks. Laws barring blacks from entering Northern states, testifying in court, and voting were made null and void by the Civil Rights Act of 1866 and the postwar constitutional amendments. Blacks pressing damage claims against railroads and streetcars that barred them from first-class compartments or excluded them altogether invoked these new laws to support their cases. In 1867 the Pennsylvania state legislature prohibited streetcar segregation; and, in a pioneering move six years later Republicans in New York in 1873 enacted a civil rights law that outlawed discrimination in all public accommodations. Moreover, the political climate in New York shifted so dramatically that the state's Republican Party supported a referendum as early as 1869 that would have granted equal suffrage to blacks. Despite the failure to gain passage, 90 percent of the party's voters supported the referendum. In much of the North, discrimination in transportation had disappeared, although state courts generally held that segregated facilities, if truly equal, did not violate the Fourteenth Amendment. Blacks also made progress in access to public schools in states where they had earlier been denied. Some cities with sizable black populations such as New York and Cincinnati refused to integrate their schools, but others such as Chicago, Cleveland, and Milwaukee instituted integrated school systems and occasionally hired a black teacher. In Michigan and Iowa, integrated education was common throughout the state.[24]

Despite the advances made by Northern blacks during Reconstruction, most of them, like blacks in the South, remained trapped in poverty and confined to inferior housing. Many counted themselves lucky to be employed in what were usually menial and unskilled jobs. Often they were undercut in their efforts to obtain even low-level jobs by the influx of European immigrants coming into the North. Furthermore, labor unions barred blacks from membership and employers customarily discriminated against them, preferring to give the lowest-rung jobs to the new immigrants. Indicative of the economic plight of Northern blacks is the fact that a survey of New York City's black community in 1871 found some four hundred waiters and five hundred longshoremen, but only two physicians and a handful of skilled craftsmen. This situation was due to some extent to the lack of militancy of Northern black politicians, who failed to develop a viable strategy for addressing the economic plight of their communities. Owing to the fact that most politicians came from a minute business class and represented a tiny black political constituency of less than 2 percent, this failure was perhaps inevitable. Still, the North's public life was now open to blacks in ways that were inconceivable before the Civil War.[25]

THE STRUGGLE OF CHEROKEE FREEDMEN

Those blacks who had been held as slaves by the Cherokee Indians also vigorously struggled for equal rights within the Cherokee Nation. Although Cherokee freedmen were able to vote in local and national elections, they were caught between two political parties, neither of which cared very much for advancing their interests. Because it was not popular to advocate equality for freedmen and because both major parties were shrewd, they refused to make equal rights a top priority. However, the two parties desired the votes of freedmen and aggressively courted them for their political support. From the outset, most Cherokee freedmen were aware of the fact that Cherokee politicians did not represent their interests, and they distrusted them. For example, in 1876, Joseph Rogers told his fellow freedmen: "The leaders of both parties always told me next Council we will fix it, we almost got it through this time, just vote us in once more." He further noted, "Just so it is, next Council and next Council, like tomorrow, never comes, it is the delusive [sic] end of the rainbow, with its sacks of gold always in sight, but never in reach, a receding tantalizing will-o-the wisp, leading you further into the morass of disappointment." In Rogers's opinion, these politicians could not be taken at their word because "they may honey you with sweet words and promises of citizenship, however much they may Mr. Smith and Mr. Jones you, they are only giving you a pill, sugar coated it may be, still only a pill to work you through the election. . . . I don't believe there is anything to hope for from these politicians."[26]

While Cherokee freedmen gained access to the ballot, they were unsuccessful in their efforts to win elective offices. In the election of 1875, Joseph Brown of Tahlequah District became the first and only freedman elected to the National Council. He went on to serve one term in the lower house and was subsequently nominated by the Tahlequah District as one of the Cherokee Nation's representatives to the Grand Council of the Indian Territory. However, by the time of his nomination, this position had waned in significance, since the Grand Council had lost congressional support. And, furthermore, it was on the verge of disbanding.[27]

The disappointment felt by Cherokee freedmen over their failure to gain elective offices did little to dissuade them from pushing their case for equal rights. They vigorously campaigned for full citizenship but were careful not to invite the wrath of those in power. Many of their petitions for full citizenship struck a patriotic tone. For example, a group of Cherokee freedmen petitioned in 1879 for equal rights: "The Cherokee nation is our country; there we were born and reared; there are our homes made by the sweat of our brows; there are our wives and children, whom we love as dearly as though we were born with red, instead of black skins. There we intend to live and defend our national rights, as guaranteed by the treaties and laws of the United States, by every legitimate and lawful means."[28]

The plight of deprived Native Americans, either black or full-blooded, had been of much concern to blacks for several years. In fact, more than a few significant black figures expressed their identification with Native Americans or fought for their rights, and a number have argued that blacks and Native Americans had a common interest. For example, the father of black nationalism in the United States, Martin R. Delany, as early as 1852 in a speech denouncing slavery, made the connection between the plight of both groups: "We are identical as the subject of American wrongs, outrages and oppression, and therefore one in interest." He was so concerned with this topic that he would devote a whole chapter to it in his only novel, *Blake*, in 1859. In the book, Delany discussed ways in which both blacks and Native Americans could combat the common foe: individuals of European descent.[29] In the post-Civil War period, the U.S. government pushed its genocidal policy in regard to Native Americans into high gear, and black politicians were among some of the most vocal critics of this policy. Senator Blanch K. Bruce of Mississippi, himself a former runaway slave, launched what many scholars regard as the most stinging assault on the government's genocidal policy by a U.S. citizen who was not a Native American. Bruce came onto the floor of the Senate on April 7, 1880, and told his colleagues exactly how U.S. actions had made Native Americans fugitives and vagabonds in their own land. He got right to the point:

> Our Indian policy and administration seem to me to have been inspired and controlled by a stern selfishness, with a few honorable exceptions. Indian treaties have generally been made as the condition and instrument of acquiring the valuable territory occupied by the several Indian nations, and have been changed and revised from time to time as it became desirable that the steadily growing, irrepressible white races should secure more room for their growth and more lands for their occupancy; and war bounties, and beads have been used . . . for the purpose of temporary peace and security for the whites, and as the preliminary to further aggressions upon the red man's lands, with the ultimate view of his expulsion and extinction from the continent.

Senator Bruce closed his remarks with a special plea to "save and not destroy these people, who stood in the path of the U.S. government and its citizens." [30] Unfortunately, his words did not resonate with most whites, as the genocidal policy toward Native Americans continued to flourish in the closing decades of the nineteenth century. And, indeed, it inflicted great suffering on Native Americans, some of whom were freedmen living within the various Indian nations.

WHITE VIOLENCE AND THE ESTABLISHMENT OF THE KU KLUX KLAN

The sight of black men holding political office and making important decisions was so intolerable to Southern whites that they took vicious and illegal measures against blacks. The Ku Klux Klan, a white supremacist group organized in 1866 in Pulaski, Tennessee, by Confederate war veterans, stepped up its attacks. Working together with other white supremacists, such as the White League of Louisiana, the Klan set out to intimidate blacks so that they would fear for their lives and stop supporting the Republican Party. Hooded Klansmen broke into the homes of blacks at night and terrorized them, and many blacks lost their lives at the hands of the Klan. Gender was no exception; black women were often brutalized and raped.

The Klan was often successful in reaching its goal. As F. H. Brown, a freedman, testified, "They kept the Negroes from voting. They would whip them. They put up notices: 'No Niggers to come out to the polls tomorrow.' They would run them off of government land which they had homesteaded." At other times, Klansmen tried verbal intimidation. They told Brown's father, " 'Now, Brown, you are too good to get messed up, and we don't want to see you get hurt. So you stay 'way from the polls tomorrow.' And, tomorrow my father would stay away."[31] Eli Davison explained to an interviewer that he never voted, "cause them KKK was always at the voting places for a long time after the negro was freed."[32] Many blacks, however, continued to go to the polls and vote the Republican ticket. Former slave Bill McNeil, for example, although he was scared by the Klan, kept on voting for the Republicans. "I sticks out to de end wid de party dat freed me," he said.[33] Around election time, white bosses on the different farms where freedman Morgan Ray worked would tell him to vote Democratic. He ignored them, he said, because "I knew de Republican Party was on de side of de cullud man. So I just went to de polls on election day and put my cross under de eagle."[34]

Although the Klan concentrated on preventing blacks from voting, it intimidated and murdered them for reasons other than the franchise. Freedwoman Millie Bates recounted the story of former slave Dan Black, who never bothered anyone. After the Klan shot Black, "dey took dat nigger," she said, "and hung him to a 'simmon tree. Dey would not let his folks take him down either. He jus' stayed dar, till he fell to pieces."[35] Former slave Brawley Gilmore remembered as a young boy seeing the Klansmen come along at night "a-ridding de niggers like dey was goats. Yes sir, dey had 'em down on all fours a-crawling, and dey would be on deir backs. Dey would shoot 'em offen de banisters into de water."[36] Pierce Harper knew of Klansmen murdering industrious blacks and burning down black schoolhouses. "Dey'd go to de jails an' take de colored men out, an' knock deir brains out, an' break deir necks, an' throw 'em in de river."[37]

The threat of violence against black Republican politicians was especially real. The case of Richard H. Cain, the prominent South Carolinian, illustrates this point. Cain's adopted daughter Ann Edwards vividly described what life was like for her father during Reconstruction to WPA interviewers in the 1930s. "From the moment he became a candidate for a delegate to the Constitutional Convention, a guard was necessary night and day to watch our home." She added that "he was compelled to have a bodyguard everywhere he went. We, his family, lived in constant fear at all times." Despite the armed guards, "several attempts were made to either burn the house or injure some member of the family." Edwards concluded: "If it had not been for the fact that the officials of the city and county were afraid of reprisal from the Federal government, which gave aid in protecting him, the mob would have succeeded in harming him."[38] Cain went on to establish an excellent record of public service. Many other black politicians, however, were not so fortunate as Cain. Some were beaten and run out of town, while others were murdered.[39]

Many blacks, particularly those who had been Union soldiers, responded to the random terror and violence by organizing themselves into militia groups. They were well armed and confronted the Klan fearlessly. According to Pierce Harper, "dey'd hide in de cabins, an' when de Klu Kluxes come, dere dey was. Den's when dey found out who a lot of de Klu Kluxes was, 'cause a lot of 'em was killed."[40] George Washington Albright helped to organize a volunteer militia against the organized attacks of the landlords and former slave owners. He recalled that "we drilled frequently—and how the rich folks hated to see us, armed and ready to defend ourselves and our elected government." [41] Other freedmen fought back as individuals. For example, one man shot it out one night with Klansmen who visited his house to teach him a lesson. He "told dem dat he had done nothin' wrong, an' fo' dem to go 'way, or he would kill dem." And when the shooting stopped, two members of the Klan were dead.[42] In another case, a black man in Memphis, Tennessee, killed a member of the Klan for constantly harassing him.[43]

VIOLENCE BETWEEN BLACK REPUBLICANS
AND DEMOCRATS

Reconstruction also ushered in a period of intense political violence between black Republicans and black Democrats. While most freedmen were fiercely Republican, there were some who became loyal Democrats. Spencer Taylor proudly asserted: "I never voted anything but the Democratic ticket."[44] Ike Pringle became a Democrat when he first was enfrancized,[45] and Adam Smith noted that "we have always been Democrats and we still are, me and my ole woman."[46] And Mat Fowler explained, "I allus voted Democratic till they cut us niggers out the primary."[47] Moreover, a largely untold story of African-American history brings out the fact that some freedmen exhibited so much loyalty to the Democratic Party that they joined the Red Shirts in South Carolina in the 1870s. The Red Shirts, a terrorist organization akin to the Klan, intimidated, harassed, and

beat blacks in efforts to curtail voter participation. They were especially active and effective during South Carolina's 1876 gubernatorial race between Republican Daniel Chamberlain and Democrat
Wade Hampton, so much so that they became known as "Hampton's
Red Shirts." George Fleming explained that "de Democrats done got
scared 'cause so many niggers gwine to vote fer de other side, so dey
formed a s'ciety called de Red Shirts. Dat was jes' to scare de niggers
frum coming to de polls. I was young, but I jined right up wid dem
and wore a red shirt, too."[48] During the Reconstruction period when
Hampton was stumping the region in an effort to redeem South Carolina for the Democrats, Richard Mack followed him all over the state.
Mack maintained that he led five hundred men in this endeavor and
"wore my red jacket and cap and boots. I had a sword, too."[49] Prince
Johnson joined "the Democrat club, put on the red shirt, and heped
them run all of the scalawags away from there."[50]

Why black men would join a terrorist group such as Hampton's
Red Shirts is difficult to discern. Some men such as Asbury Green,
Aaron Mitchell, and other black Red Shirt leaders were attracted to the
paternalistic appeal of Wade Hampton, a future South Carolina governor. They searched for a solution to hard economic times, increasing
turbulence that led to the loss of black lives, and Republican corruption.
They sincerely hoped that Hampton and the Democrats would be the
answer to their prayers. As Green asserted, "I will have to try another
party, and see if they will make it no better, and if they don't I don't
know what in the world to do."[51] Some of the black Red Shirts shared
the class and anti-Yankee bias of their former owners. They saw themselves as uniquely South Carolinian, sharing with white conservatives
the perception of the Yankees as outsiders. As such, they did not trust
Northerners.[52] Furthermore, men such as Madison Griffin never forgot
the destruction Lincoln and the Yankees had wrought. Griffin recalled
that Lincoln "had us all scared to death, took our mules and burned our
places."[53] Whatever the rationale of the black Red Shirts, historian
Edmund Drago is on the mark in maintaining that these black conservatives "fit into a larger theme in African-American history, namely, a
stream of blacks who have supported conservative regimes from the
colonial period to the present."[54] Clarence Thomas, Alan Keyes, Robert
Woodson, Larry Elder, Ken Hamlin, Thomas Sowell, and Armstrong
Williams are representative of a small, yet growing, number of black
conservatives today.

As expected, most blacks regarded black Democrats as traitors to
the race. Indeed, how could they lack race consciousness? What could

possibly be wrong with these individuals? How could they align themselves with former slaveowners? Did they not know that the Republican Party was the party of Abraham Lincoln and the Thirteenth, Fourteenth, and Fifteenth Amendments as well as the Freedmen's Bureau, Civil Rights Acts of 1866 and 1875, and the 1870 and 1871 Enforcement Acts? In South Carolina, black men who had voted the so-called Reform ticket in Newberry and Barnwell County were attacked by their fellows and beaten. Similar incidents took place in Charleston, Mount Pleasant, and Beaufort, South Carolina. In some areas, freedmen were told that they would be shot by the black militia if they voted Democratic. [55] Moreover, when the first black man in James City, North Carolina, voted Democratic, he was burned in effigy and run out of the town. One member of the all-black community explained: "We made a tar man and burned it up. . . . We felt he was set up by the white man."[56]

Black women figured prominently in the efforts to prevent men from voting for Democrats. For instance, black women in Alabama formed political clubs and in some instances denied their would-be Democratic husbands the pleasures of the bedroom.[57] On the Sea Islands of South Carolina they followed the same course during the state's 1876 gubernatorial contest. According to Robert Smalls, "when John went to Massa Hampton and pledged his word to vote for him and returned back home his wife told him she would not give him any of that thing if you vote for Hampton." As a result, John returned to Hampton and said, "Massa Hampton, I can't vote for you, for woman is too sweet, and my wife says if I vote for you she won't give me any."[58]

The wife of a starving freedman allegedly struck the poor fellow with an ax when he sold his vote to Democrats in exchange for food.[59] One man who wanted to vote for a white Democratic candidate was whipped on the street by his wife. In an effort to prevent her husband from voting the Democratic ticket, another woman threw his clothes out of the house and locked the door.[60] Further, on Election Day in South Carolina in 1876 the women armed themselves. According to a witness, "women had sticks; no mens were to go to the polls unless their wives were right alongside them; some had hickory sticks; some had nails—four nails driven in the shape of a cross—and dare their husbands to vote any other than the Republican ticket." The witness further noted, "my sister went with my brother-in-law to the polls and swear to God if he voted the Democratic ticket she would kill him dead in his sleep."[61]

THE DIMINISHING INFLUENCE OF
THE REPUBLICAN PARTY

The Republican Party had always been divided into factions, especially among its Northern white members, but blacks were also divided. Those Southern black Republicans who were free before the war—often mulatto and owners of property—had on some occasions held interests different from their darker brothers in the party, many of whom had been slaves before the war and owned little or no property. Some former black slaves were suspicious of the intentions of mulattoes and loathed mulatto Republicans with a passion. William Nash, a black state senator from South Carolina, asked, "To what race do they belong—I know that my ancestors trod the burning sands of Africa, but why should men in whose veins run a great preponderance of white blood seek to specially, ally themselves with the black man, . . . when they are simply mongrels?"[62]

Furthermore, there were also tensions between some Northern and Southern black members of the party. To many Southern blacks, their Northern counterparts tended to look down upon them. The superior racial attitudes of some Northern and Southern white Republicans further exacerbated tensions within the party. Several white Northerners treated black members in paternalistic ways and believed fervently that blacks should not hold important political offices. After all, in their opinion, blacks were political neophytes and lacked not only political maturity but also intellectual capability. Of course, black Republicans resented this view. Moreover, Southern white Republicans harbored even more racist views than their Northern counterparts and were not reluctant to reveal them.

These troubles came to the surface when it was time to cast ballots on such issues as unionization, land redistribution, and disfranchisement of Southern planters who had supported the Confederacy. A large number of Northern and Southern white Republicans with a sizable minority of black politicians (particularly mulatto) refused to support these three issues, all of the utmost importance to the black masses. Yet the majority of black politicians did vote in favor of these issues. In addition, although most Northern white members of the Republican Party joined black members in supporting civil rights legislation, many of the Southern whites in the party did not. Given these serious divisions, it is remarkable that the Republican Party was able to remain in power in the South as long as it did and to accomplish so much. By the early to mid-1870s its fortunes were clearly waning.

The fortunes of the Republican Party in the South continued to diminish throughout the 1870s as the Democrats began to recapture the political machinery in one state after another. In this atmosphere, Republicans in Congress made one final effort to ensure the rights of freedmen by passing the Civil Rights Act of 1875, which applied primarily to public accommodations. Blacks were given equal access to the same hotels, restaurants, theaters, and railroads as whites. But to many white Americans the measure was too progressive. Reflecting this attitude, the U.S. Supreme Court declared one year later that parts of the 1870 and 1871 laws enforcing the Fourteenth and Fifteenth Amendments were unconstitutional in the *U.S. v. Cruikshank* and *U.S. v. Reese* decisions, and in 1883 it declared the Civil Rights Act of 1875 unconstitutional.

As soon as the conservatives were in control of the machinery of government, they began minimizing the black vote. Their methods were devious and often illegal. They deliberately withheld information from registered blacks about where ballots could be cast, arrested blacks on trumped-up charges the day before an election and released them once it was over, and stuffed ballot boxes and doctored election returns. Some whites even voted several times in one election.[63] The physical and economic intimidation that had been successfully employed by Southern whites to regain political control was also continued. Thousands of African Americans were informed that if they insisted upon voting for Republican candidates, employers could no longer retain them. And, of course, the Ku Klux Klan and other white supremacist groups continued to randomly attack, beat, and murder scores of African Americans.[64] Numerous black men and women were lynched in the 1870s, 1880s, and 1890s.[65] In fact, in the 1880s and 1890s black lynchings averaged about 100 per year, reaching their zenith in 1892 when 161 were hanged.[66] These figures represent moderate estimates, and it is likely that the actual number was considerably higher.

For a time after the Civil War, the Radical Republicans, always a minority in the party, persuaded the Northern electorate that the ultimate purpose of Southern white men was to rob the North of the fruits of victory and to reestablish slavery. Therefore, Federal intervention was essential. Their task had not been easy, for a considerable number of Northern whites, in the belief that blacks were inferior to whites, preferred to keep them in a subordinate position. No wonder that by the mid-1870s, when Northerners ceased to worry about the possibility of another Southern rebellion, there was little support within their ranks for the rights of freedmen. By this time, even some Radical Republicans had lost interest in the freedmen and began turning their attention to other crusades or choosing to retire and write their memoirs. Blacks had also lost two of their most adamant and influential supporters in Congress: Pennsylvania's Congressman Thaddeus Stevens died in 1868, and Massachusetts's Senator Charles Sumner died six years later in 1874.

In addition, the industrialism of the post-Civil War period signaled a retreat from idealism. People became more interested in making as much money as they could than in helping the less fortunate.[67] Moreover, innumerable Americans were hit hard by the depression of 1873, and, as usual, the political party in control during an economic crisis received the blame. Accordingly, the hatchet fell on the Republican Party. Democrats made a convincing argument that the exorbitant spending of Republicans had contributed substantially to the depression. They were also able to tie Republicans to the political corruption that permeated local and state governments as well as the national government in the latter nineteenth century. In a shocking reversal of political fortunes, the Democrats regained control of the House of Representatives in the elections of 1874, the first time in nearly twenty years. Thus, after 1876, the Republican Party no longer needed blacks. Eastern industrialists who had a great deal of influence within the party were now looking to the Southern markets. Because a peaceful climate was necessary in the Southern states if they were to tap into these markets, they reasoned that they should adopt a "hands-off" policy on the question of black rights and let the South deal with its black population as it saw fit.[68]

The wishes of the business community were reflected in the behavior of the Republican Party. The so-called Hayes Bargain ushered in the hands-off policy. Republican Rutherford B. Hayes and Democrat Samuel J. Tilden were involved in 1876 in one of the closest presidential elections in this country's history. The electoral votes for four states—Florida, Louisiana, South Carolina, and Oregon—were in dispute and would determine the winner. A specially created electoral commission decided in favor of Hayes, but in order to prevent Southern Democrats from contesting the decision, the Republicans, with Hayes's blessing, struck a deal. Hayes would withdraw Federal troops from the South, appoint a Southerner to his cabinet, and support Federal aid to bolster economic and railroad development, which many of the conservatives who controlled the Democratic Party in the South greatly desired. Hayes's and the Republican Party's message was clear: they would not enforce the Fourteenth and Fifteenth Amendments; and once they had removed troops from the South, Southerners would have a free hand to deal with blacks as they wanted to.[69] Republicans thus officially abandoned blacks and were ready to downplay any association with them in order to attract Southern white voters. Their abandonment of freedmen at this critical stage is one of the greatest tragedies of Reconstruction.[70]

ACCOMPLISHMENTS OF THE RECONSTRUCTION ERA

Despite the bleak record of failures in the era of emancipation and Republican rule, and the counterrevolution of white conservatives in the late nineteenth and early twentieth centuries, there were some enduring accomplishments.[71] Black politicians played a role in many of these successes. Under Republican rule, many of the undemocratic features of earlier state constitutions were eliminated. Every state approved universal men's suffrage and loosened requirements for holding office. To make the basis of representation fairer, more legislative seats were apportioned to the less-populated interior regions of Southern states. Social legislation was passed that abolished laws requiring imprisonment for owing debts. The first divorce laws in many Southern states were enacted, and laws granting married women property rights were also passed. Penal laws were modernized, and as a result, in one state, the list of crimes punishable by death was reduced from twenty-six to five.

Republican governments undertook the task of financially and physically reconstructing the South. They overhauled outdated tax systems, approved generous railroad and other capital investment bonds, and invested in the infrastructure by rebuilding bridges, harbors, and roads. They also expanded social services to the sick, poor, and elderly and established hospitals and asylums. Before the Republican governments took over, there were no state-supported systems of public education. By the time the Democrats took over, there was one in every Southern state. For the first time, both races, and rich and poor alike, had access to education.[72] Such huge investments cost money, and the Republicans had to raise taxes and increase state debts. All in all, however, the Republican governments "dragged the South, screaming and crying into the modern world."[73] This accomplishment alone made their efforts worthwhile. Moreover, the fact that blacks, who until recently had been slaves, were the architects of many of the accomplishments of the Reconstruction period is truly remarkable. These black politicians were real trailblazers, and it would take nearly another century before America again would see blacks in large numbers in so many important political offices. In fact, many of the political offices held by blacks during Reconstruction have never been recaptured by them.

Emancipation and Reconstruction occurred amid great expectations for Southern blacks. It initially appeared that they might be eventually accepted as first-class citizens in America. However, in the waning years of Reconstruction and the ensuing decades, the long arm of white supremacy reached out, grabbed Southern blacks, and launched a campaign not only to stop their progress but also to return them as nearly as possible to a state of slavery. Blacks struggled tenaciously against overwhelming obstacles to achieve first-class citizenship. That they failed to accomplish their goal completely is not due to any lack of determination and effort on their part. The fact that America missed a golden opportunity to build a truly egalitarian society is the most tragic failure of Reconstruction. Unfortunately, both Northern and Southern whites allowed racism to halt and then reverse what had been a remarkable movement to obtain freedom, justice, and equality for their black brothers and sisters. This country continues to pay a heavy price for that failure.

NOTES

CHAPTER ONE

1. Colin A. Palmer, *Passageways: An Interpretive History of Black America*, 2 vols. (New York: Harcourt Brace, 1998), 1:288–89.

2. Ibid., 289.

3. Ibid.

4. Ibid., 295.

5. Ibid., 290.

6. George P. Rawick, ed., *The American Slave: A Composite Autobiography* (Westport, CT: Greenwood Press, 1977), Vol. 10, Texas Narratives, Part 9, 4060.

7. Darlene Clark Hine, William C. Hine, and Stanley Harrold, *The African-American Odyssey* (Upper Saddle River, NJ: Prentice-Hall, 2000), 230; Benjamin Quarles, *The Negro in the Making of America*, 3d rev. ed. (New York: MacMillan, 1987), 110; John Hope Franklin and Alfred A. Moss Jr., *From Slavery to Freedom: A History of African Americans*, 7th rev. ed. (New York: McGraw-Hill, 1994), 199.

8. Quarles, *The Negro in the Making*, 110; Franklin and Moss, *From Slavery to Freedom*, 199; Clark Hine et al., *The African-American Odyssey*, 230.

9. Ibid.

10. Quarles, *The Negro in the Making*, 110–11.

11. Ibid., 111; Clark Hine et al., *The African-American Odyssey*, 230.

12. Quarles, *The Negro in the Making*, 111; Jim Cullen, " 'I's a Man Now': Gender and African American Men" in Darlene Clark Hine and Earnestine Jenkins, eds., *A Question of Manhood: A Reader in U.S. Black Men's History and Masculinity* (Bloomington and Indianapolis: Indiana University Press, 1999), 490.

13. Quarles, *The Negro in the Making*, 111.

14. Lt. Col. (Ret.) Michael Lee Lanning, *The African-American Soldier: From Crispus Attucks to Colin Powell* (Secaucus, NJ: Carol Publishing Group, 1997), 1–29; Gary A. Donaldson, *The History of African-Americans in the Military* (Malabar, FL: Krieger, 1991), 1–30; Jack D. Foner, *Blacks and the Military in American History* (New York: Praeger, 1974), 3–25.

15. Benjamin Quarles, *Lincoln and the Negro* (New York: Oxford University Press, 1962), 18; Richard N. Current, "The Friend of Freedom," in Kenneth M. Stampp and Leon F. Litwack, eds., *Reconstruction: An Anthology of Revisionist Writings* (Baton Rouge: Louisiana State University Press, 1969), 25–26.

16. Quarles, *Lincoln and the Negro*, 18; Current, "The Friend of Freedom," 27–28.

17. Current, "The Friend of Freedom," 28.

18. Ibid.

19. Ibid.

20. Ibid., 29.

21. Ibid.

22. Ibid.

23. Stephen B. Oates, *With Malice toward None: The Life of Abraham Lincoln* (New York: Harper and Row, 1977), 254.

24. James M. McPherson, *Drawn with the Sword: Reflections on the American Civil War* (New York and Oxford: Oxford University Press, 1996), 201.

25. Oates, *With Malice toward None*, 260.

26. McPherson, *Drawn with the Sword*, 201.

27. Oates, *With Malice toward None*, 298–99.

28. Ibid., 299.

29. Ibid.

30. Philip Shaw Paludan, *The Presidency of Abraham Lincoln* (Lawrence: University Press of Kansas, 1994), 145–47; David Herbert Donald, *Lincoln* (New York: Simon and Schuster, 1995), 364–65; Mark E. Neely Jr., *The Last Best Hope of Earth: Abraham Lincoln and the Promise of America* (Cambridge, MA: Harvard University Press, 1993), 108; Oates, *With Malice toward None*, 309–10.

31. Paludan, *The Presidency of Abraham Lincoln*, 146.

32. Donald, *Lincoln*, 314.

33. Paludan, *The Presidency of Abraham Lincoln*, 146.

34. Ibid., 146–47.

35. August Meier and Elliott Rudwick, *From Plantation to Ghetto: An Interpretive History of American Blacks*, 3d rev. ed. (New York: Hill and Wang, 1976), 158; Quarles, *The Negro in the Making*, 113.

36. Paludan, *The Presidency of Abraham Lincoln*, 127–28.

37. Quarles, *The Negro in the Making*, 113; Palmer, *Passageways*, 1:295.

38. Allen C. Guelzo, *The Crisis of the American Republic: A History of the Civil War and Reconstruction Era* (New York: St. Martin's Press, 1995), 136; Quarles, *The Negro in the Making*, 113–14; Dorothy C. Salem, *The Journey: A History of the African American Experience* (Dubuque, IA: Kendall/Hunt, 1997), 185; Clark Hine et al., *The African-American Odyssey*, 234; Franklin and Moss, *From Slavery to Freedom*, 206.

39. Meier and Rudwick, *From Plantation to Ghetto*, 158–59.

40. Palmer, *Passageways*, 1:293.

41. Guelzo, *The Crisis of the American Republic*, 136.

42. Ibid., 136; Quarles, *The Negro in the Making*, 114; J. G. Randall and Richard N. Current, "Race Relations in the White House," in Don E. Fehrenbacher, ed., *The Leadership of Abraham Lincoln* (New York: John Wiley and Sons, 1970), 151–52; Clark Hine et al., *The African-American Odyssey*, 234.

43. Ira Berlin, Barbara J. Fields, Steven F. Miller, Joseph P. Reidy, and Leslie S. Rowland, eds., *Free at Last: A Documentary History of Slavery, Freedom, and the Civil War* (New York: New Press, 1992), 38–42.

44. Quarles, *The Negro in the Making*, 114–15; Meier and Rudwick, *From Plantation to Ghetto*, 159.

45. McPherson, *Drawn with the Sword*, 202; William L. Barney, *The Passage of the Republic: An Interdisciplinary History of Nineteenth-Century America* (Lexington, MA: D. C. Heath and Company, 1987), 220.

46. Barney, *The Passage of the Republic*, 220.

47. Franklin and Moss, *From Slavery to Freedom*, 207.

48. William L. Barney, *Battleground for the Union: The Era of the Civil War and Reconstruction, 1848–1877* (Englewood Cliffs, NJ: Prentice-Hall, 1990), 184.

49. Franklin and Moss, *From Slavery to Freedom*, 207.

50. Victor B. Howard, *Black Liberation in Kentucky: Emancipation and Freedom, 1862–1884* (Lexington: University Press of Kentucky, 1983), 34.

51. John W. Blassingame, ed., *Slave Testimony: Two Centuries of Letters, Speeches, Interviews, and Autobiographies* (Baton Rouge and London: Louisiana State University Press, 1977), 618.

52. Rawick, ed., *The American Slave*, Vol. 6, Mississippi Narratives, Part 1, 323.

53. Blassingame, ed., *Slave Testimony*, 616–17.

54. James M. McPherson, *The Negro's Civil War: How American Negroes Felt and Acted during the War for the Union* (New York: Vintage Books, 1965), 61.

55. Ibid., 63–64; Genevieve S. Gray, ed., *Army Life in a Black Regiment* (By Colonel Thomas W. Higginson) (New York: Grosset and Dunlap, 1970), 30–32.

56. Patricia W. Romero and Willie Lee Rose, eds., *Reminiscences of My Life: A Black Woman's Civil War Memoirs* (By Susie King Taylor) (New York: Markus Wiener, 1988), 14.

57. Rawick, ed., *The American Slave*, Vol. 5, Texas Narratives, Part 4, 1646–47.

58. Neely, *The Last Best Hope of Earth*, 121.

59. Ibid.

60. Ibid.

61. Rawick, ed., *The American Slave*, Vol. 6, Mississippi Narratives, Part 1, 8, 9, 11, 12.

62. Benjamin Quarles, *The Negro in the Civil War* (Boston: Little, Brown and Company, 1969), 170–75.

63. John Mack Faragher, *Out of Many: A History of the American People*, 2 vols. (Englewood Cliffs, NJ: Prentice-Hall, 1994), 1:491.

64. Michael L. Conniff and Thomas J. Davis, *Africans in the Americas: A History of the Black Diaspora* (New York: St. Martin's Press, 1994), 202.

65. Ibid.

66. Quarles, *The Negro in the Making*, 115.

67. McPherson, *The Negro's Civil War*, 49.

68. Donald, *Lincoln*, 377–78. For a discussion of Northern and Southern white reaction to the Emancipation Proclamation, and the racial climate in the North before and during the Civil War, please consult Thomas A. Bailey, *The American Pageant: A History of the Republic*, 2 vols. (Lexington, MA: D. C. Heath and Company, 1991), 1:458–59. Oates, *With Malice toward None*, 320–21; Leon F. Litwack, *North of Slavery: The Negro in the Free States, 1790–1860* (Chicago: University of Chicago Press, 1961); James O. Horton and Lois E. Horton, *Black Bostonians: Family Life and Community Struggle in the Antebellum North* (New York: Holmes and Meier, 1979); Julie Winch, *Philadelphia's Black Elite: Activism, Accommodation, and the Struggle for Autonomy, 1787–1848* (Philadelphia: Temple University Press, 1988); Vincent Harding, *There Is a River: The Black Struggle for Freedom in America* (New York: Harcourt Brace and Company, 1981), 239–40; Eric Foner, *Reconstruction: America's Unfinished Revolution, 1863–1877* (New York: Harper and Row, 1988), 32–33; Donald Yacovone, ed., *A Voice of Thunder: The Civil War Letters of George E. Stephens* (Urbana: University of Illinois Press, 1997); Bailey, *The American Pageant*, 1:459–60; and Barney, *Battleground for the Union*, 183.

69. Barney, *Battleground for the Union*, 184–86; Bailey, *The American Pageant*, 1:458; Maulana Karenga, *Introduction to Black Studies* (Los Angeles, CA: University of Sankore Press, 1982), 103.

70. Blassingame, ed., *Slave Testimony*, 372.

71. Barney, *Battleground for the Union*, 185–86; Clark Hine et al., *The African-American Odyssey*, 236–37.

72. McPherson, *Drawn with the Sword*, 204–5.

73. Paludan, *The Presidency of Abraham Lincoln*, 301; Oates, *With Malice toward None*, 404–5.

74. LaWanda Cox, "Lincoln and Black Freedom," in Gabor S. Boritt, ed., *The Historian's Lincoln: Pseudohistory, Psychohistory, and History* (Urbana and Chicago: University of Illinois Press, 1988), 181.

75. James M. McPherson, *Battle Cry of Freedom: The Civil War Era* (New York: Ballantine Books, 1989), 839; Oates, *With Malice toward None*, 405; Paludan, *The Presidency of Abraham Lincoln*, 302.

76. Oates, *With Malice toward None*, 405.

77. Ibid., 405–6.

78. Waldo E. Martin Jr., *The Mind of Frederick Douglass* (Chapel Hill: University of North Carolina Press, 1984), 266.

79. McPherson, *Battle Cry of Freedom*, 840–41.

80. Randall and Current, "Race Relations in the White House," 152–53.

81. Ibid., 153.

82. Martin, *The Mind of Frederick Douglass*, 267; Merrill D. Peterson, *Lincoln in American Memory* (New York and Oxford: Oxford University Press, 1994), 59–60.

CHAPTER TWO

1. John Hope Franklin and Alfred A. Moss Jr., *From Slavery to Freedom: A History of African Americans*, 7th rev. ed. (New York: McGraw-Hill, 1994), 214; Vincent Harding, *There Is a River: The Black Struggle for Freedom in America* (New York: Harcourt Brace and Company, 1981), 237; Jason H. Silverman, "Mary Ann Shadd and the Search for Equality," in Leon Litwack and August Meier, eds., *Black Leaders of the Nineteenth Century* (Urbana and Chicago: University of Illinois Press, 1988), 97; Dorothy Sterling, ed., *We Are Your Sisters: Black Women in the Nineteenth Century* (New York: W. W. Norton and Company, 1984), 256–58.

2. Franklin and Moss, *From Slavery to Freedom*, 214.

3. Benjamin Quarles, *The Negro in the Civil War* (Boston: Little, Brown and Company, 1969), 312.

4. George P. Rawick, ed., *The American Slave: A Composite Autobiography* (Westport, CT: Greenwood Press, 1977), Vol. 6, Mississippi Narratives, Part 1, 11.

5. Ibid., Vol. 8, Mississippi Narratives, Part 3, 1222.

6. William S. McFeely, *Sapelo's People: A Long Walk into Freedom* (New York: W. W. Norton and Company, 1994), 67.

7. Franklin and Moss, *From Slavery to Freedom*, 214.

8. Ella Forbes, *But We Have No Country: The 1851 Christiana, Pennsylvania, Resistance* (Cherry Hill, NJ: Africana Homestead Legacy, 1998), 224–26.

9. Franklin and Moss, *From Slavery to Freedom*, 214; Maulana Karenga, *Introduction to Black Studies* (Los Angeles, CA: University of Sankore Press, 1982), 104.

10. Franklin and Moss, *From Slavery to Freedom*, 214.

11. Paul S. Boyer, *The Enduring Vision: A History of the American People*, 2 vols. (Lexington, MA: D. C. Heath and Company, 1993), 1:496.

12. Franklin and Moss, *From Slavery to Freedom*, 214–15.

13. Edwin S. Redkey, ed., *A Grand Army of Black Men: Letters from African-American Soldiers in the Union Army, 1861–1865* (New York: Cambridge University Press, 1992), 243.

14. Noah Andre Trudeau, ed., *Voices of the 55th: Letters from the 55th Massachusetts Volunteers, 1861–1865* (Dayton, OH: Morningside House, 1996), 62.

15. Redkey, ed., *A Grand Army of Black Men*, 211.

16. Ibid., 243.

17. Trudeau, ed., *Voices of the 55th*, 62.

18. Redkey, ed., *A Grand Army of Black Men*, 249.

19. Ibid., 260–61.

20. Trudeau, ed., *Voices of the 55th*, 73–74.

21. Redkey, ed., *A Grand Army of Black Men*, 262.

22. Joseph T. Glatthaar, *Forged in Battle: The Civil War Alliance of Black Soldiers and White Officers* (New York: Meridian Books, 1990), 114.

23. Karenga, *Introduction to Black Studies*, 104; Franklin and Moss, *From Slavery to Freedom*, 216.

24. Virginia M. Adams, ed., *On the Altar of Freedom: A Black Soldier's Civil War Letters from the Front* (By Corporal James Henry Gooding) (Amherst: University of Massachusetts Press, 1991), 66–67.

25. Jack D. Foner, *Blacks and the Military in American History* (New York: Praeger, 1974), 47–48; Lt. Col. (Ret.) Michael Lee Lanning, *The African-American Soldier: From Crispus Attucks to Colin Powell* (Secaucus, NJ: Carol Publishing Group, 1997), 55–59; Gary A. Donaldson, *The History of African-Americans in the Military* (Malabar, FL: Krieger, 1991), 42–43; Redkey, ed., *A Grand Army of Black Men*, 269–71; Benjamin Quarles, *The Negro in the Making of America*, 3d rev. ed. (New York: MacMillan, 1987), 121; Mary F. Berry and John W. Blassingame, *Long Memory: The Black Experience in America* (New York and Oxford: Oxford University Press, 1982), 301.

26. Franklin and Moss, *From Slavery to Freedom*, 215.

27. Boyer, *The Enduring Vision*, 1:497.

28. Franklin and Moss, *From Slavery to Freedom*, 215.

29. Adams, ed., *On the Altar of Freedom*, 48–49.

30. Franklin and Moss, *From Slavery to Freedom*, 215.

31. Redkey, ed., *A Grand Army of Black Men*, 237.

32. Ibid.

33. Trudeau, ed., *Voices of the 55th*, 83.

34. Ibid., 86.

35. Adams, ed., *On the Altar of Freedom*, 83.

36. Trudeau, ed., *Voices of the 55th*, 93.

37. Ibid., 83–84.

38. Redkey, ed., *A Grand Army of Black Men*, 241; Foner, *Blacks and the Military*, 43.

39. Redkey, ed., *A Grand Army of Black Men*, 241–42.

40. Trudeau, ed., *Voices of the 55th*, 156.

41. Redkey, ed., *A Grand Army of Black Men*, 247.

42. Trudeau, ed., *Voices of the 55th*, 156.

43. Ibid., 154–55.

44. Adams, ed., *On the Altar of Freedom*, 24.

45. Franklin and Moss, *From Slavery to Freedom*, 217.

46. Glatthaar, *Forged in Battle*, 160.

47. Franklin and Moss, *From Slavery to Freedom*, 217.

48. Ira Berlin, Barbara J. Fields, Steven F. Miller, Joseph P. Reidy, and Leslie S. Rowland, eds., *Free at Last: A Documentary History of Slavery, Freedom, and the Civil War* (New York: Free Press, 1992), 447.

49. Ibid., 447–49.

50. Franklin and Moss, *From Slavery to Freedom*, 216.

51. Dudley T. Cornish, *The Sable Arm: Negro Troops in the Union Army, 1861–1865* (New York: W. W. Norton and Company, 1956), 267–69; Trudeau, ed., *Voices of the 55th*, 91.

52. Trudeau, ed., *Voices of the 55th*, 91.

53. Ibid., 59–60.

54. Foner, *Blacks and the Military*, 44; Lanning, *The African-American Soldier*, 53; Donaldson, *The History of African-Americans*, 45.

55. Noah Andre Trudeau, *Like Men of War: Black Troops in the Civil War, 1862–1865* (Boston: Little, Brown and Company, 1998), 168.

56. Cornish, *The Sable Arm*, 175.

57. Jack Hurst, *Nathan Bedford Forrest: A Biography* (New York: Alfred A. Knopf, 1993), 176, 177; Brian S. Wills, *A Battle from the Start: The Life of Nathan Bedford Forrest* (New York: HarperCollins, 1992), 180, 185, 187–96.

58. Hurst, *Nathan Bedford Forrest*, 175; Cornish, *The Sable Arm*, 175.

59. Trudeau, ed., *Like Men of War*, 169.

60. Cornish, *The Sable Arm*, 176; Trudeau, *Like Men of War*, 172.

61. Cornish, *The Sable Arm*, 176.

62. Donaldson, *The History of African-Americans*, 45.

63. Colin A. Palmer, *Passageways: An Interpretive History of Black America*, 2 vols. (New York: Harcourt Brace, 1998), 1:304–5.

64. Cornish, *The Sable Arm*, 176.

65. Gregory J. W. Urwin, " 'We Cannot Treat Negroes . . . As Prisoners of War': Racial Atrocities and Reprisals in Civil War Arkansas," *Civil War History* 42, no. 3 (1996): 196–97.

66. Ibid., 197.

67. Ibid.

68. Ibid.

69. Cornish, *The Sable Arm*, 177.

70. Urwin, " 'We Cannot Treat Negroes,' " 207–8.

71. Ibid., 208.

72. Redkey, ed., *A Grand Army of Black Men*, 276.

73. Ibid., 274.

74. Foner, *Blacks and the Military*, 44; Lanning, *The African-American Soldier*, 53.

75. Franklin and Moss, *From Slavery to Freedom*, 216.

76. Cornish, *The Sable Arm*, 178.

77. Redkey, ed., *A Grand Army of Black Men*, 165.

78. Berlin et al., eds., *Free at Last*, 449–51.

79. Redkey, ed., *A Grand Army of Black Men*, 60.

80. Genevieve S. Gray, ed., *Army Life in a Black Regiment* (By Colonel Thomas W. Higginson) (New York: Grosset and Dunlap, 1970), 29.

81. Quarles, *The Negro in the Civil War*, 211.

82. Ibid.

83. R. J. M. Blackett, ed., *Thomas Morris Chester: Black Civil War Correspondent, His Dispatches from the Virginia Front* (Baton Rouge: Louisiana State University Press, 1989), 96–97.

84. Quarles, *The Negro in the Civil War*, 211–12.

85. Blackett, ed., *Thomas Morris Chester*, 118–19; Berlin et al., eds., *Free at Last*, 484–86.

86. Glatthaar, *Forged in Battle*, 115.

87. Foner, *Blacks and the Military*, 45.

88. Harding, *There Is a River*, 241.

89. Trudeau, ed., *Voices of the 55th*, 113–14.

90. Redkey, ed., *A Grand Army of Black Men*, 135–36.

91. Blackett, ed., *Thomas Morris Chester*, 118–19.

92. Trudeau, ed., *Voices of the 55th*, 116.

93. Redkey, ed., *A Grand Army of Black Men*, 214.

94. Ibid.

95. Adams, ed., *On the Altar of Freedom*, 13.

96. Ibid.

97. Trudeau, ed., *Voices of the 55th*, 125.

98. Ibid., 40.

99. Ibid., 51.

100. Redkey, ed., *A Grand Army of Black Men*, 205.

101. Berlin et al., eds., *Free at Last*, 359–60.

102. Ibid., 389–92.

103. Ibid., 464; Ira Berlin and Leslie S. Rowland, eds., *Families and Freedom: A Documentary History of African-American Kinship in the Civil War Era* (New York: New Press, 1992), 97.

104. Berlin and Rowland, eds., *Families and Freedom*, 100.

105. Ibid., 99.

106. Ibid.

107. McFeely, *Sapelo's People*, 78–79.

108. Redkey, ed., *A Grand Army of Black Men*, 159.

109. Wilbert L. Jenkins, *Seizing the New Day: African Americans in Post-Civil War Charleston* (Bloomington and Indianapolis: Indiana University Press, 1998), 40.

110. Reginald Hildebrand, "Methodism, the Military and Freedom" (Paper presented at the annual conference of the Association for the Study of Afro-American Life and History, Chicago, 1990), 5.

111. Rawick, ed., *The American Slave*, Vol. 2, Arkansas, Colorado, Minnesota, Missouri, Oregon, and Washington Narratives, 106.

112. Ibid., Vol. 9, Mississippi Narratives, Part 4, 1877.

113. Ibid., Vol. 12, Oklahoma Narratives, 242.

114. Ibid., Vol. 6, Mississippi Narratives, Part 1, 136.

115. Ibid., Vol. 12, Oklahoma Narratives, 177.

116. Ibid., Vol. 1, Alabama, Arizona, Arkansas, District of Columbia, Florida, Georgia, Indiana, Kansas, Maryland, Nebraska, New York, North Carolina, Oklahoma, Rhode Island, South Carolina, and Washington Narratives, 20.

117. Ibid., Vol. 6, Mississippi Narratives, Part 1, 193.

118. Berlin and Rowland, eds., *Families and Freedom*, 69.

119. Ibid., 69–70.

120. Ibid., 71–72.

121. Ibid., 199–201; Berlin et al., eds., *Free at Last*, 493–95.

122. Berlin et al., eds., *Free at Last*, 394–95.

123. Berlin and Rowland, eds., *Families and Freedom*, 201.

124. Berlin et al., eds., *Free at Last*, 530.

125. Berlin and Rowland, eds., *Families and Freedom*, 137–38.

126. Marion B. Lucas, *A History of Blacks in Kentucky*, 2 vols. (Lexington: Kentucky Historical Society, 1992), 1:168.

127. Trudeau, ed., *Voices of the 55th*, 52, 82.

128. Ibid., 42.

129. Lucas, *A History of Blacks in Kentucky*, 1:167.

130. Ibid.

131. Gray, ed., *Army Life in a Black Regiment*, 20; Glatthaar, *Forged in Battle*, 159.

132. James M. McPherson, *The Negro's Civil War: How American Negroes Felt and Acted during the War for the Union* (New York: Vintage Books, 1965), 211.

133. Ibid., 212–13; Lucas, *A History of Blacks in Kentucky*, 1:169; Glatthaar, *Forged in Battle*, 226.

134. McPherson, *The Negro's Civil War*, 211.

135. Glatthaar, *Forged in Battle*, 226–27.

136. Lucas, *A History of Blacks in Kentucky*, 1:169.

137. Adams, ed., *On the Altar of Freedom*, 85–86.

138. Redkey, ed., *A Grand Army of Black Men*, 119–21.

139. Ervin L. Jordan Jr., *Black Confederates and Afro-Yankees in Civil War Virginia* (Charlottesville: University Press of Virginia, 1995), 283.

140. Ibid., 285; Hampton Institute, *The Negro in Virginia: Compiled by Workers of the Writers' Program of the Work Projects Administration in the State of Virginia* (New York: Hastings House, 1940), 199.

141. Ella Forbes, *African American Women during the Civil War* (New York: Garland, 1998), 41–42.

142. Sterling, ed., *We Are Your Sisters*, 259.

143. Donald Yacovone, ed., *A Voice of Thunder: The Civil War Letters of George E. Stephens* (Urbana: University of Illinois Press, 1997), 201.

144. Patricia W. Romero and Willie Lee Rose, eds., *Reminiscences of My Life: A Black Woman's Civil War Memoirs* (By Susie King Taylor) (New York: Markus Wiener, 1988), 11–12.

145. Rawick, ed., *The American Slave*, Vol. 9, Mississippi Narratives, Part 4, 1903–1904.

146. Redkey, ed., *A Grand Army of Black Men*, 123–25.

147. Jordan, *Black Confederates and Afro-Yankees*, 283.

148. Redkey, ed., *A Grand Army of Black Men*, 170.

149. Whittington B. Johnson, *Black Savannah, 1788–1864* (Fayetteville: University of Arkansas Press, 1996), 166.

150. Harding, *There Is a River*, 253.

151. Hampton Institute, *The Negro in Virginia*, 188.

152. Johnson, *Black Savannah*, 166.

153. Quarles, *The Negro in the Making*, 121–22.

154. Jordan, *Black Confederates and Afro-Yankees*, 128.

155. Russell Duncan, ed., *Blue-Eyed Child of Fortune: The Civil War Letters of Colonel Robert Gould Shaw* (Athens: University of Georgia Press, 1992), 372.

156. Jordan, *Black Confederates and Afro-Yankees*, 128.

157. Ibid., 130.

158. Martha Hodes, *White Women, Black Men: Illicit Sex in the 19th-Century South* (New Haven: Yale University Press, 1997), 139–40.

159. Jordan, *Black Confederates and Afro-Yankees*, 131.

160. Ibid., 132.

161. Hodes, *White Women, Black Men*, 141–42.

162. Jordan, *Black Confederates and Afro-Yankees*, 132.

163. Hodes, *White Women, Black Men*, 141, 143.

164. Jordan, *Black Confederates and Afro-Yankees*, 133.

165. Ibid.

166. Ibid.

167. Ibid.

168. Rawick, ed., *The American Slave*, Vol. 2, Arkansas, Colorado, Minnesota, Missouri, Oregon, and Washington Narratives, 125.

169. Peter Bardaglio, "The Children of Jubilee: African American Childhood in Wartime," in Catherine Clinton and Nina Silber, eds., *Divided Houses: Gender and the Civil War* (New York: Oxford University Press, 1992), 218–19.

170. Ibid., 219.

171. Ibid.

172. Ibid.

173. Ibid.

174. Ibid., 220.

175. Ibid., 220–21.

176. Ibid., 221.

177. Ibid.

178. Franklin and Moss, *From Slavery to Freedom*, 212.

179. Hampton Institute, *The Negro in Virginia*, 193.

180. Rawick, ed., *The American Slave*, Vol. 9, Mississippi Narratives, Part 4, 1475.

181. Ibid., Vol. 7, Mississippi Narratives, Part 2, 618.

182. Ibid., Vol. 7, Mississippi Narratives, Part 2, 553.

183. Ibid., Vol. 5, Texas Narratives, Part 4, 1852.

184. Ibid., Vol. 6, Mississippi Narratives, Part 1, 185.

185. Ibid., Vol. 8, Mississippi Narratives, Part 3, 1107.

186. Ibid., Vol. 7, Mississippi Narratives, Part 2, 398.

187. Ibid., Vol. 8, Mississippi Narratives, Part 3, 890.

188. Jordan, *Black Confederates and Afro-Yankees*, 191.

189. Richard Rollins, "Black Southerners in Gray," in Richard Rollins, ed., *Black Southerners in Gray: Essays on Afro-Americans in Confederate Armies* (Redondo Beach, CA: Rank and File Publications, 1994), 12.

190. Ibid., 15.

191. Rawick, ed., *The American Slave*, Vol. 1, Alabama, Arizona, Arkansas, District of Columbia, Florida, Georgia, Indiana, Kansas, Maryland, Nebraska, New York, North Carolina, Oklahoma, Rhode Island, South Carolina, and Washington Narratives, 139–41.

192. Ibid., Vol. 7, Mississippi Narratives, Part 2, 451.

193. Jordan, *Black Confederates and Afro-Yankees*, 225.

194. Rawick, ed., *The American Slave*, Vol. 10, Texas Narratives, Part 9, 4260.

195. Rollins, "Black Southerners in Gray," 2.

196. Franklin and Moss, *From Slavery to Freedom*, 213.

197. See, for example, James G. Hollandsworth Jr., *The Louisiana Native Guards: The Black Military Experience during the Civil War* (Baton Rouge: Louisiana State University Press, 1995).

198. Rollins, "Black Southerners in Gray," 2.

199. Ibid., 20.

200. Jordan, *Black Confederates and Afro-Yankees*, 228.

201. Johnson, *Black Savannah*, 157–58.

202. Jenkins, *Seizing the New Day*, 23.

203. Rollins, "Black Southerners in Gray," 4.

204. Jordan, *Black Confederates and Afro-Yankees*, 226.

205. Rollins, "Black Southerners in Gray," 4.

206. Hampton Institute, *The Negro in Virginia*, 250.

207. Rawick, ed., *The American Slave*, Vol. 7, Texas Narratives, Part 6, 2857.

208. Marli F. Weiner, *Mistresses and Slaves: Plantation Women in South Carolina, 1830–80* (Urbana: University of Illinois Press, 1998), 165.

209. Johnson, *Black Savannah*, 161.

210. Rollins, "Black Southerners in Gray," 7; Hollandsworth, *The Louisiana Native Guards*, 4–6; Jenkins, *Seizing the New Day*, 23.

211. Rollins, "Black Southerners in Gray," 8–9.

212. Robert F. Durden, "Georgia's Blacks and Their Masters in the Civil War," *Georgia Historical Quarterly* 69, no. 3 (Fall 1985): 358.

213. Jeffrey J. Crow, Paul D. Escott, and Flora J. Hatley, *A History of African Americans in North Carolina* (Raleigh: North Carolina Division of Archives and History, 1992), 74.

214. Yacovone, ed., *A Voice of Thunder*, 138.

215. Berlin et al., eds., *Free at Last*, 5.

216. Ibid., 132–33.

217. James M. McPherson, *For Cause and Comrades: Why Men Fought in the Civil War* (New York: Oxford University Press, 1997), 162.

218. James M. McPherson, *Battle Cry of Freedom: The Civil War Era* (New York: Ballantine Books, 1989), 835.

219. Ibid.

220. Ibid., 836; Berlin et al., eds., *Free at Last*, 164–65.

221. McPherson, *Battle Cry of Freedom*, 836–37; McPherson, *For Cause and Comrades*, 171; Robert F. Durden, *The Gray and the Black: The Confederate Debate on Emancipation* (Baton Rouge: Louisiana State University Press, 1972), 289.

222. Rollins, "Black Southerners in Gray," 26–27.

223. Blackett, ed., *Thomas Morris Chester*, 248.

224. Ibid., 248–49; Harding, *There Is a River*, 253–54; W. E. B. DuBois, *Black Reconstruction: An Essay toward a History of the Part Which Black Folk Played in the Attempt to Reconstruct Democracy in America, 1860–1880* (New York: Harcourt Brace, 1935), 119–20.

225. Redkey, ed., *A Grand Army of Black Men*, 217.

226. Lanning, *The African-American Soldier*, 40.

227. Foner, *Blacks and the Military*, 51.

228. James Mellon, ed., *Bullwhip Days: The Slaves Remember, An Oral History* (New York: Avon Books, 1988), 339.

CHAPTER THREE

1. George P. Rawick, ed., *The American Slave: A Composite Autobiography* (Westport, CT: Greenwood Press, 1977), Vol. 6, Mississippi Narratives, Part 1, 220.

2. Ibid., Vol. 9, Mississippi Narratives, Part 4, 1483.

3. Ibid., Vol. 3, Texas Narratives, Part 2, 551.

4. Peter Bardaglio, "The Children of Jubilee: African American Childhood in Wartime," in Catherine Clinton and Nina Silber, eds., *Divided Houses: Gender and the Civil War* (New York: Oxford University Press, 1992), 221.

5. Walter J. Fraser Jr., *Charleston! Charleston! The History of a Southern City* (Columbia: University of South Carolina Press, 1989), 259.

6. Harvey Wish, "Slave Disloyalty under the Confederacy," *Journal of Negro History* 23, no. 4 (October 1938): 443; Vincent Harding, *There Is a River: The Black Struggle for Freedom in America* (New York: Harcourt Brace and Company, 1981), 229.

7. Wish, "Slave Disloyalty under the Confederacy," 443.

8. William F. Messner, "Black Violence and White Response: Louisiana, 1862," *Journal of Southern History* 41, no. 1 (February 1975): 21.

9. Ibid.

10. Ibid.

11. Wish, "Slave Disloyalty under the Confederacy," 443–44.

12. Messner, "Black Violence and White Response," 22–23.

13. Wish, "Slave Disloyalty under the Confederacy," 444.

14. Rawick, ed., *The American Slave*, Vol. 10, Texas Narratives, Part 9, 4140.

15. Ibid., Vol. 12, Oklahoma Narratives, 69.

16. B. A. Botkin, ed., *Lay My Burden Down: A Folk History of Slavery* (Chicago and London: University of Chicago Press, 1945), 233.

17. Leon F. Litwack, *Been in the Storm So Long: The Aftermath of Slavery* (New York: Vintage Books, 1979), 181.

18. Ibid.

19. Joel Williamson, *After Slavery: The Negro in South Carolina during Reconstruction, 1861–1877* (Hanover, NH, and London: University Press of New England, 1990), 33–34.

20. Ibid., 34.

21. Gary B. Nash, *The American People: Creating a Nation and a Society*, 2 vols. (New York: Harper and Row, 1990), 1:543.

22. Ibid.

23. C. Vann Woodward, ed., *After the War: A Tour of the Southern States, 1865–1866* (By Whitelaw Reid) (New York: Harper and Row, 1965), 389.

24. Paul S. Boyer, *The Enduring Vision: A History of the American People*, 2 vols. (Lexington, MA: D. C. Heath and Company, 1993), 1:515.

25. Rawick, ed., *The American Slave*, Vol. 9, Mississippi Narratives, Part 4, 1601.

26. Arnold H. Taylor, *Travail and Triumph: Black Life and Culture in the South since the Civil War* (Westport, CT: Greenwood Press, 1976), 4.

27. James West Davidson, *Nation of Nations: A Narrative History of the American Republic*, 2 vols. (New York: McGraw-Hill, 1990), 1:621, 624.

28. Ibid., 624; John Mack Faragher, *Out of Many: A History of the American People*, 2 vols. (Englewood Cliffs, NJ: Prentice-Hall, 1994), 1:523.

29. James Mellon, ed., *Bullwhip Days: The Slaves Remember, An Oral History* (New York: Avon Books, 1988), 349–50.

30. Ibid., 347–48.

31. Williamson, *After Slavery*, 37.

32. Boyer, *The Enduring Vision*, 1:531.

33. Nash, *The American People*, 1:544.

34. Ibid., 545.

35. Ibid.

36. Jacqueline Jones, *Labor of Love, Labor of Sorrow: Black Women, Work, and the Family, From Slavery to the Present* (New York: Vintage Books, 1985), 69.

37. Ibid., 69.

38. Ibid., 68.

39. Ibid., 69; Wilbert L. Jenkins, *Seizing the New Day: African Americans in Post-Civil War Charleston* (Bloomington and Indianapolis: Indiana University Press, 1998), 42.

40. Jenkins, *Seizing the New Day*, 47, 49–50; Peter J. Rachleff, *Black Labor in the South: Richmond, Virginia, 1865–1890* (Philadelphia: Temple University Press, 1984), 14–15; Eric Foner, *Reconstruction: America's Unfinished Revolution, 1863–1877* (New York: Harper and Row, 1988), 81.

41. William A. Byrne, "The Burden and Heat of the Day: Slavery and Servitude in Savannah, 1733–1865" (Ph.D. diss., Florida State University, 1979), 337; John W. Blassingame, "Before the Ghetto: The Making of the Black Community in Savannah, Georgia, 1865–1880," in Donald G. Nieman, ed., *Church and Community among Black Southerners, 1865–1900* (New York and London: Garland, 1994), 464–65.

42. Jenkins, *Seizing the New Day*, 50.

43. Bert James Loewenberg and Ruth Bogin, eds., *Black Women in Nineteenth-Century American Life: Their Words, Their Thoughts, Their Feelings* (University Park: Pennsylvania State University Press, 1976), 70; Dorothy Sterling, ed., *We Are Your Sisters: Black Women in the Nineteenth Century* (New York: W. W. Norton and Company, 1984), 245, 248–51; Benjamin Quarles, *The Negro in the Civil War* (Boston: Little, Brown and Company, 1969), 128–29; Benjamin Quarles, *Lincoln and the Negro* (New York: Oxford University Press, 1962), 200–204.

44. Rawick, ed., *The American Slave*, Vol. 4, Texas Narratives, Part 3, 1270.

45. Sterling, ed., *We Are Your Sisters*, 245–48, 403.

46. Ibid., 255.

47. Ibid., 405.

48. Ibid.

49. Penelope Majeske, "Your Obedient Servant: The United States Army in Virginia during Reconstruction, 1865–1867" (Ph.D. diss., Wayne State University, 1980), 34, 35, 40, 41, 42.

50. Jenkins, *Seizing the New Day*, 50–51.

51. Armstead L. Robinson, "Plans Dat Comed from God: Institution Building and the Emergence of Black Leadership in Reconstruction Memphis," in Donald G. Nieman, ed., *Church and Community among Black Southerners, 1865–1900* (New York and London: Garland, 1994), 93; John W. Blassingame, "Before the Ghetto," in Nieman, ed., *Church and Community*, 1–2; Jonathan Woolard McLeod, "Black and White Workers: Atlanta during Reconstruction" (Ph.D. diss., University of California at Los Angeles, 1987), 13; Colin A. Palmer, *Passageways: An Interpretive History of Black America*, 2 vols. (New York: Harcourt Brace, 1998), 2:14; Boyer, *The Enduring Vision*, 1:531; Foner, *Reconstruction*, 81–82; Howard N. Rabinowitz, "A Comparative Perspective on Race Relations in Southern and Northern Cities, 1860–1900, with Special Emphasis on Raleigh," in Jeffrey J. Crow and Flora J. Hatley, eds., *Black Americans in North Carolina and the South* (Chapel Hill: University of North Carolina Press, 1984), 138–39.

52. Palmer, *Passageways*, 2:14–15.

53. Mellon, ed., *Bullwhip Days*, 346, 376–77.

54. Byrne, "The Burden and Heat of the Day," 340.

55. Ibid., 340–41.

56. Genevieve S. Gray, ed., *Army Life in a Black Regiment* (By Colonel Thomas W. Higginson) (New York: Grosset and Dunlap, 1970), 89–90.

57. Bernard E. Powers, *Black Charlestonians: A Social History, 1822–1885* (Fayetteville: University of Arkansas Press, 1994), 103.

58. Ibid., 104.

59. Ibid., 103.

60. Quarles, *The Negro in the Civil War*, 321, 325.

61. Byrne, "The Burden and Heat of the Day," 335.

62. Ibid.

63. Jenkins, *Seizing the New Day*, 31.

64. Quarles, *The Negro in the Civil War*, 329.

65. Ibid. Author's emphasis.

66. Ibid.

67. R. J. M. Blackett, ed., *Thomas Morris Chester: Black Civil War Correspondent, His Dispatches from the Virginia Front* (Baton Rouge: Louisiana State University Press, 1989), 289, 290.

68. Quarles, *The Negro in the Civil War*, 331; Hampton Institute, *The Negro in Virginia: Compiled by Workers of the Writers' Program of the Work Projects Administration in the State of Virginia* (New York: Hastings House, 1940), 201.

69. Blackett, ed., *Thomas Morris Chester*, 290.

70. Edwin S. Redkey, ed., *A Grand Army of Black Men: Letters from African-American Soldiers in the Union Army, 1861–1865* (New York: Cambridge University Press, 1992), 175.

71. Ibid., 175–76; Litwack, *Been in the Storm So Long*, 169; Blackett, ed., *Thomas Morris Chester*, 293.

72. Blackett, ed., *Thomas Morris Chester*, 294.

73. Rawick, ed., *The American Slave*, Vol. 1, Alabama Narratives, 139.

74. Blackett, ed., *Thomas Morris Chester*, 294–97; Quarles, *The Negro in the Civil War*, 333–35; Hampton Institute, *The Negro in Virginia*, 213.

75. Quarles, *The Negro in the Civil War*, 335; Blackett, ed., *Thomas Morris Chester*, 297.

76. Quarles, *The Negro in the Civil War*, 332; Litwack, *Been in the Storm So Long*, 169–70.

77. Blackett, ed., *Thomas Morris Chester*, 304–5.

78. Jenkins, *Seizing the New Day*, 36, 38, 39; Williamson, *After Slavery*, 47–49; Quarles, *The Negro in the Civil War*, 336–39.

79. Litwack, *Been in the Storm So Long*, 170.

80. Williamson, *After Slavery*, 49.

81. Ibid.

82. Litwack, *Been in the Storm So Long*, 177.

83. Redkey, ed., *A Grand Army of Black Men*, 187–88.

84. Rawick, ed., *The American Slave*, Vol. 8, Mississippi Narratives, Part 3, 1119.

85. Ibid., Vol. 12, Oklahoma Narratives, 195.

86. Ibid., Vol. 8, Mississippi Narratives, Part 3, 1065.

87. Ibid., Vol. 8, Mississippi Narratives, Part 3, 1223.

88. Rupert Sargent Holland, ed., *Letters and Diary of Laura M. Towne: Written from the Sea Islands of South Carolina, 1862–1884* (Cambridge, MA: Riverside Press, 1912), 88; Quarles, *Lincoln and the Negro*, 244.

89. Rawick, ed., *The American Slave*, Vol. 8, Mississippi Narratives, Part 3, 1345.

90. Jenkins, *Seizing the New Day*, 40; Frank [Francis] A. Rollin, *Life and Public Services of Martin A. Delany, Sub-Assistant Commissioner, Bureau of Refugees, Freedmen, and Abandoned Lands, and Late Major 104th U.S. Colored Troops* (Boston: Lee and Shepard, 1883), 204–5; Quarles, *Lincoln and the Negro*, 245.

91. Quarles, *The Negro in the Civil War*, 342–43.

92. Quarles, *Lincoln and the Negro*, 244–245.

93. Elizabeth Hyde Botume, *First Days amongst the Contrabands* (New York: Arno Press and New York Times, 1968, reprint), 174–75.

94. Quarles, *The Negro in the Civil War*, 345.

95. Rawick, ed., *The American Slave*, Vol. 4, Texas Narratives, Part 3, 1271.

96. Quarles, *The Negro in the Civil War*, 345.

97. Hampton Institute, *The Negro in Virginia*, 214.

98. Quarles, *Lincoln and the Negro*, 246.

99. John T. O'Brien Jr., "From Bondage to Citizenship: The Richmond Black Community, 1865–1867" (Ph.D. diss., University of Rochester, 1974), 76.

100. Quarles, *Lincoln and the Negro*, 245–46.

101. Redkey, ed., *A Grand Army of Black Men*, 221–22.

102. Hampton Institute, *The Negro in Virginia*, 214.

103. Quarles, *Lincoln and the Negro*, 244.

104. Rachleff, *Black Labor in the South*, 39.

105. Ibid., 40.

106. Ibid.

107. Daniel F. Littlefield, *The Cherokee Freedmen: From Emancipation to American Citizenship* (Westport, CT: Greenwood Press, 1978), 61.

108. Ibid., 61–63.

109. Foner, *Reconstruction*, 119.

110. Rawick, ed., *The American Slave*, Vol. 4, Texas Narratives, Part 3, 1160.

111. Foner, *Reconstruction*, 121; Sidney Andrews, *The South since the War: As Shown by Fourteen Weeks of Travel and Observation in Georgia and the Carolinas* (Boston: Ticknor and Fields, 1866), 221.

112. Littlefield, *The Cherokee Freedmen*, 68.

113. Daniel F. Littlefield, *The Chickasaw Freedmen: A People without a Country* (Westport, CT: Greenwood Press, 1980), 94–95.

114. Taken from Dr. Martin Luther King Jr.'s speech on December 11, 1961, before the Fourth Constitutional Convention of the AFL-CIO in Bal Harbour, Florida.

CHAPTER FOUR

1. Wilbert L. Jenkins, *Seizing the New Day: African Americans in Post-Civil War Charleston* (Bloomington and Indianapolis: Indiana University Press, 1998), 47; Alan Brinkley, *American History: A Survey*, 8th rev. ed. (New York: McGraw-Hill, 1991), 452–53; Paul S. Boyer, *The Enduring Vision: A History of the American People*, 2 vols. (Lexington, MA: D. C. Heath and Company, 1993), 1:515; Thomas A. Bailey, *The American Pageant: A History of the Republic*, 2 vols. (Lexington, MA: D. C. Heath and Company, 1991), 1:478–79.

2. Brinkley, *American History*, 452–53.

3. Charles H. Wesley, *Negro Labor in the United States, 1850–1925: A Study in American Economic History* (New York: Vanguard Press, 1927), 147.

4. Ibid.

5. Eric Foner, *Reconstruction: America's Unfinished Revolution, 1863–1877* (New York: Harper and Row, 1988), 102.

6. Ruthe Winegarten, *Black Texas Women: 150 Years of Trial and Triumph* (Austin: University of Texas Press, 1995), 51.

7. William A. Byrne, "The Burden and Heat of the Day: Slavery and Servitude in Savannah, 1733–1865" (Ph.D. diss., Florida State University, 1979), 350.

8. Bailey, *The American Pageant*, 1:480–81.

9. John T. O'Brien Jr., "From Bondage to Citizenship: The Richmond Black Community, 1865–1867" (Ph.D. diss., University of Rochester, 1974), 79.

10. Martin Abbott, *The Freedmen's Bureau in South Carolina, 1865–1872* (Chapel Hill: University of North Carolina Press, 1967), 52.

11. C. Vann Woodward, ed., *After the War: A Tour of the Southern States, 1865–1866* (By Whitelaw Reid) (New York: Harper and Row, 1965), 564.

12. Ibid., 59.

13. Ibid., 564.

14. Loren Schweninger, *Black Property Owners in the South, 1790–1915* (Urbana and Chicago: University of Illinois Press, 1990), 145.

15. Foner, *Reconstruction*, 104.

16. George P. Rawick, ed., *The American Slave: A Composite Autobiography* (Westport, CT: Greenwood Press, 1977), Vol. 9, Mississippi Narratives, Part 4, 1649.

17. Ibid., Vol. 8, Mississippi Narratives, Part 3, 1035.

18. Ibid., Vol. 7, Mississippi Narratives, Part 2, 629.

19. Ibid., Vol. 10, Mississippi Narratives, Part 5, 1986.

20. Jacqueline Baldwin Walker, "Blacks in North Carolina during Reconstruction" (Ph.D. diss., Duke University, 1979), 64.

21. Elizabeth Hyde Botume, *First Days amongst the Contrabands* (Boston: Lee and Shepard, 1893), 170.

22. Donna J. Benson, " 'Before I Be a Slave': A Social Analysis of the Black Struggle for Freedom in North Carolina, 1860–1865" (Ph.D. diss., Duke University, 1984), 171.

23. Byrne, "The Burden and Heat of the Day," 365.

24. William L. Barney, *The Passage of the Republic: An Interdisciplinary History of Nineteenth-Century America* (Lexington, MA: D. C. Heath and Company, 1987), 250.

25. Gary B. Nash, *The American People: Creating a Nation and a Society*, 2 vols. (New York: Harper and Row, 1990), 1:544.

26. James A. Henretta, *America's History*, 2 vols. (New York: Worth, 1997), 1:491.

27. Rawick, ed., *The American Slave*, Vol. 3, Texas Narratives, Part 2, 853.

28. Ibid., Vol. 3, Texas Narratives, Part 2, 877.

29. Jenkins, *Seizing the New Day*, 62.

30. Michael Fellman, "Lincoln and Sherman," in Gabor S. Boritt, ed., *Lincoln's Generals* (New York: Oxford University Press, 1994), 149–50.

31. Byrne, "The Burden and Heat of the Day," 366–67.

32. Henretta, *America's History*, 1:491; Arnold H. Taylor, *Travail and Triumph: Black Life and Culture in the South since the Civil War* (Westport, CT: Greenwood Press, 1976), 70.

33. Hampton Institute, *The Negro in Virginia: Compiled by Workers of the Writers' Program of the Work Projects Administration in the State of Virginia* (New York: Hastings House, 1940), 218.

34. Leslie A. Schwalm, *A Hard Fight for We: Women's Transition from Slavery to Freedom in South Carolina* (Urbana and Chicago: University of Illinois Press, 1997), 191–92.

35. Ibid., 192.

36. Ibid., 193.

37. Ibid.

38. Colin A. Palmer, *Passageways: An Interpretive History of Black America*, 2 vols. (New York: Harcourt Brace, 1998), 2:18; Edmund L. Drago, *Black Politicians and Reconstruction in Georgia: A Splendid Failure* (Athens and London: University of Georgia Press, 1992), 86–87; Thomas Holt, *Black over White: Negro Political Leadership in South Carolina during Reconstruction* (Urbana and Chicago: University of Illinois Press, 1977), 128; Taylor, *Travail and Triumph*, 18.

39. Palmer, *Passageways*, 2:18.

40. Schweninger, *Black Property Owners*, 145.

41. Ibid., 145–46.

42. Woodward, ed., *After the War*, 564–65.

43. Henry M. Christman, ed., *The South As It Is: 1865–1866* (By John Richard Dennett) (New York: Viking Press, 1965), 108.

44. Sir George Campbell, *White and Black: The Outcome of a Visit to the United States* (New York: R. Worthington, 1879), 276.

45. Edward Royce, *The Origins of Southern Sharecropping* (Philadelphia: Temple University Press, 1993), 114.

46. Rawick, ed., *The American Slave*, Vol. 7, Texas Narratives, Part 6, 2732.

47. Ibid., Vol. 4, Georgia Narratives, Part 2, 603.

48. Ibid., Vol. 4, Texas Narratives, Part 3, 1084.

49. Hampton Institute, *The Negro in Virginia*, 223.

50. Foner, *Reconstruction*, 106.

51. Hollis R. Lynch, ed., *The Black Urban Condition: A Documentary History, 1866–1971* (New York: Thomas Y. Crowell Company, 1973), 5.

52. Foner, *Reconstruction*, 106.

53. Benson, "Before I Be a Slave," 173.

54. Rawick, ed., *The American Slave*, Vol. 2, Arkansas, Colorado, Minnesota, Missouri, Oregon, and Washington Narratives, 133.

55. Ibid., Vol. 4, Texas Narratives, Part 3, 1303.

56. Ibid., Vol. 2, Arkansas, Colorado, Minnesota, Missouri, Oregon, and Washington Narratives, 206.

57. Ibid., Vol. 9, Texas Narratives, Part 8, 3703.

58. Ibid., Vol. 12, Oklahoma Narratives, 132.

59. Ibid., Vol. 12, Oklahoma Narratives, 30.

60. Ibid., Vol. 12, Oklahoma Narratives, 219.

61. Ibid., Vol. 12, Oklahoma Narratives, 64–66.

62. Hampton Institute, *The Negro in Virginia*, 219.

63. Rawick, ed., *The American Slave*, Vol. 7, Texas Narratives, Part 6, 2539–2540.

64. Schweninger, *Black Property Owners*, 148.

65. Ibid., 150–51.

66. Wesley, *Negro Labor in the United States*, 142–43.

67. Ibid., 143.

68. Carl R. Osthaus, *Freedmen, Philanthropy, and Fraud: A History of the Freedman's Savings Bank* (Urbana: University of Illinois Press, 1976), 98, 100.

69. Ibid., 98.

70. Walker, "Blacks in North Carolina," 63.

71. Wesley, *Negro Labor in the United States*, 144–45.

72. Dorothy Sterling, ed., *We Are Your Sisters: Black Women in the Nineteenth Century* (New York: W. W. Norton and Company, 1984), 361.

73. Ibid., 361–62.

74. Ruthe Winegarten, *Black Texas Women: 150 Years of Trial and Triumph* (Austin: University of Texas Press, 1995), 50.

75. Wesley, *Negro Labor in the United States*, 145–46.

76. Jenkins, *Seizing the New Day*, 65–66.

77. Foner, *Reconstruction*, 107; Peter J. Rachleff, *Black Labor in the South: Richmond, Virginia, 1865–1890* (Philadelphia: Temple University Press, 1984), 42–44.

78. Rachleff, *Black Labor in the South*, 44.

79. Eric Arnesen, *Waterfront Workers of New Orleans: Race, Class, and Politics, 1863–1923* (New York and Oxford: Oxford University Press, 1991), 21–23.

80. Ibid., 22, 24, 30.

81. Sterling, ed., *We Are Your Sisters*, 355–56.

82. Winegarten, *Black Texas Women*, 50.

83. William L. Barney, *Battleground for the Union: The Era of the Civil War and Reconstruction, 1848–1877* (Englewood Cliffs, NJ: Prentice Hall, 1990), 308.

84. The most comprehensive piece of scholarship on emigration movements, particularly with respect to Singleton and Adams, is Nell Irvin Painter, *Exodusters: Black Migration to Kansas after Reconstruction* (New York and London: W. W. Norton and Company, 1986).

85. Noralee Frankel, *Break Those Chains at Last: African Americans, 1860–1880* (New York and Oxford: Oxford University Press, 1996), 92–93.

86. Ibid., 93.

87. Dorothy C. Salem, *The Journey: A History of the African American Experience* (Dubuque, IA: Kendall/Hunt, 1997), 231.

88. Lt. Col. (Ret.) Michael Lee Lanning, *The African-American Soldier: From Crispus Attucks to Colin Powell* (Secaucus, NJ: Carol Publishing Group, 1997), 65; William Loren Katz, *Black Indians: A Hidden Heritage* (New York: Atheneum Books, 1986), 176.

89. Jack D. Foner, *Blacks and the Military in American History* (New York: Praeger, 1974), 53–54.

90. Gary A. Donaldson, *The History of African-Americans in the Military* (Malabar, FL: Krieger, 1991), 67.

91. Ibid., 66.

92. Ibid., 65–66.

93. Katz, *Black Indians*, 174–75.

94. Lanning, *The African-American Soldier*, 70; Monroe Lee Billington, *New Mexico's Buffalo Soldiers, 1866–1900* (Niwot: University Press of Colorado, 1991), preface xi.

95. Foner, *Blacks and the Military*, 53; Lanning, *The African-American Soldier*, 73.

96. Lanning, *The African-American Soldier*, 73–74; Frank N. Schubert, *Black Valor: Buffalo Soldiers and the Medal of Honor, 1870–1898* (Wilmington, DE: Scholarly Resources, 1997), 19–22.

97. Donaldson, *The History of African-Americans*, 61–62.
98. Foner, *Blacks and the Military*, 57.
99. Katz, *Black Indians*, 175–76.
100. Donaldson, *The History of African-Americans*, 58.
101. Foner, *Blacks and the Military*, 53; Lanning, *The African-American Soldier*, 76.
102. Katz, *Black Indians*, 176; Donaldson, *The History of African-Americans*, 66.
103. See, for example, Kenneth L. Kusmer, *A Ghetto Takes Shape: Black Cleveland, 1870–1930* (Urbana and Chicago: University of Illinois Press, 1976), 38; and Salem, *The Journey*, 226.

CHAPTER FIVE

1. George P. Rawick, ed., *The American Slave: A Composite Autobiography* (Westport, CT: Greenwood Press, 1977), Vol. 10, Mississippi Narratives, Part 5, 2155.
2. Ibid., Vol. 3, Texas Narratives, Part 2, 477.
3. Ibid., Vol. 3, Texas Narratives, Part 2, 564.
4. Ibid., Vol. 3, Texas Narratives, Part 2, 923.
5. Peter Randolph, *Sketches of Slave Life* (Boston, 1855), 53–54.
6. Reverend Philo Tower, *Slavery Unmasked: Being a Truthful Narrative of a Three Years' Residence and Journeying in Eleven Southern States* (1856; reprint ed., New York: Negro Universities Press, 1969), 307–8.
7. Elizabeth Hyde Botume, *First Days amongst the Contrabands* (Boston: Lee and Shepard, 1893), 164.
8. Rawick, ed., *The American Slave*, Vol. 6, Mississippi Narratives, Part 1, 179.
9. Ibid., Vol. 7, Mississippi Narratives, Part 2, 410.
10. Ibid., Vol. 9, Mississippi Narratives, Part 4, 1399–1400.
11. Ibid., Vol. 1, Alabama Narratives, 138.
12. Ibid., Vol. 3, Georgia Narratives, Part 1, 79–80.
13. Ibid., Vol. 8, Mississippi Narratives, Part 3, 1080.
14. Fredrika Bremer, *The Homes of the New World; Impressions of America*, 2 vols. (New York: Harper and Brothers, 1853), 1:376.
15. Rawick, ed., *The American Slave*, Vol. 6, Texas Narratives, Part 5, 2345–2346.
16. Ibid., Vol. 5, Texas Narratives, Part 4, 1704.
17. James Mellon, ed., *Bullwhip Days: The Slaves Remember, An Oral History* (New York: Avon Books, 1988), 146–47.
18. John W. Blassingame, ed., *Slave Testimony: Two Centuries of Letters, Speeches, Interviews, and Autobiographies* (Baton Rouge and London: Louisiana State University Press, 1977), 592.
19. Rawick, ed., *The American Slave*, Vol. 9, Texas Narratives, Part 8, 3651.
20. Ibid., Vol. 7, Mississippi Narratives, Part 2, 381–82.
21. Ibid., Vol. 5, Texas Narratives, Part 4, 1853–1854.
22. Hampton Institute, *The Negro in Virginia: Compiled by Workers of the Writers' Program of the Work Projects Administration in the State of Virginia* (New York: Hastings House, 1940), 85.
23. Robert H. Abzug, "The Black Family during Reconstruction," in *Key Issues in the Afro-American Experience*, ed. Nathan I. Huggins, Martin Kilson, and Daniel M. Fox (New York: Harcourt Brace Jovanovich, 1971), 31.

24. C. Vann Woodward, ed., *After the War: A Tour of the Southern States, 1865–1866* (By Whitelaw Reid) (New York: Harper and Row, 1965), 126.

25. Ira Berlin and Leslie S. Rowland, eds., *Families and Freedom: A Documentary History of African-American Kinship in the Civil War Era* (New York: New Press, 1992), 163–64.

26. Ibid., 168–70.

27. Botume, *First Days*, 158.

28. Rawick, ed., *The American Slave*, Vol. 2, Texas Narratives, Part 1, 120.

29. Ibid., Vol. 1, Alabama Narratives, 467.

30. Ibid., Vol. 6, Texas Narratives, Part 5, 2286–2287.

31. Ibid., Vol. 8, Mississippi Narratives, Part 3, 926.

32. Ibid., Vol. 5, Texas Narratives, Part 4, 1543–1544.

33. Ibid., Vol. 9, Texas Narratives, Part 8, 3450.

34. Ibid., Vol. 6, Texas Narratives, Part 5, 2096–2098.

35. Botume, *First Days*, 157.

36. Woodward, ed., *After the War*, 127.

37. Rawick, ed., *The American Slave*, Vol. 5, Texas Narratives, Part 4, 1585.

38. Blassingame, ed., *Slave Testimony*, 483.

39. Ibid., 499.

40. Mellon, ed., *Bullwhip Days*, 278–79.

41. Rawick, ed., *The American Slave*, Vol. 4, Texas Narratives, Part 3, 1058.

42. Ibid., Vol. 7, Mississippi Narratives, Part 2, 721.

43. Ibid., Vol. 8, Mississippi Narratives, Part 3, 854.

44. Ibid., Vol. 3, Texas Narratives, Part 2, 538.

45. Ibid., Vol. 5, Indiana and Ohio Narratives, 441.

46. Ibid., Vol. 6, Mississippi Narratives, Part 1, 158.

47. Ibid., Vol. 2, Texas Narratives, Part 1, 344.

48. Ibid., Vol. 7, Mississippi Narratives, Part 2, 444–45.

49. Ibid., Vol. 10, Mississippi Narratives, Part 5, 1996.

50. Botume, *First Days*, 159–60.

51. Rawick, ed., *The American Slave*, Vol. 3, Georgia Narratives, Part 1, 261–62.

52. Mellon, ed., *Bullwhip Days*, 423–24.

53. Rawick, ed., *The American Slave*, Vol.10, Mississippi Narratives, Part 5, 2234.

54. Ibid., Vol. 10, Texas Narratives, Part 9, 4105.

55. Mellon, ed., *Bullwhip Days*, 352.

56. Rawick, ed., *The American Slave*, Vol. 10, Texas Narratives, Part 9, 4117–4123; Wilma King, *Stolen Childhood: Slave Youth in Nineteenth-Century America* (Bloomington and Indianapolis: Indiana University Press, 1995), 149.

57. Berlin and Rowland, eds., *Families and Freedom*, 171–72.

58. Rawick, ed., *The American Slave*, Vol. 2, Texas Narratives, Part 1, 100.

59. Ibid., Vol. 6, Mississippi Narratives, Part 1, 232.

60. Ibid., Vol. 9, Mississippi Narratives, Part 4, 1734.

61. Eric Foner, *Reconstruction: America's Unfinished Revolution, 1863–1877* (New York: Harper and Row, 1988), 84.

62. Rawick, ed., *The American Slave*, Vol. 5, Texas Narratives, Part 4, 1901.

63. Gary B. Nash, *The American People: Creating a Nation and a Society*, 2 vols. (New York: Harper and Row, 1990), 1:543; C. Peter Ripley, "The Black Family in Transition: Louisiana, 1860–1865." *Journal of Southern History* 41, no. 3 (August 1975): 379.

64. Leslie A. Schwalm, *A Hard Fight for We: Women's Transition from Slavery to Freedom in South Carolina* (Urbana and Chicago: University of Illinois Press, 1997), 244.

65. Noralee Frankel, *Break Those Chains at Last: African Americans, 1860–1880* (New York and Oxford: Oxford University Press, 1996), 102.

66. Berlin and Rowland, eds., *Families and Freedom*, 172–73.

67. Abzug, "The Black Family," 31.

68. Foner, *Reconstruction*, 82.

69. Wayne E. Reilly, ed., *Sarah Jane Foster: Teacher of the Freedmen, A Diary and Letters* (Charlottesville and London: University Press of Virginia, 1990), 104.

70. Foner, *Reconstruction*, 84.

71. Botume, *First Days*, 163–64.

72. Jacqueline Baldwin Walker, "Blacks in North Carolina during Reconstruction" (Ph.D. diss., Duke University, 1979), 129.

73. Jeffrey J. Crow, Paul D. Escott, and Flora J. Hatley, *A History of African Americans in North Carolina* (Raleigh: North Carolina Division of Archives and History, 1992), 83.

74. Rawick, ed., *The American Slave*, Vol. 8, Texas Narratives, Part 7, 3269.

75. King, *Stolen Childhood*, 144.

76. Peter J. Rachleff, *Black Labor in the South: Richmond, Virginia, 1865–1890* (Philadelphia: Temple University Press, 1984), 15–16.

77. Paul S. Boyer, *The Enduring Vision: A History of the American People*, 2 vols. (Lexington, MA: D. C. Heath and Company, 1993), 1:531–32.

78. Abzug, "The Black Family," 33.

79. Edwin S. Redkey, ed., *A Grand Army of Black Men: Letters from African-American Soldiers in the Union Army, 1861–1865* (New York: Cambridge University Press, 1992), 175–77.

80. Crow, Escott, and Hatley, *A History of African Americans*, 82–83.

81. Joseph T. Glatthaar, *The March to the Sea and Beyond: Sherman's Troops in the Savannah and Carolinas Campaigns* (Baton Rouge and London: Louisiana State University Press, 1985), 60–61.

82. Berlin and Rowland, eds., *Families and Freedom*, 17–20.

83. Ibid., 214–15.

84. King, *Stolen Childhood*, 145.

85. Jonathan Woolard McLeod, "Black and White Workers: Atlanta during Reconstruction" (Ph.D. diss., University of California at Los Angeles, 1987), 18.

86. Walker, "Blacks in North Carolina," 128.

87. Joel Williamson, *After Slavery: The Negro in South Carolina during Reconstruction, 1861–1877* (Hanover, NH, and London: University Press of New England, 1990), 307.

88. Berlin and Rowland, eds., *Families and Freedom*, 173, 176.

89. Walker, "Blacks in North Carolina," 133.

90. Botume, *First Days*, 163.

91. James West Davidson, *Nation of Nations: A Narrative History of the American Republic*, 2 vols. (New York: McGraw-Hill, 1990), 1:624.

92. Rawick, ed., *The American Slave*, Vol. 7, Texas Narratives, Part 6, 2615–2616.

93. Ibid., Vol. 3, Texas Narratives, Part 2, 636.

94. Hampton Institute, *The Negro in Virginia*, 85–86.

95. Mellon, ed., *Bullwhip Days*, 352.

96. Rawick, ed., *The American Slave*, Vol. 8, Texas Narratives, Part 7, 3240.

97. King, *Stolen Childhood*, 144.

98. Marion B. Lucas, *A History of Blacks in Kentucky: From Slavery to Segregation, 1760–1891*, Vol. 1 (Lexington: Kentucky Historical Society, 1992), 206.

99. Rawick, ed., *The American Slave*, Vol. 10, Mississippi Narratives, Part 5, 2351.

100. King, *Stolen Childhood*, 151–52.

101. Berlin and Rowland, eds., *Families and Freedom*, 214.

102. Rebecca Scott, "The Battle over the Child: Child Apprenticeship and the Freedmen's Bureau in North Carolina," *Prologue* 10, no. 2 (Summer 1978): 107.

103. Rawick, ed., *The American Slave*, Vol. 10, Mississippi Narratives, Part 5, 2168–2169.

104. King, *Stolen Childhood*, 152.

105. Berlin and Rowland, eds., *Families and Freedom*, 231–33.

106. Ibid., 237.

107. Ibid.

108. King, *Stolen Childhood*, 152–53.

109. Scott, "The Battle over the Child," 105–7.

110. Ira Berlin, Barbara J. Fields, Steven F. Miller, Joseph P. Reidy, and Leslie S. Rowland, eds., *Free at Last: A Documentary History of Slavery, Freedom, and the Civil War* (New York: New Press, 1992), 533–35.

111. Ibid., 535–36.

112. Berlin and Rowland, eds., *Families and Freedom*, 227–30.

113. Ibid., 230–31.

114. Rachleff, *Black Labor in the South*, 21.

115. Rawick, ed., *The American Slave*, Vol. 2, Arkansas, Colorado, Minnesota, Missouri, Oregon, and Washington Narratives, 141.

116. Walter Hill, "A Sense of Belonging: Family Functions and Structure in Charleston, S.C., 1880–1910" (Paper prepared at Howard University, 1984), 6–7.

117. Rawick, ed., *The American Slave*, Vol. 10, Mississippi Narratives, Part 5, 2385.

118. Walker, "Blacks in North Carolina," 132.

119. Ibid., 133.

120. Abzug, "The Black Family," 33–34.

121. Rawick, ed., *The American Slave*, Vol. 10, Mississippi Narratives, Part 5, 2234–2235.

122. Mary Beth Norton, *A People and a Nation: A History of the United States*, 2 vols. (Boston: Houghton-Mifflin Company, 1990), 2:456.

123. Jacqueline Jones, *Labor of Love, Labor of Sorrow: Black Women, Work, and the Family, from Slavery to the Present* (New York: Vintage Books, 1985), 76–77.

124. Jones, *Labor of Love, Labor of Sorrow*, 76.

125. Alan Brinkley, *American History: A Survey*, 8th rev. ed. (New York: McGraw-Hill, 1991), 469.

126. Foner, *Reconstruction*, 86.

127. Noralee Frankel, *Freedom's Women: Black Women and Families in Civil War Era Mississippi* (Bloomington and Indianapolis: Indiana University Press, 1999), 74–75.

128. Foner, *Reconstruction*, 86.

129. Schwalm, *A Hard Fight for We*, 211–12.

130. Frankel, *Freedom's Women*, 71, 76.

131. Davidson, *Nation of Nations*, 1:624.

132. Foner, *Reconstruction*, 86–87.

133. Ibid., 87.

134. Ibid.

135. Mellon, ed., *Bullwhip Days*, 225.

136. Rawick, ed., *The American Slave*, Vol. 9, Texas Narratives, Part 8, 3498.

137. Ibid., Vol. 5, Texas Narratives, Part 4, 1696.

138. Ibid., Vol. 5, Indiana and Ohio Narratives, 165.

139. Ibid., Vol. 5, Texas Narratives, Part 4, 1533.

140. Ibid., Vol. 8, Texas Narratives, Part 7, 3257.

141. Ibid., Vol. 7, Texas Narratives, Part 6, 2589.

142. Mellon, ed., *Bullwhip Days*, 225.

143. Herbert G. Gutman, *The Black Family in Slavery and Freedom, 1750–1925* (New York: Pantheon Books, 1976), 230–56.

144. Rawick, ed., *The American Slave*, Vol. 7, Texas Narratives, Part 6, 2764.

145. Ibid., Vol. 8, Mississippi Narratives, Part 3, 1240.

146. Daniel F. Littlefield, Jr. *Africans and Seminoles: From Removal to Emancipation* (Westport, CT: Greenwood Press, 1977), 193.

147. Woodward, ed., *After the War*, 147.

148. Norton, *A People and a Nation*, 2:456.

149. Ibid.

150. Joe A. Mobley, "In the Shadow of White Society: Princeville, A Black Town in North Carolina, 1865–1915," in Donald G. Nieman, ed., *Church and Community among Black Southerners, 1865–1900* (New York and London: Garland, 1994), 28–72; Joe A. Mobley, *James City: A Black Community in North Carolina, 1863–1900* (Raleigh: North Carolina Division of Archives and History, 1981); James M. Smallwood, *Time of Hope, Time of Despair: Black Texans during Reconstruction* (Port Washington, NY: Kennikat Press, 1981), 118.

151. Dorothy Sterling, ed., *We Are Your Sisters: Black Women in the Nineteenth Century* (New York: W. W. Norton and Company, 1984), 339.

152. Ibid.

153. Ibid., 339–40.

154. Ibid., 339.

155. Ibid., 341.

156. Ibid.

157. Ibid., 340–41.

158. Ibid., 341–42.

159. Ibid., 342.

160. Ruthe Winegarten, *Black Texas Women: 150 Years of Trial and Triumph* (Austin: University of Texas Press, 1995), 57, 58.

161. Sterling, ed., *We Are Your Sisters*, 341, 342.

162. Winegarten, *Black Texas Women*, 58.

163. Ibid., 57.

164. Berlin and Rowland, eds., *Families and Freedom*, 182–84.

165. King, *Stolen Childhood*, 112.

166. Wilbert L. Jenkins, *Seizing the New Day: African Americans in Post-Civil War Charleston* (Bloomington and Indianapolis: Indiana University Press, 1998), 107.

167. Ibid., 107–8.

168. Willard B. Gatewood, "The Remarkable Misses Rollin: Black Women in Reconstruction South Carolina," *South Carolina Historical Magazine*, 92, no. 3 (July 1991): 179.

169. William E. Montgomery, *Under Their Own Vine and Fig Tree: The African-American Church in the South, 1865–1900* (Baton Rouge and London: Louisiana State University Press, 1993), 260.

CHAPTER SIX

1. Wilma King, *Stolen Childhood: Slave Youth in Nineteenth-Century America* (Bloomington and Indianapolis: Indiana University Press, 1995), 78.

2. George P. Rawick, ed., *The American Slave: A Composite Autobiography* (Westport, CT: Greenwood Press, 1977), Vol. 1, Alabama Narratives, 412.

3. Ibid., Vol. 3, Texas Narratives, Part 2, 950.

4. Ibid., Vol. 10, Mississippi Narratives, Part 5, 2358.

5. Ibid., Vol. 10, Mississippi Narratives, Part 5, 2337.

6. Ibid., Vol. 2, Texas Narratives, Part 1, 231.

7. Ibid., Vol. 8, Mississippi Narratives, Part 3, 1292.

8. Ibid., Vol. 9, Texas Narratives, Part 8, 3711.

9. Ibid., Vol. 4, Texas Narratives, Part 3, 1110; Vol. 2, Texas Narratives, Part 1, 421; Vol. 1, Alabama Narratives, 352.

10. Ibid., Vol. 4, Texas Narratives, Part 3, 1110; Janet Cornelius, "We Slipped and Learned to Read: Slave Accounts of the Literacy Process, 1830–1865," *Phylon* 44, no. 2 (September 1983): 179.

11. Ibid., Vol. 7, Texas Narratives, Part 6, 2643–2644.

12. King, *Stolen Childhood*, 77.

13. Rawick, ed., *The American Slave*, Vol. 2, Texas Narratives, Part 1, 96–97.

14. King, *Stolen Childhood*, 77.

15. Rawick, ed., *The American Slave*, Vol. 5, Indiana and Ohio Narratives, 424.

16. King, *Stolen Childhood*, 78.

17. Rawick, ed., *The American Slave*, Vol. 7, Mississippi Narratives, Part 2, 497.

18. Ibid., Vol. 9, Mississippi Narratives, Part 4, 1664.

19. Ronald E. Butchart, *Northern Schools, Southern Blacks, and Reconstruction: Freedmen's Education, 1862–1875* (Westport, CT: Greenwood Press, 1980), 176.

20. James D. Anderson, *The Education of Blacks in the South, 1860–1935* (Chapel Hill: University of North Carolina Press, 1988), 5.

21. Eric Foner, *Reconstruction: America's Unfinished Revolution, 1863–1877* (New York: Harper and Row, 1988), 96–97.

22. Anderson, *The Education of Blacks*, 18; Butchart, *Northern Schools, Southern Blacks*, 176.

23. Ira Berlin, ed., *Herbert Gutman, Power and Culture: Essays on the American Working Class* (New York: The New Press, 1987), 269.

24. Ibid.

25. Wilbert L. Jenkins, *Seizing the New Day: African Americans in Post-Civil War Charleston* (Bloomington and Indianapolis: Indiana University Press, 1998), 72–73.

26. For an excellent study that chronicles the efforts of African Americans to extend literacy to freedmen in the South, see Clara Merritt DeBoer, *His Truth Is Marching On: African Americans Who Taught the Freedmen for the American Missionary Association, 1861–1877* (New York: Garland, 1995).

27. Linda M. Perkins, "The Black Female American Missionary Association Teacher in the South, 1861–1870," in Jeffrey J. Crow and Flora J. Hatley, eds., *Black Americans in North Carolina and the South* (Chapel Hill: University of North Carolina Press, 1984), 132.

28. Ibid.

29. Ibid.

30. Ibid.

31. Ibid.

32. Ibid., 133.

33. Joseph T. Glatthaar, *Forged in Battle: The Civil War Alliance of Black Soldiers and White Officers* (New York: Meridian Books, 1990), 245

34. William E. Montgomery, *Under Their Own Vine and Fig Tree: The African-American Church in the South, 1865–1900* (Baton Rouge and London: Louisiana State University Press, 1993), 147.

35. Reginald F. Hildebrand, *The Times Were Strange and Stirring: Methodist Preachers and the Crisis of Emancipation* (Durham, NC, and London: Duke University Press, 1995), 61.

36. Ibid.

37. Perkins, "The Black Female," 129; Bertram Wyatt-Brown, "Black Schooling during Reconstruction," in Walter J. Fraser Jr., R. Frank Saunders Jr., and Jon L. Wakelyn, eds., *The Web of Southern Social Relations: Women, Family, and Education* (Athens: University of Georgia Press, 1985), 150.

38. Perkins, "The Black Female," 131.

39. Ibid.

40. Butchart, *Northern Schools, Southern Blacks*, 176.

41. Peter Kolchin, *First Freedom: The Responses of Alabama's Blacks to Emancipation and Reconstruction* (Westport, CT: Greenwood Press, 1972), 84.

42. C. Peter Ripley, *Slaves and Freedmen in Civil War Louisiana* (Baton Rouge: Louisiana State University Press, 1976), 144.

43. Butchart, *Northern Schools, Southern Blacks*, 170.

44. Kolchin, *First Freedom*, 84–85.

45. Sidney Andrews, *The South since the War: As Shown by Fourteen Weeks of Travel and Observation in Georgia and the Carolinas* (Boston: Ticknor and Fields, 1866), 337–38.

46. John T. Trowbridge, *The South: A Tour of Its Battlefields and Ruined Cities, A Journey through the Desolated States, And Talks with the People* (Hartford, CT: L. Stebbins, 1866), 337.

47. Mary Beth Norton, *A People and a Nation: A History of the United States*, 2 vols. (Boston: Houghton Mifflin Company, 1990), 2:454.

48. William A. Byrne, "The Burden and Heat of the Day: Slavery and Servitude in Savannah, 1733–1865" (Ph.D. diss., Florida State University, 1979), 348; Jenkins, *Seizing the New Day*, 89–90; Trowbridge, *The South*, 509.

49. Anderson, *The Education of Blacks*, 19.

50. Norton, *A People and a Nation*, 2:454.

51. William Preston Vaughn, *Schools for All: The Blacks and Public Education in the South, 1865–1877* (Lexington: University Press of Kentucky, 1974), 15.

52. Ibid., 15; *New York Times*, July 3, 1874.

53. Butchart, *Northern Schools, Southern Blacks*, 170.

54. Gary B. Nash, *The American People: Creating a Nation and a Society*, 2 vols. (New York: Harper and Row, 1990), 1:557.

55. Wayne E. Reilly, ed., *Sarah Jane Foster: Teacher of the Freedmen, A Diary and Letters* (Charlottesville and London: University Press of Virginia, 1990), 47.

56. Ibid.

57. Ibid.

58. Wyatt-Brown, "Black Schooling during Reconstruction," 159.

59. Ibid.

60. Robert C. Morris, ed., *Semi-Annual Report on Schools for Freedmen*, Vol.1, Numbers 1–10, January 1866–July 1870 (New York: AMS Press, 1980), (Semi-Annual Report for January 1, 1867), 11.

61. John T. O'Brien Jr., "From Bondage to Citizenship: The Richmond Black Community, 1865–1867" (Ph.D. diss., University of Rochester, 1974), 81.

62. Robert H. Abzug, "The Black Family during Reconstruction," in Nathan I. Huggins, Martin Kilson, and Daniel M. Fox, eds., *Key Issues in the Afro-American Experience*, 2 vols. (New York: Harcourt Brace Jovanovich, 1971), 2:38.

63. Butchart, *Northern Schools, Southern Blacks*, 169.

64. Jacqueline Baldwin Walker, "Blacks in North Carolina during Reconstruction" (Ph.D. diss., Duke University, 1979), 97.

65. Wyatt-Brown, "Black Schooling during Reconstruction," 160.

66. Ibid.

67. Anderson, *The Education of Blacks*, 7.

68. Ibid., 6–7.

69. Foner, *Reconstruction*, 97.

70. Anderson, *The Education of Blacks*, 6–7.

71. Ripley, *Slaves and Freedmen*, 138.

72. Foner, *Reconstruction*, 97; Joe M. Richardson, *Christian Reconstruction: The American Missionary Association and Southern Blacks, 1861–1890* (Athens and London: University of Georgia Press, 1986), 4; Perkins, "The Black Female," 125.

73. Walker, "Blacks in North Carolina," 98.

74. Foner, *Reconstruction*, 98; Kolchin, *First Freedom*, 86.

75. Abzug, "The Black Family," 37–38; C. Vann Woodward, ed., *After the War: A Tour of the Southern States, 1865–1866* (By Whitelaw Reid) (New York: Harper and Row, 1965), 511.

76. Foner, *Reconstruction*, 96, 98; Ripley, *Slaves and Freedmen*, 139.

77. Willard B. Gatewood, "The Remarkable Misses Rollin: Black Women in Reconstruction South Carolina," *South Carolina Historical Magazine* 92, no. 3 (July 1991): 177.

78. Maxine Deloris Jones, "A Glorious Work: The American Missionary Association and Black North Carolinians, 1863–1880" (Ph.D. diss., Florida State University, 1982), 66–67.

79. Ibid., 67.

80. Marion B. Lucas, *A History of Blacks in Kentucky: From Slavery to Segregation, 1760–1891* (Lexington: Kentucky Historical Society, 1992), 1:239.

81. Jones, "A Glorious Work," 65.

82. Ibid., 67.

83. William Loren Katz, *Black Indians: A Hidden Heritage* (New York: Atheneum Books, 1986), 145–46.

84. Foner, *Reconstruction*, 98.

85. Anderson, *The Education of Blacks*, 10.

86. Ibid., 11; Butchart, *Northern Schools, Southern Blacks*, 173.

87. Butchart, *Northern Schools, Southern Blacks*, 171.

88. James M. Smallwood, *Time of Hope, Time of Despair: Black Texans during Reconstruction* (Port Washington, NY: Kennikat Press, 1981), 102–3.

89. Lucas, *A History of Blacks in Kentucky*, 1:239.

90. Smallwood, *Time of Hope, Time of Despair*, 103.

91. Montgomery, *Under Their Own Vine and Fig Tree*, 150–51.

92. Ibid., 151.

93. Ibid.

94. Ibid.

95. Ibid., 148–49.

96. Ibid., 151.

97. Foner, *Reconstruction*, 98.

98. Woodward, ed., *After the War*, 152.

99. Nash, *The American People*, 1:557.

100. Rawick, ed., *The American Slave*, Vol. 5, Indiana and Ohio Narratives, 111.

101. Nash, *The American People*, Vol. 1, 557.

102. Rawick, ed., *The American Slave*, Vol. 5, Texas Narratives, Part 4, 1648.

103. Butchart, *Northern Schools, Southern Blacks*, 186–87.

104. Reilly, ed., *Sarah Jane Foster*, 51.

105. Ibid.

106. Ibid., 52

107. Trowbridge, *The South*, 377.

108. John W. Alvord, *Letters from the South Relating to the Condition of Freedmen Addressed to Major General O. O. Howard* (Washington, DC: Howard University Press, 1870), 22.

109. Rawick, ed., *The American Slave*, Vol. 8, Mississippi Narratives, Part 3, 991.

110. Anderson, *The Education of Blacks*, 25; Kolchin, *First Freedom*, 99.

111. Hildebrand, *The Times Were Strange*, 62.

112. Bernard E. Powers, *Black Charlestonians: A Social History, 1822–1885* (Fayetteville: University of Arkansas Press, 1994), 155; E. Horace Fitchett, "The Role of Claflin College in Negro Life in South Carolina," *Journal of Negro Education* 12, no. 1 (Winter 1943): 43–45.

113. Lenwood G. Davis, *A Travel Guide to Black Historical Sites and Landmarks in North Carolina* (Winston-Salem, NC: Bandit Books, 1991), 172–73.

114. Evelyn Brooks Higginbotham, *Righteous Discontent: The Women's Movement in the Black Baptist Church, 1880–1920* (Cambridge, MA: Harvard University Press, 1993), 21–23; Benjamin Brawley, *History of Morehouse College* (College Park, MD: McGrath, 1970), 9; Addie Louise Joyner Butler, *The Distinctive Black College: Talladega, Tuskegee, and Morehouse* (Metuchen, NJ: The Scarecrow Press, 1977), 102–3; Powers, *Black Charlestonians*, 155; Davis, *A Travel Guide*, 167–68.

115. Davis, *A Travel Guide*, 107–8, 169.

116. Lester C. Lamon, *Blacks in Tennessee, 1791–1970* (Knoxville: University of Tennessee Press, 1981), 41; Butler, *The Distinctive Black College*, 18; Rayford W. Logan, *Howard University: The First Hundred Years, 1867–1967* (New York: New York University Press, 1968), 18, 20; Clarence A. Bacote, *The Story of Atlanta University: A Century of Service, 1865–1965* (Atlanta, GA: Atlanta University, 1969),

16–17; Robert Francis Engs, *Freedom's First Generation: Black Hampton, Virginia, 1861–1890* (Philadelphia: University of Pennsylvania Press, 1979), 142; Adele Logan Alexander, *Ambiguous Lives: Free Women of Color in Rural Georgia, 1789–1879* (Fayetteville: University of Arkansas Press, 1991), 170; Clarice T. Campbell and Oscar Allan Rogers, Jr., *Mississippi: The View from Tougaloo* (Jackson: University Press of Mississippi, 1979), 6–7.

117. Davis, *A Travel Guide*, 159.

118. Alexander, *Ambiguous Lives*, 170; Rogers, *Mississippi*, 14; Davis, *A Travel Guide*, 159; Hildebrand, *The Times Were Strange*, 62–63.

119. Logan, *Howard University*, 12–14; Davis, *A Travel Guide*, 169; Lamon, *Blacks in Tennessee*, 41–42.

120. Davis, *A Travel Guide*, 167–68, 192–93.

121. Engs, *Freedom's First Generation*, 149–50.

122. Bacote, *The Story of Atlanta University*, 37; Butler, *The Distinctive Black College*, 22–23.

123. Engs, *Freedom's First Generation*, 143–45; August Meier, *Negro Thought in America, 1880–1915: Racial Ideologies in the Age of Booker T. Washington* (Ann Arbor, MI: University of Michigan Press, 1963), 91.

124. Logan, *Howard University*, 25.

125. Dorothy Sterling, ed., *We Are Your Sisters: Black Women in the Nineteenth Century* (New York: W. W. Norton and Company, 1984), 406.

126. Jennifer Lund Smith, "The Ties That Bind: Educated African-American Women in Post-Emancipation Atlanta," in John C. Inscoe, ed., *Georgia in Black and White: Explorations in the Race Relations of a Southern State, 1865–1950* (Athens and London: University of Georgia Press, 1994), 95–97, 99.

127. Engs, *Freedom's First Generation*, 147.

128. Alexander, *Ambiguous Lives*, 173–75.

129. Logan, *Howard University*, 36–38.

130. Hildebrand, *The Times Were Strange*, 62.

131. Ibid., 63.

132. Edwin S. Redkey, ed., *A Grand Army of Black Men: Letters from African-American Soldiers in the Union Army, 1861–1865* (New York: Cambridge University Press, 1992), 222–23.

133. Lamon, *Blacks in Tennessee*, 42.

134. Calculated from the U.S. Bureau of the Census, Tenth, Eleventh, and Twelfth Censuses; Jenkins, *Seizing the New Day*, 91.

CHAPTER SEVEN

1. John B. Boles, "Evangelical Protestantism in the Old South: From Religious Dissent to Cultural Dominance," in Charles R. Wilson, ed., *Religion in the South* (Jackson: University Press of Mississippi, 1985), 30–32; Wilson Fallin Jr., *The African-American Church in Birmingham, Alabama, 1815–1963: A Shelter in the Storm* (New York and London: Garland, 1997), 10.

2. Fallin, *The African-American Church*, 9.

3. Allan D. Charles, "Black-White Relations in an Antebellum Church in the Carolina Upcountry," *South Carolina Historical Magazine*, 89, no. 4 (October 1988): 220–22.

4. George P. Rawick, ed., *The American Slave: A Composite Autobiography* (Westport, CT: Greenwood Press, 1977), Vol. 7, Mississippi Narratives, Part 2, 345.

5. Ibid., Vol. 3, Georgia Narratives, Part 1, 219.

6. Ibid., Vol. 3, Georgia Narratives, Part 1, 198.

7. Ibid., Vol. 1, Alabama Narratives, 176.

8. Ibid., Vol. 3, Georgia Narratives, Part 1, 92.

9. Ibid., Vol. 3, Georgia Narratives, Part 1, 238.

10. Fallin, *The African-American Church*, 11.

11. Rawick, ed., *The American Slave*, Vol. 6, Mississippi Narratives, Part 1, 123–24.

12. Ibid., Vol. 8, Mississippi Narratives, Part 3, 845.

13. Ibid., Vol. 8, Mississippi Narratives, Part 3, 1221.

14. Albert J. Raboteau, *Slave Religion: The "Invisible Institution" in the Antebellum South* (Oxford: Oxford University Press, 1978), 293.

15. Rawick, ed., *The American Slave*, Vol. 3, Texas Narratives, Part 2, 555–56.

16. Raboteau, *Slave Religion*, 291–92.

17. Rawick, ed., *The American Slave*, Vol. 7, Mississippi Narratives, Part 2, 744.

18. Ibid., Vol. 3, Georgia Narratives, Part 1, 26.

19. Ibid., Vol. 7, Mississippi Narratives, Part 2, 757.

20. Ibid., Vol. 3, Georgia Narratives, Part 1, 258.

21. Ibid., Vol. 7, Mississippi Narratives, Part 2, 595.

22. Ibid., Vol. 3, Georgia Narratives, Part 1, 7–8.

23. Ibid., Vol. 6, Mississippi Narratives, Part 1, 202.

24. Joel Williamson, *After Slavery: The Negro in South Carolina during Reconstruction, 1861–1877* (Hanover, NH, and London: University Press of New England, 1990), 197; Eric Foner, *Reconstruction: America's Unfinished Revolution, 1863–1877* (New York: Harper and Row, 1988), 91.

25. Foner, *Reconstruction*, 91.

26. Jacqueline Baldwin Walker, "Blacks in North Carolina during Reconstruction" (Ph.D. diss., Duke University, 1979), 150.

27. Arnold H. Taylor, *Travail and Triumph: Black Life and Culture in the South since the Civil War* (Westport, CT: Greenwood Press, 1976), 146.

28. Donna Johanna Benson, "'Before I Be a Slave': A Social Analysis of the Black Struggle for Freedom in North Carolina, 1860–1865" (Ph.D. diss., Duke University, 1984), 225.

29. John Hope Franklin and Alfred A. Moss Jr., *From Slavery to Freedom: A History of African Americans*, 7th rev. ed. (New York: McGraw-Hill, 1994), 231; Taylor, *Travail and Triumph*, 146.

30. Benson, " 'Before I Be a Slave,' " 225.

31. Taylor, *Travail and Triumph*, 146, 147.

32. Benson, " 'Before I Be a Slave,' " 224.

33. Ibid.

34. August Meier and Elliott Rudwick, *From Plantation to Ghetto: An Interpretive History of American Blacks*, 3d rev. ed. (New York: Hill and Wang, 1976), 174.

35. Walker, "Blacks in North Carolina," 148.

36. Franklin and Moss, *From Slavery to Freedom*, 232.

37. Foner, *Reconstruction*, 92.

38. Taylor, *Travail and Triumph*, 147.

39. James M. Smallwood, *Time of Hope, Time of Despair: Black Texans during Reconstruction* (Port Washington, NY: Kennikat Press, 1981), 106.

40. Foner, *Reconstruction*, 90; Armstead L. Robinson, "Plans Dat Comed from God: Institution Building and the Emergence of Black Leadership in Reconstruction Memphis," in Donald G. Nieman, ed., *Church and Community among Black Southerners, 1865–1900* (New York and London: Garland, 1994), 87; Hampton Institute, *The Negro in Virginia: Compiled by Workers of the Writers' Program of the Work Projects Administration in the State of Virginia* (New York: Hastings House, 1940), 247–48.

41. Kenneth M. Hamilton, *Black Towns and Profit: Promotion and Development in the Trans-Appalachian West, 1877–1915* (Urbana and Chicago: University of Illinois Press, 1991), 17.

42. Smallwood, *Time of Hope, Time of Despair*, 101.

43. Ruthe Winegarten, *Black Texas Women: 150 Years of Trial and Triumph* (Austin: University of Texas Press, 1995), 61.

44. Ibid.

45. Lenwood G. Davis, *A Travel Guide to Black Historical Sites and Landmarks in North Carolina* (Winston-Salem, NC: Bandit Books, 1991), 17.

46. Fallin, *The African-American Church*, 13–14.

47. Hampton Institute, *The Negro in Virginia*, 248.

48. Fallin, *The African-American Church*, 14.

49. Smallwood, *Time of Hope, Time of Despair*, 105.

50. Ibid., 100–101.

51. Ibid., 101.

52. Fallin, *The African-American Church*, 13.

53. Winegarten, *Black Texas Women*, 61.

54. Robinson, "Plans Dat Comed from God," 88; Kathleen C. Berkeley, "Colored Ladies Also Contributed: Black Women's Activities from Benevolence to Social Welfare, 1866–1896," in Nieman, ed., *Church and Community*, 329.

55. Wilbert L. Jenkins , *Seizing the New Day: African Americans in Post-Civil War Charleston* (Bloomington and Indianapolis: Indiana University Press, 1998), 119.

56. J. W. Alvord, *Letters from the South Relating to the Condition of Freedmen Addressed to Major General O. O. Howard* (Washington, DC: Howard University Press, 1870), 24.

57. Hampton Institute, *The Negro in Virginia*, 250.

58. William E. Montgomery, *Under Their Own Vine and Fig Tree: The African-American Church in the South, 1865–1900* (Baton Rouge and London: Louisiana State University Press, 1993), 304–5.

59. Ibid., 107–8.

60. Carl Schurz, *Report on the Condition of the South* (New York: Arno Press and New York Times, 1969, Reprint), 26.

61. Benson, " 'Before I Be a Slave,' " 223.

62. J. T. Trowbridge, *The South: A Tour of Its Battlefields and Ruined Cities, A Journey through the Desolated States, And Talks with the People* (Hartford, CT: L. Stebbins, 1866), 454.

63. Hollis R. Lynch, ed., *The Black Urban Condition: A Documentary History, 1866–1971* (New York: Thomas Y. Crowell Company, 1973), 6.

64. C. Vann Woodward, ed., *After the War: A Tour of the Southern States, 1865–1866* (By Whitelaw Reid) (New York: Harper and Row, 1965), 100.

65. Montgomery, *Under Their Own Vine and Fig Tree*, 275–76.

66. Ibid.

67. John W. Blassingame, *Black New Orleans, 1860–1880* (Chicago and London: University of Chicago Press, 1973), 151.

68. Ibid., 151–52; Montgomery, *Under Their Own Vine and Fig Tree*, 292.

69. Leon F. Litwack, *Been in the Storm So Long: The Aftermath of Slavery* (New York: Vintage Books, 1979), 467.

70. Joe M. Richardson, *Christian Reconstruction: The American Missionary Association and Southern Blacks, 1861–1890* (Athens and London: University of Georgia Press, 1986), 199.

71. Montgomery, *Under Their Own Vine and Fig Tree*, 288.

72. E. Franklin Frazier, *The Negro Church in America* (New York: Schocken Books, 1974), 40; Peter J. Rachleff, *Black Labor in the South: Richmond, Virginia, 1865–1890* (Philadelphia: Temple University Press, 1984), 23; John W. Blassingame, "Before the Ghetto: The Making of the Black Community in Savannah, Georgia, 1865–1880," in Nieman, ed., *Church and Community*, 11–12; William L. Barney, *The Passage of the Republic: An Interdisciplinary History of Nineteenth-Century America* (Lexington, MA: D. C. Heath and Company, 1987), 249–50; Foner, *Reconstruction*, 92.

73. Minutes of Morris Street Baptist Church, April 1, 1867.

74. Rawick, ed., *The American Slave*, Vol. 6, Mississippi Narratives, Part 1, 30.

75. Rachleff, *Black Labor in the South*, 23.

76. Rawick, ed., *The American Slave*, Vol. 10, Mississippi Narratives, Part 5, 2291.

77. Montgomery, *Under Their Own Vine and Fig Tree*, 293–94, 302–3.

78. Joe A. Mobley, *James City: A Black Community in North Carolina, 1863–1900* (Raleigh: North Carolina Division of Archives and History, 1981), 75.

79. Montgomery, *Under Their Own Vine and Fig Tree*, 302–3.

80. Winegarten, *Black Texas Women*, 61–62.

81. Jenkins, *Seizing the New Day*, 128.

82. Marion B. Lucas, *A History of Blacks in Kentucky: From Slavery to Segregation, 1760–1891* (Lexington: Kentucky Historical Society, 1992), 1:163–64.

83. Montgomery, *Under Their Own Vine and Fig Tree*, 300.

84. Lucas, *A History of Blacks in Kentucky*, 1:169.

85. Berkeley, "Colored Ladies Also Contributed," in Nieman, ed., *Church and Community*, 327–28.

86. Lucas, *A History of Blacks in Kentucky*, 1:199–200.

87. Blassingame, "Before the Ghetto," in Nieman, ed., *Church and Community*, 13.

88. Montgomery, *Under Their Own Vine and Fig Tree*, 299.

89. Lucas, *A History of Blacks in Kentucky*, 1:200; Montgomery, *Under Their Own Vine and Fig Tree*, 300.

90. Blassingame, *Black New Orleans*, 170; Henry M. Christman, ed., *The South As It Is: 1865–1866* (By John Richard Dennett) (New York: Viking Press, 1965), 304; Herbert G. Gutman, *The Black Family in Slavery and Freedom, 1750–1925* (New York: Pantheon Books, 1976), 227–28.

91. Montgomery, *Under Their Own Vine and Fig Tree*, 261; Berkeley, "Colored Ladies Also Contributed," in Nieman, ed., *Church and Community*, 337, 340.

92. For an excellent coverage of the black church today, consult C. Eric Lincoln and Lawrence H. Mamiya, *The Black Church in the African American Experience* (Durham and London: Duke University Press, 1990).

93. Lucas, *A History of Blacks in Kentucky*, 1:224–25.

94. Jenkins, *Seizing the New Day*, 129–32.

95. Taylor, *Travail and Triumph*, 13.

96. Frazier, *The Negro Church*, 47–48; Foner, *Reconstruction*, 93.

97. Edmund L. Drago, *Black Politicians and Reconstruction in Georgia: A Splendid Failure* (Athens and London: University of Georgia Press, 1992), 66–100.

98. Jacqueline Jones, *Labor of Love, Labor of Sorrow: Black Women, Work, and the Family, from Slavery to the Present* (New York: Vintage Books, 1985), 67.

99. Jualynne Dobson, "Nineteenth-Century A.M.E. Preaching Women: Cutting Edge of Women's Inclusion in Church Policy," in Hilah E. Thomas and Rosemary S. Keller, eds., *Women in New Worlds* (Nashville: Abingdon, 1981), 277–83.

100. Ibid., 283–85.

101. Jacquelyn Grant, "Black Women and the Church," in Gloria T. Hull, Patricia B. Scott, and Barbara Smith, eds., *All the Women Are White, All the Blacks Are Men, But Some of Us Are Brave* (New York: The Feminist Press, 1982), 143–44.

102. Dobson, "Nineteenth-Century A.M.E. Preaching Women," in Thomas and Keller, eds., *Women in New Worlds*, 284, 285, 288.

103. For an excellent discussion of the trials and tribulations that African-American women preachers continue to go through in black churches, see Bettye Collier-Thomas, *Daughters of Thunder: Black Women Preachers and Their Sermons, 1850–1979* (San Francisco: Jossey-Bass, 1998).

CHAPTER EIGHT

1. John Hope Franklin, *Reconstruction: After the Civil War* (Chicago and London: University of Chicago Press, 1961), 88–92; Mary F. Berry and John W. Blassingame, *Long Memory: The Black Experience in America* (New York and Oxford: Oxford University Press, 1982), 152–54; John Hope Franklin and Alfred A. Moss Jr., *From Slavery to Freedom: A History of African Americans*, 7th rev. ed. (New York: McGraw-Hill, 1994), 239–43; Arnold H. Taylor, *Travail and Triumph: Black Life and Culture in the South since the Civil War* (Westport, CT: Greenwood Press, 1976), 15–16.

2. Joseph T. Glatthaar, *Forged in Battle: The Civil War Alliance of Black Soldiers and White Officers* (New York: Meridian Books, 1990), 249; Eric Foner, *Reconstruction: America's Unfinished Revolution, 1863–1877* (New York: Harper and Row, 1988), 472.

3. See, for example, Edmund L. Drago, *Black Politicians and Reconstruction in Georgia: A Splendid Failure* (Athens and London: University of Georgia Press, 1992); Thomas Holt, *Black over White: Negro Political Leadership in South Carolina during Reconstruction* (Urbana and Chicago: University of Illinois Press, 1977); Peter Kolchin, *First Freedom: The Responses of Alabama's Blacks to Emancipation and Reconstruction* (Westport, CT: Greenwood Press, 1972).

4. Taylor, *Travail and Triumph*, 18.

5. W. E. B. DuBois, *Black Reconstruction in America, 1860–1880* (New York: Atheneum, 1969), 417–25; Kenneth M. Stampp, *The Era of Reconstruction, 1865–1877* (New York: Alfred A. Knopf, 1965), 177–80.

6. *New York Times*, April 24, May 2, May 9, 1867; *New York Daily Tribune*, May 4, 1867; Wilbert L. Jenkins, *Seizing the New Day: African Americans in Post-Civil War Charleston* (Bloomington and Indianapolis: Indiana University

Press, 1998), 143–45; John W. Blassingame, *Black New Orleans, 1860–1880* (Chicago and London: University of Chicago Press, 1973), 189–90; Peter J. Rachleff, *Black Labor in the South: Richmond, Virginia, 1865–1890* (Philadelphia: Temple University Press, 1984), 42; Taylor, *Travail and Triumph*, 49.

7. Dorothy Sterling, ed., *We Are Your Sisters: Black Women in the Nineteenth Century* (New York: W. W. Norton and Company, 1984), 254.

8. Willard B. Gatewood, "The Remarkable Misses Rollin: Black Women in Reconstruction South Carolina," *South Carolina Historical Magazine* 92, no. 3 (July 1991): 172, 177.

9. Colin A. Palmer, *Passageways: An Interpretive History of Black America*, 2 vols. (New York: Harcourt Brace, 1998), 2:121.

10. Ruthe Winegarten, *Black Texas Women: 150 Years of Trial and Triumph* (Austin: University of Texas Press, 1995), 73–74.

11. Sterling, ed., *We Are Your Sisters*, 363–64.

12. Patricia W. Romero and Willie Lee Rose, eds., *Reminiscences of My Life: A Black Woman's Civil War Memoirs* (By Susie King Taylor) (New York: Markus Wiener, 1988), 123–24.

13. Winegarten, *Black Texas Women*, 71–73.

14. Rachleff, *Black Labor in the South*, 31–32.

15. Winegarten, *Black Texas Women*, 66.

16. Rosalyn Terborg-Penn, *African-American Women in the Struggle for the Vote, 1850–1920* (Bloomington and Indianapolis: Indiana University Press, 1998), 24, 26, 27, 28, 31.

17. For an in-depth discussion of the debate over the Fifteenth Amendment, consult Terborg-Penn, *African-American Women in the Struggle for the Vote*, 24, 26, 27, 28, 31, 32, 33; Ellen Carol DuBois, *Feminism and Suffrage: The Emergence of an Independent Women's Movement in America, 1848–1869* (Ithaca, NY: Cornell University Press, 1980), 69–70, 166–67, 178; Paula Giddings, *When and Where I Enter: The Impact of Black Women and Sex in America* (New York: Bantam Books, 1984), 65–68; Sterling, ed., *We Are Your Sisters*, 415; Rosalyn Terborg-Penn, "Discrimination against Afro-American Women in the Woman's Movement, 1830–1920," in Sharon Harley and Rosalyn Terborg-Penn, eds., *The Afro-American Woman: Struggles and Images* (Port Washington, NY: Kennikat Press, 1978), 20; Winegarten, *Black Texas Women*, 65–66; Bert James Loewenberg and Ruth Bogin, eds., *Black Women in Nineteenth-Century American Life: Their Words, Their Thoughts, Their Feelings* (University Park: Pennsylvania State University Press, 1976), 238; Foner, *Reconstruction*, 448.

18. Darlene Clark Hine, William C. Hine, and Stanley Harrold, *The African-American Odyssey* (Upper Saddle River, NJ: Prentice Hall, 2000), 294–95.

19. Joel Williamson, *After Slavery: The Negro in South Carolina during Reconstruction, 1861–1877* (Hanover, NH, and London: University Press of New England, 1990), 337–38.

20. Leonard I. Sweet, *Black Images of America, 1784–1870* (New York: W. W. Norton and Company, 1976), 166.

21. Drago, *Black Politicians and Reconstruction*, 84–85.

22. Victor B. Howard, *Black Liberation in Kentucky: Emancipation and Freedom, 1862–1884* (Lexington: University Press of Kentucky, 1983), 155–56; Marion B. Lucas, *A History of Blacks in Kentucky*, 2 vols. (Lexington: Kentucky Historical Society, 1992), 1:301.

23. Peggy Lamson, *The Glorious Failure: Black Congressman Robert Brown Elliott and the Reconstruction in South Carolina* (New York: W. W. Norton and Company, 1973), 100. For a lively discussion of the responses of white Radi-

cals and white Democrats to the Fifteenth Amendment, see Jason H. Silverman, "Mary Ann Shadd and the Search for Equality," in Leon Litwack and August Meier, eds., *Black Leaders of the Nineteenth Century* (Urbana and Chicago: University of Illinois Press, 1988), 98.

24. Foner, *Reconstruction*, 471–72.

25. Ibid.

26. Daniel F. Littlefield, *The Cherokee Freedmen: From Emancipation to American Citizenship* (Westport, CT: Greenwood Press, 1978), 63–64.

27. Ibid., 64.

28. William Loren Katz, *Black Indians: A Hidden Heritage* (New York: Atheneum Books, 1986), 147.

29. Ibid., 172.

30. Ibid., 173.

31. James Mellon, ed., *Bullwhip Days: The Slaves Remember, An Oral History* (New York: Avon Books, 1988), 396.

32. George P. Rawick, ed., *The American Slave: A Composite Autobiography* (Westport, CT: Greenwood Press, 1979), Vol. 4, Texas Narratives, Part 3, 1106.

33. Mellon, ed., *Bullwhip Days*, 397.

34. Ibid.

35. Ibid., 404.

36. Ibid., 401.

37. Ibid., 399.

38. Rawick, ed., *The American Slave*, Vol. 4, Texas Narratives, Part 3, 1269–1275.

39. See, for example, Foner, *Reconstruction*, 426–27. White Republicans were also susceptible to violence at the hands of the Democratic Ku Klux Klan. See, for example, Foner, *Reconstruction*, 427.

40. Mellon, ed., *Bullwhip Days*, 399–400.

41. Rawick, ed., *The American Slave*, Vol. 6, Mississippi Narratives, Part 1, 17–18.

42. Mellon, ed., *Bullwhip Days*, 400–401.

43. *New York Times*, March 19, 1868.

44. Rawick, ed., *The American Slave*, Vol. 1, Alabama Narratives, 400–401.

45. Ibid., Vol. 9, Mississippi Narratives, Part 4, 1760.

46. Ibid., Vol. 10, Mississippi Narratives, Part 5, 1975.

47. Ibid., Vol. 4, Texas Narratives, Part 3, 1401.

48. Ibid., Vol. 11, North Carolina and South Carolina Narratives, 137.

49. Ibid., Vol. 1, Alabama, Arizona, Arkansas, District of Columbia, Florida, Georgia, Indiana, Kansas, Maryland, Nebraska, New York, North Carolina, Oklahoma, Rhode Island, South Carolina, and Washington Narratives, 390.

50. Ibid., Vol. 8, Mississippi Narratives, Part 3, 1177.

51. Edmund L. Drago, *Hurrah for Hampton! Black Red Shirts in South Carolina during Reconstruction* (Fayetteville: University of Arkansas Press, 1998), 29.

52. Ibid., 32.

53. Ibid., 35.

54. Ibid., 3.

55. James E. Sefton, "A Note on the Political Intimidation of Black Men by Other Black Men," *Georgia Historical Quarterly* 52 (March 1968): 447; *Charleston Courier*, November 9, 1876.

56. Joe A. Mobley, *James City: A Black Community in North Carolina, 1863–1900* (Raleigh: North Carolina Division of Archives and History, 1981), 67.

57. Sefton, "A Note on the Political Intimidation," 447; Elsa Barkley Brown, "The Labor of Politics," in Thomas C. Holt and Elsa Barkley Brown, eds., *Major Problems in African-American History*, 2 vols. (Boston and New York: Houghton Mifflin Company, 2000), 1:414.

58. Sterling, ed., *We Are Your Sisters*, 369–70.

59. Holt, *Black over White*, 35.

60. Drago, *Hurrah for Hampton!*, 42.

61. Sterling, ed., *We Are Your Sisters*, 370; Brown, "Labor of Politics," 413–14.

62. Holt, *Black over White*, 60.

63. Benjamin Quarles, *The Negro in the Making of America*, 3d rev. ed. (New York: MacMillan, 1987), 141.

64. Ibid., 139–40.

65. Berry and Blassingame, *Long Memory*, 348; Taylor, *Travail and Triumph*, 42; John Hope Franklin and Alfred A. Moss, Jr., *From Slavery to Freedom: A History of Negro Americans*, 6th rev. ed. (New York: Alfred A. Knopf, 1988), 282.

66. August Meier and Elliott Rudwick, *From Plantation to Ghetto: An Interpretive History of American Blacks*, 3d rev. ed. (New York: Hill and Wang, 1976), 204.

67. Quarles, *The Negro in the Making*, 141.

68. Ibid.

69. Ibid., 141–42; Gary B. Nash, *The American People: Creating a Nation and a Society*, 2 vols. (New York: Harper and Row, 1990), 1:566.

70. For coverage of the political, economic, and social fates of Southern African Americans in the post-Reconstruction era, consult Franklin and Moss, *From Slavery to Freedom*, 7th rev. ed., 259–61; Taylor, *Travail and Triumph*, 39; James L. Underwood, "The Contributions of Black Delegates to the Framing of the South Carolina Constitution of 1868" (Paper presented at the South Carolina Supreme Court Historical Society First Annual Colloquium, 1998), 12, 14; C.Vann Woodward, *The Strange Career of Jim Crow*, 3d rev. ed. (New York: Oxford University Press, 1974), 84, 85, 97–102; I. A. Newby, *The South: A History* (New York: Holt, Rinehart, and Winston, 1978), 351–52; W. Marvin Dulaney, *Black Police in America* (Bloomington and Indianapolis: Indiana University Press, 1996), 17; Walter J. Fraser Jr., *Charleston! Charleston! The History of a Southern City* (Columbia: University of South Carolina Press, 1989), 297, 308; and Jenkins, *Seizing the New Day*, 161–62.

71. For coverage of the accomplishments of the Reconstruction era, consult Foner, *Reconstruction*, 602; and Jenkins, *Seizing the New Day*, 160–63.

72. Nash, *The American People*, 1:559; Quarles, *The Negro in the Making*, 136; Underwood, "The Contributions of Black Delegates," 1, 7, 10, 11, 15, 16, 18, 19.

73. Nash, *The American People*, 1:559.

BIBLIOGRAPHICAL ESSAY

Local conditions pertaining to education, economics, politics, social life, and race relations as well as invaluable insight into the civil affairs of freedmen can be gleaned from the extensive Records of the Bureau of Refugees, Freedmen, and Abandoned Lands, Record Group 105, and the Department of the South Papers, Record Group 393, in the National Archives in Washington, DC. However, thanks to the Southern History Project, much of this material has been published in several edited volumes under the guidance of historian Ira Berlin. The volumes most important for this study are Ira Berlin et al., eds., *Free at Last: A Documentary History of Slavery, Freedom, and the Civil War* (New York: New Press, 1992), and Ira Berlin and Leslie S. Rowland, eds., *Families and Freedom: A Documentary History of African-American Kinship in the Civil War Era* (New York: New Press, 1992).

Although black source material for this study is limited, a large collection of slave testimony, recorded as part of the Federal Writers' Project in the 1930s, is available. The Federal Writers' Project interviews are reproduced in George P. Rawick, ed., *The American Slave: A Composite Autobiography*, 19 vols. and supplements (Westport, CT: Greenwood Press, 1972). Slave narratives are also published in John W. Blassingame, ed., *Slave Testimony: Two Centuries of Letters, Speeches, Interviews, and Autobiographies* (Baton Rouge: Louisiana State University Press, 1977); B. A. Botkin, ed., *Lay My Burden Down: A Folk History of Slavery* (Chicago: University of Chicago Press, 1945); and James Mellon, ed., *Bullwhip Days: The Slaves Remember, An Oral History* (New York: Avon Books, 1988).

Published travel accounts, letters, memoirs, journals, and diaries by Northerners and Europeans who made excursions into the South during this period comment on relations between blacks and whites and on the social and economic conditions and everyday lives of slaves and free blacks. Travel accounts are useful in ascertaining how former slaves perceived their relations with whites and how freedmen interacted with the propertied class of blacks. The best travel accounts of the economic, social, and political activities of blacks during emancipation and Reconstruction are Sidney Andrews, *The South since the War: As Shown by Fourteen Weeks of Travel and Observation in Georgia and the Carolinas* (Boston: Ticknor and Fields, 1866); Henry M. Christman, ed., *The South As It Is: 1865–1866* (By John

267

Richard Dennett) (New York: Viking Press, 1965); J. T. Trowbridge, *The South: A Tour of Its Battlefields and Ruined Cities: A Journey through the Desolated States, and Talks with the People* (Hartford, CT: L. Stebbins, 1866); and C. Vann Woodward, ed., *After the War: A Tour of the Southern States, 1865–1866* (By Whitelaw Reid) (New York: Harper and Row, 1965). Diaries, journals, memoirs, and letters written by both Northern and Southern blacks and whites who spent some time in various capacities in the South round out the picture provided by the writings of travelers. The best of these are R. J. M Blackett, ed., *Thomas Morris Chester: Black Civil War Correspondent, His Dispatches from the Virginia Front* (Baton Rouge: Louisiana State University Press, 1989); Donald Yacovone, ed., *A Voice of Thunder: The Civil War Letters of George E. Stephens* (Urbana: University of Illinois Press, 1997); Patricia W. Romero and Willie Lee Rose, eds., *Reminiscences of My Life: A Black Woman's Civil War Memoirs* (By Susie King Taylor) (New York: Markus Wiener, 1988); Frank [Francis] A. Rollin, *Life and Public Services of Martin A. Delany, Sub-Assistant Commissioner, Bureau of Refugees, Freedmen, and Abandoned Lands, and Late Major 104th U.S. Colored Troops* (Boston: Lee and Shepard, 1883); John W. Alvord, *Letters from the South Relating to the Condition of Freedmen Addressed to Major General O. O. Howard* (Washington, DC: Howard University Press, 1870); Elizabeth Hyde Botume, *First Days amongst the Contrabands* (New York: Arno Press and New York Times, 1968, reprint); and Rupert Sargent Holland, ed., *Letters and Diary of Laura M. Towne: Written from the Sea Islands of South Carolina, 1862–1884* (Cambridge, MA: Riverside Press, 1912).

On the question of Lincoln and the issue of black freedom, see Benjamin Quarles, *Lincoln and the Negro* (New York: Oxford University Press, 1962); Stephen B. Oates, *With Malice toward None: The Life of Abraham Lincoln* (New York: Harper and Row, 1977); LaWanda Cox, "Lincoln and Black Freedom," in Gabor S. Boritt, ed., *The Historian's Lincoln: Pseudohistory, Psychohistory, and History* (Urbana: University of Illinois Press, 1988), 175–96; Richard N. Current, "The Friend of Freedom," in Kenneth M. Stampp and Leon F. Litwack, eds., *Reconstruction: An Anthology of Revisionist Writings* (Baton Rouge: Louisiana State University Press, 1969), 25–47; J. G. Randall and Richard N. Current, "Race Relations in the White House," in Don E. Fehrenbacher, ed., *The Leadership of Abraham Lincoln* (New York: John Wiley and Sons, 1970), 150–55; Waldo E. Martin Jr., *The Mind of Frederick Douglass* (Chapel Hill: University of North Carolina Press, 1984); and James M. McPherson, *Drawn with the Sword: Reflections on the American Civil War* (New York: Oxford University Press, 1996).

The black military experience in the Civil War is covered superbly by several scholars. Black soldiers in the Union army are discussed in Benjamin Quarles, *The Negro in the Civil War* (Boston: Little, Brown and Company, 1969); James M. McPherson, *The Negro's Civil War: How American Negroes Felt and Acted during the War for the Union* (New York: Vintage Books, 1965); Dudley T. Cornish, *The Sable Arm: Negro Troops in the Union Army, 1861–1865* (New York: W. W. Norton and Company, 1956); Joseph T. Glatthaar, *Forged in Battle: The Civil War Alliance of Black Soldiers and White Officers* (New York: Meridian Books, 1990); and Noah Andre Trudeau, *Like Men of War: Black Troops in the Civil War, 1862–1865* (Boston: Little, Brown and Company, 1998). Although the military experience of blacks in the Confederate armed services has not been dealt with extensively by scholars, some excellent works have been published on the topic. For example, see Richard Rollins, ed., *Black Southerners in Gray: Essays on Afro-Americans in Confederate Armies* (Redondo Beach, CA: Rank and File Publications, 1994); Ervin L. Jordan Jr., *Black Confederates and Afro-Yankees in Civil War Virginia* (Charlottesville: University Press of Virginia, 1995); James G. Hollandsworth Jr., *The Louisiana Native Guards: The Black Military Experience during the Civil War* (Baton Rouge: Louisiana State University Press, 1995); and Robert F. Durden, *The Gray and the Black: The Confederate Debate on Emancipation* (Baton Rouge: Louisiana State University Press, 1972).

The literature on the black family, women, and children during the Civil War, emancipation, and Reconstruction has steadily increased in volume in recent years. Much of this work is solid. Herbert G. Gutman, *The Black Family in Slavery and Freedom, 1750–1925* (New York: Pantheon Books, 1976), is still the most thorough study and emphasizes the strength of the black family despite the brutality and destructiveness of slavery. Readers should also find the following works particularly insightful: C. Peter Ripley, *Slaves and Freedmen in Civil War Louisiana* (Baton Rouge: Louisiana State University Press, 1976); Robert F. Durden, "Georgia's Blacks and Their Masters in the Civil War," *Georgia Historical Quarterly* 69, no. 3 (Fall 1985): 355–64; and Robert H. Abzug, "The Black Family during Reconstruction," in Nathan I. Huggins, Martin Kilson, and Daniel M. Fox, eds., *Key Issues in the Afro-American Experience* (New York: Harcourt Brace Jovanovich, 1971), 2:26–41. Black women and children are superbly covered in Wilma King, *Stolen Childhood: Slave Youth in Nineteenth-Century America* (Bloomington: Indiana University Press, 1995); Jacqueline Jones, *Labor of Love, Labor of Sorrow: Black Women, Work, and the Family, from Slavery to the Present* (New York: Vintage Books,

1985); Ella Forbes, *African American Women during the Civil War* (New York: Garland, 1998); Noralee Frankel, *Freedom's Women: Black Women and Families in Civil War Era Mississippi* (Bloomington: Indiana University Press, 1999); and Leslie A. Schwalm, *A Hard Fight for We: Women's Transition from Slavery to Freedom in South Carolina* (Urbana: University of Illinois Press, 1997).

Eric Foner, *Reconstruction: America's Unfinished Revolution, 1863–1877* (New York: Harper and Row, 1988), is the most thorough synthesis of the period and presents blacks as central players in the story of Reconstruction. W. E. B. DuBois, *Black Reconstruction: An Essay toward a History of the Part Which Black Folk Played in the Attempt to Reconstruct Democracy in America, 1860–1880* (New York: Harcourt Brace, 1935), though published more than sixty-five years ago, is a classic and must be read by those interested in the study of this period. The best general work on blacks during emancipation and Reconstruction in the South is Leon F. Litwack, *Been in the Storm So Long: The Aftermath of Slavery* (New York: Vintage Books, 1979). Although the definitive work on the social and economic adjustment of freedmen after slavery on the state level is Joel Williamson, *After Slavery: The Negro in South Carolina during Reconstruction, 1861–1877* (Hanover, NH: University Press of New England, 1990), there are additional excellent studies by state. For example, see James M. Smallwood, *Time of Hope, Time of Despair: Black Texans during Reconstruction* (Port Washington, NY: Kennikat Press, 1981); and Peter Kolchin, *First Freedom: The Responses of Alabama's Blacks to Emancipation and Reconstruction* (Westport, CT: Greenwood Press, 1972).

On the Freedmen's Bureau and the struggle by blacks to obtain land, open bank accounts, establish businesses, and engage in other economic activities, see Martin Abbott, *The Freedmen's Bureau in South Carolina, 1865–1872* (Chapel Hill: University of North Carolina Press, 1967); George R. Bentley, *A History of the Freedmen's Bureau* (New York: Octagon Books, 1970); Claude F. Oubre, *Forty Acres and a Mule: The Freedmen's Bureau and Black Land Ownership* (Baton Rouge: Louisiana State University Press, 1982); Carl R. Osthaus, *Freedmen, Philanthropy, and Fraud: A History of the Freedman's Savings Bank* (Urbana: University of Illinois Press, 1976); Eric Arnesen, *Waterfront Workers of New Orleans: Race, Class, and Politics, 1863–1923* (New York: Oxford University Press, 1991); Loren Schweninger, *Black Property Owners in the South, 1790–1915* (Urbana: University of Illinois Press, 1990); and Peter J. Rachleff, *Black Labor in the South: Richmond, Virginia, 1865–1890* (Philadelphia: Temple University Press, 1984).

There is a wealth of fine literature on black education. Those interested in the antebellum period in the South should consult Janet Cornelius, "We Slipped and Learned to Read: Slave Accounts of the Literacy Process, 1830–1865," *Phylon* 44, no. 2 (September 1983): 171–86. The definitive work is James D. Anderson, *The Education of Blacks in the South, 1860–1935* (Chapel Hill: University of North Carolina Press, 1988), which offers a detailed analysis of the efforts of blacks to establish and maintain schools. A chapter by Herbert Gutman titled "Schools for Freedom: The Post-Emancipation Origins of Afro-American Education," in Ira Berlin, ed., *Herbert Gutman, Power and Culture: Essays on the American Working Class* (New York: New Press, 1987), 260–97, also highlights the efforts by blacks to support their own educational endeavors. The establishment of historically black colleges and universities are nicely dealt with in Clarence A. Bacote, *The Story of Atlanta University: A Century of Service, 1865–1965* (Atlanta, GA: Atlanta University, 1969); Rayford W. Logan, *Howard University: The First Hundred Years, 1867–1967* (New York: New York University Press, 1968); and Robert Francis Engs, *Freedom's First Generation: Black Hampton, Virginia, 1861–1890* (Philadelphia: University of Pennsylvania Press, 1979).

Several excellent works on black religion exist. Although dated, E. Franklin Frazier, *The Negro Church in America* (New York: Schocken Books, 1974), and Carter G. Woodson, *The History of the Negro Church* (Washington, DC: Associated Publishers, 1921), are both still solid. Wilson Fallin Jr., *The African-American Church in Birmingham, Alabama, 1815–1963: A Shelter in the Storm* (New York: Garland, 1997), provides good coverage of the black church on the local level. Reginald F. Hildebrand, *The Times Were Strange and Stirring: Methodist Preachers and the Crisis of Emancipation* (Durham, NC: Duke University Press, 1995), is the best book on black Methodist preachers during emancipation. William E. Montgomery, *Under Their Own Vine and Fig Tree: The African-American Church in the South, 1865–1900* (Baton Rouge: Louisiana State University Press, 1993), is probably the best book on the black church during emancipation and Reconstruction.

Although Thomas Holt, *Black over White: Negro Political Leadership in South Carolina during Reconstruction* (Urbana: University of Illinois Press, 1977), is by far the most thorough work on black politicians during Reconstruction, there are many fine works on the subject that proved beneficial to this study. For example, see Edmund L. Drago, *Black Politicians and Reconstruction in Georgia: A Splendid Failure* (Athens: University of Georgia Press, 1992); Howard N.

Rabinowitz, ed., *Southern Black Leaders of the Reconstruction Era* (Urbana: University of Illinois Press, 1982); and Peggy Lamson, *The Glorious Failure: Black Congressman Robert Brown Elliott and the Reconstruction in South Carolina* (New York: W. W. Norton and Company, 1973).

INDEX